The Enterprise of Florida

Pedro Menéndez de Avilés, 1519–1574, Adelantado de la Florida, Comendador de Santa Cruz de la Zarza, Orden de Santiago. (Reproduced from Cesaréo Fernández Duro, *Armada Española*. Photo enlargement by Homer N. Cato.)

The Enterprise of Florida

Pedro Menéndez de Avilés and the Spanish Conquest of 1565–1568

EUGENE LYON

A University of Florida Book

The University Presses of Florida

Gainesville

University Presses of Florida is the central agency for scholarly publishing of the State of Florida's university system. Its offices are located at 15 NW 15th Street, Gainesville, FL 32603.

Works published by University Presses of Florida are evaluated and selected for publication, after being reviewed by referees both within and outside of the state's university system, by a faculty editorial committee of any one of Florida's nine public universities: Florida A&M University (Tallahassee), Florida Atlantic University (Boca Raton), Florida International University (Miami), Florida State University (Tallahassee), University of Central Florida (Orlando), University of Florida (Gainesville), University of North Florida (Jacksonville), University of South Florida (Tampa), University of West Florida (Pensacola).

Library of Congress Cataloging in Publication Data

Lyon, Eugene, 1929–
    The enterprise of Florida.

    "A University of Florida book."
    Bibliography: p.
    Includes index.
    1. Florida—History—Spanish colony, 1565–1763.
    2. Menéndez de Avilés, Pedro, 1519–1574. I. Title.
F314.L98   975.9 '01   76-29612
ISBN 0–8130–0777–1

The picture on the cover is the coat of arms of the City of Avilés, Spain. It incorporates the Menéndez family *escudo* and shows an episode in the taking of Seville from the Moslems in the thirteenth century. A Menendez relative broke the chain the Moslems had placed in the Guadalquivir River, and the city fell.

Preface

This work arose out of a long interest in the founding of Spanish Florida by Pedro Menéndez de Avilés. Initial research on the topic was performed for a doctoral program at the University of Florida but was continued after the program had been completed. After first surveying the primary Spanish materials available in Florida, I spent three academic years studying Spanish archives. During this time, I examined materials in the Archive of the Indies (A.G.I.) and the Seville and Cádiz notaries' archives. In Madrid, I consulted the archive of the Royal Academy of History, the manuscript collection of the *Biblioteca Nacional*, the notaries' archive of Madrid, and the archive of the *Instituto de Valencia de Don Juan*. In the summer of 1975, I studied in the archive of Simancas.

In an attempt to uncover the underlying nature of the Florida enterprise of 1565–68, I endeavored to examine all possible primary material which might bear upon sixteenth-century Spanish Florida or its founder. Work began in the document collections from the A.G.I. located at the P. K. Yonge Library of Florida History at the University of Florida. The largest and most important of these, the John B. Stetson Collection, was gathered by Irene Wright in Seville prior to 1930; it is calendared with the index numbers in use at the A.G.I. at that time. Aided by Paul E. Hoffman's table for conversion of these numbers to those now in use in the archive, I was able to compare Stetson Collection holdings with the original materials in Seville. Miss Wright had covered several sections of the archive generally well—*Patronato Real*, *Contratación*, and *Gobierno: Santo Domingo* and *Indiferente General*—although some additional documentation from those areas was found. On the other hand, it became clear that Miss Wright had utilized the *Justicia*, *Escribanía de Cámara*, and *Contaduría* sections to only a small degree. The civil and criminal lawsuits, investigations, *residencias*, and audits from those parts of the archive contain rich accretions of data about Pedro Menéndez de Avilés, his key supporters, and the Florida conquest. One such item, a *legajo* from *Escribanía de Cámara*, proved to be the main body of the legal case prosecuted by Menéndez and his heirs over his Crown contract to settle Florida. The Spanish notarial archives were also of great utility, and furnished contracts, wills, and other data relating to the dramatis personae of the enterprise of Florida. The records at Cádiz proved to be of particular importance in establishing that port as the fiscal nerve-center for the support of Menéndez' colonizing effort.

The data which emerged from this research provide the basis for a better understanding of Pedro Menéndez as a many-sided figure and of the founding of sixteenth-century Spanish Florida as a mixed and multidimensional enterprise. It has led me to analyze the kinship network which supported the *adelantado* and became the basis for the later socioeconomic structure of Spanish Florida. The richness of materials also enabled a better correlation of events in Europe and in the Indies which led to the Florida establishment.

The generally expressed but erroneous belief that Pedro Menéndez de Avilés was sent as a mere military subordinate to Florida because Philip II had learned of the French incursion at Fort Caroline has encouraged a shallow view of the Spanish effort of 1565–68. Actually, the Hapsburg King's actions were the culmination of decades of attempts to conquer, settle, and exploit eastern North America. A series of contracts with adelantados, from the time of Ponce de León, through that of the second Ayllón in 1563, to the date of the agreement with Pedro Menéndez, emphasized settlements to be organized around Spanish municipalities. Through these, which were to be maintained by agricultural and commercial enterprise, a framework was to be erected for the conversion of the native populations. The Crown's purposes were always continental in scope, and their foci lay to the north and west of peninsular Florida, although that area held strategic importance in the defense of the *Carrera de Indias*.

To characterize the costly Florida enterprise of Pedro Menéndez and his sovereign as strictly one of expulsion of an invader and the subsequent defense of a perimeter is to ignore the range and depth of the Iberian culture which was brought to Florida and the means by which it was to be established in the land. The holder of such a view would also overlook the complex and very human reasons for the presence of Menéndez and his men in Florida, and would thus neglect the entire "private side" of a Spanish conquest.

Although this study is oriented toward the Spanish conquest, it may shed some additional light upon the French side of the clash of 1565. The testimony of French prisoners (taken in Cuba, Hispaniola, Jamaica, or Florida), the report of Gabriel de Enveja, and the evidence of the papers found in Jean Ribault's room in Fort Caroline give weight to Charles-André Julien's belief that the French Florida expeditions were part of a French national policy. The little-known and ill-fated relief expedition sent from Bordeaux in 1565 seems also to have had direct or indirect sponsorship by the Valois rulers.

Both Crowns, therefore, dealt with the Florida matter indirectly, by the use of proprietary champions. If the French approach was a more covert one, evidently made at a double remove of the Crown from the acting party, the perilous royal position may have justified this. For both the parties, France and Spain, this procedure befitted the ambiguities of the nonsettlement (during and after the negotiations at Cateau-Cambrésis) of the Franco-Spanish Indies question.

The years of the Florida conquest not only featured the conflict of men representing two European powers, but also involved traumatic contacts with the native peoples of Florida. The story of these interactions is imperfectly and incompletely told here. It is to be hoped that an ever increasing access by scholars to the plentiful sources of Spanish primary material and the very useful anthropological studies now being performed in Florida will eventually yield much more complete knowledge of this vital aspect of the history of Florida in those years.

Finally, this work can be characterized as incomplete for it contains the description of the Menéndez conquest to the year 1568. A second volume is planned which would carry the narrative forward, past the death of the adelantado to the termination of the *adelantamiento* in 1634.

There is no way to acknowledge properly or completely my many debts of gratitude to those who have helped to increase my knowledge and deepen my understanding of the Spaniard in Florida. With no intention to slight any of those who have helped me, I will mention those which come to mind as being the most outstanding.

Lyle N. McAlister, who directed my academic program, consistently guided the project into the broadest possible relationship with Iberian and Latin-American history—to the place where Spanish Florida studies belong. His high standards, the depth of his erudition, and his ever fruitful suggestions were essential to the completion of the work.

Several other members of the faculty of the University of Florida greatly influenced my desire to work with primary colonial documentation: John K. Mahon, Paul Smith, George D. Winius, and Cornelius Goslinga. Francis Hayes' instruction reawakened a long-dormant interest in the beauty and utility of the Spanish language. Antonio Oliveira-Marques' patient work with me in paleography afforded me the key to sixteenth-century Spanish documents.

Several persons have encouraged me to work in the field of Florida history. The first was Samuel Proctor, whose instruction in 1947–48 awakened my interest in the field. His never failing advice and friendship over the years have been invaluable. I owe a special and affectionate debt to Bessie Wilson DuBois of Jupiter, Florida; it was she who urged me to return to a full-time commitment to Florida studies. No one who knows her can resist her infectious enthusiasm for the history of this state. Charles H. Fairbanks of the University of Florida has inspired me with a continuing interest in the Florida Indians whom Pedro Menéndez found when he began his conquest. Charles Arnade and Michael Gannon have listened patiently to my questions and responded with good advice and encouragement, as has Luis Arana, long-time historian for the National Parks Service at the Castillo de San Marcos in St. Augustine.

At the P. K. Yonge Library of Florida History at the University of Florida, I found an academic home. Elizabeth Alexander, its librarian, and her staff assistants have aided me in becoming acquainted with the fine collection of secondary works and the great Spanish document collections in that library.

For more than eight years, Paul E. Hoffman of Louisiana State University has been my principal collaborator in the study of sixteenth-century Spanish Florida. He has shared freely with me the fruits of his own extensive archival work. I have found his insights into the personages and primary materials of the Menéndez years to be invariably cogent and compelling, and I prize our long association.

Many persons have helped to make my sojourns in Spain both pleasant and fruitful. To none of these do I owe a greater debt than Rosario Parra Cala, directora of the Archive of the Indies. She and all of her staff have served their nation well, as they have preserved its documental patrimony and courteously aided those who have come from overseas to study there. At the A.G.I., Louis-André Vigneras and Juan Friede acted as mentors to me, initiating me into the mysteries of the indices and inventories.

I am grateful for the means of financing my various periods of study which have been provided from several sources. My support during my initial period of work was furnished by an NDEA Title VI fellowship, which was granted through the Center for Latin American Studies of the University of Florida under the successive direction of Lyle N. McAlister and William E. Carter. Vivian Nolan of the CLAS was most helpful in arranging for the banking and transfer of funds and in many other ways. Archival research in Spain in 1974–75 was sponsored by St. Augustine Restoration, Inc., under the direction of William E. Rolleston. The publication of this book was assisted by the American Council of Learned Societies under a grant from the Andrew W. Mellon Foundation.

Finally, I want to express my appreciation to my daughter, Peggy, for her aid in the correction and preparation of the manuscript for this book and to my wife, Dorothy, for her constant and continual encouragement and the sacrifices she has made so that this work could go forward.

·· { *To Dot* } ··

Contents

Contractors in Conquest and Defense

The sixteenth-century Castilian expansion into the Western Hemisphere proceeded in several waves. After the voyages of Columbus, Spaniards occupied the islands of Hispaniola, Puerto Rico, Cuba, and Jamaica. These islands then served as advance bases from which to launch expeditions of exploration and conquest around the Caribbean basin. During these years, probing attempts had also been made to discover the North American coasts. By mid-century, Spaniards had met and interacted with many native peoples in widely scattered areas.

The purposes and methods of the conquerors reflected much, if not all, of the diversity of the lands from which they came.[1] The motivation and organization of conquest was as complex as the make-up of sixteenth-century Spanish Iberia. At any single *entrada* in the Indies, Spaniards pursued many diverse personal, dynastic, and religious objectives. On this advancing frontier, elements of medievalism—in commerce, law, and the institutions of government—coexisted with more modern concepts of kingship and personal enterprise.

The very means of conquest itself were also a mixture of ancient tradition and newer practice. The rulers in whose names the seas, islands, and mainlands of the Indies were appropriated represented an advancing absolutism. A preoccupation with the step-by-step increase of royal prerogatives can, however, obscure the extent to which

1. The writer is indebted to those anthropologists who have studied and written about acculturation theory, and especially to George M. Foster for his work *Culture and Conquest: America's Spanish Heritage*. Foster has demonstrated the origin of many elements of Spanish colonial culture in their Iberian agricultural, religious, social, and governmental models and stresses the totality of a culture conquest. (Complete information on references may be found in the Bibliography.)

limitations upon kingly power still existed. The fiscal and organizational weaknesses of the Castilian rulers through the whole first era of conquest insured that their reach would always exceed their grasp. From the time of Columbus through that of Balboa, Cortés, Pizarro, Alvarado, Montejo, Mendoza, and de Soto, conquest was accomplished or recognized through contract by licensed entrepreneurs, many of whom carried the title of adelantado.[2]

The institution of adelantamiento in Castile can be traced back at least to the twelfth century, and possibly further.[3] The earlier officer, called *adelantado mayor*, functioned primarily as a surrogate of the King in hearing legal appeals, although he also bore responsibility for the maintenance of order in his district. The unification of Castile and León in the early thirteenth century led to a revival of the Reconquest from the Moslems. Under the leadership of Ferdinand III, the forces of Castile drove deeply into Andalusia, captured Córdova and Seville, and opened a path to the sea by 1241. The older office of adelantado was reconstituted and was given wider authority under the title of *adelantado menor*. Now the peace-keeping functions of the adelantados were expanded to include those of the commanders of frontier military districts. Within his district, an adelantado had great juridical and governmental powers; these were outlined and limited by law.[4] His services were rewarded by the grant of revenue-producing estates along the frontier. He could expect to profit from his lands if he proved able to defend them. Thus was the private defensor aided by the grant of benefices from the Crown so that he might more easily mount his private effort.

When the subjugation of new kingdoms began in the Western world, the institution of private conquest was transmitted, without visible alteration, from Castile to the Indies.[5] The expansion policies

2. Itemized listings of the adelantados of the Indies exist. Two of these are incomplete but nonetheless helpful. The first is "Noticias extractadas de asientos y Capitulaciones que se hicieron para descubrir en Indias despves de Colón," from Cesáreo Fernández Duro, *Armada Española*, 1:452–59; Roscoe R. Hill included a chart of Indies adelantados in his article "The Office of Adelantado," p. 656.

3. An excellent summary of the history of adelantamiento in medieval Spain has been prepared by Manuel Dánvila y Collado in *Historia del poder civil en España*, 1:77–83. The Iberian background of the institution is also examined thoroughly by Hill in "The Office of Adelantado," pp. 646–51.

4. Royal laws and ordinances governing adelantados were promulgated by the Castillian King Alfonso X in a special code entitled *Leyes para los Adelantados Mayores*. See Marcelo Martínez Alcubilla, *Códigos Antiguos de España*, 1:175–76. For jurisdiction of adelantados, see Leyes XIX and XXII, Titulo IX, part II, in *Las Siete Partidas*. These have been reproduced in *Códigos Antiguos de España*, 1:301–2. When the Cortes was held at Alcalá de Henares in 1348, Laws VII and XX of Titulo XX of the *Ordenamiento de Alcalá* were concerned with the authority of the adelantado.

5. The precise identity of Castilian with Indies adelantamiento was discussed and

the Spanish Crown developed during its dealings with Christopher Columbus became a model for future outreach, in which adelantamiento had its proper part. Columbus received several titles as a result of his contract with Ferdinand and Isabella, which made him the primary entrepreneur of the Indies which he was to discover. Among these was the title of adelantado mayor, which he proceeded to subdivide by naming his brother Bartolomé as adelantado of Hispaniola in 1497. The descendants of the discoverer litigated for continuation of the title of adelantado mayor of the Indies, which exists today.[6] Although Hernando Cortés began his conquest of Mexico under the authority of the licensed adelantado, Diego Velásquez, his success enabled him to deal directly with the Crown. The royal "Instructions" and grants to Cortés constituted him as a major contractor in conquest even though he did not become adelantado of New Spain.[7] Francisco Pizarro, the last of the three great *conquistadores*, also obtained his royal contract after he had begun his enterprise under the aegis of another official, the governor of Panama. His *asiento* of 1529 was a standard one which granted him the title of adelantado of Peru as well as a number of other offices and benefits. Francisco Montejo accomplished the conquest of Yucatan as an adelantado whose efforts and expenditures for many years overcame difficult obstacles.[8]

Adelantamiento in the Spanish Indies rested upon the juridical basis of personal royal title to the new lands. This ownership and overlordship, called *señorío natural*, had been confirmed by the donations of Pope Alexander VI.[9] Although the papal bulls laid spiritual

affirmed in the *consulta* of the Council of the Indies dealing with the successors in title to Pedro Menéndez de Avilés. See *Archivo General de Indias* (hereafter A.G.I.) *Santo Domingo* 231; the consulta is given at Madrid on November 28, 1671, and is found in the John B. Stetson Collection at the P. K. Yonge Library of Florida History (hereafter Stetson Coll.).

6. A good summary of the benefits, titles, and legal cases related to Christopher Columbus is found in the work of Otto Schoenrich, *The Legacy of Christopher Columbus*. Columbus' contract, the *Capitulaciones de Santa Fé*, was signed by Ferdinand and Isabella outside Granada on April 17, 1492, and has been reprinted in *Colección de documentos inéditos relativos al descubrimiento . . . de América y Oceania* (hereafter *D.I.*), 17:572–74.

7. Hernando Cortés' instructions and ordinances of government have been reprinted in *D.I.*, 12:349, 355; 13:355 ff.; 26:19, 65, 135, 149, 160, 170, 185.

8. The Pizarro *Capitulación* was dated at Toledo on July 26, 1529, and has been reprinted in *D.I.*, 22:271–85. A detailed account of the Montejo conquest is in Robert S. Chamberlain, *The Conquest and Colonization of Yucatan*.

9. A good summary of the Castilian title to the Indies is found in the packet of documents gathered by the Council of the Indies in preparation for the consulta furnished to Philip II on May 5, 1565, and found in A.G.I. *Indiferente General*, 738, ramo 7. The papal bulls *Inter caetera* and *Dudum siquidem* were issued by Alexander VI in 1493; they are reproduced in full in Frances G. Davenport, ed., *European Treaties Bearing on the History of the United States*, 1:80–82. The laws of the Indies formally conferred the title of

obligations upon the Castilian rulers in their new lands, their right to dispose of the territories was legally intact. The monarch, as señor natural, was the sole suzerain who could license exploitation of his properties. The Indies adelantados were granted the privilege of discovering, populating, and exploiting the royal lands. The Crown also granted certain incomes, exemptions, and monopolies to its entrepreneurs. These were of varying duration; some were perpetual in scope, while many were to endure for the lifetime of the grantee. The emoluments promised to an adelantado included inheritable estates and titles. For the ambitious sixteenth-century *caballero* the hoped-for benefits constituted high rewards in both the material and the psychic sense.

In return for their license and privileges, the adelantados bore the essential burden of the cost and risk of their conquest. As the private instruments of their sovereign's will, they were required to agree to carry out royal policies of fortification for defense, the implanting of Castilian municipal institutions in desired areas, and the fair treatment of the Indians. The duration and extent of their effort was dictated in substantial detail.

Final sovereignty over its territories had not been surrendered by the Crown to its designated representative. The history of the royal disputes with Columbus and later conquerors demonstrates that the Spanish rulers always guarded their prerogatives with jealous zeal. The adelantados might receive enduring title to lands and lasting privileges, but their control over the government of the lands they had conquered was limited; within one or two lifetimes the monarch would recapture the offices of governor and captain-general. During the life of the agreement, however, effective civil and military authority was in the hands of the adelantado. Within the boundaries of his district, the adelantado was supreme. The viceroyalties founded in New Spain in 1535 and Peru in 1544 had no territorial jurisdiction over the adelantamientos established by royal fiat. Neither could the *Audiencias* appointed in the Indies after 1511 interpose their judgments in the legal appeal channel for cases arising in the adelantamiento—these proceeded from local justices to the adelantado and from there to the Council of the Indies. The King would also appoint royal financial officials to assure that Crown revenues would be accounted for and forwarded to Spain. The ancient devices of

---

Señor Natural upon the monarch; see *Recopilación de leyes de los reinos de las Indias,* Libro III, Titulo I, Ley 1–A. The theoretical background of royal authority over and ownership of the Kingdoms of the Indies has been thoroughly developed by Frank Jay Moreno, "The Spanish Colonial System: A Functional Approach."

visita and residencia could also help to check excesses in the use of granted powers.[10]

All the reciprocal arrangements between the Castilian monarchs and their adelantados were formalized in their asientos y capitulaciones—a series of negotiated contracts. An examination of a number of these accords discloses that they were, in the main, very similar. By the middle of the sixteenth century they had become largely standardized. The asientos are therefore good indices of the abiding aims and purposes of Crown and contractors alike.[11]

In every case, the twofold mission of the conquest—pacification and settlement—was impressed upon the contractor. He would receive the titles and properties promised and could enjoy the short-run incomes, exemptions, and more enduring privileges, if he complied with his obligation to fortify, populate, and provide an atmosphere in which evangelization of the natives could go forward. On both sides of the contract—benefit as well as obligation—the promises and requirements were most specific.

As captains and explorers set forth in every direction in attempts to expand the dominions of Castile and their own fortunes, it was inevitable that the unknown northern continent should come within the expanding Spanish sphere of interest. The North American coasts became a field for conquest.

From Puerto Rico, Juan Ponce de León launched two expeditions to his licensed area of "Bimini" and made two voyages, the last of which culminated in his death. He carried out his ill-starred enterprise at his own cost as adelantado. When it was done, the general geographic outline of the lovely, deadly land he had named Florida had become somewhat clearer to the Spanish.[12]

The next systematic attempt to move northwestward to conquest arose in Santo Domingo. Two men, Lucas Vázquez de Ayllón and the *Licenciado* Matienzo, *oidores* of the Audiencia there, sent two caravels northward along the coast discovered by Ponce de León and found fertile land lying in thirty-five to thirty-seven degrees north latitude.

10. The injunction against interference from viceroyalties is formalized in the code of laws enacted by Philip II, promulgated at Segovia on July 13, 1563, to govern adelantamientos, in "Ordenanzas sobre descubrimiento nuevo e población," in *D.I.*, vol. 8, no. LXIX, p. 508. The applicable appeals route and legal jurisdiction are covered ibid., no. XLIII, p. 501; no. LXVIII, pp. 507–8, and no. LXX, p. 508. Provision for officials to guard the royal treasury is located ibid., no. LXIV, p. 507; the residencia, no. LXXXIV, p. 512; visita, no. CIII, p. 518.

11. See Appendix 2 for an itemizing of a number of clauses from sixteenth-century asientos. For a detailed analysis of the terms and requirements of such an agreement, see the description of that negotiated with Pedro Menéndez de Avilés, on pp. 47–54.

12. Ponce de León's patent for Bimini is found in *D.I.*, 22:26–32.

Vázquez Ayllón determined to attempt its settlement. His petition for an asiento was approved in 1523, but storm and shipwreck destroyed the expedition. The failure of this would-be adelantado left the field open again.[13]

In the meantime, Castile's claim to the Western Hemisphere lands west of the line of demarcation established by the Tordesillas agreements came under challenge. Castile-Aragon and its Mediterranean and overseas possessions had been drawn into the Hapsburg orbit after King Ferdinand began the long struggle with the Valois rulers of France. With the beginning of intense rivalry between Francis I and Emperor Charles V, the lands and waters of North America became a theater of contest. The French monarch sponsored Giovanni di Verrazano on a voyage of exploration and discovery along the eastern coasts of the continent during 1524.

At Granada, on December 11, 1526, yet another adelantado was licensed for an attempt upon Florida. A resident of Cuba who had been involved in the conquest of Mexico, Pánfilo de Narváez, was given his asiento to pacify and populate an area between New Spain and the areas granted to Ponce de León and to Vázquez Ayllón—from the River of Palms to the Cape of Florida. Narváez left Spain in mid-1527, and only reached Florida the next spring. As his dwindling forces traversed the Gulf Coast, the expedition lost touch with its sources of supply and ended in disaster. Only four men, including Cabeza de Vaca, reached New Spain, eight years after their Florida landing.[14]

After the battle of Pavia and the capture of Francis I by Charles V, another short-lived peace prevailed. When Francis was released, however, war began again in Europe, and this time the first French commerce-raiders appeared in the Spanish Indies. Ignoring the Spanish and Portuguese pretensions to exclusive title in the Americas, Francis I also sent Jacques Cartier in 1534 and 1535 to explore Newfoundland, seeking a passage westward to the Orient.

After Cabeza de Vaca returned to Spain to report in 1537, the Crown passed over his application to take up the contract of Narváez and awarded it to Hernando de Soto. The asiento of de Soto required him to fortify and settle and made him the usual concessions for

13. Vázquez Ayllón reported to the emperor about the northern discoveries; a summary of his narrative is appended to the body of his asiento, which was approved at Valladolid on June 12, 1523, and is found in A.G.I. *Indiferente General* 415, fol. 32–40. The original discoveries which led to Ayllón's application are described in A.G.I. *Justicia* 3, no. 3.

14. The contract of Narváez is found in A.G.I. *Indiferente General* 415, A.G.I. *Contratación* 3,309, and has been reprinted in *D.I.*, 8:224–45.

profit and prestige. It was continental in scope; de Soto was given all of the areas previously promised to Vázquez Ayllón and to Narváez.[15] The vast expanse of his territories swallowed up Hernando de Soto and his men; his expedition never passed beyond the exploration stage and ended in death for its leader and many of his men.

In the meantime, preparation for the third voyage of Jacques Cartier was well advanced. Word of its arming reached and alarmed the emperor and his councillors, for it was to be a thoroughgoing colonization attempt. The Spanish viewed the coming voyage as an act of aggression in the rightful lands of the rulers of Castile. Charles V considered sending a war fleet to intercept Cartier at sea, but an armada sent later was only an ordinary one to protect a treasure fleet. In June 1541, the Council of the Indies suggested to the King that he send scout vessels to follow the movements of Cartier, and practice defensive settlement by giving another asiento to a Spanish nobleman to check the French in North America.[16]

After the Cartier voyage came to naught (as far as lasting settlement was concerned), no further Spanish contracts for the Florida conquest were issued for many years. In June 1549, Father Luis Cáncer de Barbastro, a Dominican priest who had taken part in the peaceable evangelization of Verapaz, was killed with two of his fellows at Tampa Bay while attempting to convert the Florida Indians. After more than thirty-five years the Spanish still had not made successful establishments on the southeastern mainland.

The year of Father Cáncer's sacrifice also represented a peak year in the intrusion of French vessels, which came in numbers to raid and trade in the Spanish Indies. By now, the distinction between peace and war had become blurred. Corsairs sailed continually to the "hotspots" between Cuba and Hispaniola where inter-island commerce and a plentiful supply of hides and sugar attracted the French.

By this time, Spanish trade with the Indies had grown until it represented immense value which had to be protected. The commer-

15. The agreement with Hernando de Soto is in A.G.I. *Indiferente General* 415. It was entered into at Valladolid on April 20, 1537. De Soto, who had served notably in Peru with Francisco Pizarro as his principal military supporter, had gained there a patrimony estimated to be worth more than 100,000 pesos. It was out of this that he expected to finance the Florida enterprise. See Theodore Maynard, *DeSoto and the Conquistadores*, p. 113.
16. The writer is indebted to Paul E. Hoffman for the citation of the consulta of the Council of the Indies. It was dated June 10, 1541, and has been reproduced in Buckingham Smith, *Colección de varios documentos para la historia de la Florida y tierras adyacentes*, pp. 109–11. Hoffman has a most cogent introductory essay about the corsair threat and the development of Spanish defense in his "Defense of the Indies, 1535–1574: A Study in the Modernization of the Spanish State," pp. 1–18.

cial system called the Carrera de Indias was a near monopoly in which the Crown licensed merchants to engage in commerce. During the first four or five decades of the Carrera, trade was diffused among many ports. In Spain, in 1529, the emperor gave permission to La Coruña and Bayona in Galicia, Avilés in Asturias, Laredo in Santander, Bilbao in Vizcaya, and San Sebastián in Guipúzcoa to load cargoes for the Indies. Permission was also extended to Cádiz and Seville in Andalusia.[17]

Many *norteños* engaged in the Atlantic commerce made commercial ties with the Caribbean trade centers—Santo Domingo, La Yaguana, Monte Cristi, Puerto Plata and Puerto Real on the island of Hispaniola, Santiago in Cuba, and San Juan in Puerto Rico. Sugar, hides, placer gold, and copper were exchanged for the wines, iron goods, and cloth of Spain. As the century advanced, the agricultural products and bullion from New Spain and Peru began slowly to eclipse the island commerce. San Juan de Ulua, Nombre de Dios, and Cartagena became the main ports for the ingress and egress of organized fleets. Across the Atlantic, except for limited separate privileges granted to Cádiz, all of this trade was funneled through Seville.

As merchants from the north of Spain lost their one-time privileges in the Indies commerce, some of them gravitated to Cádiz and continued their shipping from there. Considerable tension arose between them and the shippers' guild at Seville.

The royal *Casa de Contratación* at Seville (founded in 1503) and the guild of sea merchants (*Consulado de la Universidad de Mercaderes*, established in 1543) composed a symbiotic community of interests. The traders of Seville had achieved monopoly through royal patronage, becoming a strong and wealthy power center. Through the Casa, the Crown insured the safe passage of its Indies revenues, including those taxes levied on the commerce itself. The functionaries of the Casa came to represent the merchants' guild as much as they did the King. An official at Cádiz insured that ships from that port conformed to the rules. Crown policies were also carried out through the Carrera regulation. The inspections by the Casa enforced controls over outgoing passengers, who had to conform to the Spanish laws of religious purity and moral fitness before they could sail.[18]

17. See *cédula*, Toledo, January 15, 1529, in Diego de Encinas, *Cedulario Indiano*, 4:133.
18. A complete compendium of the Spanish colonial navigation laws is Joseph de Veitia Linaje, *Norte de la contratación de las indias occidentales*. A standard work on the Spanish commercial system is Clarence H. Haring, *Trade and Navigation between Spain and the Indies in the Time of the Hapsburgs*. Interpretation of the legal aspects of the Carrera de Indias, a deep understanding of the institutions involved in it, and the best itemized chronology of the trade from 1500 to 1650 is the multivolume work of Pierre and

To protect the Spanish ships against Berber pirates and the commerce-raiders who swarmed in the waters west of Spain, the emperor assessed the trade for its own defense. The Crown, operating through its officials in the Casa de Contratación, used the funds realized from the *avería* to lease ships, purchase cannon and ammunition, and pay soldiers and sailors to defend the fleets. By mid-century, the practice of joint sailing in fleet convoy for defense purposes had begun but was not yet regularized. Coastal patrols also protected the Mediterranean shoreline and the other Spanish coasts.[19]

On the north coast, conditions were particularly favorable for the development of a vigorous culture based upon the sea. The very nature of the rugged shore, cut by endless inlets alternating with rocky headlands, thrust men onto the oceans for livelihood. In addition to fishing, from an early date they engaged in trade with northern Europe and the Indies. To the east, in Vizcaya, the combination of rich iron ore deposits, ample supplies of wood, and a sea-oriented people produced a long and vital tradition of shipbuilding.

With excellent ships and fine seamen, the norteños made lasting reputations as mariners and the builders of fleets. The stimulus which activated them was essentially that of war, and its more particular impetus was privateering. During the lengthy Italian wars and the many Mediterranean campaigns mounted by Ferdinand and Emperor Charles V, the Crown freely gave letters-of-marque to Spanish shipowners to prey upon enemy vessels in the Bay of Biscay, the near approaches to Europe, and the waters of the Indies.[20]

The major incentive for privateering was the taking of enemy prizes. The wealth which thus accrued to the north coast was substantial. In 1542, Vizcayan privateers captured thirty-one French prizes; another Basque group captured forty-two French vessels from the Newfoundland fishing trade. Juanot de Villaviciosa from Asturias captured more than sixty prizes during his wartime career. Other

Huguette Chaunu, *Séville et l'Atlantique: 1504–1650*. The Carrera was, of course, the only route for the return of the Indies revenues of the Crown, including customs duties (*almojarifazgo*), tithe (*diezmo*), tribute, the royal fifth of mined bullion (*quinto*), court fines (*penas de cámara*), and sales taxes (*alcabala*). The machinery of cargo registries and ship visitations and the requirement that cargoes be cleared only through Seville were used aggressively to enhance and promote the monopoly.

19. The best study of the avería is that of Guillermo Céspedes del Castillo, *La Avería en el comercio de Indias*. See also Chaunu, *Séville et l'Atlantique*, 1:175–82. An excellent summary of the development of fleet defense methods in the sixteenth century is Hoffman, "The Defense of the Indies," pp. 1–18.

20. On June 30, 1498, at Saragossa, Ferdinand and Isabella issued unlimited license for the armadores of Guipúzcoa and Vizcaya to go privateering. Prince Philip, on November 24, 1551, issued a similar cédula. These are cited in Duro, *Armada Española*, 1:63, 427.

successful *contra-corsario* captains were Domingo de Villaviciosa, Bartolomé Carreño, and Álvaro Sánchez of Avilés. One *memorial* contains
twenty-two Guipuzcoan captains who had made prize captures during
war with France.[21]

In addition to independent adventuring, the captains and ship-
builders of the north coast early gained access to royal funds and
favor through the furnishing of ships. They sailed on expeditions
against the Berbers and Turks and took part in the Mediterranean
sea-actions connected with the Italian wars. The Crown would pay a
sueldo, or ship-charter fee, for the use of the vessel, and would also
furnish supplies, artillery, munitions, and pay for the seamen. The
entrepreneur who provided the ships would also be given a royal
commission as captain-general to lead them in battle. One of the
most notable of the *armador* families was that of Bazán. Before the
end of the fifteenth century, Sancho de Bazán was already known
for furnishing vessels. Galleys and other fighting ships from the
north coast were important contingents in the expeditions against
the Berbers and Turks in 1510, 1519, 1530, 1535, and 1540–41. In
1543, Álvaro de Bazán, who had served with distinction in the Mediterranean since the 1520s, was commissioned to form an armada to
counter a large French fleet. His forty ships met the enemy off
Galicia in the battle of Muros and defeated them handily, taking
twenty-three prizes and much other booty.

Pedro Menéndez de Avilés was very much a part of this sea-borne
culture and of the anti-corsair milieu. Born in 1519 at Avilés,
Menéndez was the descendant of minor Asturian *hidalgos* and had
blood and marriage connections with the important Valdés family as
well as with other noble norteño families.[22] After an early marriage to

21. Ibid., 1:270–74. The memorial is "Información hecha en la villa de San Sebastián
para acreditar las acciones marineras de los capitanes armadores de Guipúzcoa, durante
la guerra con Francia."
22. The genealogy of Pedro Menéndez de Avilés can be learned, or inferred, from a
variety of sources. The four main narrative sources do not furnish data of a precise
nature, but are useful in establishing some of the relationships. These are "Barcia"
(Andrés González de Carballido y Zúñiga), *Ensayo cronológico para la historia general de la
Florida*; Bartolomé Barrientos, *Pedro Menéndez de Avilés; su vida y hechos*; Eugenio Ruidiaz
y Caravía, *La Florida: su conquista y colonización por Pedro Menéndez de Avilés*; and a contemporary biography of the Florida adelantado during the conquest, Gonzalo Solís de Merás,
Pedro Menéndez de Avilés. This work is found in ms. in the *Archivo de los Condes de
Revillagigedo* (A.C.R.) (microfilm, P. K. Yonge Library), Legajo 2, no. 2; it was
translated by Jeannette T. Connor and published at Deland in 1923. A facsimile edition
was reprinted by University of Florida Press in 1965, with introduction by Lyle N.
McAlister. Ciriaco Miguel Vigil, in *Noticias biográficas-genealógicas de Pedro Menéndez de
Avilés*, provides more detail, particularly about the relationships contemporary to and
since the time of the adelantado. Ruidiaz relied upon Vigil substantially, and they shared
some errors, e.g., their confusion of Pedro Menéndez Marquéz with Pedro Menéndez de

Doña María de Solís, Menéndez went to sea and entered the world of privateering. He had before him the example of his elder brother, Álvaro Sánchez, and such luminaries as Álvaro Bazán. It appears that he served in Bazán's fleet for two years beginning in 1543.[23] This experience led him to buy his own *patache* (a small, rapid sailing craft) and become a privateer. Within a very few years he was well known for his decisive, daring seamanship and for the number of prizes that he took. For Pedro Menéndez this proved to be a path to preferment at the court. He received two royal commissions to pursue corsairs, one granted by Maximilian in 1548, acting as regent for the emperor, and another granted by Charles V himself.[24] Manifestly, the Asturian's rise was aided by his exploits, but family influence may have also been a factor.

Pedro Menéndez armed a galleon at his own cost and went with a crew of relatives and friends to pursue French ships which had seized eleven Vizcayan prizes off Galicia. He tracked down the French near La Rochelle, captured three of the corsair's vessels, and mortally wounded the leader, Jean Alphonse.

Menéndez' second royal letter-of-marque, issued by the emperor in 1550, granted a wider sphere of action to the young sea captain. He could now pass to the Indies to seek illegal intruders corsairing in time of peace.[25] With this instruction he built two galleons and went to Seville, where the Casa de Contratación registered his two ships to *Tierra Firme*. In 1550, he left for the Indies and returned the next year.[26]

During the next voyage made by Pedro Menéndez, war erupted again with France, and all-out incursions in force by French corsairs

---

Avilés *el mozo*. Insights into relationships gleaned from various interrogatories, testimonies, and legal cases have been valuable. The noted sixteenth-century historian Gonzalo Fernández de Oviedo y Valdés and the Inquisitor Hernando de Valdés came from the Valdés family. See Appendix 3.

23. Solís de Merás, *Pedro Menéndez de Avilés*, p. 40, describes Menéndez' enlistment in an armada "against corsairs"; it probably was the Bazán fleet.

24. Pedro Menéndez says that when he was twenty-eight or twenty-nine years of age, in 1548, he was given a royal order to sail from Asturias against an "infestation" of corsairs. See "Servicios del general Pedro Menéndez de Avilés" (hereafter "Servicios"), Seville, 1564, A.G.I. *Patronato* 257, no. 3, ramo 2, fol. 1 (Stetson Coll.). The first commission is described in Solís de Merás, pp. 41–42.

25. The writer appreciates the citation of the 1550 commission: *Archivo General de Simancas* (A.G.S.), *Guerra Antigua, Libros de despachos*, Legajo 18, fol. 86–88 vto. It was furnished by Paul E. Hoffman.

26. Although the detailed registry of his vessels is not available in the Archive of the Indies, Menéndez' ships are recorded in the "Libro de Registros," A.G.I. *Contratación* 2,898, 1550 *Ida* and 1551 *Venida*. Pedro Menéndez took the *Nao Santa Maria de la Antigua*. His other vessel was probably *La Concepción*, whose master was Alonso Menéndez.

began. Under leaders such as Jacques LeClerc, called "Wooden-leg," and Jacques Sores, they prepared to assault shipping near Spain, in the Canary and Azores islands, and in the Caribbean. In the midst of this tense situation, the Asturian had an exciting journey. While carrying merchandise in the Caribbean in 1552, he was captured by a sizeable French galeass. For fifteen days Menéndez was kept prisoner as he negotiated with the corsairs for his ransom and release. In Santiago de Cuba he borrowed 1,098 gold pesos to ransom his person and his ship.[27]

Menéndez had learned of French plans to raid the Indies on a large scale. After refitting his ship in Santiago, Menéndez carried some stranded sailors as paid passengers to Vera Cruz.

Once in New Spain, Pedro Menéndez went to the city of Mexico and reported personally to Viceroy Luis de Velasco, advising him of the danger of the coming French assault. Then he sailed to Havana, where he conferred with Juan de Rojas, the most powerful man in that port, and with Juan de Lobera, *alcaide* of the fort. Menéndez next went to Santo Domingo and appeared before the Audiencia. The thirty-four-year-old ship captain then returned to Spain, bearing signed testimony, from the highest authorities in the Spanish Caribbean, of the threat to the Indies.

To meet the danger, Menéndez had a plan. He appeared before the Council of the Indies as an expert seaman experienced in dealing summarily with the corsair menace. Drawing upon this reputation and his expertise, Menéndez proposed to counter the French and build four ships and four smaller *zabras* at his own cost. He urged the Crown to bear the expense of outfitting the ships and paying him a salary as captain-general. With the pay of his officers and the men, the cost would be about 40,000 ducats a year. Clearly, the Asturian aspired to be another Álvaro Bazán.

Pedro Menéndez made his point. He received a commission as captain-general for the Indies voyages and prepared to sail. His appointment sparked conflict with strong influences within the Carrera de Indias. Menéndez was only one of several captains-general of the Azores and Indies fleets imposed upon the merchants of Seville by the Crown. Diego López de las Roelas and his brother Pedro, Gonzalo and Luis de Carvajal, Álvaro Bazán, Álvaro Sánchez de Avilés, and Pedro Menéndez de Avilés were all shipowners and expert mariners. They were also norteños. Menéndez represented a semi-independent power, Asturian in origin, with a reputation and high-

27. Menéndez describes his adventures in a memorial to the Council of the Indies dated 1553, and found in A.G.I. *Santo Domingo* 71 (Stetson Coll., misdated 1567).

level connections. His appointment also implied a more direct intervention of the Crown in fleet defense. In the face of the burgeoning corsair threat, new ordinances had been promulgated for the arming of convoy ships.[28] The powers of fleet generals and captains-general were now considerable and touched the interests of merchants at vital points—the control of the seaworthiness of vessels, some aspects of cargo lading, and sailing times. Pierre and Huguette Chaunu have written a striking description of the captain-general of this period: "with the economic force of a merchant, strong in his own military and naval puissance, at times an adelantado, almost always a ship-armer, first provider of armadas for the King, a grandee in his nepotism, defrauder of the customs laws for his own account and for that of others, carrying contraband aboard his own vessels and favoring contraband, absolute master in the ports of the Indies . . . such was the Captain-General."[29] For its part, the merchant guild in Seville had enough influence upon the Casa officials to insure selective enforcement of the regulations against the generals. In measuring a vessel, bonding its master, and approving the outgoing and incoming registry, many delays and obstructions were possible. In contests between fleet general or captain-general and the Casa, final appeal was to the Crown through the Council of the Indies. Thus each opposed power center sought support from the throne to buttress its position in the polycentric organism of sixteenth-century Spain. All three parties involved in the Carrera were inextricably bound together through the institution of the avería. Salaries and ship-charter fees paid to the generals came out of this assessment levied for the Crown upon the trade. The administration of the avería was, however, often in the hands of the merchants themselves, through various asientos with the Crown, for which they acted as tax-farmers. The three-way relationship among the King, his trade officials, and semi-autonomous fleet generals like Pedro Menéndez de Avilés was replete with opportunities for conflict. The antagonisms aroused by the assignment of Pedro Menéndez to the Indies fleets were not long in erupting.

Before he could take his office, however, Pedro Menéndez was recalled by Prince Philip. As Charles V neared the end of his long reign, it was decided that the Prince should marry Mary Tudor, the

28. See Crown to Casa, February 13, 1552, A.G.I. *Contratación* 5,010.
29. *Séville et l'Atlantique*, 1:114. The laws relating to the authority of the generals are found in *Recopilación de leyes de los reinos de las Indias*, III, Libro IX, Titulo 15, Ley 13 ff. A result of the clash between interests was a continuing argument over respective powers of the Seville officials and the captains-general. In 1559, a dispute arose in Seville when Pedro de las Roelas displayed a cédula outlining the powers of the captain-general. See Casa to Crown, Seville, March 7, 1559, from A.G.I. *Contratación* 5,167.

eldest daughter of the late Henry VIII, in hope that the union with England would bolster and support Philip's dominions in the Netherlands. Philip asked Menéndez to be one of the troop which escorted him to England for the wedding, and when a fleet of 150 sails left La Coruña on July 12, 1554, the Asturian went along. After the royal marriage, Pedro Menéndez returned to Spain with dispatches to the regents in Valladolid, and then, in Seville, resumed his interrupted preparations to sail. After much delay, his ships sailed in October 1555. Some of the Cádiz vessels were forced to return to port by stormy weather. A Casa representative from Seville inspected them in Cádiz and found many violations of shipping laws. His attempts to enforce the laws resulted in open fighting in the town, and he was thrown in jail by the Cádiz magistrate. A young merchant named Pedro del Castillo was one of those involved in the illegal transactions. Pedro Menéndez had permitted Castillo, who was a distant relative, to send goods under his command in violation of the laws of the Casa de Contratación. Enmity against Cádiz, Pedro del Castillo, and Pedro Menéndez de Avilés began to build in Seville.[30] Álvaro Sánchez, Menéndez' brother, went with the other ships as admiral of the fleet. The brothers and their convoy of eighty-one ships sailed directly into danger. A new urgency gripped the traders of the Carrera de Indias and the Spaniards in the Indies.

As the last of the Italian wars began in Europe, there was a new peak of raids and attacks by Frenchmen upon towns and shipping in the Spanish overseas possessions. La Yaguana in Hispaniola, Santiago de Cuba, and Havana were seized by large, determined bands of corsairs. On July 10, 1555, Jacques Sores had landed, thoroughly sacked Havana, and put many of its residents to the sword. Damage to the agricultural and mercantile productivity of the Caribbean islands was severe and enduring.

The stormy winter of 1554–55 had been even more disastrous for the Seville merchants than had the pirate raids. Three ships from the New Spain fleet of that year had been lost off Padre Island, on the modern Texas coast, while two from the Tierra Firme contingent sank in the Bahama Channel. The *almiranta* of Tierra Firme, rich in

---

30. The incident of 1555 in Cádiz is detailed in "Información hecha en la ciudad de Cádiz acerca de lo ocurrido entre Francisco Duarte, factor . . . de la Casa de Contratación, y el Licenciado Quevedo, Alcalde Mayor de la ciudad de Cádiz," from A.G.I. *Justicia* 970. Castillo, a *vecino* of Cádiz, was married to the former Isabel de Ribera and was probably of northern origins. His relationship to Pedro Menéndez de Avilés was affirmed by Menéndez in his will, dated at Sanlúcar de Barrameda on January 7, 1574. The will is found in A.C.R., Legajo 9, no. 21, and is also found in the *Archivo de Protocolos de Cádiz* (A.P.C.), *Escribanía* of Diego de Ribera, fol. 276–77 for 1577.

her own cargo and heavily laden with contraband, was shipwrecked on the Andalusian shore near Tarifa.[31]

Pedro Menéndez' first charge as Indies fleet captain-general was, therefore, a heavy and responsible one. The manner in which he accomplished it was typical of the man—it aroused both acclaim and abuse. By all accounts his return passage to Spain was rapid. The captain-general had gone personally to Vera Cruz with the New Spain ships while Álvaro Sánchez took charge of the section which discharged and collected goods and bullion at Nombre de Dios and Cartagena. Although his return was not anticipated until the following spring, Menéndez brought the ships back in September 1556, richly laden with merchant goods and Crown revenues. After the ships had been inspected by the Casa, Pedro Menéndez and his brother were arrested and charged with having brought a half million ducats' worth of cochineal and sugar outside of legal registry. They were also charged with having brought passengers disguised as soldiers. The men were jailed, and litigation on their case began. After the brothers were condemned by the Audiencia of the Casa de Contratación, they won a reversal of the verdict on appeal to the Council of the Indies.[32] Menéndez was then praised by the Crown for his diligence in the 1555–56 voyage, and directed to return as captain-general of the next armada departing to the Indies.[33] Before this could take effect, however, events in Europe led to a change in plans. The military operations of the Spaniards and their English allies in Flanders required heavy naval support across the Channel and from Iberian ports.

At first it was planned that Álvaro de Bazán divert his guard armada from Spanish waters and from the convoy of fleets between the Azores and Seville and move it to Flanders. Pursuant to this idea, Pedro Menéndez was named to take over his duties.[34] This idea was later abandoned, and the Asturian entered a period of two years busy service to the courts and armies in England and Flanders. He was

31. The loss of the New Spain vessels was described in A.G.I. *Contratación* 2,898, fol. 193 vto., and in A.G.I. *Contratación* 58. Material on the ill-starred Tierra Firme ships under General Farfan is profuse, as the salvage of the almiranta became a notable case of theft and contraband; see A.G.I. *Contratación* 58, and A.G.I. *Contratación* 2,898, 1555, *Venida*, inter alia. The Tarifa shipwreck is described in detail by Duro, *Armada Española*, 1:215–16.

32. Menéndez describes the contraband charges as mere harassment. See "Servicios," A.G.I. *Patronato* 257, no. 3, ramo 2. The case is found in A.G.I. *Justicia* 842, no. 9. Menéndez' fleet audit for 1555–56 is at A.G.I. *Contaduría* 455.

33. Crown to Pedro Menéndez de Avilés, n.p., February 26, 1557, A.G.I. *Indiferente General* 425.

34. *Nombramiento*, Pedro Menéndez de Avilés by Philip II, March 22, 1557, in A.C.R., Legajo 2, no. 3, A., 1. This order has also been printed in *D.I.*, 14:245, and in Ruidiaz, *La Florida*, 2:379 ff. It is discussed by Duro, *Armada Española*, 2:449.

posted as subordinate to Luis de Carvajal of Guipúzcoa in the arduous task of protecting supply lines and transporting personnel across waters active with French privateers. In making up his squadron, Pedro Menéndez armed ten ships and two zabras and operated on Crown charters while taking occasional prizes to bolster his income and that of his supporters. Now his brother Bartolomé Menéndez, Diego Flores Valdés, Pedro Menéndez Marquéz (the son of Álvaro Sánchez), and Esteban de las Alas of Avilés had joined his service. Menéndez' family had grown: his son Juan was now a young man, who served with his father. Of his three legitimate daughters, Ana and Catalina had not yet married, and María had become a nun. Pedro Menéndez had fathered an illegitimate daughter, also named María.[35]

As a result of his voyages in support of Spanish commitments in northern Europe, Pedro Menéndez came directly to the favorable notice of his sovereigns and further enhanced his reputation. His successful escort of 1.2 million ducats to Flanders was credited with having helped support the Spanish offensive which ended in the victory at St. Quentin in August 1557. In blockade and convoy duty from Dover to Calais in company with Carvajal, he aided the English allies so efficiently that he was commended by Queen Mary. In the culmination of his northern duties, Menéndez was selected for the signal honor of escorting Philip II to Spain from Flanders. The Prince had become King, and peace had been signed at Cateau-Cambrésis in April 1559. The young Asturian brought his King to Laredo in safety, and a new era began for him and for Spain.[36]

While Pedro Menéndez had been occupied in the last struggles of the war with France in Europe, the "corsair war" in Atlantic waters and in the Spanish Indies had reached a new level of bitterness. It had long been the practice that Frenchmen caught in the overseas dominions of Castile should be returned as prisoners for trial in

35. See "Renunciation of María Menéndez, nun," 1554, A.G.I. *Escribanía de Camara* 1,024-A. The other daughter named María later was married to Don Diego de Velasco.

36. The northern assignments of Menéndez are described in detail by Solís de Merás, *Pedro Menéndez de Avilés*, pp. 45–63. They are also discussed by Pedro Menéndez himself in "Servicios," A.G.I. *Patronato* 257, no. 3, ramo 2. Fernández Duro puts the exploits of Pedro Menéndez into the larger tradition of the Spanish marine in *Armada Española*, 1:320–21. It was at this same time that the Asturian was proposed by the King for the habit of a caballero of the religious-military order of Santiago. The initial proposal is found in a letter from Philip II to Don Diego de Acuña of the order sent from Valladolid on May 17, 1558. It has been printed in Ruidiaz, *La Florida*, 2:739–40. Next, the long procedure of examining the background, orthodoxy, and purity of Menéndez' Catholicism began. The corpus of the investigation has also been printed by Ruidiaz as "Memorial de los padres y abuelos de Capitán Pero [sic] Menéndez de Avilés . . . ," in *La Florida*, 2:742–801.

Seville. Now, Álvaro de Bazán decreed that French captives should be sentenced to serve at the oar in Spanish galleys, while their officers should be hanged or thrown in the sea.[37]

Continued concern about further French attempts to settle North America also led to another Crown venture in Florida. To protect other castaways, Philip II wished to evangelize the heathen Gulf coast Indians who had murdered Father Cáncer and harassed the shipwreck survivors in the 1554 fleet disaster. The King decided to undertake the Florida settlement, fund it from the royal treasury, and administer it through the viceroy of New Spain, the able Luis de Velasco.[38]

After reconnaissance in the northeastern Gulf by Guido de Labazaris in 1558, Velasco launched two expeditions. The first, commanded by Tristán de Luna, left Vera Cruz in midsummer of 1559, landed in Pensacola Bay, and was still unloading when it was scattered by a hurricane. The viceroy also sent Ángel de Villafañe with a skilled Asturian pilot, Gonzalo de Gayón, to explore and take possession of the Santa Elena area of the east coast. By summer of 1561, both efforts had failed completely, and the forces had been withdrawn. The cost to the New Spain treasuries was substantial.[39]

The pressures of the war had led to the launching of such costly adventures. Peace brought a realization that Castilian finances were in parlous state. A state bankruptcy had occurred in 1557; the end of

37. The earlier order for the disposition of corsairs was formalized in a cédula from the Queen to the Audiencia of Peru written from Valladolid on September 4, 1549, and found in Encinas, *Cedulario Indiano*, 1:406. The order of Bazán was dated December 31, 1558, and is cited by Duro in *Armada Española*, 2:462.

38. The plan for the colonization of Florida was outlined by Pedro de Santander in a letter to the Crown dated July 15, 1557. See *Colección de documentos inéditos para la historia de España (D.I.E.)*, 26:340–65. The King, overcoming a hesitation that his viceroys undertake discoveries and settlement, authorized the effort in a cédula sent to Luis de Velasco from Valladolid on December 29, 1557. It is found in A.G.I. *Santo Domingo* 115 (Stetson Coll.). Philip emphasized the importance of making a settlement at Santa Elena on the east coast to impede the French "who might wish to go to this land of Florida to settle in it and take possession." This is in a letter to Tristán de Luna sent from Toledo on December 18, 1559, and found in A.G.I. *Justicia* 1,013, no. 2.

39. The Labazaris voyage was described by the viceroy in a letter to the Crown from Mexico, February 1, 1559, A.G.I. *Indiferente General* 738, ramo 7, no. 73–A (Stetson Coll.). Villafañe's report is found in his letter to the Crown from Santa Elena dated May 27, 1561, and found in A.G.I. *Indiferente General* 738, ramo 7, no. 73–B (Stetson Coll.). The finding of Don Luis, the Indian chieftain, in the Chesapeake region was described in a letter from the Casa to the Crown written at Seville on September 29, 1561, from A.G.I. *Contratación* 5,167. De Luna's report on the disastrous storm in Pensacola Bay is dated September 24, 1559, and is found in A.G.I. *Patronato* 179, ramo 1. It has also been reproduced in *The Luna Papers*, translated and edited by Herbert I. Priestley, 2:244–47. Gayón, who was a native of Pola de Lena in Asturias, was the most experienced pilot in Florida waters. A body of information about him is found in "Services of Gonzalo de Gayón, 1558–1566," from A.G.I. *Santo Domingo* 11 (Stetson Coll.).

the war meant that substantial cutbacks in Crown spending were imperative. The armada of Álvaro de Bazán was dismissed and some of its war matériel sold. The coming of peace, however, did little to relieve the most pressing problems of defense. When Philip announced to his Indies officials the signing of the treaty at Cateau-Cambrésis, he warned them that it was no time to relax their vigilance against corsairs: "See that the said peace is observed on our part and because, as you know, in peacetime we are accustomed to having corsairs going to rob against the will of their prince, it is well that during this time, the ships which come from that area do not come unprepared."[40]

In the diplomatic negotiations which had preceded the execution of the treaty, the whole question of French intrusion in the domains claimed by Spain had been treated at length. After debating the matter for weeks, the parties reached no settlement on the issue of trespass. In 1560, when the discussions finally broke down for lack of agreement, both sides were left essentially where they had been. For their part, the Spanish maintained the integrity of the areas set aside for them by the Papal bulls and the Tordesillas treaty, while the French continued to insist that they might sail in and colonize any areas not actually occupied by the Spanish. Matters were left in that uneasy and unsettled state, a fertile field for future misunderstanding.[41]

40. Cédula to all officials in the Indies, Valladolid, May 23, 1559, A.G.I. *Indiferente General* 427, Book of 1543–1601.

41. Felix Zubillaga has summarized the disputes over the right of navigation and settlement in the Indies in *La Florida: La Mission Jesuítica (1566–1572) y la colonización española*, pp. 134–35. A more recent and exhaustive study of the matter has been undertaken: see Paul E. Hoffman, "Diplomacy and the Papal Donation."

Philip II, Florida, and Pedro Menéndez de Avilés

The unresolved questions of overseas jurisdiction between the courts were only part of the concerns of Philip II. He feared that a flood tide of heresy threatened to overwhelm all of Catholic Europe. The keen and fervent apostles of militant Protestantism, aided by the output of the busy printing presses in Geneva, spread Calvinism to many areas of France where the threat to the Catholic faith seemed immediate and urgent. France dissolved into chaos after the death of Henry II and the ensuing weakness of a regency. After the insurrection at Amboise in March 1560, leading noble families pursued their rivalries which were now sharpened by religious differences. In the Mediterranean there was a renewed threat of Turkish naval invasion, while the Barbary raiders continued to endanger Spanish shipping from Gibraltar to Cape St. Vincent.

Philip II, pressed as never before by his external problems, also directed his attention to internal concerns. During the years after 1556, Philip moved to regularize and control the complex organisms which composed the Spanish governmental system. He sought to improve the efficiency and revenues of the commercial network between Spain and his possessions overseas and to strengthen defenses in the Indies. The management and financing of conquest and settlement in new lands were also areas for royal initiative.

Although he consistently sought to draw the reins of his power ever tighter, Philip II did not abandon the traditional means of licensing private conquerors. It is more correct to say that he supplemented the device of adelantamiento or used it selectively to carry out his policies. In 1557, the King gave an asiento to Jaime Rasquín to settle and populate the area of the Rio de la Plata.[1] As has been seen, the Crown authorized the royal expedition to Florida in that same year. The exhaustion of the state treasury at the end of the 1550s clearly posed a dilemma to the Castilian King: he sought to avoid heavy expenditures in the conquest of new lands, yet still to exercise control over their exploitation. Philip II wrestled with the problems involved, but for the moment the pressure of fiscal necessity outweighed other considerations.

The atmosphere of 1560 was thus one in which the talents of Pedro Menéndez de Avilés were in greater demand than ever. After Menéndez had escorted the King to Laredo, however, he had no immediate personal employment until the next fleet was ready to depart. Then he served for three years as captain-general of the combined New Spain and Tierra Firme fleets, alternating with Pedro de las Roelas and Nicholas de Cardona. During these years, Menéndez used his own vessels as lead ships in the fleets which he commanded, gaining Crown charter fees as well as his salary. The Asturian also sent his ships in other fleets on royal errands and commercial enterprises. His private income came largely from freight charges and passenger fares; he does not appear to have been a major trader dealing for his own account on any sizeable basis.

In Andalusia, Pedro Menéndez had made direct and profitable connection with a number of norteños engaged in the Carrera de Indias. Many of these merchants operated from Cádiz and possessed opposite numbers in the Caribbean island ports, at San Juan de Ulúa and the City of Mexico, and the entrepôts of Tierra Firme. Pedro del Castillo was spokesman for the Cádiz traders and was still closely associated with Pedro Menéndez.[2]

Menéndez and Castillo were unfavorably linked together by officials of the Casa de Contratación in accusations arising out of the return of the 1561 fleets. Pedro Menéndez had enjoyed a prosperous voyage.

---

1. The agreement with Rasquín has been printed in *D.I.*, 26:273 ff. It is mentioned in the work of Duro, *Armada Española*, in "Noticias extractadas de asientos y capitulaciones que se hicieron para descubrir en Indias despves de Colón," 1:459.

2. Castillo appears as a leading merchant in Cádiz and spokesman for the other traders of that city in a royal cédula sent by Philip II to "a certain merchant of Cádiz" from Valladolid on May 23, 1559. The letter, which discusses conditions surrounding the special license given to Cádiz merchants to deal in hides and sugar from Hispaniola and Puerto Rico, is from A.G.I. *Indiferente General* 425, Book 23, fol. 396 and vto. In 1561, the King responded to a complaint by Castillo that the royal *corregidor* had been sending the cases of Cádiz shipmasters to the Audiencia at Granada, where they languished. At that time, Castillo had just become a *regidor* of the *cabildo* of Cádiz. The King's letter was dated May 10, 1561, and is also from A.G.I. *Indiferente General* 425, Book 24.

He captured several English and French prizes on the return voyage to Spain, but the day after the ships crossed the bar and anchored at Sanlúcar, the Casa authorities inspected them and made inquiries among the crew and in the vicinity.

Pedro del Castillo was arrested and charged with smuggling goods outside of registry. Witnesses swore that Castillo had come aboard Menéndez' galleon at his invitation after dark on the evening of its arrival and had been closeted with the captain-general and a certain Domingo Hernandez, the master of Castillo's ship in the convoy. Others reported that thirty-seven chests of contraband silver were taken from the ship at midnight and transported to Puerto Santa María, where they were put into a small boat, then loaded into a cart, which disappeared into the darkness. Castillo was jailed in Seville. He denied that he had received any goods except those in the official registry. Castillo admitted that he had come to visit Pedro Menéndez at Sanlúcar, but he said that this was because the two men were long-time friends.

The Casa de Contratación put Pedro del Castillo under 6,000-ducat bond. His bondsmen were two bankers of Seville—Pedro de Morga and Gaspar de Astudillo. Although Castillo was lodged in an apartment rather than a cell and was well treated, he became ill and was finally released.[3]

The mutual animosity between Pedro Menéndez de Avilés and his friends and supporters, on the one hand, and the merchants' guild in Seville and the Casa de Contratación, on the other, is evident throughout the proceedings. As Pedro Menéndez prepared for the voyage of 1562, he could be assured that his every act would be closely watched and reported to Seville.

During these years, the tension between the broadening scope of Spanish foreign concerns and the limited royal resources continued. Heavy Spanish losses in ships and men at Tripoli in 1560 had been a drain upon the Crown. Philip's marriage to Elizabeth of Valois, daughter of Catherine de Medici, had brought no reassuring stability to the French scene. Indeed, after Charles IX succeeded Francis II, the weakness of the French Crown encouraged rapid polarization and dissension among the nobility. The disturbances, which shortly became localized warfare, led to the seizure of several ports by the Huguenot forces. Gaspard de Coligny, who had become admiral of

3. The case against Pedro del Castillo is found in "Pedro del Castillo, 1561," from A.G.I. *Justicia* 855. Menéndez advises that he was shortly set free because he was "without any guilt." The statement is found in "Servicios," A.G.I. *Patronato* 257, no. 3, ramo 2, fol. 11, vto.

France, prepared an expedition from the Huguenot ports for the colonization of Florida. On February 18, 1562, Jean Ribault and René de Laudonnière left Le Havre; by the end of April, the French had made landfall in Florida and proceeded to plant their colony at Port Royal.

Ironically, the general depression of the Spanish royal treasury had coincided with delayed reports of the costly failure of the Luna and Villafañe expeditions, to produce completely negative feelings about further colonization in Florida. While the French established their colony, the Spanish King formally eschewed further royal support for Florida. This resolve was urged on him in March of 1562.[4]

Meanwhile, Pedro Menéndez de Avilés had undertaken another Indies voyage as captain-general of the combined fleets. He now owned several sizeable ships. In addition to the *Magdalena*, he had built a large galeass, *San Sebastián*, and a galleon, *Santa María*. The galeass, under the command of Pedro Menéndez Marquéz, had sailed the previous year as *capitana* of New Spain while Esteban de las Alas commanded the New Spain division.[5] When Menéndez sailed in April 1562, he left under strict command from Philip II to intercept and castigate corsairs whom he might find in the Indies. The orders reflected the harsh tone of the period: "We are informed that in the Indies sailing routes go some French, English, and Scotch corsair ships, seeking to steal what comes and goes from there. This is a disservice to God our Lord, to us, and is against the peace agreed upon between us and the princes of those kingdoms. Because these corsairs should, by rights, be hanged as peace-breakers and robbers and violators of the orders of their own lords and rulers, I order you, if you capture any of the said corsairs, to proceed against them and punish them in conformity with justice, executing it then upon the sea with all rigor; in order that you might do this, we give you full powers."[6]

In accordance with previous practice, Pedro Menéndez divided his

4. See Crown to Luis de Velasco, September 23, 1561, from A.G.I. *Patronato* 19, ramo 12. When the royal order to study the matter of Florida was in the hands of the viceroy of New Spain, he convoked a council which included Ángel de Villafañe and several captains from the expeditions of 1557–61. Their judgment was that no further such ventures should be attempted from New Spain. Any future attempts upon Florida would best be mounted, they believed, from Spain directly, and should be concerned only with the areas north of Santa Elena. Velasco concurred in the findings. The *parecer* of the council of New Spain is from Woodbury Lowery's "Manuscripts of Florida" (microfilm, P. K. Yonge Library, reel 1, box 141–A).

5. See "1561, Ida," from A.G.I. *Contratación* 2,898.

6. "Instructions to General Pedro Menéndez, 1562," A.G.I. *Indiferente General* 415. These are also reprinted in Ruidiaz, *La Florida*, 2:407.

fleet into two parts; he went with the New Spain vessels while his brother, Bartolomé, took those of Tierra Firme. Juan Menéndez accompanied his father. The outbound voyage proved costly; seven ships were found unfit for further travel in San Juan de Ulúa, while several of the Tierra Firme group were scarcely seaworthy.[7] To allow more time for commercial transactions and to permit the refitting of the ships, Bartolomé and Pedro Menéndez decided to lay over in port during the winter months and to depart early in the New Year. Bartolomé had sent a courier vessel to Spain under the command of Diego de Hevia. When it reached Sanlúcar with its news, the captain was put in prison by the Casa de Contratación; there he joined Esteban de las Alas, who had been imprisoned earlier on the same charge, carrying contraband goods.[8]

Royal orders reached Pedro Menéndez in New Spain in February 1563. He was commanded to delay there until May or June and then to return via the usual route to Europe. The King directed Bartolomé Menéndez to leave immediately and be back in Spain by the end of April with the Tierra Firme ships and the bullion of Peru. Pedro Menéndez did not obey the order, or rather, he did not obey it completely. He determined to sail straightaway from San Juan de Ulúa to Havana, join his brother there, and return to Spain with the Tierra Firme vessels. Since the lead ships were not in condition to navigate, Menéndez prepared and designated his own two galleons, *Santa María* and *Magdalena*, and the patache *Santiago* as capitana, almiranta, and escort. Only his own ships left New Spain, while the others were left behind. The registries of Menéndez' ships show that they were laden with cochineal.[9] The shipments were from norteños resident in New Spain to consignees in Cádiz and Seville, including Pedro del Castillo. The ships left port on February 17, and made an uneventful passage to Havana. Once he had reached Havana, Pedro Menéndez sent his son Juan back as general in charge of escorting the remaining vessels to Spain. Bartolomé Menéndez, who had contracted fever in Nombre de Dios, was somewhat delayed in his arrival at Havana, but both brothers and their combined fleets sailed April 1, en

7. Menéndez describes the condition of the vessels in his letter to Philip II from Havana (n.d., probably March 1563), which is found in A.G.I. *Patronato* 257, no. 3, ramo 2 (Stetson Coll.).

8. Ibid.

9. Detail of the ships armed by Menéndez in San Juan de Ulúa is found, together with the registries of his vessels, in "Fiscal con Pedro Menéndez de Avilés sobre sueldos de dos galeones," A.G.I. *Justicia* 872, no. 1, The case began when the captain-general sought payment from avería for the charter of his ships. The Casa advised the King that Menéndez also carried gold, silver, and hides. See Crown to Casa, Madrid, July 16, 1563, from A.G.I. *Contratación* 5,167, Book III.

route to Spain. They dropped their anchors off the Guadalquivir bar on June 10, 1563.

It is likely that Pedro Menéndez only heard of the new French initiative in Florida when he arrived in Spain. The King had received word of the Ribault settlement from his ambassador in France in mid-February. He had immediately written to Menéndez and to Diego de Mazariegos, the royal governor at Havana, telling them of the fort the French had built at the "point of Santa Elena." The two men were ordered to discuss the matter, investigate, and take immediate action to expel the intruders. The letter could scarcely have reached the captain-general before his departure for Spain. Governor Mazariegos did not send out an expedition for more than a year.[10]

To counteract the French menace further, Philip II determined to follow the same procedure which had been considered in 1541: preventive settlement on the mainland. By the end of April 1563, he had decided to grant an asiento in Florida to Lucas Vázquez de Ayllón, namesake and successor to the patent-holder of 1523.[11] The contract with Vázquez de Ayllón was a typical and classic one. It made no mention whatever of the French but contained the standard benefits and obligations. The contractor was to launch a full-scale colonization, taking married settlers and a quantity of livestock. The Indians, whom he was not permitted to put into *encomienda*, were to be gathered by missionaries into villages near the Spanish towns. He could, however, use Indian tribute to provide pensions for his men. The colonies, which were to be in the area of Santa Elena, would concentrate upon planting sugarcane, cassia fistula, vineyards, and olive trees. The asiento was issued on June 4, 1563.[12]

At the same time, the King matured in his concept of the role of the Crown and its contractors in conquest. At Segovia, on July 13, Philip II approved 149 comprehensive ordinances for conquest and population. These laws provided for every detail of the exploration, occupation, and development of new lands by *asientistas*, whether designated adelantados, corregidores, *gobernadores*, or *alcaldes*. They also contained a particular injunction against royal expenditure, which served to put discovery and settlement upon a strictly private basis:

10. See the separate cédulas from the Crown to Diego de Mazariegos and to Pedro Menéndez de Avilés, Madrid, February 13, 1563, A.G.I. *Indiferente General* 427. Notice was also sent to officials in Santo Domingo, Venezuela, Cartagena, Tierra Firme, and San Juan, Puerto Rico.

11. In a letter from the Crown to the Casa, sent from Madrid on April 25, 1563, the King asked his trade officials to accommodate Vázquez de Ayllón in his difficulties in gathering sufficient settlers for his expedition.

12. It is found in "Asientos de Armada," A.G.I. *Contratación* 3,309.

Even though (due to the zeal and desire which we have that all unknown lands in the Indies might be discovered, so that the Holy Evangel might be proclaimed, and the natives of them might come to a knowledge of our Holy Catholic Faith) we count as little that which might be spent from our Royal Treasury for such a holy purpose, experience has shown that, in many discoveries and voyages undertaken at our cost (due to a lack of care and diligence), those who have carried them out have tried to enrich themselves from the Royal Treasury rather than carry out their designated purposes.

Thus we order that no discovery, new exploration, and settlement be undertaken at expense to our Royal Treasury, neither may those who govern expend anything from it, even though they possess our written authority and instructions to discover and explore, unless they should have special authorization to do it at our cost.[13]

Although Vázquez de Ayllón was not permitted to place any Indians into encomienda, the 1563 ordinances made no such general prohibition. On the contrary, as added incentive for private initiatives in conquest, the laws permitted two- and three-life encomienda.[14]

While Lucas Vázquez de Ayllón was in Sanlúcar preparing three vessels for the Florida journey, Pedro Menéndez de Avilés had left his ships there on the evening of June 14 and had gone up the Guadalquivir toward Seville in a small boat. He took with him a priest who

13. From "Ordenanzas," *D.I.*, vol. 8, no. XXV, pp. 494–95. To a degree, the resurgence of adelantamiento during the reign of Philip II has been overlooked. In the study of the strengthening of the early modern dynastic state, some writers have viewed the coming of the Spanish viceregal system as coincident with the termination of the phase of discovery and exploitation by private persons licensed by the Crown. An example of this viewpoint is the statement of Robert S. Chamberlain, speaking of the 1550s: ". . . the time was past when the Crown would permit the development of personal control anywhere in the Indies, especially when authority of a semi-feudal nature was concerned. The absolute monarchs of Castile were determined to bring their overseas possessions, which belonged to the Crown of Castile alone, not to the nation, under their own rigid authority. Therefore, they began early to create imposing machinery of royal, absolute government which left no place for personal governmental power or wide personal holdings of a political character" (*The Conquest and Colonization of Yucatan*, p. 184). On the other hand, George P. Hammond recognizes that the 1595 asiento of Juan de Oñate was issued under the royal colonization ordinances as an adelantamiento. See his article "Oñate's Effort to Gain Political Autonomy for New Mexico." Roscoe R. Hill, in "The Office of Adelantado," also recognizes the longer duration of adelantamiento under Philip II.

14. The provision for encomienda is found in "Ordenanzas," *D.I.*, vol. 8, no. LVIII, p. 505. For a discussion of how financial necessity had almost impelled Philip II to make encomienda in Peru perpetual in 1560, see C. H. Haring, *The Spanish Empire in America*, pp. 54–55.

was a distant relative, some servants, and a quantity of unregistered bullion. While his boat sailed northward through the night, the prosecutor of the Casa de Contratación was being rowed southward, searching for evidence of the smuggling of contraband. The two craft met briefly on the dark river, and the captain-general evaded the boat from the Casa. At dawn on June 15, the Menéndez party was seen to land on the riverbank just south of the city gates of Seville. Witnesses stated that the priest and sailors appeared to be heavily laden as they walked toward the city, where closer examination revealed that they carried bars of silver and several chests. Once inside the city, Menéndez and his party went to the houses of the archbishop of Seville, Hernando de Valdés, where they received hospitality and lodging.[15]

When the news of Menéndez' arrival came to the Casa de Contratación, its officials went to summon him to appear and answer charges of carrying contraband into Seville. Menéndez faced the judges in the Audiencia hall of the Alcázar and firmly denied their jurisdiction over him. He stated further that he had come upriver from Sanlúcar with the full knowledge of other Casa officials, and that his baggage had held only his own clothing, his arms, and enough silver for personal necessities. While the judges deliberated, the Asturian left, and when they finally issued their order to jail him and seize the silver, he had fled. Pedro Menéndez had gone to Madrid to seek royal support against his enemies.

Once at court, the captain-general quickly gained the ear of his King. Philip II responded to Menéndez' pleas by sending an immediate order to Seville that the monies due Menéndez for his galleon escort be calculated and paid. He then concluded an agreement with the Asturian to escort the Licenciado Castro to Tierra Firme on Crown business in the early fall. For the projected voyage, Menéndez would use his fine new galeass *San Pelayo*, just delivered from the Vizcaya shipyards. He also took the precaution of retaining an attorney to represent him at court in his disputes with the Casa de Contratación.[16] On July 3, the King sent his officials in Seville a

15. The main body of the 1563 case against Pedro Menéndez de Avilés is found in "Proceso de los cargos y culpas que resulta contra el General Pedro Menéndez de Avilés . . . en la flota y armada que vinó de Tierra Firme este año de 1563," from A.G.I. *Justicia* 970. Much material is also in A.G.I. *Contratación* 135-A.

16. The order of June 17 to pay Menéndez is referred to in Crown to Casa, Barcelona, February 26, 1564, from A.G.I. *Indiferente General* 1,966. The King decided not to accept Menéndez' offer to escort the Juan Menéndez ships from the Azores; see Crown to Casa, Madrid, July 16, 1563, A.G.I. *Contratación* 5,167. On July 28, 1563, the King notified the Casa de Contratación of the arrangement for the escort of Castro; the

strongly worded defense of Menéndez in which he pointed out that jurisdiction over the captains-general belonged to the crown, not the Casa.

Meanwhile, the escape of Pedro Menéndez de Avilés and the evidence of royal favor in his behalf had stirred the merchants and officials of Seville to angry action. A negative reply was sent to the King about Menéndez' request for payment for the 1563 escort galleons, as the traders' guild and the avería deputies rejected the claim. This was hardly surprising, for the administration of the avería, from which any payment would have to come, was firmly in the hands of the merchants of Seville.[17] After he received their opinion that Menéndez had evidently made his return voyage for profit and not for fleet defense, the King replied by ordering the officials to deduct from Menéndez' payment the sums he had earned from freight and passenger fees and settle the matter rapidly.[18] The Casa officials' only response to Philip's defense of Menéndez in the main dispute was to hasten the gathering of evidence against him. Witnesses from the fleet painted a picture of criminal laxity aboard the ships in which massive amounts of contraband bullion were allegedly carried by representatives of the recent viceroy of Peru and by the royal visitors to that province. They accused the captain-general of allowing a felon to escape with his funds at Tercera, of taking a bribe in New Spain, and of being caught with personal contraband in his possession. By the time Menéndez returned to Seville on July 26, 1563, his enemies were prepared to level criminal charges against him.

When he faced his detractors, Menéndez was confident that his backing at court would protect him and that only minor offenses could be proven, so his testimony was bold and forthright. He denied that he carried unregistered funds of any importance, but merely sufficient monies for his voyage, in keeping with long practice in the fleets. He blandly admitted accepting money from New Spain merchants, but denied that this had influenced his actions and stated that in any case it was no mortal sin.[19]

---

letter is also from A.G.I. *Contratación* 5,167. The power of attorney from Pedro Menéndez to Juan Gómez de Argomedo was originally recorded in the notaries' archives, but has been reproduced with its date of June 24, 1563, in A.G.I. *Justicia* 872 and also in *Justicia* 865.

17. Pierre and Huguette Chaunu point out that the consulado controlled the Indies avería contract from 1562 to 1564 (*Séville et l'Atlantique*, 1:203).

18. Crown to Casa, Madrid, July 16, 1563, A.G.I. *Contratación* 5,167, Book III.

19. Elements of the documentation of the 1563–65 case between Pedro Menéndez de Avilés and the Casa de Contratación have also survived in A.G.I. *Justicia* 865, no. 1, entitled "El fiscal de Su Magestad con el General Pedro Menéndez sobre dos barras de plata que trajo de las Indias sin registrar." Aspects of the case are also found in "Fiscal

After the captain-general had posted bond and given his testimony, he had every reason to expect that he could go about his affairs. Much to his surprise, however, the officials of the Casa de Contratación seized his brother, Bartolomé, and then came, on August 19, 1563, to place Menéndez himself in custody. The commerical powers were determined to punish him and his entire coterie through the laws of the Casa de Contratación for the threat he represented to their sphere of influence. In the course of a short time, Esteban de las Alas, Hevia, Pedro del Castillo, and now the Menéndez brothers felt the power of Seville.

Although he was made comfortable as a prisoner of distinction and was lodged in the *atarazanas* of the Casa between the old city walls and the Guadalquivir, Pedro Menéndez was distressed at the slow pace with which his case proceeded. The *fiscal* of the Casa gathered his evidence at a leisurely rate. Although Menéndez had given bond for his presence, he could not obtain release from custody. His appeals to the King produced royal letters to the Casa de Contratación but yielded little immediate result. No rapid settlement was made of his galleon-lease case, and he could not get his freedom to supervise the preparation of his galleons for their journey.[20] Worse troubles were in the making, however.

Without his knowing it as yet, Pedro Menéndez had suffered some grievous losses. His galeass, the *San Sebastián*, had sailed with Roelas' fleet in May with a cargo of royal mercury and other goods. Early in the morning of July 22, the *San Sebastián* and four other vessels were

---

de Su Magestad con Pedro de Menéndez de Avilés y sus fiadores Juan Antonio Corzo y Gaspar Astudillo, vecinos de Sevilla, sobre su quiebra del prisión donde estaba," from A.G.I. *Justicia* 868, no. 9. Thirteen of the charges against Menéndez are detailed in the captain-general's own complaint to Philip II in "Servicios," A.G.I. *Patronato* 257, no. 3, ramo 2. Solís de Merás, in *Pedro Menéndez de Avilés*, pp. 64–70, describes the 1563 case in some detail, from a viewpoint thoroughly sympathetic to his brother-in-law's. The unregistered bar silver was brought by Cristobal Carrecho, master of the *Magdalena*. Witnesses for the Casa alleged that it was worth 688 pesos and was intended to be given to one Diego de Molina by Captain Diego de Amaya by orders of Pedro Menéndez. See A.G.I. *Justicia* 865, no. 1, fol. 1.

20. A letter from the Casa to the Crown on August 2, 1563, contained in A.G.I. *Contratación* 5,167, Book II, acknowledged royal letters of July 13, 16, and 18, and noted that Menéndez had the commercial cargoes arranged for his galleons and had obliged himself to have them loaded aboard by September 10. Menéndez described the arrest of Bartolomé, in a letter to the King on July 27, and his own imprisonment, in a letter on August 21; both are found in Ruidiaz, *La Florida*, 2:34–43. The King also corresponded with his trade officials about the galleons of Pedro Menéndez in letters dated July 28 and August 11, 1563, and affirmed the arrangements for the passage of Licenciado Castro. These letters are also found in A.G.I. *Contratación* 5,167, Book III.

shipwrecked along the reefs in the area known as the Jardines de la Reina on the southwest coast of Cuba.[21]

As Menéndez chafed at the restriction of his prison apartment, his only son, Juan, was drawing closer to mortal danger in the Indies. The main body of the New Spain fleet sailed from San Juan de Ulua on June 15, but was delayed by calms and contrary winds, and only reached Havana on August 1. The eleven ships in the original convoy were increased by two Honduran vessels; all thirteen left Havana together on August 15.[22] In so doing, Juan Menéndez disobeyed an order of his father, for Pedro Menéndez had warned him not to sail if his departure time would put him into the hurricane season. As Menéndez told the King: "I left express commands to Don Juan, my son, that in the whole month of July he could come out of the Bahama Channel, because in the beginning of August, some years, they often have very great hurricanes."[23]

For almost a month the voyage went well. On the eighth of September, however, when the convoy had reached the latitude of Bermuda, they were scattered by rising winds and seas. By the morning of September 10, they were in a full-scale hurricane. One of the ships lost steering control; its hull worked open and it sank west of Bermuda, while three vessels drifted or were blown southward to the north coast of Hispaniola—the almiranta *Santa Catalina* and the two Honduras merchantmen. One of the Honduras ships sank before it could reach port; its bullion was off-loaded onto the almiranta; the other barely made it to the port of Monte Christi with the *Santa Catalina*. The eight ships which had escaped serious damage from the storm made rendezvous at the Azores and continued to Spain together, arriving in the first week of November.[24] When the several

21. The loading of the *San Sebastián* at Sanlúcar is described in testimony before Juan Gutierrez Tello on March 22, 1563, found in A.G.I. *Contratación* 5,101. Pedro Menéndez Marquéz was her master. The shipwrecks are described by Duro in *Armada Española*, 2:465, and by the Chaunus in *Séville et l'Atlantique*, 1563 *aller*, 3:41. See also the marginal notes in A.G.I. *Contratación* 2,898, 1563 *Ida*.

22. See Casa to Crown, Seville, November 2, 1563, A.G.I. *Contratación* 5,167. Juan Menéndez, before his departure from Havana, wrote to the Casa (on August 9, 1563) in a letter found in A.G.I. *Contratación* 5,104.

23. Pedro Menéndez to Crown, August 21, 1563, printed in Ruidiaz, *La Florida*, 2:38–43.

24. The return of the surviving ships to Spain was announced in Casa to Crown, Seville, November 12, 1563, A.G.I. *Contratación* 5,167. Data on the shipwrecks were inscribed on the margin of the registry book, A.G.I. *Contratación* 2,898, fol. 231 vto. In a letter sent from that place on December 20, 1563, and contained in A.G.I. *Santo Domingo* 71 (Stetson Coll.), the Royal Officials from Santo Domingo advised the King of the three vessels which arrived in their waters from the ill-fated fleet. The Chaunus

accounts which arrived at Seville were finally sifted and analyzed, it was evident that the capitana—*La Concepción*—was missing, together with General Menéndez. The lead ship had last been seen, sailing well, in the midst of the storm, but its later fate was unknown.

As bits of information about the shipwrecks reached Seville, Pedro Menéndez learned what little he could. If he were only free, he could lead the search for the lost ship. Chafing at his confinement, Menéndez attempted to move his legal cases forward, but met only frustrating inertia. The pressure that he exerted at court resulted in an inquiry by the King about Menéndez' imprisonment. When the charges against him were sent to the Council of the Indies in October, that body agreed that the indictment was for "grave and ugly" faults and seemed content for the moment to leave prosecution in the hands of the Casa de Contratación.[25] The captain-general would have welcomed a definite decision. Instead, the prosecuting officer of the Casa had been granted a three-month delay in which to gather further evidence.

In response to pressure from the licenciado Castro, the man designated to sail for Peru as new president of the Audiencia of Lima (and scheduled to sail on Menéndez' ship), the Casa officials gave a short term of liberty to Pedro Menéndez to go to Cádiz and dispatch his three ships. Since Menéndez had given a 40,000-ducat bond to leave on the royal mission by September 30, he was anxious to meet his overdue obligation but was still unable to be present when the ships sailed on November 9, 1563. After leaving in a rising storm, the vessels were scattered and damaged before they could return to port, and one of them landed near Gibraltar in battered condition. Instead

discuss the matter in *Séville et l'Atlantique*, 1563 *retour*, 3:61, 66. See also Eugene Lyon, "A Lost Son." Pilot Noriega, who had been aboard one of the ships which reached the Azores, testified before the Casa de Contratación, which advised the King that the storm struck the ships about 180 miles south and west of Bermuda, in about 32 degrees latitude. Another account, cited by Dave Horner in *The Treasure Galleons*, p. 227, placed the ships above the latitude of Bermuda. It was from A.G.I. *Indiferente General* 2,003. In 1595, several witnesses testified that the ships had been in the vicinity of Bermuda when they ran into hurricane winds. See "Información de algunos servicios prestadas por el adelantado Pedro Menéndez de Avilés," Mexico, April 3, 1595, reprinted in Ruidiaz, *La Florida*, 2:590 ff. Two accounts from Florida, so to speak, testified that the capitana of Juan Menéndez had been wrecked in the Indian River section of the peninsula. Hernando d'Escalante Fontaneda, in *Memoir of Hernando d'Escalante Fontaneda*, p. 33, claimed to have interviewed survivors from the Menéndez fleet. More testimony came in the deposition of Stephan de Rojomonte (A.G.I. *Patronato* 19, no. 1, ramo 14), one of the Frenchmen captured by the Spanish in Hispaniola in January 1565. Rojomonte stated, as had Fontaneda, that two Spanish ships had been lost, the one of Juan Menéndez being wrecked close to Cape Canaveral.

25. See Council of the Indies to Casa, Madrid, October 11, 1563 (copied as 1564 in error), in A.G.I. *Contratación* 5,167, Book III.

of the 20,000 ducats the ships would have earned, Menéndez now faced repair costs which he estimated at 20,000 ducats.[26]

Finally, the *proceso* against Pedro Menéndez was complete. The deliberations of the Casa de Contratación were forwarded to the Council of the Indies. Juan Gómez de Argomedo, attorney for Menéndez, filed the plea of his client before the Council on December 16.[27] The Asturian was not hopeful, however; his expectations of justice and satisfaction seemed to be at a low ebb indeed. He composed several desperate appeals to the court and Council of the Indies. In a long memorial to the King, Menéndez reviewed his entire career and recounted the history of his struggles with the merchants of Seville and the Casa de Contratación. He outlined each of the charges against him and gave his own defense against them. Pedro Menéndez expressed particular anger at the allegations of conflict-of-interest and he forcefully contradicted the complaint that he had become rich through royal service. When he began to serve the Crown, Menéndez told Philip II, he possessed two galleons. Now, after sixteen years, he only had three ships, and these were heavily mortgaged. At length he detailed his losses and sacrifices in recent years, including the bereavement suffered in the evident loss of his son and many other relatives and friends in the 1563 New Spain fleet disaster. Again Pedro Menéndez begged for settlement of his monetary affairs and for release from prison. He then made statements about the settlement of Florida which are of particular interest here. He labeled the Luna and Villafañe expeditions as wasteful and misdirected and alleged that more than a half-million ducats and five hundred lives had been expended with no visible effect. It would be far better and much less costly, said Menéndez, to plant colonies in Florida directly from Spain. Thus the expedition would avoid the dangerous currents of the Bahama Channel and the poor, low land of the extreme southeastern coast and the peninsula. For about 50,000 ducats, claimed Menéndez, a profitable settlement could be implanted closer to Newfoundland where it would be of more strategic value.

Menéndez wrote another letter to Juan de Sarmiento, president of the Council of the Indies, in a humble, almost despairing tone. It expressed emotions which Pedro Menéndez had not been able to

26. See Officials of the Casa to Castro, Seville, October 23, 1563, from A.G.I. *Justicia* 868, no. 9. Pedro Menéndez described his plight in "Servicios," from A.G.I. *Patronato* 257, no. 3, ramo 2. The ships were the *San Pelayo*, the new galeass, the *Santa Clara*, and the *Magdalena*.

27. See inscription of Juan Gómez de Argomedo, December 16, 1563, in A.G.I. *Justicia* 865, no. 1.

reveal to the King and displayed a father's grief and anger at his impotence to help in the search for his son. He proposed to go with four pataches to collect the monies left in Hispaniola from his son's fleet and also to seek the lost capitana. His proposal was rejected, and the officials of Seville named General Juan de Velasco de Barrio to arm two heavy galleons for the task.[28]

The mood of dejection which had assailed Pedro Menéndez proved well founded. When the Council of the Indies heard the arguments of its fiscal and read the testimonies sent from Seville, they found Menéndez guilty on the main charge of bringing unregistered silver on his ship. The sentence and verdict they handed down on January 17 levied a fine of 100 gold pesos upon the captain-general. Lawyer Gómez immediately began an appeal.[29]

One positive benefit for Menéndez did result from the letters he had sent in January. The King wrote peremptorily to his officials at Seville, accused them of malicious delay in the settlement of the 1563 galleon-lease case, and directed termination of the matter "within fifteen days."[30] Early in March, hearings resumed on the case and Pedro Menéndez was taken from confinement to testify in the Audiencia hall of the Casa de Contratación in the Alcázar at Seville. The Casa judges were in the position of mediating a dispute between Menéndez, who sought payment from avería for his ships, and the prior and consuls of the guild of sea-merchants and the deputies of the avería. In the face of the commands of Philip II, the Casa officials were compelled to find for Menéndez. On March 8 they decreed the payment of a sueldo to him for his two galleons, less what he had collected in freights and passenger fares on the voyage.[31]

Now a storm of protest arose from the mercantile interests. The whole matter was a fraud, they said. Menéndez had brought his galleons and patache from New Spain for his own profit, and they served the interests of the fleet not at all. It was illegal, they maintained, for a captain-general to use his own ships as paid escort vessels

28. The letter to Juan de Sarmiento is dated "primero de enero" in the copy found in A.G.I. *Patronato* 257, no. 3, ramo 2 (Stetson Coll.). Menéndez' offer was rejected in a letter from the Council of the Indies to the Crown, dated at Madrid on February 14, 1564, from A.G.I. *Indiferente General* 738, ramo 6, no. 73. General Velasco described his successful journey in a letter to the Casa from Sanlúcar dated September 25, 1564, and found in A.G.I. *Contratación* 5,101.

29. The sentence of the Council of the Indies and the appeal notations of Menéndez' case are from A.G.I. *Justicia* 865, no. 1.

30. Crown to Casa, Barcelona, February 26, 1564, from A.G.I. *Indiferente General* 1,966.

31. From "Fiscal con Pedro Menéndez de Avilés sobre sueldos de dos galeones," A.G.I. *Justicia* 872, no. 1.

in his own convoy.[32] They averred that the expenses that Menéndez claimed were false, and his supporting papers were not properly certified by a notary.

Pedro Menéndez, scenting victory over his enemies, appeared and made a strong plea for a substantial advance, for his ships had still not sailed for Tierra Firme, and he badly needed 4,000 ducats to finish their refit and to pay some of his crewmen. On March 10, the Casa awarded him 1,500 ducats. He protested strongly, but the Casa stood by its decision: It was that or nothing. Menéndez contested the case, saying that he had received nothing for his patache, and the matter became bogged down on appeal. Frustration continued to be the lot of the imprisoned Asturian. While guards paced outside his apartment door, his financial affairs seemed as far as ever from solution. But somehow Menéndez managed to raise the funds to send his ships off to the Indies under the command of Esteban de las Alas and Pedro Menéndez Marquéz.

In the meantime, although the Spanish had as yet done nothing to erase Jean Ribault's Port Royal settlement in Florida, the French colonists had become thoroughly discouraged. Ribault himself had been in England, a part of the time in prison. The confusion in France before the pacification of Amboise had prohibited the sending of reinforcements. Finally, René de Laudonnière left Le Havre April 22, just as the French prepared to leave Port Royal and abandon their colony. On May 12, 1564, Governor Mazariegos of Havana finally dispatched the small search ship *Santa Catalina* with Hernando Manrique de Rojas as captain. Rojas, a thirty-year-old nephew of Juan de Rojas, chose experienced pilot Gonzalo de Gayón to guide the expedition to seek the French settlement. None of the three groups was destined to meet any of the others.[33]

When the Cuban vessel reached the Florida coast, north of Cape Canaveral, Manrique de Rojas traversed the shoreline, carefully searching for signs of enemy settlement. Finally, in 32.25 degrees

32. Philip II had made such a ruling in a cédula to the Casa dated July 15, 1562. It is cited by the Chaunus in *Séville et l'Atlantique*, 1563 *aller*, 3:41.

33. Both the first Ribault and the Laudonnière expeditions are described in a long narrative entitled "Información del Gobernador Blas de Merlo," from A.G.I. *Justicia* 212. René de Laudonnière's own narrative, "L'Histoire Notable de la Floride," has been reprinted in a number of places; the writer prefers the version in the work of Suzanne Lussagnet, *Les Français en Amérique pendant la deuxième moitié du XVIᵉ siècle*, vol. 2, *Les Français en Floride*, pp. 37–200. The dispatch of the Manrique de Rojas ship is described in "Report on the French who went to populate Florida," Havana, July 9, 1564, from A.G.I. *Santo Domingo* 99 (Stetson Coll.), and has been translated by Lucy Wenhold in "Manrique de Rojas' Report, 1564." See also "Services of Gonzalo Gayón," from A.G.I. *Santo Domingo* 11 (Stetson Coll.).

north latitude, they located a sizeable inlet with Indian settlements. There they encountered one Guillaume Rouffi, a sixteen-year-old boy. Rouffi told them that the other Frenchmen had left in a small craft some days before, leaving him behind with the Indians. Searching further they found and burned a wood blockhouse the French had built. They also discovered the six-foot marble column, bearing the arms of France, which had been planted by Jean Ribault. The column and Rouffi were brought aboard ship and returned to Havana, where Mazariegos reported to Spain that the French threat was over for the present.

While the Rojas party was making its report in Havana, the ships of Lucas Vázquez de Ayllón, which had left Sanlúcar in October, had only reached Santo Domingo. By mid-summer, Vázquez de Ayllón had made little progress in preparing for departure for Florida. The royal officials of Hispaniola began to suspect that the expedition might never sail.[34]

During the early summer of 1564, when so many events affecting Florida and the Indies were occurring overseas, events at court began at last to develop more favorably for Pedro Menéndez de Avilés. In May, his ship-charter case had been transferred to the Council of the Indies. On June 18, Philip II had decided to bring the main dispute for which Menéndez had been jailed to Madrid for hearing. He sent Menéndez a formal royal summons to report within twenty days to the Council of the Indies.[35]

When the summons from the King reached Pedro Menéndez in his prison apartment in Seville, he had decided to break out of his confinement. He saw clearly that he would never be free as long as he remained in the power of the Seville interests. On Saturday, July 1, Menéndez bribed or evaded his guards and left his jail. The same day, the Menéndez brothers executed a power of attorney in Seville to a banker, Domingo de Ocaris, and a trusted young Asturian, Hernando de Miranda, and left to them the responsibility of collecting monies forthcoming from the Casa in Seville. By the sixth of July, Pedro Menéndez was in Madrid where he was placed in the royal jail.[36]

34. Report of the dispatch of Vázquez de Ayllón's ships from Sanlúcar came in a report from Captain Juan de Texeda to the Casa written on October 4, 1563, from A.G.I. *Contratación* 5,167 (Stetson Coll.). For reaction to the delays in Santo Domingo, see the letter from Licenciado Echegoyen to the Crown, Santo Domingo, August 10, 1564 (enclosing letter from April 1564), A.G.I. *Santo Domingo* 71 (Stetson Coll.).

35. Crown to Pedro Menéndez de Avilés, Madrid, June 18, 1564, from A.G.I. *Justicia* 868, no. 9.

36. The jailbreak was described by the discomfited fiscal of the Casa in a report

When Menéndez' servants came to take away his chests and other furniture, the Casa de Contratación belatedly discovered that their prisoner was gone. A hearing was held, and the angry officials determined to take up the 30,000-ducat bonds. On July 14, they also seized and jailed the bondsmen, Gaspar de Astudillo and Juan Antonio Corzo, who had given surety for Pedro Menéndez.[37]

Now the accused captain-general had finally succeeded in having his litigation transferred from the biased atmosphere of Seville, but it brought him no immediate satisfaction. After an initial flurry of legal action, Pedro Menéndez languished in the court jail. On July 24, he launched a fervent appeal to the Council of the Indies, and complained that he was confined with common criminals and other persons of low estate. This treatment, he said, was an affront to the dignity of his person and to the prestige of the offices which he had held through royal patronage. Menéndez asked that he be released from the jail and be given the court as his area of detention. On August 7, the Council of the Indies agreed that while the litigation was under study he might leave the jail and be placed in house arrest at his inn.[38]

While the legal affairs of Pedro Menéndez were moving somewhat closer to resolution in Madrid, the Spanish authorities had no clear view of what had occurred in Florida. René de Laudonnière and his colony were established within the mouth of the river May where they had erected a fortification named Fort Caroline.[39] The Castilian

---

dated July 15, 1564, from A.G.I. *Justicia* 868, no. 9. The power of attorney was executed on July 1, 1564, and was originally from the *Archivo de Protocolos de Sevilla* (hereafter A.P.S.), *Escribanía* of Juan de la Cobaco. It has been reproduced in A.G.I. *Contratación* 4,802 (Stetson Coll.). The main body of the Menéndez case in 1564 is found in A.G.I. *Justicia* 869.

37. Corzo was a shipowner, merchant, and slaver, while Astudillo served as banker and financial agent in Seville. Astudillo was also fiscal representative for Pedro del Castillo and his wife, Dona Isabel de Ribera, for certain juros the Castillos held in the Casa de Contratación. See revocation of *poder* of July 28, 1563, in A.P.C., *Escribanía* of Medina, fol. 287, 287 vto.

38. Order of August 7, 1564, from A.G.I. *Justicia* 868, no. 9.

39. An excellent description of the construction, dimensions, and armament of the fort is found in "Information of Governor Blas de Merlo," from A.G.I. *Justicia* 212. Fort Caroline was also described in an account and map sent with the letter of Governor Mazariegos to the Crown, written at Havana on December 22, 1564, and found in A.G.I. *Patronato* 267, no. 1, ramo 37. It has been depicted by Jacques Le Moyne du Morgues, the contemporary artist who served in the fort; see the color reproductions in *The New World* by Stefan Lorant, p. 55. Charles Bennett has also reproduced these in *Settlement of Florida*, pp. 21, 23. The reconstruction of the fort by the National Parks Service at St. Johns' Bluff has closely followed the contemporary depictions. The fort on the river May (the present St. Johns River) may not necessarily have been precisely like Le Moyne's painting, however. It appears that his paintings may have been created after his return to France, and it has been demonstrated that

King had no knowledge of the French establishment. Intelligence from the Indies in the summer of 1564 was a blend of fact and rumor. On August 30, the Audiencia of Santo Domingo notified Philip II that a one-eyed Portuguese named Mimoso was supposed to have come from Calais with five ships of Frenchmen and three of the ships had landed at Santa Elena in Florida.[40] In this case, the actual intrusion of the Laudonnière expedition was obscured by the multitude of corsair reports which flowed continually to the Spanish Crown from France, the Atlantic islands, and the Indies.

The instrument chosen by Philip II to deny the mainland to the French through colonization proved to be a feeble one. Lucas Vázquez de Ayllón, embroiled in some financial difficulties in Santo Domingo, was forced to sell one of his ships, and many of his men deserted. Finally, in early August 1564, Vázquez de Ayllón fled Santo Domingo by night in a small craft, reportedly heading for Peru. The latest chapter in the long history of attempts to settle Florida had come to an inglorious end.[41]

While the Spanish were failing to discover or counter the French moves in Florida, the armada of galleons that belonged to Pedro Menéndez moved around the Caribbean with the Tierra Firme ships. Esteban de las Alas brought the *San Pelayo*, the *Santa Clara* and the *Magdalena* to Nombre de Dios. On August 13, they left that port for Cartagena, and, three days later, the *Magdalena* was wrecked on the Darien coast.[42] The diminished fleet left Cartagena on September 20. After the ships sailed from Havana, the *Santa Clara* ran aground on the eastern side of the Gulf Stream. All the crew were rescued and the treasure transferred to the ample holds of the great galeass *San Pelayo*, while the *Santa Clara* was abandoned as a hopeless wreck. Heavily laden (the ship carried more than 1,400 bars of silver), the *Pelayo* returned to Spain and landed at Cádiz on December 4.[43] The

---

they contain errors. See Jerald T. Milanich and William Sturtevant, eds., *Francisco Pareja's 1613 Confessionario*, p. 4.

40. The report of the Audiencia, dated August 30, 1564, from A.G.I. *Patronato* 254, ramo 38 (Stetson Coll.), recounts a route of the supposed Portuguese-French fleet which does not square with the actual course of the Laudonnière vessels. The Huguenots, who had left from Le Havre, touched at the Canary Islands, watered at Dominica, and went directly from the Virgin Islands to the eastward of the Bahamas, and thence westward to the river May. See the description in "Information of Governor Blas de Merlo," from A.G.I. *Justicia* 212. The Santo Domingo story placed the French ships in the vicinity of Cape San Antonio on the western tip of Cuba.

41. See letter from Licenciado Echegoyen to the Crown, August 10, 1564, from A.G.I. *Santo Domingo* 71 (Stetson Coll.).

42. See Chaunu, *Séville et l'Atlantique*, 1564 *aller*, 3:58.

43. The return of the *San Pelayo* and the loss of the *Santa Clara* are described in the text and margins of A.G.I. *Contratación* 2,898, fol. 230 vto., and by the Chaunus in

reports of disaster it brought to Pedro Menéndez de Avilés were tempered no whit by the news that there was no further trace of his missing son.

Meanwhile, trouble had also visited the small French Huguenot colony on the river May. Laudonnière explored the area and traded with the Indians near the fort. An increasing shortage of supplies and the desire for adventure provoked some of the garrison to mutiny. Eleven mutineers fled the fort first, taking a small shallop, and setting course for the Caribbean. Three weeks later, on December 18, 1564, seventy men from the garrison held René de Laudonnière prisoner long enough to extort from him a document authorizing their journey. They then departed on a voyage of adventure among the Antilles in two small sailing craft.[44]

The year of 1564 had thus far held little cause for rejoicing for Pedro Menéndez de Avilés. When the Council of the Indies ruled on the whole battery of charges against him on November 23, it found him guilty on nine of the fourteen charges, fined him 3,000 ducats, and sentenced him to three years without office in the Indies.[45] But immediately after this low point in his fortunes his affairs seemed to improve. On November 24, he was given the court as his jail pending his latest appeal. On December 7, the Council ruled favorably for Menéndez in the galleon-lease case and granted him the sueldo for his ships. Menéndez pressed his advantage and asked that his freight earnings not be deducted from the payment, and that he be reimbursed for the pay of the soldiers who accompanied the ships. The councillors took the requests under advisement.[46]

Early in the new year, the Council of the Indies reconsidered the main Menéndez case, and finally reduced its sentences to six guilty charges and the exile from Indies offices to one year. Menéndez' fine was cut to 1,000 ducats.[47] Now that the tide of influence seemed at last to be running in his favor, a major question at court must have been that of the future of this valuable, contentious man.

Séville et l'Atlantique, 1564 *aller*, 3:60, 62. The officials at Seville reported the arrival of the *San Pelayo* in a letter to Philip II dated at Seville on December 5, 1564, and found in A.G.I. *Contratación* 5,167, Book III.

44. René de Laudonnière describes the mutiny in "L'Histoire Notable," in Lussagnet, *Les Français en Amérique*, 2:124–25. Some of the mutineers recounted their version of events, which was recorded in the "Information of Governor Blas de Merlo," from A.G.I. *Justicia* 212.

45. See the sentence of November 23, 1564, from A.G.I. *Justicia* 869.

46. See the petitions of Pedro Menéndez and his attorney in A.G.I. *Justicia* 872, no. 1.

47. From A.G.I. *Justicia* 869, sentence of January 24, 1565.

From Asiento to Joint Venture

W hile Pedro Menéndez pressed for favorable settlement of his law-suits and was still technically a prisoner in Madrid, events were taking place rapidly in the Indies. Although the Spanish were as yet unaware of Laudonnière's settlement at Fort Caroline, some Frenchmen from that place took a course of action that would shortly bring their colony to open and dramatic attention in the Spanish Indies.[1] The two little vessels which had left the river May together in mid-December 1564 had been separated in a storm. One of these arrived at Cagay, a Spanish town within the great bay on the southwest coast of Hispaniola. The men aboard captured a small prize, which they ransomed; after trading their own vessel for a larger, finer Spanish ship, they sailed off on further adventures. The other French crew soon came to La Yaguana, a port thirty miles from Cagay. When they appeared off the harbor entrance, Spanish ships sailed out to intercept them and the Frenchmen fled. Not aware of their compatriots' earlier raid on Cagay, the corsairs went there. Their landing force had surrounded some settlers' houses when armed Spaniards attacked them and killed or captured several of the French, while the rest were put to flight.

1. The material which follows is taken from the "Information of Governor Blas de Merlo," taken at La Vega, Jamaica, on March 6, 1565, and found in A.G.I. *Justicia* 212. The "Information" is a 51-folio narrative of events of all the French expeditions to Florida, taken from the prisoners captured in Jamaica by Merlo on January 25, 1565, together with testimonies by Spanish eyewitnesses to the corsairing activities of the French. Merlo had the document copied at Bayamo, Cuba, and sworn to before the *alcalde ordinario* there on May 13, 1566. That copy eventually found its way into the papers relating to the French prisoners in A.G.I. *Justicia* 212.

Near Cape Tiburón, at the extreme southwest point of Hispaniola, the two groups of Frenchmen rejoined forces. They then crossed the Windward Passage together, came within sight of the mountains of Oriente, and landed at the Cuban port of Baracoa. There they raided the town for supplies, ransacked houses, and took a small caravel which they found in the bowl-shaped harbor. The little fleet then recrossed to Hispaniola. On January 16, 1565, the ships assaulted a Spanish ship anchored close to Cape Tiburón. The men aboard it were well armed and determined to sell their lives dearly, and their surrender came only after three of their force had been killed—a soldier, a slave, and one Antón Núñez.[2] This action of the Frenchmen was certain to bring them to the notice of Spanish officialdom, for Núñez was secretary of the Audiencia of Santo Domingo, and had been traveling to Cuba on a mission for that body. In addition to the wines and other goods they seized, the French captured more than twenty Spaniards. Now they abandoned the last remaining vessel of those brought from Florida. The little fleet, now composed entirely of prizes, set a course for the southwest and Spanish Jamaica where they hoped to exchange their prisoners for food.[3]

Meanwhile the Frenchmen in the third small craft from Fort Caroline had decided to try their luck in Cuban waters. At the town of Savanna, they captured a mulatto and seized some supplies. When they raided the port of Arcos, the man escaped and made his way to the governor at Havana. As soon as the notice reached him, Governor Mazariegos readied two small boats, sailed for Arcos, and surprised and captured all eleven of the French raiders. When the prisoners were brought to Havana, they were interrogated by Guillaume Rouffi, the French lad whom the Spanish had found at the site of Ribault's deserted colony at Port Royal. The captives' narrative was written down on December 22, 1564.

A careful description was made of the French craft and the stolen goods it contained. Five of the men testified, and their stories contained a startling message: the French had again settled in Florida! They had built a fort at a location between twenty-eight and twenty-

2. On October 2, 1565, the Council of the Indies advised the King of the French raids on Santo Domingo; in July, word had come to the Council from that Audiencia about Núñez' death. The correspondence is found in A.G.I. *Indiferente General* 1,218. Another account of the capture of the ship off Cape Tiburón is the "Deposition of Francisco Ruiz Manso," which has been translated and printed in Charles Bennett, *Laudonnière and Fort Caroline*, pp. 103–6.

3. Jamaica was well known in the Indies for its production of beef and cassava. A comprehensive description of Jamaica as a sixteenth-century center for the export of cassava is found in Francisco Morales Padrón, *Jamaica española*, pp. 282–84.

nine degrees north latitude. The French prisoners described the fort, its garrison, and its armament in detail. The men, who claimed to be Catholics, said that they had fled Florida to avoid the harsh labors their "Lutheran" officers imposed upon them. Governor Mazariegos prepared to send three of the prisoners with their vital news to Spain.[4]

Less than a month after the capture of the men at Arcos, on January 20, 1565, three sails appeared off Point Morant, the southeast cape of the isolated island of Jamaica. As soon as he sighted the ships, Governor Blas de Merlo hastened to put his forces in a state of defense. The Frenchmen dropped anchor and sent their smallest craft into the harbor of Caguaya, near the capital of Santiago de la Vega (near old Port Royal harbor and the modern city of Kingston). They chased down and boarded a small caravel. Governor Merlo learned from one of the caravel's crew that the raiders were French, and he prepared to attack. First, he put the Frenchmen off their guard by parleying with them and promised to trade them food for the Spanish captives they held. While they waited for the food to arrive, the governor attacked with several ships. The action was short but sharp, and when it was over, two vessels and thirty-two Frenchmen were prisoners. One of their ships had escaped, however. It made its way out of the harbor and began the long voyage back to Florida.[5]

The corsairing of the three little craft from Laudonnière's Florida was, after all, no more than small-bore piracy and they had posed no major threat to the Carrera de Indias. Some concern had been aroused in the Spanish Indies, but property damage was minor. The effects of the adventures were, however, major ones and would spell disaster to the French in Florida.

Now, at last, the location of the French settlement was unmasked, and the vague menace was given definite shape. The prisoners said

4. The prisoner interrogation is found in A.G.I. *Patronato* 267, no. 1, ramo 37. The names of the men (as given by the Spanish) were Alberto Melenes, Francisco Juan, Miguel Cobin, Juanes de Sigaray, and Martin Joaber. One of them, Joaber, testified that he had been a part of the 1562 Ribault expedition, had returned to France, and had left Le Havre with Laudonnière in April 1564. Another deposition, made on February 28, 1565, was given by one Stefan de Rojomonte, who had been with the corsairs on the Hispaniola coast. Although the folder is marked "Cuba" and presumably had been taken there, Rojomonte was evidently captured at Cagay and had no knowledge of the eleven Frenchmen taken at Arcos. His testimony is found in A.G.I. *Patronato* 19, no. 1, ramo 14, and in A.G.I. *Indiferente General* 2,081.

5. René de Laudonnière advises that the ringleaders of the corsairing expedition —Desfourneaux, LaCroix, and De Gênes—got away safely from Jamaica in the vessel which escaped; from Laudonnière's "L'Histoire Notable," in Lussagnet, *Les Français en Amérique*, 2:126. On the other hand, Governor Merlo states that he had captured the French captain in charge.

that the offending colony was at about twenty-eight to twenty-nine degrees north latitude, clearly within the territories of the Crown of Castile, and those who had settled there were guilty of trespass under Spanish law. The raiders from the settlement had also added piracy to their crimes. The punishment thus merited by the Huguenot colony and compounded by its mutineers would eventually be forthcoming. Only the factors of time and distance could delay it, as the news slowly filtered back to Spain. The message the governor of Cuba had sent in the ship *La Vera Cruz* was the first to arrive. The urgent and momentous dispatch about the French fort would not reach Seville until March 26.[6]

In the meantime, on February 3, 1565, the Council of the Indies finally terminated the two cases affecting Pedro Menéndez. The long *pleito* with the Casa de Contratación was definitively ended, in his favor. The two bars of silver, now the only remaining issue, were ordered returned to Menéndez; that matter at last came to an end. At the same meeting the council also terminated the case involving charter fees and reimbursements for Menéndez' two galleons and patache, from the 1563 fleet. In their decision, the councillors agreed to the terms Menéndez' attorney had asked the previous December—he would receive full repayment for the pay of the soldiers he brought aboard the ships.[7]

Now this able, vital, and troublesome figure could again serve his King. In the Indies there was an area of real concern where his abilities and knowledge might be most useful. Philip II formally asked Menéndez to study and report on the problems of Florida. What, asked the King, did he know about its coasts and lands? What did he believe could be done to settle it, after so many failures to do so? What measures should be taken in the event corsairs had gone there to establish a base for raids against Spanish ships?

In reply, Menéndez sent a lengthy memorial.[8] He began by recounting current rumors about corsairs who might have settled in Florida; he had heard of two groups. The first, captained by the infamous Portuguese Mimoso, had been reported by the Audiencia of Santo

6. The officials of the Casa advised the King of the vessel's arrival, in Casa to Crown, A.G.I. *Contratación* 5,167, Book III.
7. The final sentences are found in A.G.I. *Justicia* 865 and *Justicia* 872, no. 1, respectively. The settlement of the main case with the Casa described in A.G.I. *Justicia* 865 is at variance with its description by Solís de Merás in *Pedro Menéndez de Avilés*, pp. 67–68.
8. The memorial, from A.G.I. *Patronato* 19, has been reprinted in Ruidiaz, *La Florida*, 2:320–26. It bears no date, but internal evidence indicates that it can hardly have been written before February 1, 1565, and must have been presented before negotiations began on the asiento signed by Menéndez on the following March 15.

Domingo the preceding August.[9] In Menéndez' version of the story, Mimoso had been seen at Tenerife in the Canaries in the late spring of 1564; possibly he was now in Florida. The second expedition was composed of five heavily armed English galleons. When it touched briefly at El Ferrol on Spain's north coast at the end of December, Galician fishermen learned that the squadron was planning to go to Florida. If, said Menéndez, these tales were true and an enemy colony was established in Florida, homeward-bound ships would stand in danger of being taken by fast galleys from the corsair settlement. He also raised the spectre of enemy-incited slave insurrections in the Spanish Caribbean, which could lead to the loss of vital island strong points. Menéndez also expressed his great concern that such an establishment, if not quickly eradicated, might quickly take deep root in the land, as the English or French found favor with the Indians there. He was strongly convinced that Protestant heretics and American aboriginals held similar beliefs, probably Satanic in origin. These shared beliefs would naturally lead them to affinity, unless they were kept apart. An alliance between foreign intruders and the Indian peoples would prove most difficult, if not impossible, to break.

Shifting his emphasis to the geographic features of the North American mainland, Pedro Menéndez told Philip II of the rumors he had heard of the great passage to the South Sea. He was certain that "an arm of the sea" extended from Newfoundland twelve hundred miles to the westward where it came into close proximity with another waterway. This last passage, Menéndez believed, gave access to the mines of Zacatecas in New Spain and led ultimately to the South Sea. It was only necessary to explore the first water route and make a short overland journey to the second passage, and the way to the Pacific lay open.[10] It was vital, he asserted, to let no enemy learn the secrets of this strategic waterway and threaten the trade of the East, or seize the rich silver mines. Menéndez was also concerned that the French could easily create trade routes to a North American colony, since many vessels already came each year to the Newfoundland fishing banks from France. He could even foresee the possibility that they might establish sugar works and flocks to provide them with the sugar and wool they continually sought through trade or piracy.

Pedro Menéndez then outlined concrete proposals for Florida's set-

9. See p. 36. Menéndez had spoken in May 1564, at Seville, to a group of sailors returning from the Canary Islands. His story added little to the version sent from Santo Domingo.

10. There is an excellent appreciation of the geographical concepts of Pedro Menéndez, as well as some discussion of earlier hopes of the western passage, in L. A. Vigneras, "A Spanish Discovery of North Carolina in 1566," pp. 398–402.

tlement. If no actual intruders were in the land, an expedition should proceed directly to Santa Elena. A force of five hundred sailors, soldiers, and farmers would probably suffice. Menéndez urged that four Jesuits accompany the expedition to establish *doctrinas* and teach the faith to the sons of the native chiefs. While small vessels explored and mapped the coasts north to Newfoundland, agricultural settlements would be made in fertile inland areas. The cost of such an enterprise was estimated at 80,000 ducats for all expenses of initial outfitting and a year's supplies. Menéndez suggested that the Crown bear the cost of the undertaking in order to do it more quickly and secretly. If there should turn out to be Frenchmen in the land, a different approach would be advisable. In that case, a punitive expedition should be mounted with four well-armed galleons and one thousand soldiers and sailors. For a six-month military effort of this kind, Menéndez estimated a cost of 50,000 ducats.

After receiving and studying the memorial, Philip II and his Council of the Indies determined to carry out the Florida enterprise. They chose not to undertake it as a Crown-sponsored activity, but to license it as an adelantamiento, with Pedro Menéndez as adelantado. Now that the bothersome legal obstacles were out of the way, the decks were clear for meaningful negotiation. At this point one can analyze the diverse motivations of the parties to these negotiations and the purposes which they held in common. First, from the standpoint of the Crown of Castile, a number of considerations justified another attempt at the settlement of Florida. The King and his advisers were never forgetful of the continuing threat of French or English incursion along the long North American coastline. Whether or not this had already occurred, it remained always a possibility. Aggressive population and fortification could deny any establishment to another power and at the same time protect the legal rights of Castile. Exploration would unlock the secrets of the ports, currents, and shoals, and more accurate marine charts would lead to more secure navigation. Perhaps the fabled Northwest Passage could be found, thereby enabling a more direct trade with the East. The Carrera de Indias would be buttressed and protected from enemy assault by the very existence of mainland settlements. If Havana were adequately defended and the Florida coast fortified, the strategic Bahama Channel would be protected.

The evangelistic mission of the Catholic faith, so inextricably mixed with the other purposes of conquest and colonization, was an important consideration in preparing the Florida asiento. As royal authority for conquest was delegated to the adelantado as surrogate for the

King, so was a portion of responsibility for carrying out the *patronato*. All previous experience in Florida indicated that this would be a difficult and challenging mission. In the face of such difficulties, the winning of the souls of the Florida Indians would be an enterprise of great spiritual merit for the Crown of Castile and its adelantado. Conversely, for those souls to remain in their heathen state or, even worse, to become infected with the deadly virus of heresy would be reproach in the eyes of God.

As for Pedro Menéndez himself, one might wonder at his interest in the enterprise, after his disparaging remarks about Florida as a graveyard of hopes. For one thing, he must have held a lingering hope that his explorations might uncover the fate of his son, Juan.[11] Another was the strong inducement to build further his family name, reputation, and estate. An enterprise which promised lands, revenues, high titles, and expectation of exalted service to God and prince would stir any sixteenth-century hidalgo. In such an undertaking, moreover, there would be honor and profit, lands and offices enough for the whole circle of kinsmen and friends in the Menéndez orbit. In the bargaining Menéndez pressed for the title of marqués and the lands which would support it.[12] He had before him the example of the marquisate of Hernando Cortés in New Spain, which was granted in 1529. By 1565, the extent of the private holdings of the Marqués del Valle, held by the successor to Hernando Cortés, was well known. Cortés' economic empire was founded upon Indian labor and tribute which probably amounted to 30,000 pesos in value annually by 1560. This income permitted further investment in stock-raising, sugar production, money-lending, and mining ventures, while Indian and Negro slaves worked the agricultural properties. It was this kind of empire that Pedro Menéndez de Avilés had in mind when he petitioned for the title and lands of a marquis.[13] Pedro Menéndez also sought ways to gain privileged entrée into the Carrera de Indias for his maritime operations—shipping licenses granted by the Crown. At the same time, he wished to be freed from some of the onerous

11. See pp. 29–30. Stephan de Rojomonte's deposition, which advised that Juan Menéndez' ships had been lost near Cape Canaveral, could not yet have reached Spain to raise Menéndez' hopes.

12. See Appendix 1.

13. Hernando Cortés described the richness of his dominions, his 23,000 vassals, and his struggle against the municipalities to maintain political power in his land grant in a letter to Francisco Núñez, his attorney in Spain, dated June 25, 1532. The letter is reproduced in a work by Jorge Fernando Iturribarria entitled *Oaxaca en la historia*, pp. 64–65. An excellent discourse on the commercial side of Cortés' affairs was written by France V. Scholes in "The Spanish Conqueror as a Business Man; A Chapter in the History of Fernando Cortés."

regulations imposed upon shipowners by the Casa de Contratación.

Certain motives were shared by the parties. The establishment of a prosperous, thriving colony was a matter of mutual interest—revenues from it would flow both to the King and to his privileged adelantado. Such a flourishing settlement would be the best defense against any enemy and the most sure guarantee of profit from trade and agriculture. It would lend value to the land which could, in turn, support a high rank for the holder of that land.

The attempt to populate Florida was thus to be accomplished through the ancient institution of the adelantado. Even had they wished to do so, Philip II and his advisors would scarcely have been able to conquer Florida through the viceroyalty of New Spain. Luis de Velasco, the aggressive viceroy who had sent Miguel de Legazpi to the Philippines the past year and who had dispatched the de Luna and Villafañe expeditions to Florida, was dead. The government of New Spain was currently under the control of the Audiencia of Mexico until a new viceroy could arrive.

It has been pointed out that royal financial limitations had discouraged Crown financing of discovery, and that Philip II had determined in 1563 that the funding of exploration and settlement should, as a general rule, be private.[14] At this point, there was no reason to depart from this policy. After all, no grave and immediate threat was yet known to be in Florida. On the contrary, every circumstance dictated the continuance of the "no-cost" tactic; a host of urgent necessities pressed in upon Philip II from every quarter.

For four years and more, Spanish ships and men had been lavishly used to stem the Moslem assaults upon the North African bases of Oran and Mazalquivir. Now the main Turkish fleet threatened to break into the western Mediterranean by taking the island of Malta. Don Álvaro de Bazán's armada of galleys had to be sent there to bolster the Christians, but unfortunately the asiento undertaken by the merchant guild of Seville to support his ships had expired. Embarrassed for funds because of dislocations in the Indies trade, the Sevillians were dragging their feet at renewing the agreement.[15] The merchants felt that the galleys should be used to protect the Indies fleets against corsairs near Spain instead of sending them eastward to do battle with the Turks. Anxious to increase his flow of revenues from overseas, Philip II had proposed (in late 1564 and early 1565) a

14. See pp. 24–25.
15. See Prior and Consuls to the Crown, Seville, April 13, 1565, A.G.I. *Indiferente General* 1,093.

major re-working and tightening of fleet sailing laws and defense.[16] Because of his own lack of money, the King himself was constrained to borrow from the probate deposits in the Casa at Seville, until the next fleet should arrive.[17]

The Spanish Crown, moreover, faced other grave diplomatic problems. Amid a climate of hardening ideological conflict, Philip II had been pursuing his own counter-Reformation in his dominions in the Netherlands where he had published the Tridentine decrees in 1564. The King was irritated at the slowness of their implementation and the growth of opposition to the royal commands, and he felt gradually compelled to show a stronger hand.

In neighboring France, personal, dynastic, and religious involvements complicated the diplomacy of Philip II. His own ties to the Valois kingdom were close—his wife, Isabel, was daughter to the Queen Mother, Catherine de Medici, and sister of Charles IX, the King. Catherine and her son held tenuous control over a nation in an increasingly ambiguous and difficult internal situation. After the Pacification of Amboise in 1563, rival noble families, whose differences were compounded by religious loyalties, lived in uneasy proximity within the court and ministries of the French Crown. Philip II, who took a dogmatic position for the Catholic faith, stood ready to furnish his mother-in-law with concrete support against the Huguenot nobles. Under the circumstances, he had to watch events in France closely, for they might require substantial commitment at any time.

In spite of the collapse of the adelantamiento of Lucas Vázquez de Ayllón, and the failures of the other would-be adelantados of Florida, there seemed no better way to conquer Florida at minimum royal cost. Menéndez' suggestion of Crown underwriting was therefore rejected, and the adelantamiento of Florida was approved. Pedro Menéndez de Avilés fitted the needs of the moment by offering, in addition to his skill and zeal, one fine ship as the nucleus of a fleet. He could also call upon a host of friends and relatives in Asturias and the rest of the north coast of Spain who would pledge their persons, ships, and followers to his cause. In Cádiz, Seville, and in the Indies, Menéndez had credit sources to aid in arming of vessels and carrying out the expedition. Without question, moreover, his drive, ability, and reputation could act as a lodestone to draw support to the enterprise of Florida.

The Council of the Indies chose one of its members, Dr. Juan

16. Casa to Crown, Seville, December 8, 1564, A.G.I. *Contratación* 5,167, Book III, and Ordinances of the Fleets, March 6, 1565, A.G.I. *Indiferente General* 1,966.
17. Casa to Crown, Seville, April 8, 1565, A.G.I. *Indiferente General* 1,093.

Vázquez de Arce, to negotiate with Menéndez and agree upon the conditions under which the Florida expedition and settlement would be carried out. The bargaining ended on March 15, 1565, when both men signed a lengthy asiento.[18] To appreciate the underlying nature of this contract and to understand the relation of the parties to it, one must examine the relative positions of Pedro Menéndez and his sovereign. First of all, this was clearly not an accord between two parties of legally equal standing; one cannot view the asiento as a modern business contract. Neither the would-be adelantado nor his King was able, as is done today, to deal in contractual terms limited strictly to the business at hand. Their mutual binding on the enterprise of Florida was done within the framework of their broader relationship as ruler and subject. An example of this was the final clause which the King inserted in the last version of Menéndez' agreement. It stated that non-compliance by Pedro Menéndez would not be a mere contract violation; it would be "treason to his natural Lord." An agreement with a sixteenth-century monarch would always exhibit this disconcertingly open-ended feature: there always existed the possibility of unilateral, prejudicial action.

Yet Philip II was not a totally unlimited despot. Among other restraints upon his power, the legalism present in all of Spanish life also affected the King's agreements with his subjects. In this tradition, therefore, the terms of the asiento had been set forth in great detail. For his part, Menéndez could rely upon receiving what had been promised to him in the contract, provided he lived up to his obligations—and provided Philip II did not decide to recast the nature of their relationship.

The asiento contained a rough quid pro quo of duties and rewards, obligations, and benefits which approximated what is termed in modern business law "consideration." This bilateral contractual balance

18. The 1565 Florida asiento can be found in many places in the Archive of the Indies. A signed copy of the March 15 agreement is in *Patronato* 257, no. 3, ramo 3; it has been reproduced for the Stetson Collection. A signed copy of the March 20 contract was found in A.G.I. *Escribanía de Cámara* 1,024-A. Entire copies are located in *Patronato* 19, no. 1, ramo 15; *Contratación* 3,309, 1°; *Justicia* 918, no. 3; *Indiferente General* 415 and 2,673. A copy is in A.C.R. Legajo 2°, no. 5; positive microfilm of this, obtained through the kindness of Michael Gannon, is in the P. K. Yonge Library. The asiento of March 20 has been printed in Ruidiaz, *La Florida*, 2:415–27, and in *D.I.*, 2d ser., 23:242–58. As they were needed to support the claims of Pedro Menéndez or his followers for certain privileges and exemptions, sections of the asiento were put piecemeal into various records in Spain and in the Indies. The agreement is summarized in A.G.I. *Contaduría* 941, fol. 4; this is available on negative microfilm at the P. K. Yonge Library. The contract was dissected minutely by the *Contadores Mayores* in the audit they undertook for the 1567 legal case over the asiento, in A.G.I. *Escribanía de Cámara* 1,024-A. The March 15, 1565, agreement is translated and reproduced here in Appendix 1.

must also be considered in its broader setting of an agreement between a loyal subject and a patrimonial monarch.[19]

The contract agreed to by the representative of the King and Pedro Menéndez embodied many of the provisions proposed by Menéndez in his earlier memorial. It was divided into two main parts. The first contained an enumeration of the tasks and obligations undertaken by Menéndez. In the second half, the Crown listed the privileges which it agreed to grant as recompense for his efforts.[20]

The asiento began with a promise that Menéndez would prepare four fast zabras and six shallops, fully equipped with oars, artillery, arms, and munitions for any action on the sea. Next, he agreed to bring a force of five hundred men on his expedition, of which one hundred would be farmers, one hundred sailors, and the rest armed men and officers. He agreed to carry two clerics and to bring stone-cutters, carpenters, farriers, blacksmiths, barbers, and surgeons. All of his men would have to be fully armed with arquebuses, crossbows, helmets, and shields. The expedition was to leave by May 31, 1565.

Because the smaller vessels had neither the tonnage nor the facilities to carry large numbers of men and their requisite equipment and supplies, Menéndez was instructed to prepare his fine new galeass, the *San Pelayo*, to take part in the journey. The *San Pelayo* was sizeable enough to transport three hundred of his men and most of their supplies and was thus admirably suited to accompany the expedition. It was, moreover, relatively fast and maneuverable for its size and was large enough to constitute a formidable gun platform. Since, however, this was Menéndez' finest and largest ship and his best single source of income, a bargain was struck. He could load it with goods for his own account or carry merchandise for others for the freight income, up to one-half or even two-thirds of the ship's tonnage. At some point in the West Indian islands, he would then off-load the men and supplies intended for Florida onto the smaller vessels, and the *San Pelayo* could then proceed on its profitable journey.[21]

19. With certain reservations about the application of the terms "fief" and "feudal" to sixteenth-century Castile, I have accepted the model of the "decentralized patrimonial state" as applicable to the European and Indies kingdoms of the Hapsburg ruler Philip II. This conceptualization is set forth by Max Weber in *The Theory of Social and Economic Organization*, esp. pp. 346–58.

20. See pp. 3–5 for a general discussion of the privileges and obligations in the asientos of adelantados.

21. See pp. 36–37 for the earlier (1564) voyage of the *San Pelayo*. Although the asiento recites merely that she was "of more than 600 tons," she was far greater in size than 600 tons. Just before her Florida journey, she was measured officially at 906 tons burden; see the audit of the Contadores Mayores, 1567, A.G.I. *Escribania de Cámara* 1,024-A.

Next, Menéndez was required to sail to the coast of Florida and seek the most advantageous places for settlement. He was also to search for traces of any corsairs or other unauthorized intruders in the lands of Philip II and expel them, if such should exist. Upon landing, Menéndez was to claim and take Florida in the King's name.

The geographic limits set upon the mission of Menéndez were immense. No bounds were set upon inland expansion, save the implicit limitation of the existing frontiers of the viceroyalty of New Spain. Expressed in terms of shoreline, the confines of the adelantamiento ranged from the Ancones, or St. Joseph's Bay, on the Gulf of Mexico around the Florida Keys and up the east coast to *Terra Nova*, in from fifty to sixty degrees north latitude. Thus the coastal expanses which Menéndez had to explore, chart, and protect were extremely extensive. The distances involved were reasonably well comprehended by the Spanish, for they had a good grasp of the measurements of latitude. The worst distortions of their geography seemed to arise out of an imperfect understanding of longitude and, hence, of the east-west dimension. The wanderings of De Narváez, de Soto, and Coronado had given some indications of the extent of the North American land mass, but its true limits were not appreciated. In any event, the areas granted in the asiento afforded a great scope for enterprise. Completion of the first phase of exploration was required to be done as soon as possible, but had to be completed by the end of three years.

Next, the King dictated definite terms for the effort of population and settlement. The initial thrust of conquest was to endure for one year, and supplies would have to be furnished for that period. An additional four hundred settlers were to be put onto the land before the first three years had elapsed. Of the total of five hundred settlers, at least two hundred would have to be married men, and at least one hundred of them farmers, the essential purpose being to found viable agricultural settlements. As in Spain, the farmers were to cluster around villages; the town was to be the spearhead for the advance of Castilian civilization. Menéndez was to found two or three towns, and to fortify each with a stronghouse of stone, adobe, or wood and with a moat and drawbridge. It was intended that these fortified villages would then serve as refuges for the settlers in the event of Indian troubles or corsair attack.

Menéndez was required to bring in five hundred slaves as the basic labor force to construct the towns, build fortifications, and cultivate the land. These slaves were to plant sugarcane and build the sugar works with which to grind it. It was the contractor's responsibility to provide the livestock essential for the self-support of the colonies and for future commercial hide production—one hundred horses and mares, two hundred calves, four hundred hogs, four hundred sheep, some goats, and other domestic animals and birds. The effort of colonization was to continue for the three-year term.

Relatively little was said in the asiento about relations with the Florida Indians. It provided that every attempt should be made to bring the natives into the Christian faith and to loyal obedience to the King. For the religious life of the settlers and the conversion of the Indians, Menéndez was obliged to bring to Florida ten or twelve religious, of any order desired, during the long-term effort of conquest and colonization. More specifically, four additional Jesuit missionaries had to come to establish doctrinas among the Indians. It was further ordered that the Florida enterprise be carried out in peace, friendship, and Christianity. As to the rest, the contract advised that the usual instructions applied as they were given in regulations for those who go to make such settlements. With regard to land tenure and Indian service, the 1563 ordinances specified that, in such population efforts, an adelantado might make two-life *repartimientos* of Indians in each village, for himself and his heirs. They also permit three-life encomiendas to be granted to other settlers in areas apart from the ports or main towns. It should be noted that Lucas Vázquez Ayllón's 1563 asiento for Florida had cautioned him that he could establish no encomiendas of Indians. Pedro Menéndez' agreement, however, is totally silent on this point, except for the reference to the 1563 ordinances.[22]

Pedro Menéndez had, then, obligated himself for a mission of exploration, population, and religious conversion. These purposes were interdependent, were of a piece with the requirements made of others who had signed sixteenth-century asientos, and were consistent with the general aims of Spanish expansion.

The second part of the asiento began with the statement that Menéndez' mission would impose such great efforts and expenses upon him that the King offered certain benefits and privileges to him in remuneration. The first benefit promised was an immediate cash payment of 15,000 ducats. This, the only royal outlay in the entire agreement, was to be paid if Menéndez sailed before the end of May. He was required to post a valid performance bond that he would return the funds if he failed to meet the sailing date.

22. In the "Ordenanzas," *D.I.*, vol. 8, provisions are made as follows: encomienda, no. LVIII, p. 505, no. CXLIX, p. 536; repartimiento, no. LXI, p. 506, no. CXLV, p. 535; with regard to tribute, see no. CXLVI, pp. 535–36.

A number of titles and offices were immediately granted to Pedro Menéndez, or were held out to him as future possibilities. He was to enjoy the title of adelantado of Florida and could bequeath it to his heirs in perpetuity. To insure that both the civil and military government of the adelantamiento would be in his hands, the offices of governor and captain-general were conceded to him for two lives—his own and that of a son or son-in-law. A salary of 2,000 ducats a year, to be paid from royal profits, accompanied the posts. If an Audiencia were ever established in Florida, the position of *alguacil mayor* would be set aside perpetually for Menéndez and his family. He was to be named captain-general of the ships which were to go on the Florida expedition. The adelantado was allowed to name a properly qualified lieutenant to take his place during absences from Florida. He could, therefore, be a part-time official and would thus be free to pursue his own economic interests elsewhere in the Indies, return to Spain, or serve in other posts of privilege and honor to which his sovereign might call him. This whole assemblage of offices and titles can be described as a substantial grant of authority for Menéndez' lifetime, with some elements of it planned to continue after his death.

One of Menéndez' more valuable authorizations, and one which would help to attract eager followers to his enterprise, was the power to distribute lands in Florida. The asiento granted him the authority to grant tracts of land for plantations, farms, and stock-breeding facilities as he might see fit, provided that he did not impede the rights of Indians. As to his own lands, the King granted him an estate, or estates, totaling 25 leagues squared. These immense tracts of land, more than 5,500 square miles, could provide the territorial backing and, it was hoped, the revenues to support the title of marqués. If, according to the asiento, the expedition was accomplished and the terms of the agreement were successfully completed, the King would consider his services and grant him the appropriate favor. Menéndez' jurisdiction over the land grant was, however, to be limited. He would not, for example, possess governmental powers there like the ones exercised by the Marqués del Valle or by the Columbus family in Jamaica, nor would he possess any subsurface mineral rights—these would be reserved for the Crown.[23]

23. In a cédula of March 22, 1565, sent from Madrid, the King promised Menéndez a letter granting the privilege in the land and advising again that the title of marquis would be forthcoming if the expedition were successful. Perpetual jurisdiction within the land grant was not to be given, however, nor were any mineral rights in the land; these were reserved to the King. Compare the powers given to the Columbus family in Jamaica, discussed at length in Morales Padrón, *Jamaica española*, pp. 125 ff. The March 22 cédula is also found in A.C.R., Legajo 2, no. 4, and may be seen on microfilm at the P. K. Yonge

A key cluster of privileges to be conceded to the Florida adelantado and to his followers were economic ones. Of these benefits, some were usually given to adelantados: Menéndez could bring five hundred slaves free of any duties, provided that they were intended only for Florida; the adelantado and other Florida residents would receive an exemption from customs duties (the almojarifazgo) for a period of time, and the usual royal quinto paid on precious metals, pearls, and other jewels would be reduced to one-tenth for a term of ten years. Pedro Menéndez was promised two fisheries—one of pearls and one of fish—of perpetual duration and was guaranteed 6⅔ per cent of all net royal profits in Florida in perpetuity. All of these provisos were generally found in sixteenth-century asientos. Only the number of slave licenses to be given Menéndez was unusual.

Some of the economic benefits were particularly linked with the Spanish trade system, the Carrera de Indias. While some limited shipping privileges and exemptions were often noted in asientos for conquest and population, these were always modest and were tied specifically to trade with the proposed new settlements. In the case of Pedro Menéndez, however, a significant departure was made. He was given permission to put into the Indies trade two galleons of from five hundred to six hundred tons' burden, together with two pataches. He was free to send these ships to any port in the Indies and to sail them with the fleets or not, as he chose. For cargoes sent in these ships, in no way tied to the Florida expedition, Menéndez did not have to pay the avería, or convoy assessment. The only restrictions placed upon this trade were that the outward-bound vessels carry only foodstuffs and beverages, and that on the return voyage, any cargo could be brought but gold, silver, or precious stones, unless they belonged to him or were earmarked for his account because he had earned them through freight payments. These ship licenses were valid for six years.

A separate trade privilege involved Menéndez' smaller vessels and was more particularly tied to the Florida enterprise. He was granted the licenses for six shallops and four zabras, to operate between Spain and Florida, Puerto Rico, Hispaniola, or Cuba. For the first year, it was understood, these ships were dedicated to the initial conquest; then the trade privilege would run (after June 1566) for six years. The cargoes of these little vessels were intended for the Florida settlement. It was provided, however, that Menéndez could bring foodstuffs or beverages to the islands and unload and sell them there. Then he could load for Florida cattle or other merchandise which

Library. Expectations of a marquisate were formalized in the "Ordenanzas" for all adelantados; in *D.I.*, vol. 8, no. LXXXV, p. 512.

could be bought in those islands. These ships could also sail freely without regard to the fleet regulations of the Casa de Contratación. The King allowed the adelantado to sail with unexamined pilots and waived the requirement that a notary or ship's secretary be aboard each of the small vessels.

Another maritime privilege given to Menéndez allowed him to send some of his ships directly from the north of Spain without examination at Sanlúcar, Seville, or Cádiz. Instead, he was to be permitted to sail directly to the Canary Islands and to have his official papers approved before the local justices there. The adelantado's small vessels were exempt from paying avería on the initial Florida expedition. After that time, if they wished to sail in convoy with the regular fleets, it had to be paid. If they preferred to sail singly or together outside of fleet protection, no avería was to be collected. The asiento specifically provided that none of Pedro Menéndez' ships could be taken, or embargoed, for royal service. Finally, the adelantado was given what amounted to an open-ended letter-of-marque. Any prizes which he might take at any time during the six-year ship license term would belong to him, subject only to the usual Crown share of one-third.

The asiento closed with a clause establishing the rights of succession for all of Menéndez' rights and privileges, if he should die before the basic three-year term had expired. It was signed by Dr. Vázquez and Pedro Menéndez.

Five days later, on March 20, 1565, Philip II affixed his signature to the formal, royal decree establishing the Florida agreement. In this instrument, no change was made in the terms agreed to in the first asiento. The King had, however, added a lengthy introduction, converted the form of address to the "Vos" mode used by a monarch to address a favored subject, and appended a closing related to compliance.

The introduction recalled the long, fruitless attempts to settle Florida. It emphasized that the need to convert the Indians to the holy Faith was the primary motive of the Crown in seeking to populate the mainland. Then it repeated the tasks Menéndez had offered to perform at his own expense and accepted the offer on those terms, by virtue of Menéndez' evident qualifications.

In the closing, Philip II reaffirmed that Pedro Menéndez would conduct the entire conquest and population at his own cost, would honor the asiento in so doing, and would agree to obey other, later instructions which the Crown might make relative to the enterprise. The King then promised to carry out his obligations and pledged his royal word that each and every proviso of the agreement would be honored if Menéndez faithfully carried out his part. If he failed to do so, he would be punished as a disloyal subject.

Comparison of the Menéndez agreement with those of four other adelantados of Florida and with the asientos for sixteenth-century settlement in Costa Rica, the Rio de la Plata, and "the province of Omagua" demonstrates the similarities and the differences between agreements and thus helps establish the distinctive characteristics of Pedro Menéndez' asiento.[24] From such a comparison, it can be concluded that the striking uniformity of many clauses and provisions in the asientos bears testimony to the marked continuity of the settlement policies of the Crown of Castile. Requirements as to population, defense, Indian policies, and the granting of privileges remained remarkably similar over the fifty years spanned by these contracts. Even the area of relations with the Indians, beset as it was during those years with dispute preceding and following the passage of the New Laws, changed little. Indeed, differences in the asientos appear to have been more a matter of degree than of kind. With particular regard to Florida, it can be affirmed that the 1565 compact with Pedro Menéndez represented the culmination of a long series of attempts to populate eastern North America through the use of the instrument of adelantamiento.

Notwithstanding the basic and underlying similarity of the asientos studied, one difference stands out clearly: the unusual nature of the benefit package afforded to Pedro Menéndez de Avilés. First, the scope of some of the benefits is far greater than usual. Five hundred slave licenses, duty free, are five times as many as the number permitted to any of the other seven contractors; in 1563, Ayllón was allowed to bring only eight slaves, and he had to pay duty on these. Menéndez was to control the government of the adelantamiento for two lives, while the other Florida grantees could govern only for one. The tracts of lands to be given him were more than double the size of those offered to Narváez, DeSoto, and the second Ayllón and were almost twice as large as those provided for the first Ayllón contract. They were, in fact, the same size as the Veragua lands tendered to Don Luis Colón, grandson of the discoverer, in 1537.[25]

By far the most remarkable privileges which the newest Florida adelantado was to receive, however, were those connected with

24. A comparative table of several asientos is found in Appendix 2. I am indebted to Roscoe R. Hill for his creative introduction to the comparative approach in the study of adelantados in his article "The Office of Adelantado," passim.

25. See "Lo que le parece a Loaysa se ha de dar a Don Luis Colón, 1536," in A.G.I. *Patronato* 10, ramos 2, 4.

maritime trade. Taken together—the out-of-fleet permission, avería exemptions, exemption from examination of ships and cargoes in Andalusia, permission to carry unlicensed pilots and to sail without a notary, and the ship licenses themselves—these represented a substantial breach of the privilege system of the Seville merchants. The whole collection appears to cater to the deepest inclinations of Pedro Menéndez de Avilés—to engage freely in the Indies trade under special royal patronage with a very minimum of restriction. The benefits were, moreover, almost all convertible into money for Menéndez. Ship licenses or slave licenses, for example, if not used could be sold.

For the Crown, the advantages given to Pedro Menéndez represented the price of the Florida conquest. This was not a price to be paid directly by the King. In part, its payment would be realized through the granting of an estate which the adelantado would be allowed to create in Florida. For the rest, it would be paid by giving Menéndez license to profit through trade—a privilege to be carved out from the sphere of the mercantile monopolists of the Carrera de Indias. In return, the Crown could hope for a bulwark of Castilian civilization against any enemy incursion upon the North American continent.

Now there was much to be done. Copies of the asiento had to be made for the parties, and another was prepared by the royal secretary to be sent to Seville for the books of contracts kept in the Casa de Contratación. Thus the maritime privileges of Menéndez could be accounted for, and his licenses could be granted as needed. It was also necessary to draw up separate cédulas, or decrees, embodying the main privileges allotted to Menéndez and also to his followers in the asiento, together with patents of the titles which he had been granted.[26] On March 22, 1565, a letter was sent from the King to the officials of the Casa de Contratación at Seville. It asked all possible aid for Pedro Menéndez, so that his armadas might be sent off as soon as might be feasible. A form letter containing the same advice was posted to the Casa representative at Cádiz, Antonio de Abalia, and to the King's officials in Vizcaya, the "four villas of the coast," Galicia, and the Canary Islands. Two days earlier, another, separate dispatch

26. These individual decrees, all dated March 22, 1565, were given to Menéndez. They were concerned with the reduction in the quinto, the 25-league-squared land grant, the two fisheries, the 6⅔ per cent of royal profits, the title of captain-general of the Florida armada, the title of adelantado, the ship privileges, the slave licenses, and the 2,000-ducat salary. These are all found in A.C.R., Legajo 2 (microfilm, P. K. Yonge Library). Menéndez signed an oath of compliance and acceptance of the asiento on March 26, 1565; this is found in A.G.I. *Patronato* 19, no. 1, ramo 15, at fol. 153.

had been sent to Abalia in Cádiz, pointing out that particular aid would be required for Menéndez in that city, and asking Abalia to see that it was available.[27]

Pedro Menéndez left Madrid, armed with the proofs of his agreement with the Crown, to begin his journey to the north coast. Later, in Seville, he could ask for immediate payment of the 15,000 ducats which the asiento promised. With a letter of judgment from the Council of the Indies, he could also press for settlement of his ship-lease case. In Cádiz he could begin outfitting his expedition.

While the adelantado was still traveling north from Madrid, the merchant ship *La Vera Cruz* had ended its long voyage from Havana and had anchored within the port of Sanlúcar de Barrameda. The urgent dispatch from Diego de Mazariegos telling of the French settlement was sent along at once by messenger to Seville, together with the three French prisoners sent by the governor. A rapid courier then forwarded the governor's letter from Seville to Philip II. Its delivery was swift indeed: the note of enclosure was dated March 26 and the King had it by March 30. Now that the momentous news was in Philip's hands, he and his counsellors knew for the first time of the French post at Fort Caroline. They had also learned that Laudonnière shortly expected substantial reinforcement from France.[28]

Pedro Menéndez' newly authorized expedition of settlement and population would go ahead, but first it would have a punitive mission to perform. The same day he received the news, Philip II wrote two insistent letters to Menéndez. In the first, Philip tersely advised the adelantado of the message from Havana. He ordered Menéndez to leave as quickly as possible, as already required by his asiento and capitulación. The second dispatch was even more importunate in tone: the King asked Pedro Menéndez to move up his departure date and leave for Florida by the first of May. He asked Menéndez to keep his destination secret, and that he spread the word that his goal was to be the Rio de la Plata.[29]

27. Crown to Abalia, Madrid, March 20, 1565, A.G.I. *Justicia* 918; also in A.C.R., Legajo 2, no. 3-B (microfilm, P. K. Yonge Library).

28. The Casa's letter is Casa to Crown, Seville, March 26, 1565, A.G.I. *Contratación* 5,167, Book III. The prisoner interrogation was also enclosed. Pedro Menéndez himself said, "when Your Majesty contracted with me for the conquest and population of the provinces of Florida, it was unknown that the Lutheran Frenchmen were already in those places"; this is from "Menéndez reports to the Crown, 1565 [*sic*]," from Manuscript Division, Library of Congress, typescript translation, 1937. A transcript is also in the P. K. Yonge Library. The fact that Carillo's vessel brought the news for the first time is also found in Crown to Casa, August 27, 1565, from A.G.I. *Contratación* 5,012 (Stetson Coll.).

29. Crown to Pedro Menéndez de Avilés (two letters), Madrid, March 30, 1565, A.G.I. *Escribanía de Cámara* 1,024-A.

The notice which Philip II had received of the French fort and colony in his Florida territory apparently did not disturb the friendly tenor of his correspondence with the French monarchs. An affectionate letter from Catherine de Medici was addressed to "the most high, excellent, and powerful Prince, our very dear and well-beloved son-in-law, son, and cousin."[30] Catherine's letter crossed with one Philip wrote on April 2 to Charles IX and his mother. It assured them that, in spite of the pressure of his affairs, he would come with Isabel to see them as many times as possible. His note closed with a warm salute "to the most Christian Queen, my mother and lady," and was signed "the good son and brother of Your Majesties."[31]

In spite of such pleasantries, however, some concern had arisen at the Castilian court about the projected meeting of the two royal families. Both Queen Isabel and her mother believed that a friendly family conference would somehow solve their mutual diplomatic problems and could even help resolve the internal religious tensions in France. Philip was unwilling to disappoint his young wife by disavowing the meeting, but his conscience was most uneasy about the possible contact with heretics at such a conference. Even after his councils had debated the issue and had recommended that the King go in person to the meeting, he demurred. At this early April date, there was real doubt that the meeting would actually take place or, if it did, that the King would attend. Philip could not, however, reject the thought that he should use every means possible to strengthen the Catholic cause in France, and the royal conference might help further this aim.

Certainly a part of the ambivalance in the King's feelings about France must have been related to his recent knowledge of Laudonnière's settlement at Fort Caroline. One thing was certain in his mind—the threat which the fort posed to the Indies and to the fleets should be erased as soon as possible. From his palace at Aranjuez, Philip sent urgent dispatches on April 5 to the commanders of his key defense points in the Caribbean—the Audiencia of Santo Domingo on the island of Hispaniola and his governors at Puerto Rico and Havana. Philip also urged the Seville officials to speed up payment to Pedro Menéndez of the 15,000-ducat *merced* promised to him in his asiento and to make rapid money settlement with him

30. Catherine de Medici to Philip II, Burdeos, April 1, 1565, *Archivo Documental Español* (hereafter *A.D.E.*), vol. 7 (1565), no. 1,019, p. 205. It originally appeared in A.G.S., *Estado*, Legajo K, 1,503, no. 50.

31. Philip II to Charles IX and Catherine de Medici, Madrid, April 2, 1565, *A.D.E.*, vol. 7, no. 1,021, p. 209. From A.G.S., *Estado*, Legajo K, 1,503, no. 51.

over the long-pending galleon-lease case. The adelantado had, the King advised, pressing need for the funds in order to mount his expedition.[32]

The dispatches warned the Indies of the dangers which the French fort represented, and initiated the necessary countermoves. With these messages the enterprise of Florida entered a new phase: now, for the first time, the Crown planned to furnish its adelantado with some material support. This fateful step permanently imposed a dual character upon the maintenance of the adelantamiento of Florida. In his letter to the Audiencia of Santo Domingo, Philip described the message he had received from Governor Mazariegos and reported the location of the French fort in Florida. He ordered the Audiencia to raise two hundred armed men for Pedro Menéndez' use under "a good captain," and to furnish a ship, horses, and ample supplies for an expedition of four months, at the cost of the royal treasury.

The message to Havana acknowledged the governor's earlier report and asked Mazariegos to provide fifty armed men, a number of horses, and a ship. When Menéndez arrived in Havana, the governor was to turn the force over to him for the Florida enterprise. Again, the estimated term of service (and the duration of expense) was to be four months. By thus setting a time limit upon royal participation, Philip demonstrated that he felt that the punitive phase of the expedition would be relatively short. The King also cautioned that all the usual controls upon expenditure from royal funds would be observed in this case.

The urgency of the King's commitment to this enterprise—and the priority which he assigned to it—can best be measured against what is known of his financial position during those days. As mentioned, Philip II was struggling with pressing needs in several key diplomatic and military undertakings. He was especially concerned with the state of the royal forces in Oran and Mazalquivir. To meet some of his obligations, the King asked the officials of the Casa de Contratación to attempt to borrow 200,000 ducats in Seville; the royal coffers there were entirely empty.[33] As for the supplemental measures the King

32. Philip's messages of April 5 to the Audiencia of Santo Domingo and to the governor at Havana are found in A.G.I. *Escribanía de Cámara* 1,024-A. His cover letter is Crown to Casa, Aranjuez, April 5, 1565, A.G.I. *Indiferente General* 1,966.

33. See Francisco Duarte to Crown, Seville, April 8, 1565, A.G.I. *Indiferente General* 1,093. The King may have taken these funds. At some date prior to July 1565, he had incurred an obligation of 80,000 ducats to Anton Fugger. That sum, with 120,000 ducats available in Seville, would have totaled the 200,000 ducats Philip was seeking. See Casa to Crown, Seville, September 4, 1565, A.G.I. *Contratación* 5,167, Book II, for the Fugger debt.

had set in motion for Florida in the Indies, they would not result in direct royal expense to Spain. Crown monies used in the Indies would, of course, never reach Seville as royal revenues. At this point, then, the expulsion of the French at Fort Caroline did not seem to call for any major effort by the Spanish Crown.

The Duke of Alba, the head of a major faction at the Spanish court and a militant hard liner in upholding his sovereign's dynastic rights and orthodox Catholicism, gave his opinion to Philip II on April 11. Alba first expressed great firmness in opposing the presence of any Huguenot nobles at the planned conference at Bayonne and advised that if any of these planned to come to the meeting, Queen Isabel should not be permitted to attend. Turning to the question of Florida, the duke urged an immediate move to dislodge the French from their fort there but did not reject the diplomatic approach. Alba pointed out that prisoner interrogations affirmed that the Queen of France and Admiral Coligny had authorized the expedition of Laudonnière. In view of this, the duke urged the King to gather together the proofs of Castilian title to the North American continent. Next he suggested that the Spanish Ambassador to France make formal presentation of the evidence before the Valois rulers and that he ask Catherine de Medici and Charles IX to recall the French Huguenots in Florida and to cancel any reinforcements that were to be sent there.

After study of the duke's *parecer*, the King gave immediate assent to the part about the coming royal conference at Bayonne. On April 16, the King ordered the ambassador to France, Don Francis de Alava y Beaumont, to give Catherine de Medici formal notice that he would not permit Isabel to attend the meeting if any religious undesirables, e.g., heretics, planned to be there. If that were the case, Philip II would cancel the visit. Ten days later, a reply came from Catherine; the French Queen had concurred with Philip's wish.

Only sporadic action had yet been taken with regard to the French incursion in Florida. The expedition of Menéndez was to be supplemented with some Crown aid from Caribbean Indies bases, and the general of the New Spain fleet, Pedro de las Roelas, was to provide naval support for the Florida adelantado. Although the King and his officials had learned from interrogation of prisoners that Laudonnière expected reinforcement soon, they were not yet aware that the arming of the Ribault fleet had already begun. At this point the adelantado returned from a trip to the north coast of Spain with some alarming intelligence. Menéndez noted that he had heard in Vizcaya that sixteen French ships, with two thousand men, were being outfitted in Le Havre for the reinforcement journey. On the first of

May, Philip wrote his French ambassador asking him to determine the truth of Menéndez' report. Alava's reply, dated just six days later, deprecated the adelantado's story. He noted that he employed able and diligent agents in Normandy and Brittany to detect any such sailings and that none of these had given him any information about it. He had heard other rumors that a fleet was being readied for Florida, but had discounted them, believing that they were probably corsair ships being prepared for raids on Spanish shipping lanes. The ambassador did promise, however, to send a skilled spy, Dr. Gabriel de Enveja, to make a special investigation.[34]

As concern grew in Madrid about the possibility of added French commitments in Florida, Philip II sent his secretary, Gonzalo Pérez, to the president of the Council of the Indies to carry an urgent request. Philip II agreed with the suggestions of the Duke of Alba and asked the Council to study the proof of his title to Florida and report quickly to him about it. The Council made a diligent search in royal archives and delivered its opinion to the King on May 5, 1565.[35]

In its findings about the rights of the Crown of Castile in Florida, the Council relied heavily upon the donation of Pope Alexander VI and enclosed a copy of the original Bull. As vicar of Christ, the Pope had chosen Ferdinand and Isabella to carry the faith to all infidels within a certain sphere of control. Since Florida was located within the limits established by the papal decree, no man could exploit or even visit the land without particular license from the rulers of Castile and León.

Next, the Council offered evidence that the rights granted to the *Reyes Católicos* had been validated in and for Florida by the recorded actions of a long series of explorers and conquerors. The time allowed to prepare the memorandum for the King had been altogether too short to permit the Council to locate proof of all these explorations, but reference was made to two specific instances, the voyage of Guido de Labazaris in 1558 and the 1561 expedition of Angel de Villafañe. The King's advisers attached sworn statements of the formal acts of

34. The parecer of the Duke of Alba, April 11, 1565, is from A.G.S.,*Estado*, Legajo K, 1503, no. 57, and has been printed in *A.D.E.*, vol. 7, no. 1,028, pp. 235–36. The consulta of the Council of the Indies, Madrid, May 12, 1565, from A.G.I. *Indiferente General* 738, ramo 7, no. 74, makes note of Menéndez' report. This consulta is also found in the Stetson Collection. Alava's letter to Philip II, from St. Micon, May 7, 1565, is in *A.D.E.*, vol. 7, no. 1,046, pp. 313–14 (A.G.S., *Estado*, Legajo K, 1,503, no. 77), and refers to the report. The emissary was identified in Alava's letter to Philip II, Bayonne, May 27, 1565, from *A.D.E.*, vol. 7, no. 1,063, p. 355 (A.G.S., *Estado*, Legajo K, 1,503, no. 93).

35. The May 5, 1565, document is found, together with supporting material, in A.G.I. *Indiferente General* 738, ramo 7, no. 73-A (Stetson Coll.). It has been cited at length in Woodbury Lowery, *The Spanish Settlements*, 2:107–8, and may be found in *D.I.*, 4:136–40.

taking possession, that essential step in the establishment of dynastic claim to the land.[36] In its haste to render its opinion to the King, the Council made some glaring geographic errors. It stated that the new French fort was built in the very place formally appropriated for the Crown by both Labazaris and Villafañe. As a matter of fact, Fort Caroline was nowhere near the Bahia Phillipina which Labazaris had discovered on the Gulf coast or the Santa Elena area where Villafañe had landed. In any event, the Council of the Indies determined that Philip's claim to Florida was perfectly clear and valid. The councillors warned the King that the French fort presented a continual threat to the safe passage of Spanish ships through the Bahama Channel. On the cover sheet of the document, a note traced in Philip's hand indicates his approval of its deliberations. The document illustrates the advancing priority of Florida as a strategic concern and demonstrates a vital stage in Philip's step-by-step escalation of his support for the Florida enterprise. The proof-of-title *parecer* was the first of a regular flurry of letters, dispatches, and *consultas* in which the new policies were developed and implemented.

As a result of the Council's report, another, higher level of royal support for Florida's conquest was approved. Now direct aid was to be sent to Menéndez in the form of troops and munitions. Five hundred men would be raised in Spain, to be paid and supplied at royal expense. An increase in the level of aid to be furnished in the Indies was also agreed upon. Letters to this effect went out to the Casa de Contratación, to the fleet general readying for departure in Cádiz, to Pedro Menéndez, and to officials in the Indies.

On the same day on which the Council of the Indies had furnished the King with proof of his title to Florida, its secretary, Eraso, wrote Pedro Menéndez, enclosing a royal order directing the adelantado to raise two hundred more armed men to be carried with him on his voyage at Crown expense. Eraso told Menéndez further that the King had written the royal officials in Seville, formally ordering them to provide the funds for the pay and provision of those men. In keeping with its function as royal factor in the equipping of sea-going expeditions, the Casa was to gather supplies, take muster of the men, and provide a ship for their passage to Florida. Menéndez, who had left for Andalusia, did not receive these orders until May 12.[37]

36. The act of taking formal possession of lands to be claimed for the rulers of Castile provided the legal formality which clearly established dynastic rights to the territories thus taken. The manner in which this was to be done was carefully circumscribed, and was dictated in "Ordenanzas sobre descubrimiento nuevo e población," *D.I.*, vol. 8, no. XIII, p. 490.

37. Francisco Eraso to Pedro Menéndez de Avilés, Madrid, May 5, 1565, A.G.I.

In the face of the threat from Fort Caroline, the Crown communicated again with the Casa de Contratación on May 6 with regard to the defenses of Havana. The new royal governor there, García de Osorio Sandoval, had complained to Philip that there were only four pieces of artillery in Havana, very few arquebuses, and scanty supplies of gunpowder. The King ordered that the necessary artillery and munitions be sent at once.[38] A third letter to Seville informed the Casa that the King had agreed to underwrite the cost of the artillery and munitions needed to batter down the walls of the French fort in Florida. If, the Council of the Indies noted, Menéndez had not obtained enough artillery for this purpose, it should be furnished at royal expense by the Casa.[39]

The King sent a notice on the ninth of May to Pedro de las Roelas, general of the New Spain fleet being outfitted for its journey, and ordered him to sail to Cape San Antonio at the western tip of Cuba and to detach his capitana. That vessel would then sail with two hundred armed men to Havana to await Menéndez' orders. The adelantado could use the ship and its men in Florida but was required to return it in time for it to rejoin the fleet for the return voyage to Spain.[40]

Next, the Audiencia of Santo Domingo was asked to increase the force being readied for Florida from two hundred to three hundred men because, said the King, "We hold it to be a very important thing to defeat those Frenchmen and expel them from the province of Florida."[41]

Although the Crown and Council had ordered measures to enlarge the Florida effort, their deliberations were hampered by a lack of clear intelligence about the size and strength of the French rein-

---

Escribanía de Cámara 1,024-A. Menéndez acknowledged that he received word when he reached Seville on May 12 of the 200 troops he was to raise. See Pedro Menéndez to Crown, Seville, May 18, 1565, from Ruidiaz, *La Florida*, 2:60–66. The letter is in the Stetson Collection, listed under the "old" legajo number of 148–4–9.

38. Crown to Casa, Valladolid, May 6, 1565, A.G.I. *Indiferente General* 1,966. Although he had communicated with the King earlier about Havana's defenses, Osorio did not take office until September 18, 1565. See García Osorio to Crown, Havana, December 18, 1565, A.G.I. *Santo Domingo* 115. The letter has been printed in Irene Wright, *Historia documentada de San Cristobal de la Habana*, 1:202.

39. Council of the Indies to Casa, Madrid, May 7, 1565, A.G.I. *Indiferente General* 738, ramo 7, no. 74-A.

40. Crown to Pedro de Roelas, Valladolid, May 9, 1565, A.G.I. *Indiferente General* 1,966. The ship, named the *Santa Catalina*, had been embargoed in Cádiz. For its owner's lengthy protest and the story of the ship's adventures, see "Ximeno de Bretendoña sobre sueldo," A.G.I. *Indiferente General* 2,673, bearing the date August 8, 1569.

41. Crown to Audiencia of Santo Domingo, Valladolid, May 9, 1565, A.G.I. *Escribanía de Cámara* 1,024-A.

forcement. Menéndez had told them of the rumor that the force was large, with sixteen ships and up to two thousand men. Two Spanish seamen, testifying in Seville, reported that they had seen three ships being prepared for Florida in Le Havre on April 16. Don Francis de Alava had doubted that any such Florida expedition existed. The situation was further complicated by the King's expressed hope that French knowledge of Menéndez' preparations might frighten the French into abandoning their attempt at reinforcement. The King's counsellors were in a quandary. On the one hand, if rumors were true, it might become necessary to increase the Spanish force substantially, both with ships and with men, for it was essential to match Menéndez' effort adequately against the French. At the same time, the Council did not wish to delay the adelantado's departure even one day. The tension generated between the need for strength and the desire for speed formed the atmosphere of urgency in which the Menéndez expedition was outfitted.[42]

When he arrived at Seville on May 12, Pedro Menéndez found awaiting him the royal order to raise two hundred royal soldiers for Florida; he immediately sent out captains to begin the task. Meanwhile, the officials of the Casa de Contratación began to accumulate supplies and equipment for the royal troops.[43] All was not going smoothly for the interests of the adelantado in Seville, however. The long-standing differences between Menéndez and the merchants had never ended, and opposition to his ship privilege for the *San Pelayo* had arisen among them. The entry of such a large vessel into the closely controlled Tierra Firme trade was an unwelcome intrusion in the eyes of the Seville monopolists. After the prior and consuls who represented the merchants' guild carried their discontent to the officials of the Casa de Contratación, the adelantado claimed that he experienced many obstructions and delays.[44] In spite of royal licenses, the Casa officials could find many ways to hold up the measurement,

---

42. The dilemma was manifested in the consulta of May 12, 1565, in A.G.I. *Indiferente General* 738, ramo 7, no. 74 (Stetson Coll.). The seamen testified in an *información* taken before the officials of the Casa de Contratación in Seville on May 5, 1565, and found in A.G.I. *Indiferente General* 738 (Stetson Coll.).

43. On May 20, authorization was given to expend 14,237 ducats for this purpose: A.G.I. *Contratación* 4,989-A, fol. 269.

44. Menéndez voices his plaint in his letter to the Crown, written at Seville on May 18, 1565, and found in the Stetson Collection at 148–4–9. It has also been printed in Ruidiaz, *La Florida*, 2:60–66. At this time, the prior and consuls of the Universidad de Mercaderes at Seville were Pero López Martínez, consul; Diego Diaz Bezerril, consul; Luis Sánchez Balvo, prior; Luis Marquéz, consul; and four councillors—Francisco Descobar, Gonzalo Jorge, Gonzalo Mustrenco, and Rodrigo de Illesecas; see listing as of March 22, 1565, Seville, in A.G.I. *Contratación* 4,981.

loading, and inspection of a ship, and Menéndez claimed that such delays made it impossible to load the goods from Seville aboard the *San Pelayo*. He further alleged that this badly damaged his credit at a critical time and made it difficult to raise the bond needed to collect the 15,000 ducats promised in the asiento. To compound his financial woes, Menéndez had not been paid one ducat of the 20,000 he claimed for the 1563 ship charter.

The King's officials in Seville were in a dilemma, for their old adversary and former prisoner had returned, armed with a royal asiento and Crown-guaranteed privileges in the Carrera de Indias. As if this were not enough, the nature of the Florida expedition had changed rapidly since the coming of the news of Laudonnière's fort. Now the Casa was thrust into the position of Crown agent in helping Pedro Menéndez with royal funds, while anxious royal dispatches urged them to meet his needs and speed his departure, to close his long-pending cases, and to settle the matter of his inability to make satisfactory bond. For his part, Pedro Menéndez was not likely to lose the opportunities inherent in such a situation; he had not forgotten the long months of confinement by the Torre del Oro. In a mood of thinly veiled conflict, negotiations began between Menéndez and the Casa de Contratación over the use of the *San Pelayo* to carry the King's troops and their supplies.

From the moment the decision was taken to furnish Crown soldiers to accompany Menéndez' own men, the major difficulty had been that of finding space for the men and their arms and supplies. The adelantado naturally preferred not to interrupt his plans to send the *San Pelayo* on a profitable voyage, but the Council of the Indies finally determined to lease the galeass to carry the men and goods. Their alternative was to embargo another ship for the purpose, and that cost might be substantially more.[45] The *San Pelayo* was already required to make the Florida journey, and it would be under the direct command of the adelantado. In itself, this would make for tighter military control in the event of action against the enemy. Another, perhaps unmentioned, pressure impelling the leasing of the *San Pelayo* was the obvious preference of the merchants of Seville that Menéndez' ship go to Florida instead of to Nombre de Dios.

There was room for argument in setting the compensation which Menéndez would receive for the use of his ship. Although the per-ton lease charge was fixed at seven *reales* per month, there were other

45. The cost of charter, for example, for the two guard ships carried to New Spain in 1562 had been more than 28,000 ducats, after all payments due had been settled. See Casa to Crown, December 8, 1564, A.G.I. *Contratación* 5,167, Book III.

expenses for which Menéndez could seek Crown payment, including the sums he had spent in outfitting the *San Pelayo*, reimbursement for salaries and rations of his crew after the date of taking for Crown service, and recompense for his inability to profit from the Panama journey. He had anticipated a profit of 12,000 ducats from freight charges on the outbound journey alone and could have expected an immediate 2,400-ducat advance from the traders who loaded goods for Nombre de Dios. He might also have realized monies for passenger fares and for the sale of goods carried for his own account. It was in Menéndez' interest to dramatize and maximize his expenditures and losses. In a letter to Philip II, Menéndez claimed, for example, that the goods loaded by Cádiz merchants had been aboard the *San Pelayo* since May 1, but that Casa interference had badly disturbed his commercial arrangements.[46]

Although discussions about placing the King's troops in the *San Pelayo* took place in Madrid and Seville prior to May 22, it appears that this was the date of the formal order to take the ship for royal service.[47] After that date, Pedro Menéndez began to argue seriously for repayment of funds he said he had expended in carpentry work, caulking, and strengthening his ship to carry heavier artillery. He also maintained that he should be paid the salary and rations of his eighty seamen, twenty ship's boys, and ten pages, retroactive to April 1, a total of 9,000 ducats. Since the Casa treasurer, factor, and accountant offered only 4,000 ducats, the parties were still far apart in their negotiations.

The adelantado was, moreover, discouraged over the slow progress of the settlement of the sums due him from the 1563 ship lease, and on May 22 he wrote the King that virtually nothing had been accomplished. Menéndez did acknowledge that the officials of the Casa de Contratación were heavily occupied with the dispatch of the New Spain fleet, and one of them had been very ill. He also admitted that he had lost or mislaid certain receipts and other supporting papers vital to his case. But, since he was so financially pressed, Menéndez

46. According to Agustín Francisco, a German resident in Seville who was financially affiliated with Menéndez, the freight charge for merchandise from Cádiz to Nombre de Dios in 1565 was 30 ducats per ton. Menéndez had noted that he had contracted for 100 tons of goods with merchants and shippers of Cádiz, and for 300 with Seville traders. Francisco's comments about the lading of the *San Pelayo* are found in A.P.C., *Escribanía de Alonso de los Cobos*, n.d., 1565. A copy is in A.G.I. *Indiferente General* 2,673.

47. On May 22, 1565, letters from the officials of the Casa de Contratación and from Madrid crossed. In these dispatches, the Casa proposed and the Crown ordered that Menéndez' galeass be taken for lease to carry the soldiers. Council of the Indies to Casa, Madrid, May 22, 1565, A.G.I. *Indiferente General* 1,966 and Casa to Crown, Seville, May 22, 1565, A.G.I. *Contratación* 5,167, Book III.

demanded at least 7,000 or 8,000 ducats on account so that he could get on with the business of getting the expedition ready to go to Florida.[48]

The Seville officials had also received a list from Menéndez, in which he estimated the additional artillery and munitions needed for his assault on the French fort in Florida. The material which Menéndez requested, which included 100 hundredweight of gunpowder, would cost 2,500 ducats. In addition, the Casa had to find the funds to pay and supply the King's soldiers, which it estimated at another 7,000 or 8,000 ducats. Neither the New Spain nor the Tierra Firme fleet had yet come into port, and the royal coffers in Seville were still empty of Indies revenues, but it was possible to borrow from various trust funds. Some avería money had also begun to come in as outbound ships loaded for their journeys. Silver from the Guadalcanal mines had also arrived in Seville. In spite of financial scarcities, imperative commands from Madrid directed the settlement of all matters with Menéndez, and authorized the release of 4,000 pounds of gunpowder to the adelantado.[49] The Crown also requested that the three French prisoners sent by Governor Mazariegos be turned over to Pedro Menéndez so that he might use their knowledge on his expedition.

After a brief journey to Cádiz, Menéndez reappeared in Seville on May 26 and offered two bondsmen for the Casa's consideration, so that he could receive the 15,000 ducats. Since it did not appear that the bondsmen could actually stand good for such a sum, they were not accepted. Menéndez then pleaded that the cash was vital to his preparation and offered to accept a lesser sum, 6,000 ducats. The money was paid to him the next day and was taken from the Guadalcanal silver.[50]

The circular nature of the money disputes in Seville is illustrated by Menéndez' dilemma over the ordering of supplies and munitions for his own account for the Florida enterprise. Lacking cash, he could order the goods, but delivery would not be forthcoming until payment was made. Thus, Menéndez complained, he could not complete his lading until the monies due to him from the Crown were paid, which made it impossible to meet the sailing deadline of May 31. Yet the royal merced was payable on a contingency basis—provided the ex-

48. Pedro Menéndez de Avilés to Crown, Seville, May 22, 1565, at 148–4–9, Stetson Coll.
49. Council of the Indies to Casa, Madrid, May 22, 1565, A.G.I. *Indiferente General* 1,966.
50. I am indebted to Paul E. Hoffman, who furnished the citation of this payment to the adelantado; it is from A.G.I. *Contratación* 4,680 (*Libro de Guadalcanal*), fol. 127 vo.

pedition sailed by the end of May. Clearly, the deadlock would have to be resolved if Menéndez were to depart soon.

On May 28, both parties to the negotiations over Menéndez' accounts outlined their respective positions in letters to Philip II. The Royal Officials of the Casa advised the King that they were still working on the adelantado's claims. They noted that this task was rendered much more difficult by the fact that Menéndez could not produce the documents of proof of his expenditures; thus it was necessary to take lengthy testimony and produce sworn statements in lieu of receipts and invoices. The Casa finally paid Pedro Menéndez 3,000 ducats on account, while the work continued. For his part, Menéndez flatly told the King that he could not undertake the Florida journey until he was completely paid.[51]

During the negotiations in Seville, essential information about the nature of the French reinforcement forces finally reached Philip's court. Ambassador Alava, who had come to Bayonne to make final preparations for the meetings between the two royal families, was contacted there by his spy, Dr. Enveja. The information the man gave was so startling and contained such a complete picture of the French preparations in Normandy that Alava sent Enveja to Spain on May 27 to report to the King.[52]

Philip II heard the spy's story on June 2 and had it written down the next day. There was every reason for the King to praise the thorough and perceptive report which Dr. Enveja had made, for it provided excellent intelligence about the enemy's plans and dispositions. The account, moreover, holds much of interest for the historian—it affords a contemporary description of Ribault's second expedition.[53]

When he had arrived in Dieppe on May 17, Dr. Enveja had found seven ships in harbor, in an advanced stage of preparation for the Florida journey. They were already almost fully loaded and many soldiers were aboard. Only Jean Ribault's insistence upon clear understanding of his lines of authority, which had compelled him to await instruction from Admiral Coligny, had delayed the departure of the fleet.

Ribault's flagship, the *Trinité*, at 150 tons, was much smaller than

51. Casa to Crown, Seville, May 28, 1565, A.G.I. *Contratación* 5,167, Book III. Pedro Menéndez to Crown, Seville, May 28, 1565, in Ruidiaz, *La Florida*, 2:66–67.
52. Alava to Philip II, May 27, 1565, *A.D.E.*, vol. 7, no. 1,063, p. 355 (originally A.G.S. *Estado*, Legajo K, 1,503, no. 93).
53. This key report has been printed in full by Antonio Tibesar, ed., "A Spy's Report on the Expedition of Jean Ribault to Florida, 1565." It comes originally from archives of the Real Academia de la Historia (Madrid). The new number is 9–30–3; 6271.

the *San Pelayo*, but it was also rigged and equipped as a galeass. Two of the other vessels were of a similar size, while the fourth was only slightly smaller. These three ships were probably the *Émerillon*, the *Épaule de Mouton*, and the *Truite*. The three remaining vessels were rather small—from 60 to 70 tons' burden; these must have been the *Perle*, the *Levrière*, and another named the *Émerillon*. Since the ships were outfitted in Le Havre and Dieppe, their officers and crews were almost all Norman seamen. The five hundred soldiers who had joined the expedition had come from more varied backgrounds; two hundred were of noble origin, and seven were German noblemen. From a military standpoint, the soldiers impressed Alava's investigator as well set up troops. Touches of color were added to their dress by their shining helmets, fine wool tunics, and long, multi-hued breeches "in the Levantine style." Almost all of the land forces, under the command of Captain François de la Grange, were equipped with arquebuses. The ships were alleged to carry two hundred dismounted cannon to use in land fortifications, with ample powder and shot.

The purpose of the French expedition appeared to be the mirror image of that being prepared by the Spanish. The spy stated that the Huguenots had planned an enterprise of thoroughgoing conquest, settlement, and improvement of the land. As evidence of this, Enveja reported that one of the seven ships had been converted into a veritable Noah's ark—it carried horses and mares, rams and sheep, bulls and cows, and even asses, for the Florida colony. A number of wives and children had been embarked for the voyage. What most alarmed the Spanish was the Huguenots' avowed aim of evangelizing with the "Lutheran" religion; seven or eight ministers of the new, heretical faith were carried for that very purpose.

With regard to the quality of French leadership, Dr. Enveja did not rely upon second-hand information. He sought and obtained an interview with Jean Ribault himself, and carried away vivid impressions of the Huguenot chief. Ribault projected the image of a man of competence and vigor, combined with determination and high temper. In these qualities, as well as in his ruddy complexion and reddish hair, Ribault strangely resembled his future antagonist, Pedro Menéndez de Avilés. The two men were, moreover, of equivalent age and had both sprung from maritime cultures of great vitality. The accidents of history had brought these into a conflict in which these men also professed contending religions.

Like Menéndez, Ribault had been given some degree of control over the terrain of Florida.[54] It is interesting to speculate upon the

54. Enveja states that Ribault had been given a two-year term of control; the title of

extent of French royal involvement in Ribault's effort; indeed, it is a vital historical question. Enveja's report contributes to our knowledge of this matter through his statement about the position of Admiral Coligny as arbiter of Ribault's authority as well as his assertion that Charles IX had pledged 100,000 francs to the expedition. This evidence seemed to convince Philip II that the French Crown was deeply involved and committed to the Florida adventure, for he was moved to "amazement" at the revelations. In a letter to his ambassador in France, Philip II expressed open shock at such an action by the French rulers at a time when both Crowns were formally at peace. To Philip, this constituted open aggression against a Spanish province. The Spanish King made a careful distinction between past Spanish actions against unauthorized corsairs and actions which would be required in this case and urgently required his ambassador to determine immediately if Ribault's fleet had already sailed. If it had not, he commanded his envoy to lay the matter directly before Charles IX and the Queen Mother in Paris, making a formal protest and asking officially that the expedition be halted at once. The King made his next order abundantly clear: if Alava found that Jean Ribault was already gone beyond recall, he should say "not one word" to the French rulers about this, but leave the matter to be discussed at Bayonne when the two courts met there. On the same day, Philip II wrote to Catherine and Charles, noted that he was sending the Duke of Alba as his representative at Bayonne and declared that he was already rejoicing at the pleasure they would all have when Isabel was in their midst.[55]

The revelations of Dr. Enveja provided the final spur to the anxieties of the Spanish King and his Council, and they redoubled the pressure upon those in Andalusia and the Indies who were preparing the forces for Florida. An order to the Santo Domingo Audiencia advised that Pedro Menéndez was about to leave; if the troops, ship, and supplies were not yet ready, they should be made so immediately. A notice was sent to Menéndez, telling him of the strength of the Huguenot forces and pointing out to him that the Frenchmen were

---

"colonel of the voyage and lieutenant of the king in New France" was allegedly given to Ribault. This latter phrase is cited by Charles de la Roncière in his *Histoire de la Marine Francaise*, 4:54–55, and came from manuscript no. 17294, *Bibliothèque Nationale*, fol. 231. For proof of Enveja's statement, see the description of the papers found in Jean Ribault's apartment at Fort Caroline, pp. 122–23.

55. In his letter of June 2, 1565, Philip acknowledged receipt of all of Alava's letters bearing May dates, expressed his gratification for Enveja's services, and issued his orders about the Ribault fleet; in *A.D.E.*, vol. 8, no. 1,072, p. 372 (from A.G.S. *Estado*, Legajo K, 1,504, no. 2).

about to sail. If Ribault reached Florida before he did with the fine troops seen in Dieppe and mounted heavy cannon upon the ramparts of Fort Caroline, Menéndez' mission might be impossible. The adelantado must speed up his departure; he had already passed the date fixed in the asiento. Now, he was told, he might raise as many troops as he could load aboard his ships in addition to those already gathered; the Crown would pay for them. To the Casa de Contratación went another letter, urging immediate payment of the balance of the 15,000 ducats to Menéndez, bond or no, deadline notwithstanding. As the outfitting of the Florida expedition in Cádiz and Seville entered its last, most frenetic stages, the feverish pace imposed by the court seemed to add another dimension to the fierce and glaring heat of the Andalusian summer.[56]

56. Crown to the Audiencia of Santo Domingo, Madrid, June 3, 1565, Crown to Pedro Menéndez de Avilés, Madrid, June 3, 1565, both in A.G.I. *Escribanía de Cámara* 1,024-A. The letter to Menéndez mentioned the king's note to the Casa de Contratación and advised of its contents.

Menéndez home, Avilés, during restoration. (Photo by Homer N. Cato.)

Parish church, Avilés, where Pedro Menéndez is buried. (Photo by Homer N. Cato.)

Torre del Oro, downtown Seville, near the place of Menéndez' imprisonment. Guadalquivir River in foreground, Giralda Tower and Cathedral in background. (Photo by Eugene Lyon.)

Asturian coast, from Salinas Beach, looking toward mouth of the river at Avilés. (Photo by Homer N. Cato.)

Menéndez monument, Avilés. (Photo by Homer N. Cato.)

Cádiz harbor. (Photo by Homer N. Cato.)

Undergirding the Expeditions

Both parties to the Florida contract faced a host of urgent tasks in preparing the expeditions for early departure. The officials of the Casa de Contratación, as Crown agents, had to assemble the royal troops, purchase supplies and munitions, and arrange ship charters; they had to finance this somehow from their treasury at Seville. To meet his contract obligations, Menéndez had to furnish and supply the ships, troops, and seamen required of him. The new royal support of the Florida expedition had in no way relieved the adelantado of these necessities but had merely added striking power to his own forces. Pedro Menéndez' main fleet was to sail from Cádiz, but he also prepared to dispatch forces from the north of Spain.

Network for Conquest

In organizing and administering the enterprise of Florida, Pedro Menéndez placed his trust in a small number of associates. At the heart of Menéndez' command structure were men who stood in close personal relationship with him, for they shared common bonds of blood or marriage.[1] All were Asturian hidalgos, and all were seamen

1. The careers of Pedro Menéndez' main lieutenants are well documented, as most of them achieved prominence as fleet generals or admirals in the Carrera de Indias, as governors or in other official posts, in positions in the Armada Real or in other fleets or expeditions. The correspondence relating to their offices, the audits of their accounts, the corpus of legal cases affecting them, and the sentences of the Council of the Indies sitting as judicial chamber contain much about these men. In secondary literature, two accounts have devoted some space to the subordinates of Menéndez. Ciriaco Miguel Vigil gives a brief sketch of each figure associated with the adelantado in his work *Noticias biográficos-genealógicos de Pedro Menéndez de Avilés*. Following Vigil, Eugenio Ruidiaz de Caravia did much the same in *La Florida*, vols. 1 and 2. Both men erred in confusing

71

with long experience in European and Mediterranean waters and in the Carrera de Indias.

In the first rank of Pedro Menéndez' lieutenants in 1565 were his brother Bartolomé, Esteban de las Alas, Pedro Menéndez Marquéz, and Diego Flores de Valdés. Bartolomé Menéndez had served long and loyally with his brother, had commanded the Tierra Firme ships in 1562–63, and had shared the lengthy imprisonment in Seville in 1563–64. Although he had been released from prison and planned to go to Florida with the Cádiz contingent, the illness he had contracted on the 1562–63 voyage still plagued him.[2]

Since 1553, another kinsman of Pedro Menéndez, Esteban de las Alas, had been his close associate. Born in the village of Avilés, he married Doña María de Valdés. He was general of the 1561 New Spain fleet. In 1562, he had been imprisoned by the Casa de Contratación upon return from the Indies, thus sharing a similar experience with his chief. During the Menéndez brothers' confinement, Alas commanded the Menéndez ships in 1564 and was responsible for taking the royal visitor Castro to Peru. It was he who had directed the salvage operation when the galleon *Santa Clara* was stranded on the eastern side of the Bahama Channel on the return voyage. The adelantado placed Esteban de las Alas in charge of the two northern elements of his Florida expedition, which were to leave Asturias and rendezvous with Menéndez in the Canary Islands. He would sail from Menéndez' native city of Avilés. With that trusted and reliable lieutenant in charge of the Asturian ships, Menéndez could safely concentrate his own efforts in the south, where the main contingent was being armed.[3]

Pedro Menéndez Marquéz with Pedro Menéndez el mozo, a son of Álvaro Sánchez de Avilés, brother of the adelantado.

2. Pedro Menéndez' own description of his brother's services and his illness during the Seville imprisonment of 1563–64 are found in "Memorial of Pedro Menéndez de Avilés asking grace from His Majesty," Seville, 1564, in A.G.I. *Patronato* 257, no. 3, ramo 2. Bartolomé's selection as fleet general is described by the adelantado in the same memorial. An accumulation of material about Bartolomé Menéndez is found in "Bartolomé Menéndez sobre sueldo," Madrid, 1570, in A.G.I. *Indiferente General* 1,219. The long service of Bartolomé Menéndez is described by the adelantado in a letter written to the King from Santander on May 15, 1568, and found in Ruidiaz, *La Florida,* 2:171.

3. Descriptions of various services by Esteban de las Alas are found in A.G.I. *Patronato,* Legajos 179, no. 5, ramo 4; 254, no. 2, ramo 1; 254, no. 3. Correspondence and legal matters relating to him are found in A.G.I. *Contratación* 2,937 and in *Contratación* 135, no. 5 (*autos fiscales*), which deal with de las Alas' presence in San Juan de Ulua in 1562. Reports of de las Alas' voyages in 1564 are in two letters, Casa to Crown, Seville, Dec. 5 and Dec. 5, 1564, A.G.I. *Contratación* 5,167, Book III. A pertinent *sentencia* of the Council of the Indies is found in A.G.I. *Escribanía de Cámara* 952. Audits of de las Alas' accounts in various posts in the fleets are in A.G.I. *Contaduría* 466, 547.

Pedro Menéndez' nephew, Pedro Menéndez Marquéz, was a skilled sailor and a long-time aide. By his uncle's own testimony in 1568, he "had served me twenty years in the armadas of my charge as captain of armada ships, and is one of the most expert mariners which your Majesty has in his kingdoms."[4] This meant that Marquéz had been affiliated with Pedro Menéndez since the date of his first entry into the Carrera de Indias in 1548. He was *maestre* of Menéndez' own ships in 1551 and 1564. Now Marquéz had been designated by the adelantado as second-in-command, or almirante, of the Asturian vessels.[5]

In the southern fleet which was to sail from Cádiz, Diego Flores Valdés had a similar position to that of Menéndez Marquéz in the north. Flores, a native of Laredo, was named almirante of the Cádiz division of ships as the adelantado's maritime lieutenant. Menéndez noted that Flores had been with him since 1550 and had greatly indebted himself in so serving, having encumbered all of the patrimony inherited from his parents. Pedro Menéndez extolled Flores' careful and loyal service and evidently thought highly of him as a subordinate.[6]

All of these top-level lieutenants of Menéndez could count many years of command experience and were thus qualified to serve in the Florida expedition by virtue of their accomplishments as well as by their relationship with the adelantado. Their careers, however, like that of their chief, had been oriented entirely around the sea—in

4. Pedro Menéndez de Avilés to Crown, Santander, May 15, 1568, from Ruidiaz, *La Florida*, 2:171.

5. Pedro Menéndez Marquéz does not lack for archival data of a biographical nature. Material about him as fleet general may be found in the "Papeles de armada" series for the fleets under his command, in A.G.I. *Contratación* 2,946–48. Marquéz is listed as maestre of one of Pedro Menéndez' ships in 1561 in Chaunu, *Séville et l'Atlantique*, 3:6. Bonds of Marquéz are listed in A.G.I. *Contratación* 9. Sentences against him are found in A.G.I. *Patronato* 177, no. 1, ramo 25, *Escribanía de Cámara* 967, 1,010, 1,011. An audit of Marquéz' fleet accounts is found in A.G.I. *Contaduría* 464. Various descriptions of his service are in A.G.I. *Patronato* 257, no. 4, ramos 1, 6, 8, 11. He testified at length about his early services in Florida in A.G.I. *Patronato* 257, no. 3, ramo 20, "Daños de los indios de la Florida." Consultas and cédulas about Pedro Menéndez Marquéz during his term as governor and captain-general of Florida are found in A.G.I. *Santo Domingo* 2,528 and *Indiferente General* 738, as cited later. Vigil discusses Menéndez Marquéz in *Noticias . . . de Pedro Menéndez de Avilés*, pp. 49–50, as does Ruidiaz in *La Florida*, 2:629 ff. (see pp. 71–72*n*1 for their shared error). Jeannette Thurber Connor devotes considerable space and exhibits great interest in Pedro Menéndez Marquéz in the introduction to *Colonial Records of Spanish Florida*, 1:xxiii–xxvi.

6. Pedro Menéndez had recommended Diego Flores Valdés as one of three qualified to be fleet general for Tierra Firme in 1562; see Memorial of Pedro Menéndez de Avilés to Crown, n.d., in 1564, Seville, A.G.I. *Patronato* 257, no. 3, ramo 2. Sentencias relating to Flores are found in A.G.I. *Escribanía de Cámara* 952, 967. He is praised in fulsome terms by the adelantado in his letter to Philip II dated at St. Augustine, September 11, 1565, and found in A.G.I. *Santo Domingo* 231 (Stetson Coll.).

privateering, freighting for the Indies trade, or carrying out naval functions for the Crown. Although they were accustomed to the handling of troops as men-of-war aboard ships, none of these men had become experienced in land-based operations with bodies of soldiers.[7]

A man who might have been able to supply that lack of experience was Pedro de Valdés of Tineo, in Asturias. He was the twenty-five-year-old son of the founder of the Valdés *mayorazgo* and had served the Crown for more than five years with land forces in Italy; he had also been a gentleman officer in the galleys and had received the habit of caballero in the order of Santiago. Since Valdés had been recently betrothed to Pedro Menéndez' daughter Ana, however, the adelantado had directed that he not risk his person on the expedition to Florida.[8]

Another young nobleman, Hernando de Miranda, from Avilés, was enrolled, together with his brother Gutierre, as an ordinary soldier in the Florida expedition, but he was marked out for advancement within the organization of the adelantado.[9]

A number of loyal Asturians occupied a second echelon among Menéndez' subordinates, including the Junco brothers, Juan and Rodrigo, Alonso Menéndez Marqués, Thomas Alonso de las Alas, Diego de Hevia, and Diego de Amaya, a fine pilot and skilled ship handler. The brother-in-law of the adelantado, Gonzalo Solís de Merás, also planned to join in the enterprise of Florida. Some of these men remained in the north of Spain to sail with the contingents preparing for sea in Gijón and Avilés; others joined Menéndez in Cádiz. In addition to these, a sizeable group of old associates of the adelantado in his ship crews were enrolled for Florida as soldiers, seamen, or skilled workers.

What was most remarkable about Menéndez' men was the close-knit nature of their interrelationships. Almost without exception, the men

7. It is certainly true that no clear-cut distinction between "navy" and "army" existed in the sixteenth century, and that a commission as "ordinary captain" in the King's service could be utilized on land or at sea. What is under discussion here, however, is the matter of experience.

8. Pedro de Valdés' qualifications are discussed by the adelantado in his letter to the Crown in the letter sent from St. Augustine on September 11, 1565, and found in A.G.I. *Santo Domingo* 231 (Stetson Coll.).

9. Miranda appears on a ration list of the first soldiers of the Menéndez contingent; this is "Lista de la gente de guerra que fueron con el Adelantado Pedro Menéndez a la conquista de la Florida," from A.G.I. *Contaduría* 941, fol. 9 (microfilm, P. K. Yonge Library). On June 1, 1565, he served as a witness to the appointment of Juan de Junco as *tenedor de bastimentos*; this is from "Relación de los bastimentos, artillería, armas, y municiones que recibió Juan de Junco," found in A.G.I. *Contaduría* 941, ramo 2.

who shared the confidence of Pedro Menéndez and were scheduled to hold the posts of responsibility in Florida belonged to a number of Asturian families which were tied together by complex kinship links.[10] Scores of rank-and-file soldiers and sailors from the same families also participated in the Florida enterprise. It was a family affair, or rather the affair of a small number of closely connected families from the north of Spain. In addition to the Menéndez and Valdés clans, these included the Miranda, de las Alas, Quiros, Sánchez, Arango, Solís, de Soto, Recalde, Flores, Ribera, Argüelles, Junco, Marquéz, Hevia, and LaBandera families. These families had intermarried at many points over several generations.[11]

This family complex was rooted in the fishing villages and in the valley and mountain hamlets of the rugged coast of Asturias and Santander.[12] Men came to take part in the Florida expeditions from villages which for more than fifty years had sent out conquistadores, *encomenderos*, and priests to the Indies.[13] They came from Avilés, Tineo, Villaviciosa, Gijón, Colunga, Siero, Grado, and Parilea. They came from Rivadesella, and from the "four *villas* of the coast," Santander, Santoña, Castro Urdiales, and Laredo. Some also came from as far west as La Coruña in Galicia and from San Sebastián and other towns in Guipúzcoa, near the French border. The force which linked these localities and produced men, money, ships, and supplies for the enterprise of Florida was that of family. A web of kindred provided the backing for Pedro Menéndez de Avilés, but he had not created it. The network pre-dated 1565 and was to continue its influence in the maritime and political life of Spain and the Indies long after the death of the adelantado.

Bound together by common ties, the adelantado's command and control structure shared in his hopes of patrimony in Florida. As

10. See "Genealogy of the Enterprise of Florida," Appendix 3.

11. For example, Pedro Menéndez married his cousin, Doña María de Solis, and was thus required to seek Papal dispensation for marriage within the forbidden decrees (Solís de Merás, p. 40). He was at times himself called Pedro Menéndez Valdés (see *Libro de Registros*, 1551, Ida, A.G.I. *Contratación* 2,898), and married his daughter Ana to Pedro de Valdés, who was also at times called Pedro Menéndez Valdés.

12. There are extant various lists of participants in the Florida enterprise. Several lengthy lists of officials and soldiers and some shorter ones of mariners are found in the Florida accounts in A.G.I. *Contaduría* 941, ration lists from 1566–69. Three similar lists of the royal troops in the Cádiz contingent are found in A.G.I. *Justicia* 817. In many cases, together with the names of men (or women) the birthplace and/or place of citizenship is given.

13. Peter Boyd-Bowman. *Índice geobiográfico de cuarenta mil pobladores españoles de América en el Siglo XVI*, describes (1:9 and passim) the activities of the Miranda, de la Ribera, del Busto, Junco, Valdés, Hevia, de las Alas, del Castillo, Solís, and other Asturian families in Cuba, Santo Domingo, Cartagena, Yucatán, Puerto Rico, and New Spain.

patrón of his supporters, Menéndez was the fountainhead of royal privilege, the source of present employment, and the focus of the future expectations of his subordinates. Under his asiento powers, he could divide substantial allotments of land among these men. The major civil and military offices would be theirs. Successes in Florida would evoke royal approbation and the award of honors to the adelantado. A portion of this glory would in turn be reflected upon the lieutenants and upon their houses. By establishing themselves in Menéndez' service, members of the group might also hope to rise in the service of Philip II.

Neither the command elite nor its supporting group was a static organization with a fixed membership. Individuals might enter or leave the group, but its character did not change very markedly. Menéndez' criteria for selection of men for the highest level of his establishment remained the same: that they be Asturian or at least norteño in origin, that they be noblemen and related in some mean- ingful way to himself. An administrative organism arose out of the group, as various persons were appointed to formal office within the military units and the governmental structure of Florida. Their rela- tionship with their commander was, however, deeper than the formal and legal. In a sense, they were stockholders in the Florida enterprise. They acted at least in part out of feelings of deep loyalty to their chief, mixed with hopes of substantial gain. In turn, the adelantado could delegate his powers legally to these men, but his delegation could be made with more certainty because he knew that his trust reposed in those who held his purpose in common loyalty.[14]

A genealogy chart of the enterprise of Florida, such as the one furnished in this book, does not demonstrate the full complexity of the familial matrix from which Menéndez' conquest effort sprang. Many subtle ties, perhaps even vital connections, are not completely understood. Some individuals who are termed relatives of Pedro Menéndez cannot be related directly to him by his biographers Vigil and Ruidiaz. A chart cannot illustrate the full meaning of such an interlocking organism, for it cannot depict the human forces present in such a complex. This homogenous group, bound together by common cultural and familial ties, could provide great reserves of purpose for the conquest. The fierce loyalties engendered within it and the common expectations shared by its members afforded a

14. Menéndez recognized the strength of this motivation. In a letter to the Crown, he noted that he preferred men from Asturias and Vizcaya, "who are the people best fitted to work in Florida, some because of their nature and some because of kinship and friendship" (Pedro Menéndez to Crown, Seville, December 3, 1570, A.G.I. *Indiferente General* 1,093).

source of vital energy for the tasks of conquest and population. The organism was self-reinforcing in nature and could maintain a united front against outsiders. It gave depth to the efforts of an adelantado. This was, therefore, a regional reservoir of talent. The strength of arms, the provision of ships and financial backing, and many skills and abilities could be drawn from this pool for Menéndez' use. Representatives of these Asturian families could also be found in Andalusia and in a number of ports and centers in the Indies. A certain stiffening of purpose was also added to the Florida effort by the back-up of a sizeable company of friends, relatives, and allies—their hopes could cause them to persevere in their venture in the face of any adversity. This was the matrix of the adelantamiento of Florida.

Ways and Means

In seeking to fund the effort of arming and manning the Florida expeditions, the newly named adelantado found himself hard pressed. He had emerged from his long imprisonment without substantial cash reserves, and his maritime assets had been reduced to one sizeable vessel and several smaller ones. Pedro Menéndez had an urgent need for ready money, for little of what he had to purchase could be obtained on credit, and he needed cash to keep his ship crews from deserting and to pay for supplies for the coming journey. His first approach was to press for the monies owed him by the Crown. These would not only help him meet his obligations, but would undergird his credit through the aura of royal patronage it would impart to the Florida enterprise.

Under daily pressure from the adelantado and after receiving a number of communications from Philip II about the matter, the Casa officials finally paid Pedro Menéndez the remaining 9,000 ducats of his merced, in spite of the fact that it was to have been contingent upon his leaving by May 31. They also indemnified Menéndez with 2,000 ducats for the profits lost through the diversion of the *San Pelayo* to Florida. In order to give Pedro Menéndez this money he so badly needed, the officials at Seville had to borrow from the merchants' deposits in the Casa. By June 7, however, the royal accountants had not yet been able to total the sums due to Menéndez from the 1563 ship-charter case, as they struggled with a mass of incomplete data.[15]

15. The trade officials reported to Philip II in a letter which bore no date. Apparently, it was written on June 7, 1565, for the payment it mentions was made on that day;

On June 12, Pedro Menéndez appeared before the tribunal of the Casa de Contratación and made a lengthy plea. The adelantado reviewed his total expenses in the preparation of the *San Pelayo* for its voyage to Tierra Firme and asked for reimbursement of 1,500 ducats which he spent for carpentry and caulking. He also demanded repayment of the salaries and rations for his entire 110-man crew, retroactive to April 1, and in addition asked the Casa to grant a five-month advance in pay and rations, to offset the risk and uncertainty of the hazardous journey in his fine new ship. The rate of pay Menéndez asked was, moreover, much higher than ordinary. Many Spanish seamen were paid as little as three ducats per month, and the adelantado admitted that his own men from Vizcaya would be paid five pesos. He asked, however, that the mariners aboard the *San Pelayo*, being a hand-picked, loyal crew, have seven or eight ducats' pay. Otherwise, he stated, they might desert or become so dissatisfied that the expedition might be endangered.

Menéndez' ambitious demands were disposed of coolly and rapidly. After reviewing a report of *Factor* Duarte's inspection of the *San Pelayo*, the three Royal Officials decided to allot only 500 ducats for improvements made to the vessel, to be paid when proper receipts were presented in evidence. They flatly declined to authorize any pay or allowances for Menéndez' crewmen before May 22, the date the *San Pelayo* was officially taken for Crown service.[16]

By June 14, the Casa treasurer had paid the adelantado another 8,000 ducats of the amount requested for the 1563 charter; no amount of royal compulsion could have forced any further payments of the remaining, bitterly disputed amounts. Then, on June 23, 1565, Pedro Menéndez received the last payment he was to get from the Casa de Contratación before his departure—2,300 ducats as an advance on the charter of the *San Pelayo*.[17]

Since returning to Seville from Madrid with his asiento, Pedro Menéndez had collected 30,300 ducats in cash from a variety of claims on the royal treasury.[18] Although it was less than he had asked, this

the letter is found in A.G.I. *Contratación* 5,167, Book III. Payment of the 9,000 ducats is from A.G.I. *Contratación* 4,680 (*Libro de Guadalcanal*), fol. 128; this citation was kindly furnished by Paul E. Hoffman.

16. See "Petition of Pedro Menéndez de Avilés before the *Casa de Contratación*," Seville, June 12, 1565, A.G.I. *Escribanía de Cámara* 1,024-A.

17. The payments are listed in A.G.I. *Contratación* 4,344 and A.G.I. *Contaduría* 310-B; 455: 2.

18. This includes the entire 15,000-ducat merced, the 11,000-ducat advance on the galleon-lease case settlement, and the 2,000 ducats paid as recompense for losing the Tierra Firme voyage for the *San Pelayo*. It also included the 2,300 ducats advanced on the charter of the *San Pelayo*.

money was very helpful indeed. In this way, royal funds were helping to underwrite the adelantado who was to supply the "private" effort of supporting the hand of the King in Florida.

Pedro Menéndez had to meet the rest of his money needs from other sources, and he worked to raise funds and to enlist supporters for his cause. Since Menéndez' ships were pledged to Florida for most of 1565, he could not count on much income from freight or passenger revenue. He was to collect one amount of 893 pesos which came consigned to him from Spain in the 1565 Vera Cruz ships, but the New Spain vessel which brought it did not dock in Sanlúcar until June 24. The money could scarcely have reached him before his departure.[19] Another thing Menéndez could do was to collect or assign any outstanding obligations owed him. On June 25, he discounted a debt due him from the estate of one Santiago Bozino for almost 400 ducats by turning it over to Domingo de Ocaris of Seville for cash.[20] In this way, however, only a modest sum could be realized, compared with the funds he urgently required. For the bulk of his monetary needs, Pedro Menéndez had recourse to a financial complex which merits description.

In the last half of the sixteenth century, the main source of liquid funds was commerce. The injection of bullion from Peru and Mexico into the mercantile stream undergirded the economy and added to the liquidity of the traders and bankers in Seville and elsewhere in Europe. Contained within the registries of each homeward-bound ship were sums of monies due to merchants, suppliers, and shipowners in Spain, as the result of sales transactions. A sophisticated system of exchange values easily contained a variety of bullion forms—gold and silver came in bars or were worked into plate or jewelry, while silver was coined in several forms. Quantities of various agricultural products—tobacco, sugar, hides, cochineal, and indigo —also came in the ships; these were to be sold in Spain.

Although the registry documents themselves (certified as correct by the shipmasters and accepted by the Casa de Contratación) served as valid commercial instruments in the Indies trade, other means were developed to facilitate credit. Execution of an ordinary poder, or power of attorney, proved to be a most flexible way to extend a man's financial reach. By the uncounted thousands, these poderes fill the notaries' archives of Spain; they make up the very fabric of trade.

19. I am indebted to Paul E. Hoffman for this citation; "Fé de registro, *Santa María de Ondiz*," A.G.S. *Junta de Hacienda*, 67.

20. Poder, Pedro Menéndez de Avilés to Domingo de Ocaris, Cádiz, June 25, 1565, A.P.C., *Escribanía* of de los Cobos, fol. 297.

They represent a time when money and property rights were entirely and intensely personal, when it was often essential to name a properly empowered surrogate to represent one before courts, tribunals, and justices. Such a surrogate could thus receive a delegation of the grantor's inherent prerogatives.

The poder could also be directly and immediately applied to the commercial sphere, as a means of collecting obligations due another. The grantee was given the faculty to stand in the grantor's place, receive the goods or funds which were due, and give valid receipts in the name of the originating party. Since the standard poder stated that the grantee could then proceed to substitute another party for himself, a theoretically endless chain of right and obligation could be created from a single original grant of authority.

The credit aspect of the poder becomes evident when one considers that it was usually granted for consideration. Thus, merchant A could grant trader B his poder to collect a sum due him from a third party. The sum due might not be immediately available and might not actually mature for some period of time. The first party could, however, discount his obligation and obtain immediate advantage by trading off a future collectible. As a practical matter, therefore, poder obligations could not be greatly removed in time from the real money sources which had nurtured them. An individual's credit could be extended substantially by such a paper network, but was ultimately no better than the genuine assets which backed it.

The development of late medieval commercial organizations had been centered on what might be termed "associations of trust." The earliest Italian companies were built around family groups or a small number of interrelated families. Within this circle of close relationships, business transactions could be most safely carried out.[21] Since credit obtained under this system was limited and personal, such an arrangement was best adapted to close-knit groups whose other rela-

21. Some insights into the relationships of families in commerce appear in Armando Sapori, *The Italian Merchant in the Middle Ages*, pp. 45–46. Sapori states the matter well: "in the early Middle Ages, these men [in a company] belonged to the same family, which formed a closed block of interests and individuals. They lived under the same roof, submitted to the authority of the eldest among them, and broke bread around the same table. Like the family, a compact group by reason of its ties of blood, the company had its honor to safeguard in society, and this family-company identity imposed on each of its members a line of irreproachable conduct in business affairs. Anyone who committed a fraud would ruin both his own name and that of his entire family. . . . In this way there was a rigorous reciprocal control, which was made bearable by the affection uniting the families. As the business grew, it required more capital, and therefore, outsiders, capable of supplying the necessary funds, had to be admitted. These men were chosen from a wide circle of relatives and associates and finally people who had no particular ties to the old family group."

tionships reinforced their paper obligations. Much the same tendency could be seen in sixteenth-century Spain. Commercial ties were supported by stronger underlying connections of blood, marriage, or regional identification. In the case of Pedro Menéndez de Avilés, the web of interrelated Asturian families which was involved in his command organization also had its fiscal side. Long-established ties existed between Menéndez and norteño bondsmen, bankers, and merchants living in the authorized trading centers of Seville and Cádiz. As a man deeply involved in advancing his fortunes, Pedro Menéndez de Avilés fitted well into the atmosphere of growth, prosperity, and diversity in the Andalusian ports in 1565. In Seville and in Cádiz, the socially mobile, acquisitive society described by Ruth Pike featured much interaction between upper merchants and the lower nobility.[22] Some of these men were of *converso* origin, who had, long since, created commercial bases in the Indies. For Pedro Menéndez and his associates, there were such bases at San Juan, Puerto Rico, in the City of Mexico, at Santo Domingo on the Island of Hispaniola, and in the City of San Cristobal de la Havana. In San Juan, for instance, lived Diego Montañés and Pedro Menéndez Valdés, who acted as representatives for the adelantado there.[23] The familial interconnections among Santo Domingo, Cádiz, the Indies, and the north of Spain are illustrated by a later poder from one Diego Menéndez de la Aspriella, a vecino of Santo Domingo, to Favian de Solís, merchant, a vecino of Avilés, but residing in Cádiz.[24]

The central figure of Pedro del Castillo, regidor of Cádiz, a substantial merchant there and a kinsman of Menéndez, has previously been linked to the adelantado. Pedro del Castillo was related to Menéndez, but the degree of relationship is not known. Castillo had developed trade ties to New Spain, with representatives in Vera Cruz and the City of Mexico. Gaspar de Serfate, who resided in Mexico, had shipped cochineal to Castillo as early as 1562.[25] In Seville, Castillo's banker was Gaspar de Astudillo de Burgales. Astudillo had also served as Menéndez' bondsman in 1563 and was to act for him in the future. All three men, Menéndez, Castillo, and Astudillo, employed the same norteño attorney, Sebastian de Santander. He acted

22. See Ruth Pike, *Aristocrats and Traders*; *Sevillian Society in the 16th Century*, esp. pp. 99 ff.

23. The presence of Diego Montañés and Pedro Menéndez Valdés in Puerto Rico is mentioned by Pedro Menéndez Marquéz in his visit to San Juan in September 1566. The documents are from A.G.I. *Patronato* 257, no. 4, ramo 1.

24. Poder, Diego Menéndez de la Aspriella to Favian de Solís, A.P.C., *Escribanía* of de Ribera, 1577, fol. 176.

25. See "Registro de la nao *Santa María*," A.G.I. *Justicia* 872, fol. 217, vto.-221.

as their counsel in the cases involving them before the Casa de Contratación and the Council of the Indies.[26]

Irene Wright has ably outlined the role of the linked Rojas and de Soto families in the early development of the Cuban City of San Cristobal de la Havana.[27] The real founder of the clan which was to rule the economic and political life of Havana for much of the sixteenth century was Diego de Soto, of norteño origins, who first came to Cuba in 1529. In Pedro Menéndez' time, the most influential member was Juan de Rojas, whose kinfolk dominated the cabildo of Havana and occupied most of the other local posts of honor and privilege there. Rojas' wife, Dona María de Lovera, had demonstrated her close ties to Pedro Menéndez de Avilés by naming him in her 1563 will as executor of a bequest, vital to the peace of her soul, for the building of a chapel in her memory in Spain.[28] Juan de Hinestrosa, who had testified in Seville for Menéndez in his 1564 jailbreak case, was the son of Manuel de Rojas de Bayamo and served after 1565 as one of the Royal Officials in Havana.[29]

In his need for money, therefore, Pedro Menéndez turned to those of his associates who had access to funds gained in the Indies trade. Most particularly, he turned to Pedro del Castillo. On June 25, in Castillo's house in Cádiz, Menéndez executed a lengthy poder.[30] In some ways, the instrument follows the usual pattern of documents of its kind. It lawfully establishes Castillo as Menéndez' representative in prosecuting civil or criminal actions in his name and in receiving monies due the adelantado and ends in the standard recitation that the goods and wealth of the grantor are pledged to support the powers given.

The poder to Castillo was, however, far more than a limited, ad hoc delegation. It was quite broad in nature and was deeply involved with the asiento which Pedro Menéndez had received from Philip II. In it,

26. Astudillo, a vecino of Seville, testified for Menéndez in his claim to recover funds allegedly advanced to Florida soldiers. The testimony, on March 27, 1572, is from A.G.I. *Justicia* 817. Astudillo served as bondsman for the adelantado in the 1564 jailbreak case. See "Fiscal de Su Magestad contra Pedro Menéndez de Avilés y sus fiadores," A.G.I. *Justicia* 868, pieza 9. Sebastian de Santander represented the adelantado through much of the main case involving the asiento, found in A.G.I. *Escribanía de Cámara* 1,024-A, and represented Astudillo in the jailbreak case. Pike, in *Aristocrats and Traders*, p. 123, describes the Astudillo banking family.

27. Wright, *Historia documentada de San Cristobal de la Habana en el siglo XVI*, 1:82, 83.

28. The Lovera will is found in *Archivo Histórico de Protocolos* (A.H.P.), *Escribanía* of Nicolas Muñoz, no. 635, fol. 4.

29. Hinestrosa's antecedents are discussed by Wright, p. 82. His role in the 1564 case is outlined in A.G.I. *Justicia* 868, pieza 9.

30. The poder from Pedro Menéndez to Pedro del Castillo is in A.P.C., *Escribanía* of Alonso de los Cobos. A copy is in the A.G.I., at *Indiferente General* 2,673.

the adelantado conceded full use and exploitation of the Florida contract to Pedro del Castillo, giving him the free use in his name of all clauses and sections. Castillo was given exclusive right to handle the purchase and embarkation of the five hundred Negro slaves whose licenses had been granted to Menéndez in the asiento. In fact, the entire business side of the administration of the King's contract and Menéndez' private financial affairs was given over to Pedro del Castillo. He was to have charge of the ship licenses which had been promised to Menéndez. He was empowered to buy and sell vessels, hire and dismiss masters and crews, purchase supplies, equipment and cargoes, and see that Menéndez' maritime ventures were carried out with dispatch, in Cádiz and in the north of Spain. All other poderes granted by Menéndez were annulled, except those which the adelantado stated were still valid in the north coast cities.

In order to enable Castillo to recover what he had advanced for the Florida outfitting, Menéndez gave him full power to collect monies due from the 1563 sueldo case, the carpentry work on the *San Pelayo*, and whatever might be realized from another claim that Menéndez had made against the Casa for the loss of the *Santa Clara* in 1564. He empowered Castillo to dun Factor Duarte for the balance of the *San Pelayo*'s sueldo, as it should come due. General authority was given for Castillo to collect any cash or valuables which were owed to the adelantado from his own trade enterprises. The poder especially referred to the uncollected sums due Menéndez from freight charges on goods that the merchants Alonso Rodrigues and Juan Dias Bezino had shipped in the *San Pelayo* the previous year.

The Castillo poder is a business-like document—it sets forth crisply the authority which the Cádiz entrepreneur should have in Menéndez' affairs—yet it was also a real expression of trust and confidence. Castillo could draw freely upon all the monies of the adelantado to satisfy debts which had been incurred in his name and his figures were to be accepted by Menéndez. He could set up his own accounts for these matters. This merely emphasizes the degree to which this relationship was not merely a legal and fiduciary one. The formal dealings of the two men were buttressed and enhanced by their closer ties. When Pedro del Castillo and Pedro Menéndez signed the poder on the eve of the departure of the Florida expedition from Cádiz, Castillo had acted as general factor for the Florida outfitting, expending more than 20,000 ducats for the adelantado. He had also involved his own friends and relatives in the effort.[31] It was Castillo's task to

31. Castillo describes his expenditures and those of his "friends and kinsmen" in "Requeremiento de Luna a Castillo" found in A.G.I. *Escribanía de Cámara* 1,024-A under

recover this money by collecting funds due Menéndez from the Casa and from private parties; he could then repay himself from those sources. Menéndez' royal patronage (evidenced by the asiento and its titles, privileges, and licenses), the earning power of his own ships, and the back-up of friends and relatives would, it was hoped, keep the money flow going. In carrying out his mission, Castillo proceeded to delegate his authority under the poder from Menéndez by substituting in his own place a German residing in Seville, one Agustín Francisco, who was given an instrument to that effect. Francisco was to solicit the 500 ducats which had been promised by the officials of the Casa de Contratación but which remained unpaid.[32]

Next, Pedro del Castillo established a branch office, so to speak, of Pedro Menéndez' business concerns in New Spain. He executed a poder to Gaspar Serfate, the merchant living in the City of Mexico. Castillo passed along to Serfate the rights Menéndez had ceded to Castillo in Cádiz. Serfate was given the capacity to collect monies which one Isidro de Solís owed to Pedro Menéndez and was invested with the power to receive any sums due the adelantado from other dealings. He could also handle the details of cargo purchases and the loading of ships from New Spain in Menéndez' name and could further subdivide this authority if he wished.[33]

By their own testimony, both Pedro Menéndez and Pedro del Castillo had made heavy expenditures in the preparation of the enterprise of Florida. They had both also noted that many of their own friends and relatives were also deeply encumbered as a result of the outfitting of the Florida expedition. As the main financial backer of the adelantamiento of Florida, Castillo was clearly a man of substance.[34] His own resources were essentially derived from his activities in the Indies trade, although he was also a ship chandler. Five

the date of June 28, 1565, in Cádiz. He outlines his financial sacrifices further in a letter to the King, received in Madrid on January 30, 1566, and found in A.G.I. *Indiferente General* 2,673.

32. The Agustín Francisco substitution is found in A.G.I. *Indiferente General* 2,673. It comes originally from A.P.C., *Escribanía* of Alonso de los Cobos.

33. Substitution by Pedro del Castillo, Cádiz, August 17, 1565, A.P.C., *Escribanía* of Alonso de los Cobos, fol. 409.

34. Castillo, who had served in 1563–64 as *receptor de avería* in Cádiz, was adjudged guilty of undervaluation of goods shipped for the tax. For a shortage in his books of 238,524 *maravedís*, he was fined 50,000 maravedís. Castillo had, however, also been the supplier for the galleys for which he was to have collected the avería, and was owed 224,531 maravedís for this service. See "Culpas y cargos contra Pedro del Castillo," A.G.I. *Justicia* 956. Shipments from New Spain for Castillo are listed in the Fé de registros for the vessels *La María, Santa María de Ondiz, La Trinidad, San Juan,* and *Santa María*. These were found in A.G.S. *Junta de Hacienda* 67, and furnished through the kindness of Paul E. Hoffman.

of the 1565 New Spain ships which had arrived in Sanlúcar late in June had carried a total of 12,706 pesos in silver for Castillo, which somewhat renewed the funds of the Cádiz merchant after his heavy expenditures in Menéndez' behalf. He acted as banker and factor for the adelantado out of his own commercial resources, but the financial support of the enterprise of Florida was not the work of any one man. Although its administration was centered in Pedro del Castillo, the network could enable the tapping of commercial sources and royal monies in many areas to keep the venture going. Through the associates and allies of Menéndez located in Cádiz and in the north of Spain, fresh shipments of soldiers, settlers, and supplies could be directed to Florida. Resources in the Indies could be utilized there to buttress the effort. These arrangements could serve as a partial hedge against the hazards of the sea and the vagaries and dangers of the discovery, conquest, and settlement of the new Florida colonies.

Thus it was that a combination of merchant and Crown money served to support Pedro Menéndez' efforts in Florida. Since a great part of the royal revenues used to help launch and support the effort also arose originally out of some tax upon the Carrera de Indies, it might be said that the first successful settlement of Florida was largely underwritten by trade and commerce.

Because of careful and detailed records, which have survived, one may gain a rather precise estimate of the aggregate of royal expenditure in the outfitting of the Florida expedition.[35] Direct Crown costs were 17,681 ducats. The merced paid to Menéndez was 15,000 ducats and the adelantado was also paid 2,000 ducats to recompense him for losses sustained through missing his trading voyage to Tierra Firme. He had received 2,300 ducats on account of the charter of the *San Pelayo*. This total of 36,981 ducats thus represented the down payment on the Crown share of the Florida costs. It covered all supplies bought for the royal account in Spain and the initial sueldo payments for sailors, soldiers, and vessels underwritten by the King. Set against this were the funds expended by the adelantado. For several reasons, it is not a simple task to furnish a reliable total of Menéndez' costs. In the first place, his private records are not to be found in any single continuous series comparable to the account books of the Casa de Contratación. Where his contribution was officially audited, good materials have survived. For the Cádiz effort, for example, Factor Duarte's itemized list of materials, ships, and men

35. See Appendix 4.

may serve as a reasonable basis for conjectured cost. At Avilés, Gijón, and Santander, where the northern contingents of ships and men were prepared, documentation is not as complete but can still yield enough data for some estimate of the adelantado's expenses.[36]

There is a second complicating factor; Menéndez' costs were directly shared by others in his organization. Some of his lieutenants and supporters absorbed these expenses as their own investment in the enterprise of Florida. For example, one of the Asturian ships was furnished by its master, Alonso Menéndez Marqués. Likewise, there are indications that Diego Flores de Valdés encumbered his patrimony in the Florida effort, while Francisco de Reinoso made Pedro Menéndez a loan of 2,000 ducats. The adelantado also noted that he had borrowed from brothers, relatives, and friends. In a more vital way, however, the rank and file of Menéndez' men became direct shareholders in the enterprise of Florida. The Asturian made contracts with his own soldiers through their captains, in which it was agreed that they would be paid no salary but would receive their reward in lands and booty to be gained in Florida. One of these read: "I promise in the name of His Majesty, by the commission he gives me for it, to give them in the said coast and land of Florida rations, lands and properties for their plantations, tillage and stock-breeding, and land-allotments in conformity with their service and the qualities which each one might possess, and the part which might come to them of the gold, silver, pearls and [precious] stones which there might be in the said coast, and which might be discovered. They will enjoy the rest of the exemptions and privileges which His Majesty might grant to those who participate in the settlement, discovery, and conquest of that land."[37]

Thus the adelantado was obliged to supply his men but not to pay them. The kind of supporters he recruited in this way, when bound by other ties of kinship and loyalty, might indeed be eager and enthusiastic subordinates in the venture. On the other hand, men disappointed in their hopes of land and bullion might be rebellious,

36. See Appendix 5.
37. Pedro Menéndez mentions Flores' investment in the enterprise in his October 15, 1565, letter to Philip II found in A.G.I. *Santo Domingo* 231 (Stetson Coll.). Lowery, in *The Spanish Settlements*, 2:146, advises that Flores had pawned his patrimony to support Menéndez. The adelantado discusses his loan from Reinoso in his Havana letter to the Spanish King written on Christmas Day, 1565, in A.G.I. *Santo Domingo* 231 (Stetson Coll.). It has also been reproduced in Lawson, *Letters of Menéndez*, 1:271. Menéndez reminds the King of the loans from his brothers, relatives, and friends in "Menéndez reports to the Crown, 1565 [*sic*]," from Manuscript Division, Library of Congress, typescript translation, 1937. A copy is in the P. K. Yonge Library. Menéndez' promise to his soldiers, dated at Seville, May 25, 1565, is from A.G.I. *Justicia* 879, no. 3, pieza 1.

particularly when they were not bound by the ties which united the norteños who were related to the adelantado.

All conceivable items considered, it appears that the initial outfitting of the Florida enterprise cannot have cost Pedro Menéndez and his supporters much less than 47,000 ducats. Menéndez was thus a heavy investor, but his efforts and those of his entourage represented far more than any investment of cash. It amounted to a major risk of their persons and capital. For the shipowners and their men, the vessels pledged to the Florida expedition represented their livelihood. Whether their income was earned in the Indies trade or through Crown sueldos, these ships were its source. They were the main property at hazard in the voyage.

In addition, the men and women aboard the craft—captains and soldiers, artisans, settlers, and priests—constituted a very special kind of asset, the human resources at hazard in the enterprise. Lives, careers, reputations, and patrimonies hung in the balance. Florida represented an immense speculation, a gamble undertaken for great stakes. It was not, moreover, the risk of any one man. The enterprise of Florida was a group effort. The hopes and the lives of many depended upon its outcome.

The joint nature of the undertaking made it essential that the Spanish Crown exercise a degree of control over the expenditure of its monies and the payment of its soldiery. Wherever Crown money or supplies were to be provided, it was required by law and by precedent that a Royal Official be appointed to protect the King's interest.[38] The three main offices of treasurer, accountant, and factor, called, in practice, Royal Officials, had for sixty years been a bulwark of Crown authority in the Indies and had long predated the establishment of the viceroyalties. A system of *cajas*, or royal treasuries, had spread by 1565 through the Caribbean islands and the mainland settlements of the Spanish. Royal revenues, such as customs duties, court fines, the tithe and *cruzada* income, Indian tributes, and the quinto were collected, safeguarded, and accounted for by the Royal Officials. Any expenditures from Crown funds would pass through their records. Even though the Florida asiento privileges would diminish some of these revenues or exempt the payment of some for a period of years, it was still planned that these three positions would shortly be filled. Since the salaries for the positions were to be paid out of royal

38. A good general description of the place of the Royal Officials in the Spanish colonial financial system may be found in C. H. Haring's *The Spanish Empire in America*, pp. 279–82. A more recent and far more detailed study has been done by Ismael Sánchez-Bella in *La organización financiera de las Indias, Siglo XVI*. See especially chap. 1 "Desarrollo histórico," pp. 7–68.

income, the jobs would not mean much until the settlements were a going concern. An adelantado was given the authority to propose individuals for the posts, but final confirmation of the appointments was in the King's hands.[39] Even though Royal Officials were not immediately named, a lesser position, that of tenedor de bastimentos, was created. It was the duty of the tenedor to keep records of the Crown property received and to account for its proper distribution.

Pedro Menéndez made the appointment himself, on June 1, in Seville, exercising his powers in the King's name. The circumstances were significant—Menéndez named Juan de Junco of Oviedo, a faithful member of his own retinue. Junco was not required to post any bond, which was unusual. He was to draw a salary of 300 ducats annually and would be responsible for all artillery, munitions, and other supplies furnished by the King. Junco could make distribution from royal stores as ordered by the King or the adelantado. The ostensible purpose of this office was to provide for an independent defender of the King's goods and interests. In actuality, however, the nature of the appointment of Juan de Junco made such objectivity impossible from the beginning. The close-knit structure of Pedro Menéndez' adelantamiento militated against effective royal control.[40]

Preparation for Departure

In a very short time, Pedro Menéndez de Avilés had to provide additional ships, gather his soldiers, and purchase and load supplies and munitions for the Florida journey. He took personal charge of preparations at Cádiz and delegated the tasks of equipping the three contingents from Avilés, Gijón, and Santander to trusted lieutenants. Menéndez placed Esteban de las Alas in overall command of the effort in northern Spain and named Pedro Menéndez Marquéz as his second in command.[41] Meanwhile, Casa Factor Francisco Duarte and

39. "Ordenanzas," *D.I.*, vol. 8, no. LXIV, p. 507.

40. It was, of course, difficult to guarantee a position for Indies Royal Officials independent of local power centers. This, however, was the reason for their separate salary arrangements. Sánchez-Bella discusses this problem in *La organización financiera de las Indias*, p. 28. The point here is that no member of Menéndez' own organizational apparatus was likely to establish such independence, even if he should desire to do so. Juan de Junco's brother Rodrigo was affiliated with Pedro Menéndez by 1562. See registry of the vessel *Magdalena*, in "Fiscal with Pedro Menéndez de Avilés over pay of Sueldos . . . 1563," A.G.I. *Justicia* 872. The Junco appointment, dated June 1, 1565, is found in A.G.I. *Contaduría* 941 (microfilm, P. K. Yonge Library, reel 1).

41. The documentation of the arming of the northern expeditions has been accumulated in A.G.I. *Escribanía de Cámara* 1,024-A, which contains the corpus of the suit by Pedro Menéndez over his asiento with the Crown. The adelantado and his heirs inserted the material into the record in order to prove the extent of compliance with the Florida

his representative in Cádiz, Juan Carrillo, labored diligently to prepare the Crown share of the Cádiz expedition.

It had been an unusually late and stormy winter along the coast of the Bay of Biscay, where continuous rains and heavy winds delayed the work of outfitting and equipping the vessels. On June 27, 1565, Alas appeared before Pedro de Valdés, the judge in Avilés, and made a statement of compliance with the royal asiento.[42] He averred that he had, in the name of Pedro Menéndez, readied and supplied certain ships to go from Gijón and perhaps Bilbao as well as from Avilés. When the local justices made their ship visits, he would be ready to leave with the first good weather to join the adelantado for a Canary Islands rendezvous.

The judge then required the shipmasters to open their hatches, list their cargoes, and name the officials and men who would be embarking. The men listed included 237 soldiers and 20 sailors. The man chosen as pilot of the ships from Avilés was a highly qualified Asturian, Alonso Candamo.

From Avilés eastward it is scarcely fifteen miles by land to the port of Gijón. Alongside the village mole in Gijón, two ships were being readied, and Pedro Menéndez Marquéz made application to the local justice on May 31, 1565, for a visit of his ships. The two vessels—the *Espíritu Santo* and the *Nuestra Señora del Rosario*—were small zabras, of 50 to 55 tons. Menéndez Marquéz stated that bad weather and heavy rains had delayed the work of preparing the ships for departure. This justification was put on record, since Menéndez Marquéz knew that the asiento required departure by the end of May.[43]

On the same day, one of the ships, the *Espíritu Santo*, was visited by the judge and regidor, Juan de Valdés. The ship's registry showed that she carried 55 pipes of wine, sails, anchors, rigging and other gear, two barrels of powder, 6,000 pounds of sea-biscuit, and 30 hams. Her master, Alonso Menéndez Marquéz, swore that nothing

---

contract. From the text of their works, it appears that the material was available to Gonzalo Solís de Merás and to Eugenio Ruidiaz y Caravia. The data are, however, scanty compared with that for the Cádiz section of the enterprise. I assume that perusal of the north-coast notaries' archives may uncover much more material.

42. The document is entitled "La lista que hizo el [*sic*] de las Alas en Avilés de 257 personas." It was copied in Avilés on September 27, 1567, from the original, which was dated June 27, 1565. The copy is found in A.G.I. *Escribanía de Cámara* 1,024-A. Unfortunately the ship registries, enclosed with the original, were not included, or at least are not now found with the copy. The supplies and men listed from Menéndez' native town would be invaluable.

43. "Visita y registro de los navios y gente en Gijón," Gijón, May 25, 1565, and "Visita y registro del navio *Espíritu Santo*," May 31, 1565, also at Gijón, from A.G.I. *Escribanía de Cámara* 1,024-A.

had been hidden or overlooked and presented a list of the men aboard. The two small vessels carried 50 soldiers and 17 sailors.

In the meantime, the first vessel from Vizcaya was rejected as being too small. Another vessel was prepared for the Florida voyage almost a hundred miles to the east, in Santander. This ship was a new *galeoncete*, from Vizcaya, owned by Pedro de Lexalde. She was to be used to carry 600 arquebuses made in Vizcaya, a supply of oars, and other bulky arms and munitions purchased for the account of the adelantado. Lexalde had been associated with Pedro Menéndez for nine years.[44] When, finally, the ships sailed from Avilés, Gijón, and Santander, it was so late that the possibility of making the rendezvous at the Canary Islands was very remote.

While the enlistment of ships' crews and soldiers and the outfitting of vessels continued in Asturias and Santander, work went forward rapidly in Andalusia as well. Pedro Menéndez and the Casa de Contratación engaged three caravels in order to spread the troops and cargoes more evenly among the Cádiz ships and to provide needed space. One, the *San Antonio*, of 120 tons burden, had been found in Puerto Santa María, was embargoed by the Casa de Contratación for the journey, and was rowed across the bay to Cádiz. The other two caravels were smaller. It was planned that they should all carry supplies as far as the Canary Islands, where the consumption of food and wine and the rendezvous with the Asturian ships would enable the redistribution of cargoes. The caravels would then be sent back to Spain. Work began at once upon the building of new bulkheads so that they would have sufficient storerooms and magazines.[45]

In addition to his flagship and capitana *San Pelayo* and the caravels, Pedro Menéndez armed four small one-deck shallops which ranged from 60 to 75 tons in size. These were named *Magdalena*, *San Miguel*, *San Andrés*, and *La Concepción*. The adelantado had also purchased a fine galiot with 18 banks of oars, *La Vitoria*, and a large *bergantín* of 12 banks, *La Esperanza*.[46]

44. The Lexalde ship is described briefly in "Memorial de los navios cargados de bastimentos y municiones que se perdieron el Adelantado Pero Menéndez yendo a echarlos luteranos que estavan poblando en aquella tierra de la Florida," A.G.I. *Escribanía de Cámara* 1,024-A; cf. "replica el Adelantado," ibid.

45. Pedro Menéndez describes the embargo of the *San Antonio* in his letter to the King sent from Matanzas, Cuba, on December 5, 1565, and found in A.G.I. *Santo Domingo* 231 (Stetson Coll.). Payment for the tow of the caravel, for loading water and wine into the caravels, and for the carpentry work is itemized in A.G.I. *Contaduría* 310-B; 451:4; 452:1, 2. Another description of the lading of the caravels and their subsequent journey is found in "Pedro del Castillo—información sumaria hecha en Cádiz," September 22, 1567, in A.G.I. *Escribanía de Cámara* 1,024-A.

46. The names of the vessels are found in the list of ships, men, and supplies made by

It is useful to compare the materials and supplies provided in Cádiz by the Crown and those furnished by Pedro Menéndez de Avilés under his asiento obligations, although such comparison cannot be reduced precisely to money terms, for all of the prices are not known.[47] Furthermore, the lists are not identical. The Crown's effort involved equipment and supplies for some three hundred soldiers and artillery, ammunition, and marine supplies intended to bolster the expedition and insure the ouster of the Huguenots from Florida. The broader-scale nature of Menéndez' commitment is reflected in the enumeration of the things he purchased for the expedition. First, both Crown and adelantado provided large quantities of the components of the basic sea ration, wine and sea biscuit, as well as the supplementary foodstuffs—olive oil, vinegar, rice, and beans. Menéndez was to carry supplies for one year, while the royal forces were supplied for a shorter period.

With regard to military supplies, the Crown furnished armed troops and cannon with which to besiege and capture Fort Caroline and the powder and shot with which to do it. Sixteen large bronze cannon were provided by the Crown. The adelantado bought 250 arquebuses and also provided 100 helmets, 30 crossbows and a quantity of pikes, breastplates, and harness for 50 horses. Six hundred more firearms were coming from Vizcaya for Menéndez. To supply the cannon aboard the *San Pelayo* and his other ships, Pedro Menéndez brought substantial amounts of gunpowder and iron shot.

Although the ships were fully equipped, additional marine supplies were also carried for the upkeep and repair of hulls, sails, and oars on a long voyage. The materials of husbandry and colonization were, moreover, supplied in quantity by Pedro Menéndez. For the smithy, six tons of bulk iron and a half ton of steel were brought aboard the *San Pelayo*. Fifty axes, and 450 shovels and mattocks of iron were brought to clear and work the land; 200 fishnets were provided, and shoemaking supplies were included. Cloth for trade with the Indians was loaded on the ship. For the religious life of the new colonies, the adelantado contributed eight church bells and the altar furnishings necessary for the celebration of the Mass.

Casa Factor Duarte in Cádiz, June 28, 1565, which has been reproduced in toto in A.G.I. *Escribanía de Cámara* 1,024-A. It has been printed in Ruidiaz, *La Florida*, 2:558–66, where it is cited as coming from A.G.S. *Junta de Hacienda*, Legajo 67. Menéndez described the purchase of the two ships in his letter to Philip II from Seville, May 18, 1565, which is printed in Ruidiaz, *La Florida*, 2:60–66.

47. See "Relación de los navios, gente, bastimentos, artilleria, armas, municiones . . . que lleva el adelantado Pedro Menéndez de Avilés en su armada para la conquista de la Florida," A.G.I. *Escribanía de Cámara* 1,024-A, and the royal list immediately following it.

In addition to items of supply and equipment for Florida, Pedro Menéndez brought in his Cádiz ships 138 soldiers who also held the "office," or possessed the skills, of artisans and craftsmen. These seamen were enrolled and equipped as soldiers, but were qualified by experience in their particular trade. Virtually all of the crafts of sixteenth-century Spain were represented: There were ten stone-masons, fifteen carpenters, twenty-one tailors, ten shoemakers, eight smiths, five *barberos*, and two surgeons. There were hose makers, metal smelters, cloth weavers, and cloth shearers. Two specialists in the making of lime and mortar were aboard, as well as tanners, farriers, wool carders, a hatmaker, a bookseller, and an embroiderer. Weapon experts were there in the persons of three sword makers, a gunsmith, and a crossbow repairman. There were coopers, bakers, gardeners, a dealer in silks, a blanket maker, and two men skilled in the working of flax for making linen. An apothecary, a keeper of granaries, and a master brewer rounded out the list. That essential of the paper-bound, legalistic Spaniard—the *escribano público*, the notary who would record all the formal actions—came along, together with twenty-four reams of paper and a quantity of ink. Also, 117 of the soldiers were listed as *labradores*, or farmers; these men were ready to make settlements on the land when their military duties would permit. Twenty-six of them had brought their wives and children.

The adelantado was thus preparing a full-scale transfer of Castilian civilization to the cities he planned to found in Florida. He carried in his ships enough skilled persons to service the needs of the colonies and to aid in the exploitation of their agricultural potential.

Both parties to the outfitting of the Florida expedition incurred direct expenses arising out of the purchase of equipment and supplies for the journey and the lease or purchase of ships in which to carry them. The Crown had to provide for immediate advance pay for soldiers and stood obliged to furnish continuing pay in the future for its men. Both the King and his adelantado would have to pay for supplying their men and operating the vessels involved in the Florida conquest. Of the two parties, Menéndez' obligation could have been considered the more enduring; it was to last for at least three years. As it was seen in Madrid, the royal support in Florida was intended to be a temporary thing, lasting only long enough to see the intruders defeated and ousted from the land.

The remaining days before sailing proved hectic for all parties. Much of the labor of preparing and loading the materials purchased by the Casa de Contratación fell upon the shoulders of its notary, Juan Carrillo at Cádiz. Supplies purchased by his agents came on oxcarts, on muleback, and in small boats. Wine, sea biscuit, rice, beef and pork, sides of bacon, fish, beans, cheese, garbanzos, olive oil, salt, and vinegar—even a medicine chest—were supplied by the Crown. Coopers knocked together the casks and barrels in which the bulk items would be stored. Goods, bought from many vendors, came from all of lower Andalusia—from Ronda, Jérez de la Frontera, Puerto de Santa María, and Puerto Real, from as far away as Seville, and from Cádiz itself. So much came, in fact, that it was necessary to lease storage space in the town. Some of the supplies were even stockpiled on the beach opposite the open roadstead where the *San Pelayo* and the other ships rode at anchor.[48] In the meantime, Menéndez had stowed away the supplies which he had bought.

In order that some basis might be established for the payment of the ship-lease fee for the *San Pelayo*, the Casa sent Francisco Bernal of Seville to measure the galeass. He figured it at 906 tons, and the rate of payment for the ship lease could be calculated.[49]

The 200 royal soldiers gathered by Menéndez during May 1565 embarked from Seville. In mid-June they were transported by boat to Sanlúcar, then were brought to Cádiz. The adelantado advanced them a sum of earnest-money—about one-third of a ducat apiece—for which he was shortly reimbursed by the Casa.[50] Two hundred fine new Vizcayan arquebuses were purchased for these men, together with the lead, match-cord, and powder for the weapons.

Because of the shortness of time in which the troops were recruited (Pedro Menéndez had stated that the first 200 had come on May 18, and he had only received the order to raise them on May 12), their enlistment must have taken place in Andalusia. An examination of a list of these men and their birthplaces, however, indicates that they came from villages and towns all over the peninsula. A few were from Catalonia, but most were Castilian; many places in Estremadura, the northern *meseta*, the north coast, and Andalusia were represented. These were professional soldiers, available because employment in Italy or elsewhere was not obtainable at the present. When he sought to provide the military arm to fill out his table of organization for the Florida conquest, Menéndez sought experienced men, blooded in the last of the Italian wars, in the Mediterranean galleys, and in North African expeditions.[51] By May 28, the adelantado had made a muster

48. There is a rich accretion of data on Casa pay for the *San Pelayo* and royal troops in A.G.I. *Contaduría* 310-B accounts of Factor Duarte, kindly furnished by Paul E. Hoffman.

49. See report of *Contadores Mayores*, A.G.I. *Escribanía de Cámara* 1,024-A.

50. Menéndez' advance of 23,800 maravedís to the troops was repaid by the Casa as in the record found in A.G.I. *Contaduría* 310-B, fol. 437.

51. When the adelantado described the non-commissioned officers and captains

of his own troops and presented it to the Casa de Contratación, so that each man (and wife, if she were coming on the expedition) could be examined for religious status and approved for the Indies journey.[52] In mid-June 1565, the first 200 who were to be paid by the Crown came down river from Seville to Sanlúcar de Barrameda and were then transported to Cádiz. On Sunday, June 17, a muster was held. At that time, or shortly thereafter, arquebuses were issued to the men.

Because of the exigencies of loading the ships for Florida, it was not possible to put the royal troops aboard immediately. Menéndez had to maintain and feed them ashore, before they could reach the *San Pelayo* and begin to draw upon the rations which awaited them there. He provided for the men from his own supplies until Thursday, June 22, when 99 more royal soldiers arrived. The adelantado then provided for the whole body of Crown troops ashore until they could be transported aboard ship on the twenty-sixth.[53] All the men received a payment of two months' advance salary, dating from the day of their muster.[54]

The sixteenth-century professional soldier was a hired man. The Spanish *tercios* were all composed of contract men who had been recruited by a captain and had signed agreements with him. In the case of soldiers enlisted for the royal account, each man signed his own *asiento*, received his advance pay and equipment, and began to draw rations. By terms of his contract, as long as he served, each soldier would be paid and receive his rations, worth thirty maravedís a day. Since the tools of his trade, his weapon and his accoutrements, were

whom he had appointed (including Sergeant-Major Villaroel, the *alfereces*, and other sergeants), he noted that "those without experience are few . . . they were soldiers of Italy skilled in war." Menéndez described this quality of his men in the letter dated September 11, 1565, and sent to Philip II from St. Augustine; from A.G.I. *Santo Domingo* 231 (Stetson Coll.).

52. The Royal Officials of the Casa notified Philip II of the muster in a letter sent from Seville on that date and found in A.G.I. *Contratación* 5,167, Book III.

53. Repayment to Pedro Menéndez is itemized: A.G.I. *Contaduría* 310-B, fol. 447:4; fol. 455:2.

54. Gabriel de Ayala de Salzedo, who later served as alférez for the 300 royal troops in Florida and then became a captain in Menéndez' Armada Real, describes the muster and payment in Cádiz. He noted that, as an arquebusier, he received his weapon and four ducats, representing two months' salary from June 17 at 2 ducats per month. The full pay of an arquebusier would have been 4 ducats per month ("Captain Graviel Ayala de Salzedo," A.G.I. *Indiferente General* 1,222). At the payment, which evidently was made close to the sailing date, 11 corporals and 288 soldiers, 299 men in all, were paid. Each corporal received 8 ducats and each soldier 4, as Ayala de Salzedo had said. See A.G.I. *Contaduría* 310-B, fol. 472:4. Pedro Menéndez criticized the payment Duarte made as *"ruin"* in his letter to the Crown of October 15, 1565, from St. Augustine, and found in A.G.I. *Santo Domingo* 231 (Stetson Coll.).

furnished by his employer, these were given in lieu of one month's pay. In posts or circumstances deemed to be particularly hazardous, isolated, or non-productive of loot, entertainment or additional pay might also be forthcoming.

In organizing his own assortment of soldiers at Cádiz, Pedro Menéndez did not make an appointment of a full number of captains. The non-commissioned corporals named for the voyage kept order, drew supplies, and served to keep the units organized until regular companies could be set up.

Artillerymen were in great demand and difficult to find and could command a high wage. Pedro Menéndez had looked all along the Andalusian coasts as far as Málaga and Gibraltar without finding the men he needed. Finally, he was able to fill the position of chief gunner and eventually enlisted a total of eighteen artillerymen. Diego López, who became *artillero mayor*, was only twenty-four, but could already count long years of service in his specialty. A native of Villanueva de Alcaraz, near Toledo, López had served for six years in the galleys of Don Alvaro de Bazán and had been at the taking of the *Peñón*. His *lombardero*, Antonino Escopo, forty-four years old in 1565, was a native of Naples. Escopo had been paid twenty ducats at the muster, as had Gil Talón, another lombardero who was aboard the *San Pelayo*.[55]

From the list made at the muster of the King's soldiers, it is evident that Pedro Menéndez recruited several men who had a close connection with him and let the Crown pay for their support. These included Diego de Hevia of Oviedo, Pedro de Coronas of Tineo, and Gutierre de Miranda, also of Tineo in Asturias.[56]

Meanwhile, a question which related to the Menéndez mission had been decided in Madrid. The King sent a dispatch to Ambassador Alava, asking him to determine if the Ribault expedition had sailed and proposing that the matter be brought to an open confrontation if it had not. Alava replied on June 8 that the Huguenot ships had indeed weighed anchor about May 26. He had no immediate way of

55. See Diego López to Crown and ff., Madrid, December 7, 1571, in A.G.I. *Indiferente General* 1,222, and "Antonino Escopo, Artillero," November 8, 1570, Seville, ibid. Talón's bond, in which he agrees to serve aboard the *San Pelayo* and not absent himself, and in which he acknowledges that Pedro Menéndez has paid him 20 ducats, is found at the date of June 25, 1565, in A.P.C. *Escribanía* de los Cobos, fol. 297 vto.

56. Three copies of the 1565 muster roll are found in a 115-folio section of A.G.I. *Justicia* 817, at no. 5, within testimony before the Casa de Contratación and the Council of the Indies over Pedro Menéndez' attempt to recover funds he claimed to have paid the soldiers. The dating begins with June 1570, and continues for three years. Labels on the various *numeros* of the legajo have been switched, and the pieza can be identified only by its content.

knowing that the fleet had only crossed the channel and taken refuge in England from a spring storm. They were still within recall. Insofar as Philip II was concerned, however, the die was cast. Isabel journeyed to the border of the kingdoms of France, then proceeded to Bayonne with the Duke of Alba for the long-heralded royal conference. While the parley began, preparations for conflict in Florida were to go on in Cádiz, at Gijón, Avilés, and Santander, as the ships made ready to sail.[57]

In Cádiz, financial arrangements had at last been completed, and all the men and equipment were placed aboard the vessels. Final preparations for the ships' departure were made. Castillo bought 1,500 water bottles, for which the Casa reimbursed him, for the royal soldiers. Three men filled the bottles and casks at the Cádiz wells, and the fresh water was then stowed aboard. A last muster and pay of the officials and mariners of the *San Pelayo* was arranged by the Casa's representative, Carrillo. One additional official had been added—the Crown decided to retain, at its expense, Gonzalo Gayón, a skilled Asturian pilot, who would act as chief pilot to guide the expedition to Florida waters. For this, he was to be paid 400 ducats. As a final touch, the Casa officials presented Menéndez with a ship's lantern for each of the vessels and gave him four standards painted with the royal arms, to be flown from the mastheads of the *San Pelayo* and the *San Andrés*.[58]

Shortly before Menéndez was to sail, his brother-in-law, Gonzalo Solís de Merás, appeared at Cádiz. Solís had left his studies at Salamanca and he wished to embark on the Florida adventure. Since he had almost completed the requirements for his degree and was a married man, the adelantado was much loath to permit him to come. He could not, however, resist the importunity of Solís de Merás and finally gave his consent.[59]

By this time, the matter of Menéndez' compliance with the royal asiento was already very much at issue. The King and his Council of the Indies had every intention of holding the Florida adelantado to his agreement. The Casa, charged with the overseeing of the preparation of the Crown's part of the expedition, also had the responsibility

57. Alava to Philip II, Bayonne, June 8, 1565, *A.D.E.*, vol. 7, no. 1,076, pp. 384–90.

58. The final payment to the men aboard the *San Pelayo* is in A.G.I. *Contaduría* 310-B, 472:3. Castillo's reimbursement for the water bottles is in the same legajo, at 488. The first payment of 56,250 maravedís, as part of the 400 ducats due to the pilot Gayón, is also recorded in A.G.I. *Contaduría* 310-B, fol. 452:4. His final payment on this sum was recorded in A.G.I. *Contaduría* 299; 19:3. I am indebted to Paul E. Hoffman for these citations.

59. The adelantado discusses Solís' joining the expedition in his letter to the Crown from Havana, July 1, 1566, from A.G.I. *Santo Domingo* 168 (Stetson Coll.).

of checking upon Menéndez' fulfillment of his contract. On June 23, 1565, Factor Duarte made a formal *requerimiento*. He asked Menéndez to show proof that he had carried out his obligations. In reply, Menéndez furnished him the list of equipment and supplies which he had bought, or which had been purchased for him by Pedro del Castillo.[60] Then, Duarte made a personal inspection of the vessels anchored in the Bay of Cádiz, after all lading had been completed. From Monday noon, June 25, until Wednesday, he was rowed from ship to ship in a bergantín, counting heads and verifying cargoes. He also gathered the muster rolls of the royal troops and lists of Pedro Menéndez' own personnel in the registries of each ship. His report is most useful in that it summarizes the entire effort and furnishes the best list of ships, armament, and the distribution of men. In the meantime, similar reports had been made from northern Spain, from the ports of Avilés, Gijón, and Santander directly to the Council of the Indies.

At this point, Menéndez clearly established his position on the question of compliance with the asiento. In Duarte's words: "He responded that with the ships, people, and artillery, arms, munitions, and supplies contained in this relation and with the ships which he says go from Vizcaya, Asturias, and Galicia and with the personnel, arms and artillery, munitions, and supplies which go in them, he has complied with the asiento which his Majesty ordered be taken with him more completely and in greater quantity than he was obliged to do. . . ."[61]

On Wednesday, June 27, 1565, in the afternoon, the weather appeared favorable. Pedro Menéndez' whole fleet of ships left their anchorage and passed along the bay side of the ancient city of Cádiz with sails drawing and flags flying, on their way to the Atlantic. Factor Duarte, doubtless relieved to have dispatched the fleet, sat down to write up his report.

Now there occurred an event about which much controversy was later to arise. It bore directly on the question of Menéndez' compliance with his asiento. According to the adelantado and a number of other witnesses, the ships had no sooner left the harbor entrance on

60. "Los bastimentos, armas, artilleria y municiones que el dicho Adelantado Pero Menéndez lleba en los dichos nabios de su armada . . . en quenta de lo que hes obligado conforme a su asiento . . . por una relación jurada y firmada del dicho Adelantado Pero Menéndez . . . y Pedro del Castillo . . . que es la persona por cuya mano se an comprado y probeedo la mayor parte de todo hello . . ." from A.G.I. *Escribanía de Cámara* 1,024-A. On May 28, 1565, the Casa officials had assured Philip II that they would send *veedores* to Cadiz to insure that Pedro Menéndez lived up to his asiento. From A.G.I. *Contratación* 5,167, Book III.

61. From "Los bastimentos, armas," A.G.I. *Escribanía de Cámara* 1,024-A.

Wednesday than strong and contrary winds sprang up. After endeavoring to hold the fleet together and make headway against the winds, Menéndez gave up the attempt and brought the ships back to Cádiz. Toward nightfall, he anchored off Fort San Sebastián at the farthest point of the peninsula. Here, claimed Menéndez, contact was made with the shore. Many additional men were ferried out and came aboard the vessels during the night. One witness later testified that 150 more people had come out to the ships; another stated that 300 additional passengers had embarked in Cádiz.[62] Then Pedro Menéndez and his Florida fleet set sail for the second time.

Pedro Menéndez claimed that his Cádiz expedition had sailed from Spain with a total of 1,504 souls aboard. The total of Duarte's muster was 995 persons. Duarte had not, however, included the wives or children of the 26 married soldiers aboard the *San Pelayo*, nor had he counted the sailors aboard the caravel *San Antonio*, but all of these together would probably not have exceeded 75 in number; the sums were still far apart.

It is evident, however, that some would-be voyagers to Florida had been left behind when the fleet sailed. On Thursday, the twenty-eighth, Captain Diego de Luna, a professional soldier from Málaga, arrived in Cádiz, too late to catch Menéndez' ships. De Luna immediately applied to Factor Duarte, saying that he wished to charter a vessel to carry himself and his men to meet the adelantado at the Canary Islands, so that they might yet be a part of the Florida expedition. Duarte simply told the captain to see Pedro del Castillo, who was in charge of all Menéndez' affairs, in order to make any such arrangements. The Casa de Contratación would accept neither the responsibility nor the expense.[63]

The same day, the frustrated officer went to see Castillo. He stated that he had gathered a fine group of almost seventy experienced soldiers who had served in Italy, had exhausted his own resources in bringing them to the port, and needed help to find transport to the Canaries. Since it was known that Pedro del Castillo was Pedro Menéndez' deputy in Spain, de Luna came to him, having nowhere else to turn.[64]

62. Menéndez' claims of his return to Cádiz and the loading of additional men aboard his ships is found in "Información ante el Alcalde deste Corte," Madrid, October 16, 1567, in A.G.I. *Escribanía de Cámara* 1,024-A. In their 1567 audit, found in the same legajo, the Contadores Mayores treated Menéndez' claim as a "pretension." It was, however, not refuted by any testimony appended to the trial record.

63. From "El Capitan Luna dize ante Factor Duarte," in A.G.I. *Escribanía de Cámara* 1,024-A.

64. In "Requerimiento de Luna a Castillo que le de para los fletes y costa de los soldados," A.G.I. *Escribanía de Cámara* 1,024-A.

Castillo replied directly to de Luna and stated that he had indebted himself and his kinsmen deeply, in the amount of 20,000 ducats, for the arming of Menéndez' Florida enterprise. Nevertheless, he said, the troops would be needed and he agreed to provide needed supplies so that de Luna could embark immediately. The caravel *Nuestra Señora de los Virtudes* was chartered and made ready to sail that very day.[65]

When the delayed armadas finally set sail for Florida from Cádiz and from Spain's north coast, what was the character of the effort? With regard to support of the expeditions, it was a mixed enterprise, with the larger share of the cost and risk borne by the adelantado. To sustain his part of the burden, Pedro Menéndez committed an entire coterie of relatives, friends, and associates, well experienced upon the sea. He had recruited a number of additional soldiers to round out his own organization and took into his own forces three hundred Crown-supported soldiers. More than half of his own costs were, in fact, paid indirectly by Crown grants to the adelantado. In order to underwrite his efforts, Menéndez had recourse to sources of credit linked with his regional and familial associations. He entrusted his financial and logistical maintenance to his relative Pedro del Castillo, a Cádiz merchant and long-time colleague.

The bureaucrats of the King had conscientiously furnished the funds, arms, and supplies their master had ordered. Philip II had also obligated the royal fisc, in support of the expedition, for substantial additional sums from overseas treasuries and from the New Spain fleet.

The Florida expeditions thus represented a joint venture in conquest—adelantado and Crown shared the costs of the effort. The parties had other joint considerations as well. The royal desire to erase the French presence in Florida was deeply shared by Pedro Menéndez. In their most cherished hopes, however, both parties looked beyond the coming battles. They looked for glory and profit and for the enlargement of their own domains and holdings. The ships which sailed carried more than soldiers, supplies, and cannon. They were laden with a full cargo of expectation.

65. Ibid.

Spanish Victory and First Foundation

Pedro Menéndez' basic plan of operations for the Florida conquest involved a joint rendezvous at the Canary Islands of the several contingents which had sailed at different times. The united ships would then sail to the Indies, join the Santo Domingo forces and Roelas' vessel, and proceed to Florida. The expedition which left Cádiz on June 29, however, was really Menéndez' main spearhead, for it included his largest vessel, ample artillery for land and sea use, and the bulk of the troops, private and royal.

At the time he sailed, Menéndez' main concern was to reach the French fort before Ribault's reinforcement fleet arrived. The intelligence in the hands of the adelantado was really quite complete, for he had good knowledge of the French works at Fort Caroline, and he knew exactly the composition of the forces of Jean Ribault. Since discovery of the French settlement on the river May, the Florida enterprise had assumed military, punitive, and ideological aspects. Pedro Menéndez had especial reason for hostility toward "the Lutheran French," for they stood in the way of his hopes for colonization and profits and represented the long-time enemy, now tagged unmistakably with the stigma of religious heresy. Menéndez was particularly alert to the charge that there were heretics among the crewmen aboard the *San Pelayo*, and he arrested and confined several men on the ship.[1]

The first stage of the voyage went well, for the expedition sighted

1. Pedro Menéndez to Crown, n.d. (probably October 1567), A.G.I. *Escribanía de Cámara* 1024-A. In this letter Menéndez describes the arrest of the heretics and their confinement.

the easternmost islands of the Canary group only five days after setting sail. On July 4, Menéndez' fleet entered the harbor of Las Palmas on the island of Great Canary, having come more than 750 miles. At once Pedro Menéndez saw that his ships from Asturias had missed the rendezvous. Since he could not delay further to await their arrival, Menéndez left word that, when they should arrive, they were to proceed to Puerto Rico and Havana. He would then make arrangements to meet them in the Indies.

Menéndez replenished his wood and water and rearranged the lading of his vessels in the Canaries. To correct the overcrowding which had resulted from the hasty loading of the vessels in Cádiz, it was decided to take to Florida the caravel of Jorge Dias which was originally to have returned to Spain. Menéndez then made muster of all the soldiers and seamen in the fleet, which revealed the presence of a noble stowaway, if the adelantado had not realized it before. Pedro de Valdés, the man betrothed to the adelantado's daughter, Ana, had come along in defiance of Menéndez' wishes.[2] With Valdés aboard, the fleet of eight vessels left Las Palmas on July 8, 1565, and took their departure from the great, cone-shaped peak of Teneriffe. Two of the caravels had remained in the Canary Islands to return to Spain, and the Florida fleet consisted of the capitana *San Pelayo*, the large *galeota La Vitoria*, the bergantín *La Esperanza*, the caravel *San Antonio*, and the four shallops *Magdalena*, *San Miguel*, *La Concepción*, and *San Andrés*. The last named shallop served as almiranta of the fleet, under the command of Diego Flores Valdés.

After an initial breeze carried the ships from port, they encountered light winds and began to separate, in spite of Menéndez' every effort to keep them together. In one group was the *San Pelayo*, and a smaller vessel, whose course is described in Menéndez' own account of the voyage. Five other vessels clustered around the almiranta. The expedition's chaplain, Francisco López de Mendoza Grajales, sailed in this group. Father Mendoza Grajales has left a vivid narrative of the events of the voyage of the ships which accompanied the almiranta.[3]

2. A description of the rearrangement of Menéndez' fleet at the Canary Islands is found in "Información sumaria hecha en Cádiz," Pedro del Castillo, Cádiz, September 22, 1567, A.G.I. *Escribanía de Cámara* 1024-A. The muster is described in "Información ante Alcalde," by Pedro Menéndez de Avilés, Madrid, October 16, 1567, in the same legajo. Menéndez mentions the stowaway of Valdés in his letter to the Crown from Florida dated September 11, 1565, A.G.I. *Santo Domingo* 231. This letter has also been reproduced in Ruidiaz, *La Florida* 2:74–84. It has been translated and reprinted in Bennett, *The Settlement of Florida*, pp. 148–55, and is also in the Stetson Collection.

3. The Grajales narrative comes from A.G.I. *Patronato* 19. It has been reprinted in the *Colección Muñoz*. See Real Academia de Historia, *Catálogo de la colección de J. B. Muñoz*, vol. 2, fol. 283–99 vto. It has also been reproduced in *D.I.*, 3:441–79, as

Both versions of the journey report that, in less than two weeks of their departure from the Canaries, the ships were struck by a major storm while en route to their projected landfall in the Windward Islands. Even the large and staunch *San Pelayo* was roughly treated by towering seas and gusting winds. Since the galeass was prepared for action against the French and had mounted heavy artillery on her upper decks, the *Pelayo* was in considerable danger of foundering. After the wind carried away two of the vessel's masts, Menéndez had several pieces of artillery thrown in the sea to lighten ship. After the weather moderated, he had jury-masts rigged from spare yards and was able to sail moderately well. The condition of his ship was such, however, that he determined to make straight for Puerto Rico instead of attempting the usual landfall in the Windward Islands. The *San Pelayo* and its accompanying vessel entered the harbor of San Juan on August 8.[4]

According to Father López, trouble began for the other ships even before the hurricane struck. One of the shallops began to leak badly, left the other five vessels in the convoy, and returned to the Canaries. By this time, strong winds had already begun to blow. By early morning of July 21, full hurricane winds were lashing the little vessels, while they wallowed in a wild confusion of sea and spray. All the iron cannon aboard the almiranta and many casks of water and other supplies, including seven millstones intended for use in Florida, were thrown overboard to lighten the ships. The priest had all he could do to hear the seamen's confessions and lead them in fervent prayers for deliverance. When the winds finally moderated at noon on July 23, the almiranta found itself sailing alone. Meanwhile, the galiot *La Vitoria*, which carried none of Menéndez' troops but transported large quantities of supplies, was lost on the windward coast of Guadaloupe, in the Windward Islands, and its crew drowned or fell victim to the Carib Indians. The caravel *San Antonio* was blown far westward and finally arrived at the port of Santo Domingo on Hispaniola. It was eventually lost to the Florida expedition; French corsairs took the vessel with more than a hundred of Pedro Menéndez' soldiers and substantial amounts of supplies.[5]

"Relación del capellán Francisco López de Mendoza Grajales." The narrative was translated by Benjamin F. French, and is found in his work *Historical Collections of Louisiana and Florida*, pp. 191–234. Lawson has made a translation in his book *Letters of Menéndez*, pp. 167–76, 180–95. A more effective translation is found in Bennett, *Laudonnière and Fort Caroline*, pp. 141–63.

4. See Pedro Menéndez to Crown, Puerto Rico, August 13, 1565, A.G.I. *Santo Domingo* 224 (Stetson Coll.).

5. The loss of *La Vitoria* is described in "Ship Losses of the Adelantado," n.d.

The two remaining ships anchored on the leeward side of
Dominica, and men were sent ashore to seek wood and water. They
left Dominica on August 8, passed by Guadaloupe and Montserrat,
negotiated the Virgin Islands, and entered the harbor of San Juan on
August 13.[6]

When the adelantado brought his small convoy through the rocky
harbor entrance and dropped anchor in San Juan harbor, it was
evident that the first stage of his voyage to conquer Florida had been
disastrous. There had been a serious depletion of Menéndez' striking
force, for several vessels were missing, and he could see that the ships
gathered in San Juan had been badly treated by the storm. Only hasty
repairs were possible in Puerto Rico, but the vessels were put in some
semblance of sailing condition.

Other disappointments came to the adelantado. He realized that
Pedro de las Roelas, who was to provide him with a major ship and
its soldiers, had fallen behind him on the journey. When Menéndez
left Spain, he was twenty-two days behind Roelas' fleet—at the
Canaries he had cut the time between them to eight days. Now the
adelantado had reached Puerto Rico before them. Neither this
reinforcement nor his own contingent from the north of Spain would
be immediately available. Menéndez also learned that the Santo
Domingo authorities had not yet prepared their share of the striking
force for the Florida enterprise. In view of such deficiencies,
Menéndez found it difficult to gather his scattered forces and meet
the French challenge. The adelantado could, nonetheless, perceive
some very real assets. One of these was the spearhead of the striking
force—the *San Pelayo*. The ship was fast and heavily armed, and could
carry a substantial number of soldiers and tonnage of supplies. The
adelantado also discovered a fine ally in one of the Royal Officials of
Puerto Rico, Juan Ponce de León. Ponce sprang from the founding
family of the island, that of the first adelantado of Florida; he was a

---

(November, 1567), A.G.I. *Escribanía de Cámara* 1024-A. Menéndez describes the loss of
the caravel in his letter to the Crown, Matanzas, December 5, 1565, *Santo Domingo* 115.

6. There are many discrepancies between the chronology of the Mendoza Grajales
narrative and that given by Pedro Menéndez in his letters to the Crown. The priest's
story was, however, written at some later date, while Menéndez' letters were current.
Where there is conflict between dates, therefore, I have chosen that given by the
adelantado. For instance, Mendoza Grajales states that they arrived at San Juan on
August 10 while Menéndez gives the date as the thirteenth. As a check on the correct-
ness of Menéndez' dating, the adelantado mentions the arrival of the almiranta, in
correspondence dated August 15, 1565, and found in A.G.I. *Santo Domingo* 71. A
previous letter, which bore the date of August 13, did not mention that the other ships
had yet arrived. Solís de Merás, in *Pedro Menéndez de Avilés*, p. 78, gives the date of
arrival as August 9.

large landholder, and also served as alcaide of the *fortaleza*. Pedro Menéndez met with Juan Ponce de León, gave him his poder, and thus established another base in his personal supply network. The adelantado was able in this way to tap a source of credit at San Juan, in return for which he granted Ponce some rights expected to arise out of Menéndez' trade privilege in the Caribbean. This would also facilitate the planned purchase of cattle and horses for Florida. Menéndez was able to obtain a ship in San Juan and two small boats to bolster his shattered fleet and also enlisted forty-two soldiers in San Juan. This gain was partly offset by the desertion of thirty of his men and three of the priests who had come on the adelantado's ships. Menéndez also received aboard the *San Pelayo* ten English prisoners whose Indies voyage had ended in their arrest in San Juan. The men, charged as heretics and trespassers, were to be turned over eventually to the Inquisition.[7]

While rapid repairs were being made to his ships, the adelantado rearranged his military organization to replace the hasty formations established in Cádiz. He turned for his model to the traditional Spanish tercio, perfected in the long Italian wars, which ordinarily comprised twelve to fifteen companies all under the command of a *maestre de campo*. Each company was enrolled under a captain and usually bore his name. The executive officer of the tercio was the *sargento mayor*, and each company was served by an ensign, chaplain, sergeant, piper, and drummer. Each was further subdivided into squads and a squad leader assigned to each.[8]

To command his soldiery, Pedro Menéndez chose his future son-in-law, Pedro de Valdés. This choice was consistent with Menéndez' earlier appointments, for Valdés was from a major Asturian family and closely related to the Archbishop of Seville. He was a trained soldier who had notably served the Spanish Crown in Italy. Although only twenty-five years of age, he was an experienced soldier.[9] He was, moreover, to be closely tied to Menéndez by his coming marriage. On

7. Ponce advised that the poder enabled him to buy and sell goods so as to supply ships bound for Florida; see his letter to the Crown, San Juan, April 20, 1566, A.G.I. *Santo Domingo* 71 (Stetson Coll.). The King acknowledged these services in a letter to Juan Ponce de León from Madrid dated May 12, 1566, found in A.G.I. *Justicia* 1,000 (Stetson Coll.). Menéndez' description of his connection with Ponce de León is found in his letter to the Crown, dated August 15, 1565, from A.G.I. *Santo Domingo* 71. The English prisoners are described in A.G.I. *Justicia* 888, no. 9, and in A.G.I. *Contaduría* 1,775, no. 46.

8. An effective description of the sixteenth-century Spanish military organization may be found in Rafael Altamira y Crevea, *Historia de España y de la civilización española*, pp. 293–94.

9. See p. 74.

August 13, 1565, aboard the *San Pelayo* in San Juan harbor, Pedro Menéndez de Valdés was invested with the office of maestre de campo for the Florida enterprise in the following words: "Pedro Menéndez de Avilés, governor and captain-general of the land and of the provinces of Florida and adelantado of them, says that I have need for good government of these provinces in order to expel the Lutheran French who are in the said provinces, to discover the land, and to bring its natives to the service of God our Lord, and to the obedience of His Majesty. Thus, I have need of naming a proper and sufficient person, from among those I bring with me, to be maestre de campo. Thus, Pedro Menéndez de Valdés, since you have the necessary qualities . . . in the name of His Majesty, I name you to such office for this enterprise."[10] Valdés' salary was to be 300 ducats a year, paid from the adelantado's own resources. The two men began to create a coherent organization from the formless mass of manpower aboard the ships.

With the reorganization of his forces somewhat in hand, the adelantado reviewed his strategy for the conquest of Florida. Although he knew that the French reinforcement had left Dieppe before he had departed Cádiz, Menéndez still felt fairly sure that he could arrive at the river May before Ribault's fleet. Since the French prisoners had advised him of the location of Laudonnière's fort, Menéndez planned to seize the river mouth and divide the French forces. He would next fortify his base and hold it until reinforcements from Asturias or the Indies would enable him to wipe out the French. This plan was risky but urgently necessary, for if the French should arrive first and unite their forces, it would be very difficult to dislodge them. In order to encourage the lagging officials in Santo Domingo to provide his reinforcements, Pedro Menéndez sent Hernando de Miranda there with the message that the royal contingent should immediately be sent to Havana to join the adelantado there. As added inducement, he sent along a pilot skilled in the navigation of the Bahama Channel, together with a current marine chart of the area.[11]

An essential element in Menéndez' plan was to use mounted men to give his Florida campaign power and mobility and to overawe the Florida Indians. Menéndez arranged for the purchase of some horses in Puerto Rico, but rough weather sprang up as they loaded the

---

10. "Nombramiento de Pedro Menéndez de Valdés . . . Maestre de Campo," in "Relación de los bastimentos, artillería, armas . . . municiones que recibió Juan de Junco," A.G.I. *Contaduría* 941, ramo 1 (microfilm, P. K. Yonge Library).

11. Menéndez' plans and actions in Puerto Rico are well described in his two letters to the Crown dated August 13 and August 15, 1565.

animals aboard ship in San Juan harbor. Some of the horses got loose and knocked down some of the ships' bulkheads, and most of the animals had to be destroyed. Adding further to his growing sense of unease, Menéndez learned that a French corsair had captured the King's courier vessel carrying instructions to the Audiencia in Santo Domingo about the rendezvous with the adelantado. He began to fear a French ambush somewhere along his known route to Florida.

On August 15, 1565, the little fleet left port. It consisted of the *San Pelayo*, the almiranta *San Andrés*, the shallop *San Miguel*, the galiot *La Esperanza*, and the ship which Menéndez had obtained in Puerto Rico. The vessels made their way westward along the north shore of Puerto Rico, crossed the Mona Passage, and came into sight of the Hispaniola coast on August 17, 1565. At this point, all of the doubts and concerns which had been building up in the mind of Pedro Menéndez coalesced and compelled an abrupt change in his plans. If he continued to Havana in the doubtful hope of finding reinforcement there, he would run the risk of interception by the French. The adelantado determined to forego any reinforcements and strike out directly for Florida. He chose to take an untried route through the channels, shoals, and islands of the Bahamas, by which he would avoid possible ambush and save precious days. In taking this risky step with his diminished forces, Pedro Menéndez de Avilés was staking his whole enterprise upon the gamble of first arrival in Florida.[12]

As the ships set forth on their new course, Pedro Menéndez and Maestre de Campo Valdés completed their military reorganization and announced the appointment of ten captains. Each of his captains was in command of a company of fifty men. Examination of the adelantado's military captains discloses that they were all noblemen and experienced soldiers. Only two of Menéndez' twelve captains were soldiers paid by the Crown; the rest were carried on his own account. Nine captains—Bartolomé Menéndez, Martín Ochoa, Juan Vélez de Medrano, Juan de San Vicente, Antonio Gómez, Francisco de Recalde, Gonzalo Solís de Merás, Diego de Amaya, and Francisco de Castaneda—were norteños. Two of the men—the adelantado's brother Bartolomé and Solís de Merás—were closely related to the adelantado. Pedro Menéndez thus attempted to insure control over his organization by placing his troops under the overall command of his Asturian son-in-law and by relying upon those whom he trusted most—men from the north of Spain. He appointed Gonzalo de Villa-

12. The decision to sail directly to Florida without any stop in Havana is described by the adelantado in his letter to Philip II from St. Augustine, dated September 11, 1565, A.G.I. *Santo Domingo* 231 (Stetson Coll.).

roel to the position of sargento mayor and chose sergeants and ensigns who were skilled in war and experienced in Italy.[13] Pedro Menéndez' firm organization of his troops, which included those 300 men who had been furnished by the Spanish Crown, shows clearly that he assumed full jurisdiction as captain-general for the enterprise of Florida. The royal troops were thoroughly integrated into his organization, and there was no question of separate command.[14] The seven days' journey through Bahama waters afforded time to accustom the men to their new commanders and to carry out some training for the most inexperienced. An area was provided on the *San Pelayo*'s decks where the men could practice the loading, firing, and cleaning of their arquebuses. The adelantado's fleet finally emerged into the Gulf Stream, in the vicinity of Grand Bahama Island, and sailed north and west, taking advantage of the strong current of the Gulf Stream, to seek landfall in Florida.

The chaplain's narrative describes a sign seen in the heavens by the Spanish during the first night in the Bahama channel. Toward morning, there appeared to the watcher's eyes the bright light of a comet which rapidly made its way across the sky in the direction of Florida. It seemed a good omen for the coming enterprise. After a day and a half in the channel, the low coastline was finally sighted in the vicinity of Cape Canaveral.[15]

Meanwhile, the summer months in Spain were passing in a fever of anxiety and activity for Philip II. At the time of Menéndez' departure from Cádiz, the Spanish King knew that Ribault's fleet of reinforce-

13. Father López describes the naming of the captains in his narrative (Bennett translation, p. 148). The adelantado describes and names in his letter of September 11 ten of the captains whom he had chosen. The names of the other captains were Diego de Alvarado, Pedro de Larrandia, and Francisco de Mexia.

14. A case in point was that of Graviel Ayala Salzedo, who was appointed ensign at this time. Ayala was a member of the 300-man royal contingent, but was appointed by the adelantado to the rank of ensign in the troop reorganization. Upon his return to Spain in 1570, Ayala attempted to collect from the Crown the additional pay due him for his post as ensign. The Casa de Contratación demurred, saying that when the troops left Spain there really were no officials, only squadron leaders. The Crown, however, insisted on payment. Ayala's petition is found in A.G.I. *Indiferente General* 1,222 under the date of December 9, 1570, in Seville.

15. Father Mendoza Grajales and Pedro Menéndez are far apart in the dates they assign to the sighting of Florida. In his letter of September 11, the adelantado advises that the landfall was made around noon on "Sunday the 25th." The priest advises that the landfall did not occur until "afternoon of Tuesday September 28th." Menéndez erred—the date of August 25 fell on a Saturday; Father Mendoza Grajales had the days of the week right. The adelantado's letter was, however, written much closer in time to the event. Perhaps his dating is correct even though he has erred in assigning the correct dates to the days of the week. Gonzalo Solís de Merás' account of the landfall agrees with that of the priest.

ment had already sailed. In view of its departure, he had decided not to treat directly with the French rulers about the matter, but rather to send a copy of the May 5 parecer of the Council of the Indies to his representative at Bayonne, the Duke of Alba. Alba was then to bring the matter up on the proper occasion.[16] Later it was decided that the issue of Florida should not be raised at all at Bayonne, since it might becloud the major concern of Spain at the meeting—that of the conservation and advancement of the Catholic faith in France.[17] Thus the two monarchs most concerned chose to avoid a direct confrontation over Florida while their fleets sailed to their inevitable clash there.

During the long time of waiting, before any real intelligence could come from the Indies, it was inevitable that rumors and intrigue should flourish. Early in July, Philip II heard from his ambassador in London who reported the rumor that eight French ships and 1,200 men were being prepared in England to go to Florida. Perhaps this referred to the second reinforcement which the Spanish feared was forthcoming to back up Ribault's fleet and further strengthen French fortifications in Florida.[18]

In the meantime, in Andalusia, the financial embarrassment of the Seville merchants was relieved somewhat by the arrival of the New Spain fleet on July 10, but commercial conditions continued somewhat disturbed. In one of the ships, Governor Mazariegos of Havana had sent five of the Frenchmen captured in the port of Arcos the previous December. After interrogation, the men were placed in the Casa jail. While the Frenchmen's confessions were being taken, the Seville officials were still discussing another deposition recorded four days before the fleet dropped anchor in the Bay of Cádiz, when one Juan Sánchez had stated to the Casa officials at Cádiz that he had just come from Florida. Sánchez claimed that he had been captured seven months before in the Bahama Channel by a 500-ton French ship. According to the man's story, he was carried as a prisoner to the French fort in Florida, which he described in great detail. He claimed that it was a stone fortress with four towers mounting 40 pieces of

16. Lowery, *The Spanish Settlements*, 2:111, cites a letter from Philip II to the Duke of Alba, written on June 15.

17. See Alba to Philip II, June 28, 1565, *A.D.E.*, K. 1504, p. 30.

18. Ambassador de Silva to the Crown, London, June 25, 1565, printed in *D.I.E.*, 89:173. It is evident that another French voyage of reinforcement for Laudonnière did sail in 1565, from Bordeaux, but it was broken up by storms and Spanish action in the Indies and never reached Florida. The voyage was described by French prisoners, who averred that it had been financed by Charles IX. See their description in A.G.I. *Justicia* 881, no. 6, pieza 2.

artillery and a garrison of 3,000 Englishmen and 2,000 Frenchmen. The captain of this supposed settlement, said Sánchez, was one Robert Hawkins, an Englishman. Having given his testimony, the man disappeared, and neither he nor his companions could be found by agents of the Casa de Contratación. On August 15, the Seville officials sent the message to the King.[19]

Now Philip II had occasion to weigh the adequacy of his measures to expel the French and expunge their threat to the Spanish Indies. He and his counsellors had previously understood that a sizeable French reinforcement would be forthcoming. After they learned of the departure of Ribault's ships, the Spanish came to believe that other French vessels were also being prepared to go to Florida. By the end of July, the Spanish King decided that the measures previously taken—the sending of the Menéndez expedition and the troops and ships to be provided for the adelantado in the Indies—were insufficient. Philip notified the Casa in Seville that the previous efforts were not enough to dislodge the French already in Florida and the others who had gone and would shortly go to reinforce them. The King saw the threat as substantial and widespread, extending to all the islands of the Spanish Caribbean, and told his officials in Seville that he had plans to reinforce Menéndez further by raising 1,500 armed troops and sending another armada to Florida. Philip added that he felt that this reinforcing fleet should be sent, if possible, that very August and should go supplied for a year.[20]

As the efforts to locate appropriate vessels and to recruit troops for the new expedition began, still more news and rumor came to the Spanish officials. As Pedro Menéndez' ships sighted the Florida coast and moved northward toward Fort Caroline, testimony was being taken in Seville from yet another witness of French activity. The treasurer of the Casa de Contratación received the sworn deposition of a man who claimed to have left Le Havre on the previous August 16, where he saw four ships being armed and equipped for a voyage to Florida.

As the summer of alarms and rumors drew to a close, concrete

19. Sánchez' deposition is found in A.G.I. *Patronato* 267, no. 1, ramo 41; it is also in the Stetson Collection. Notice of Sánchez' testimony was sent to Philip II in Casa to Crown, Seville, August 15, 1565, from A.G.I. *Contratación* 5,167, Book III. It is obvious that Sánchez' description of Fort Caroline is extravagant, if not totally imaginary. It is, further, doubtful that any French vessel of the size he described was near the French colony at the end of 1564 or the beginning of 1565. Lowery expresses his complete skepticism of Sánchez' testimony in "Manuscripts of Florida" (microfilm, P. K. Yonge Library, reel 1).

20. See Crown to Casa, Bosque de Segovia, July 30, 1565, A.G.I. *Contratación* 5,012 (Stetson Coll.).

activity for the arming of the second Florida expedition slowly got under way, but the fleet was not ready to sail by the end of September. On September 4, however, the Seville officials reported to Philip II that captains had been appointed to recruit 1,500 troops and that supplies and munitions for the armada were being slowly gathered and placed in the storehouses in Seville. The Casa had previously advised Philip of their difficulty in finding suitable, seaworthy vessels and cannon. It was now clear that the Spanish reinforcement could not arrive in Florida in time to aid Pedro Menéndez in his immediate tactical situation. They might still arrive in time to bolster what the Crown now saw as a lengthy effort to dislodge a numerous and dangerous foe.[21] Meanwhile, the issue lay firmly in the hands of the adelantado. Since he had decided to strike directly with the slim forces at his disposal, the contest would be decided in Florida.

As Pedro Menéndez sighted Cape Canaveral and turned his course northward, the French fleet of reinforcement under Jean Ribault was just about to arrive at the mouth of the river May. Its outbound voyage from France had taken place in two stages. As the Spanish had been told, Ribault had indeed sailed from Dieppe on May 22, 1565, after receiving his final orders from Admiral Coligny. It is evident that the French commander had also received some word of the Menéndez expedition being prepared in Cádiz.[22] Weather compelled the French fleet to take refuge on the Isle of Wight for more than two weeks. After their Atlantic crossing, the French arrived at the Gulf Stream in the vicinity of twenty-seven degrees north latitude, and they crossed directly to Florida in the Indian River area. When they landed to seek fresh water at a small inlet, the Frenchmen traded with Indians for silver from wrecked Spanish ships and found a Spanish castaway who had been captive there for twenty years. Ribault took the man aboard his ships and sailed northward to find Laudonnière's fort.[23]

21. The Casa's letter of August 22, 1565, is referred to in Crown to Casa, Bosque de Segovia, September 6, 1565, A.G.I. *Contratación* 5,012 (Stetson Coll.). The letter of September 4, 1565, from Seville is found in A.G.I. *Contratación* 5,167, Book II.

22. See Admiral Coligny to Jean Ribault, cited in Lowery, *The Spanish Settlements*, 2:95. One of the best descriptions of the departure of the French reinforcement fleet is found in Nicholas Le Challeux, "Discourse de l'histoire de la Florida," in Suzanne Lussagnet, *Les Français en Amérique*, 2:208–9; Le Challeux, who shipped as a carpenter with the expedition, has given a simple and graphic narrative of the Ribault expedition and its fate.

23. The episode is described in Le Challeux, "Discourse," p. 209. It appears that this man was Pedro de Bustinçury, who is probably the man known as Don Pedro Vizcaíno, of the Escalante Fontenada narrative. See Eugene Lyon, "Captives of Florida," pp. 6, 15.

There is striking contrast between the voyages of Pedro Menéndez and Jean Ribault. Although both fleets required two months for their ocean crossings, the French dissipated the two-week lead they held over the Spanish. While Pedro Menéndez was driven by urgency to risk the Bahama passage with his reduced forces, Ribault was leisurely cruising the Florida coast on his way to Fort Caroline. Thus, on the day that Jean Ribault dropped anchor off the St. Johns River, Pedro Menéndez had already made his Florida landfall at Cape Canaveral.

While the opposing fleets made their ways to Florida, the Laudonnière settlement had undergone a summer of crisis. After the return of the mutineers from the Caribbean in late May and the punishment of their ringleaders, René de Laudonnière had found himself increasingly hard pressed to keep order among his men, especially as their needs for supplies increased. The reinforcements he had long expected from France had not arrived, and the search for food among the Indians had endangered the good relations that Laudonnière had sought to maintain with the natives. On August 3, the colony had been revived by the visit of John Hawkins, who brought food and sold a small ship to the Frenchmen. After the English corsair had left, Laudonnière and his men prepared to vacate Fort Caroline and return to France. By August 15, their supplies were ready, and only a fair wind was lacking to speed their departure.

When the Indians brought word to the French fort that several sails were in sight off the river mouth, Laudonnière feared that his Spanish enemy had come upon him. His suspense was ended the next afternoon when seven small craft crossed the river bar, loaded with armed soldiers and with their banners snapping in the breeze. The Huguenots ashore could see the hulls of seven larger vessels anchored offshore, and finally the forces met, to be mutually identified as French. The Ribault reinforcement had almost come too late, but it had at last arrived.

Ribault began the lengthy process of unloading supplies, munitions, and troops from his ships. He had arrived with written royal orders that he replace René de Laudonnière and send him home, but the newly arrived French leader offered instead to keep his predecessor in charge at Fort Caroline. Laudonnière set to work with his own men and the newly arrived Frenchmen to put the defenses of the fort in better order, while the discharge of the ships was accomplished by Pierre d'Ully, Ribault's chief of finance and supply. Laudonnière, worn by strain and labor, fell ill for more than a week while unloading continued. Finally the three smaller vessels Ribault had brought from France were lightened enough by the discharge of their cargoes to pass over the bar and enter the river, which they did on September 4. Off the inlet, the four main French ships had swung around their anchors to face a steady south wind.

By midafternoon of the same day, lookouts aboard the anchored vessels could see five sails coming north before the wind. Then they were blotted from view by a summer thunderstorm, which swept torrents of rain, laced with lightning, across the sea. The oncoming ships, pushed ahead by squally winds, came to within a mile and a half of the French anchorage before the breeze lightened and then died completely. As the Frenchmen strained to identify the limp flags on the mastheads of the strange ships, they could not help but wonder if the Spanish had at last arrived in Florida.

They were indeed the ships of Pedro Menéndez. Since the French prisoners had told him that the French fort lay between twenty-eight and twenty-nine degrees north latitude, the adelantado had coasted northward from his landfall, exploring every inlet and every plume of smoke arising from the shore. On September 2, he had reached the latitude of twenty-nine and a half degrees and sent a shore party to examine an Indian settlement.[24] After its captain reported to the adelantado that the Indians seemed to possess information about the French fort, Menéndez went ashore himself to parley with them. It was most important for Menéndez to impress upon the natives his own personal authority as surrogate of the Castilian King, in order to seek allies against the French and to aid in his future plans for colonization. The visit was most successful and convinced the adelantado that even though he had passed the latitude where the French fort was supposed to be, he should continue to the north to seek it.

On the next morning, which was September 4, the five Spanish vessels picked their way along a shoreline of very wide and spacious beaches. About two in the afternoon, they sighted four anchored vessels moored off the mouth of a great river. As the afternoon thunderstorm swelled and burst in a shower of rain, Menéndez' lookouts discerned French standards flying from the *Trinité*, Ribault's flagship. Immediately the news was brought to him, and Pedro Menéndez experienced a bitter feeling of disappointment. Since he had learned in Cádiz that French reinforcements had sailed from Dieppe, every fiber of Menéndez' being had been stretched to beat

24. It is quite likely that this landfall was at the Ponce de León inlet, between present-day New Smyrna Beach and Daytona Beach, where there was a sizeable concentration of Indian population. This description of Menéndez' northward journey from Cape Canaveral and the first clash with Ribault's ships was taken from his letter of September 11, 1565.

the French to Florida. His entire voyage, and his vital decision to go directly to Florida without reinforcements was predicated on one thing—to arrive first at the mouth of the river May. Now he had lost the race and Jean Ribault had won. As the gusty winds of the summer squall died and choppy waters became glassy calm, the Spanish ships drifted, making no headway toward the enemy. The adelantado quickly weighed the state of his forces and determined, as soon as the wind would permit, to attack at sea.[25]

Finally, well after night had fallen, the breeze began to blow again, filling the sails of the Spanish ships and bringing them closer to the anchored French. Menéndez determined to proceed in the dark, anchor closely among the French ships, and be in position to attack them at first light. In that way, the Frenchmen within the river would not have time to furnish any aid to their four larger ships. As the great *San Pelayo* and the four smaller Spanish vessels glided among the French ships and let go their anchors, hails and shouts were exchanged. The first questions were meant, by both sides, to furnish positive identification. The Spanish asked specifically who commanded the French forces and were told in reply that Jean Ribault was the leader authorized by the King of France. The French then queried the Spanish flagship, put the same question, and received the reply that they were indeed Spanish, led by the designated adelantado of the provinces of Florida, Pedro Menéndez de Avilés. They were further told that the rightful ruler of these lands and waters, King Philip II, had given his adelantado orders to burn and hang the Lutheran French he might find there. In the morning, the French vessels would be boarded, and if they proved to be such people, the justice of the Spanish King would surely be carried out.

After this exchange, an outburst of shouts and curses came in a babble of tongues. Someone called out from the *Trinité*, taunting the Spanish men and asking why they should wait until morning. Pedro Menéndez decided to attack, even though it was dark. He had anchored the *San Pelayo* so close to the French flagship that the current had swung the great galeass' stern right around to the bow of the *Trinité*. Menéndez ordered his anchor line to be paid out, so that the two vessels would come alongside each other for boarding. As he gave this order, all the French ships cut their anchor lines, raised their

25. Menéndez described no deliberation in reaching his decision. Gonzalo Solís de Merás, however, states that a council of officers was held. He advised that the majority of his lieutenants proposed an immediate return to Santo Domingo to collect the forces prepared by its Audiencia and await the vessels of de las Alas and Pedro Menéndez Marquéz and the galleon of Roelas. Menéndez, says Solís de Merás, then said "no," believing that he had the advantage of surprise (*Pedro Menéndez de Avilés*, p. 84).

sails, and began to move away to leeward. Since the large bronze cannon on the *San Pelayo*'s decks were shotted for action against the French, the artillerymen got off five shots at the fleeing Frenchmen, but could not discern in the darkness what damage had been done to the *Trinité* by the Spanish fire.

As soon as they could get under way, Menéndez and Diego Flores Valdés led the Spanish fleet in a night-long chase of the French, but, with vessels still bearing the marks of the July hurricane, the Spanish were unable to catch the more rapid French. At dawn, it was evident to Menéndez that his enemy had escaped, so he determined to put his original plan into motion. Calling his scattered forces together, he sailed back again to the river mouth, where he proposed to seize the point of land adjoining the inlet. By denying the river to the French forces offshore, he could carry out his first objective. What the adelantado had not counted on, however, was that almost all of the French soldiery had disembarked and was, in fact, drawn up in fine order on shore, while the three smaller French vessels had stationed themselves as a barrier right across the mouth of the river. Since the *Pelayo* could not cross the bar and heavy forces opposed him ashore, Menéndez decided not to accept the challenge. He sailed south to make his own establishment and take up what might prove to be a long campaign.

Examination of the opposing forces in Florida at this point can provide us some evaluation of their relative strengths as they faced each other for mastery. Insofar as naval tonnage was concerned, the Spanish held an almost two-for-one edge, but a large part of this tonnage was in one ship—the galeass *San Pelayo*. That great gun platform could indeed outrange any opponent, but was still not fully rigged after the hurricane had struck it west of the Canaries. The French had, in fact, just demonstrated that they could outsail Menéndez' vessels.[26] In the holds of the French vessels lay an enormous wealth of bronze artillery, which remained only a potential weapon until the dismounted guns could be put into service. Insofar as manpower was concerned, the two opponents were nearly equal. Menéndez commanded some 800 men—500 soldiers, 200 seamen, and 100 others. On the French side, there was an equivalent number of soldiers—possibly 200 officers and sailors and the remainder of

26. The spy's report (see pp. 67–68) assigned the flagship *Trinité* a tonnage of 150 to 160, two of the other French vessels 150 tons apiece, one of 120, and three smaller craft between 60 and 70 tons. On the Spanish side, their chief vessel was rated at more than 900 tons, with the bergantín *La Esperanza* at 150 tons and the *San Miguel* and the *San Andrés* at 60 and 70, respectively. The tonnage of the vessel purchased in San Juan is not known.

Laudonnière's original garrison of 300, depleted by death, disease, and corsairing in the Caribbean.[27] The main striking force in any land action would be the armed and trained arquebusier, of which each side possessed 500. With regard to the matter of supply, it appears that the ship losses Pedro Menéndez had suffered to date had not destroyed his basic store of supplies, food, and munitions, much of which was still safely stowed aboard the *San Pelayo*. On their side, the French had come well supplied for an expedition of settlement and conquest. Part of these supplies had been unloaded. In sum, after striking some balance of advantages and disadvantages, the two sides were roughly equal. Under such circumstances, the decisive factor as the action began would be that of leadership.

The Spanish fleet sailed southward, then anchored off the wide bar of St. Augustine, which they had discovered a few days before. On September 8, with ceremony and ritual, the adelantado of Florida was landed from his vessel and formally took possession of the land in the name of the King of Spain. Pedro Menéndez de Avilés was then sworn in as the adelantado as well as captain-general and governor, together with the captains and officials of the expedition. The occasion was not a mere ceremony nor did it simply mark a beginning date for the Spanish occupation of Florida. It held much greater significance.

The first stage of a Spanish conquest—that of the construction of the political foundation upon which its social and economic structure should be built—was then and there accomplished. The first essential, the act of taking possession, done with solemnity and made a public record, fulfilled the requirements of the King's ordinances for conquest.[28]

To halt at this point, however, would be to overlook a vital part of the machinery for Spanish conquest and settlement. A major purpose of an adelantado was to introduce a most significant instrument of conquest—the municipal institutions of Spain.[29] One of these

27. Menéndez' estimate of forces is found in his letter of September 11, 1565. The French forces are estimated in the spy's report and Laudonnière's "L'Histoire Notable." It appears that Menéndez' September 11 estimate gives the lie to his later claim that some 1,504 left from Cádiz under his command (see p. 98). It appears, in fact, that Factor Duarte's original muster must have been essentially correct and that few, if any, additional persons could have embarked at Cádiz. This evaluation comes from deducting the men lost through the sinking of *La Vitoria*, the turning-back of *La Concepción*, and the straying and eventual loss of the caravel *San Antonio*. It further involves allowance for the gain of 43 men at San Juan balanced against the desertion of 33 others.

28. See "Ordenanzas," *D.I.*, vol. 14, no. XII, p. 490.

29. Many historians have discussed the significance of the *concejo* and other munici-

institutions—the concejo—was juridically based on the military and governmental center which was the city proper, but its limits and its influence extended far beyond that area. In St. Augustine, each man could expect to become a vecino or citizen of the municipality and be granted a city lot, his *solar*, and land to cultivate in the rural sections of the concejo. Through the estates thus granted, the Spanish municipality would reach out into the countryside as the primary institution of settlement. The role of the adelantado was essential in establishing, protecting, and commanding this organism. In each of the Florida settlements, beginning with St. Augustine, Menéndez named the alcalde and regidores of the first cabildo. Royal treasury officials would be named later. There was thus created a microcosm of Castilian civilization to effect the conquest, as the Spanish ventured forth into new and uncertain territory, basing their enterprise firmly upon their ancient urban customs.[30] Pedro Menéndez moved to fulfill these traditions. As noted by Barcia, "The adelantado had set up the courts and the municipal government in St. Augustine and left as alcalde his brother Bartolomé, who had always been a governor. He held the first session of the cabildo with the officers of the *ayuntamiento*, who were the captains. It was decided that appeal from the sentences handed down by the alcalde and regidores would be handled by the maestre de campo, whom he had named his lieutenant general, in accordance with the royal authority he possessed."[31]

---

pal institutions in Castilian conquest and settlement. Richard M. Morse has done a fruitful analysis of the concejo in "Some Characteristics of Latin American Urban History." His cogent statement (p. 325) runs: "The city is the point of departure for the settlement of the soil." Francisco Domínguez y Compañy, in "Funciones económicas del cabildo colonial hispano-Americano," has the following comment (p. 166): "The municipality is in fact the juridical agent authorized by the Crown to effect concessions and allotments of land, whether rural or urban." Perhaps the most detailed outline of the functioning of the Castilian municipality in the Indies has been done by John Preston Moore in *The Cabildo in Peru under the Hapsburgs*, pp. 15–28. James Lockhart discusses a variety of applications of the basic municipal institutions in different parts of the Spanish Indies. He also proposes an evolutionary connection between the colonial city and the *hacienda* system. Of particular value to me was his article "Encomienda and Hacienda: The Evolution of the Great Estate in the Spanish Indies."

30. See Manuel Ballesteros Gaibrois in *La Idea Colonial de Ponce de León: un ensayo de interpretación*, p. 14. Speaking of Ponce de León, Ballesteros says: "He had no utopian ideas of creating a new society, but simply wished to reproduce, on a small scale, that of Castile." A good example of the way an adelantado moved in practice in the Indies to create the municipal framework is found in the way that young Montejo founded Ciudad Real at Chichenitza in Yucatán. He appointed the first cabildo, designated one hundred of his soldiers as vecinos, and assigned plots of land to each. This is described by Chamberlain in *The Conquest and Colonization of Yucatan*, p. 136.

31. Barcia, *Chronological History*, p. 98. Although no books of the acts of the Florida cabildos have been found, a number of documents refer to these acts and bear the signatures of the alcaldes and the escribanos of the cabildos in St. Augustine, San

At St. Augustine, the first step had been made. To those who took part that day in the ceremonies of establishment, the other steps would shortly follow. Their expectations were great, for every free man, no matter how humble, could at least hope for the status of labrador (farmer) and would gain land for his own cultivation. Each man hoped to raise his status, but this advance would be along a well-known and traditional scale. As a matter of course, the hierarchical society of Asturias or Andalusia would be reproduced in Florida. The higher the rank of the settler, the more exalted his vision of his future estate. If he were but a soldier, he could hope for land and profit. If he were noble, his expectations were greater—he could picture his city and country homes, complete with Spanish and Indian vassals, land, cattle, and horses. He hoped for profit through familiar and established agricultural enterprise: the raising of cattle for local consumption and hides and the cultivation and refining of sugar for export.

It was evident that this utopia of mutual hopes could be built only where there were peaceful and fruitful relationships with the Florida Indians, a number of whom attended and observed the ceremonies of possession-taking and governmental establishment that day in St. Augustine. The Spaniards who came to Florida found themselves in the midst of one of the great culture areas of native peoples in the southeast of the continent. In the whole northeast Florida peninsula and up the St. Johns River lived the people known as Timucuan. Although these Indians generally shared cultural characteristics, they were divided into separate, warring groups. Their most powerful chief was Saturiba, whose seat of authority was located near present-day Mayport, close to Fort Caroline. Further north dwelt the Tacatacuru. Upriver to the south was the home of Chief Calibay, while Utina, a major rival to Saturiba, lived even further south.

Some of the best descriptions of the life and culture of the northeastern Florida Indians came from French sources. Sixteenth-century Spanish adelantados, such as Pedro Menéndez, had no appreciation of comparative religions; neither did they often display any objective

---

Mateo, and Santa Elena. See certifications of Alcalde Pelaez and his escribano in "Probanza hecha a pedimento de Gonzalo Gayón," St. Augustine, October 28, 1566, A.G.I. *Santo Domingo* 11 (Stetson Coll.); those of Diego de Valles as escribano of the cabildo at St. Augustine during September 1566, from A.G.I. *Contratación* 58, ramo 2, no. 3 ("Criminales"); the memorial of the settlers and cabildo at Santa Elena, July 15, 1569, from A.G.I. *Contaduría* 941 (microfilm, P. K. Yonge Library, reel 1, frame 35). Formal requirements for the foundation of the concejo, *república*, and appointment of the legal officials for the cabildo in newly discovered territories are outlined in "Ordenanzas," *D.I.*, vol. 14, no. XLIII, p. 501.

interest in native cultures as such. Menéndez, however, described the northeastern Florida Indians with some insight: "The ceremonies of these natives, for the greater part, are to worship the sun and moon; they have dead stags and other animals for idols. Each year they make three or four feasts for their devotions, where they worship the sun. They are three days without food, drink or sleep; these are their fasts. He who is weak, who cannot suffer this, is taken for a bad Indian. He goes about scorned by the noble people. He who passes best through these troubles is taken for the principal, and is given the most courtesy. They are a people of many strengths, swift, and great swimmers. They have many wars with each other, and no chief among them is recognized as powerful."[32]

The Spaniards' relations with the Florida Indians were in a very primitive first stage at this time, one of mutual exploration at arm's length, and would have far to go if Spanish expectations were to be realized. In this time of first contact, Menéndez elected to act with caution because of legal proscriptions against the exploitation of the Indians and because of the existing state of affairs in Florida. The Spanish had landed in a place where the French had clearly established a degree of influence with the Indians, and the native cultures were well organized. By contrast, the Spanish invaders had as yet insufficient numbers and power to effect a total conquest, so Menéndez sought to implant Spanish settlements alongside of the Indian cultures without disturbing their essential rights in the land. He did not endeavor to change at once their religious and political arrangements. Wherever he went in Florida, the adelantado proclaimed the overlordship of Philip II as rightful ruler of the land and sought to make agreements with the Indians based upon this concept. In a practical vein, however, the Spanish lacked the power to enforce this relationship. They were, moreover, dealing in a time of war, and even though the Crown forbade alliances with one Indian group against another, the realities of the French-Spanish struggle dictated that some Indians would be friends and some would be enemies.

Far from reaching the stage of encomienda or repartimiento, relations between the Spanish and the Florida Indians were still in the stage of trade for booty known as *rescate*. Under the agreement with his Indian friends, Pedro Menéndez was to receive tribute in the

32. Pedro Menéndez de Avilés to a Jesuit friend at Cádiz, St. Augustine, October 15, 1566, in Ruidiaz, *La Florida*, 2:155–56. Juan López de Velasco, in *Geografía universal de las Indias (1571–1574)*, pp. 159–60, provides a good description of the customs of the aboriginal Florida Indians. The matter of language and other cultural characteristics is well described and commented upon in Milanich and Sturtevant, *Francisco Pareja's 1613 Confessionario*.

name of his King. Before the pacification of the country had reached the state where outlying agricultural settlements could function in peace, tribute was to be paid at the top level—from Indian chiefs directly to the adelantado. Evangelization of the natives had to await further developments. In this first stage, when the number of interpreters was few and the language barrier relatively great, religious contact was limited. The clergymen who had come on the first expedition were intended to provide religious examples to the Indians and to furnish the sacraments to the Spaniards in the expedition. They could accustom the natives to the broad outlines of the Christian faith and give some hint of the mystic power of its chief symbols, but more complete religious instruction and the use of the doctrina would have to await the coming of trained missionaries and a more settled relationship with the Indians.

On the day of the formal possession-taking at St. Augustine, Pedro Menéndez named his brother Bartolomé governor of the district of St. Augustine, which extended from San Mateo to the river of Mosquitos. Bartolomé was also designated alcaide, or warder of the fort. As the adelantado signed the formal certificate of appointment for his brother, the men improved that part of Chief Seloy's village which they were laboring to convert into a fort. The language of the document imparts the atmosphere in St. Augustine that day: "Because the Lutheran French are fortified . . . teaching their evil sect among the Indians, I need to establish arrangements here, while I go to expel them. . . . it is necessary to make a fort in the port of St. Augustine to guard the port so that His Majesty's vessels can navigate freely. . . . they are making a place in it where the artillery and munitions will be. . . ."[33]

In the meantime, the French, having felt out the Spanish forces in their first skirmish and having reconnoitered the Spanish establishment at St. Augustine, returned to Fort Caroline where Jean Ribault and his captains assembled for a council in the bedroom of the ailing René de Laudonnière. From the friendly Indian Emola, they had word that the Spaniards had begun to build a fort and had landed in force to establish themselves there. It was decided in the council that they should descend upon the Spanish settlement with all their larger ships, for the enemy might be caught with his forces divided while unloading supplies. In spite of Laudonnière's objection to the plan, the motion carried and most of the French left the fort, even taking along 38 of Laudonnière's soldiers. Estimates of the garrison remain-

33. *Nombramiento* of Bartolomé Menéndez by Pedro Menéndez de Avilés, St. Augustine, September 7, 1565, A.G.I. *Indiferente General* 1,219.

ing in Fort Caroline ranged from 150 to 240. It had been substantially weakened in order to bolster up the marine striking force.[34] Ribault left the Sieur de Lys to aid Laudonnière in the fort. After delaying two days to assemble their forces, the four main vessels of Ribault's fleet sailed southward together with a number of small craft, carrying altogether 400 soldiers and 200 seamen.

In the meantime, Pedro Menéndez was increasingly anxious over the safety of his most valuable asset, the *San Pelayo*, and was fearful that it might be captured by the French or lost in a September storm on the little-known Florida coast. Even though its cargo was not fully discharged, Menéndez determined to send the galeass to Hispaniola. He unloaded much of the arms and ammunition from the great ship, but left the bulk of the food supplies aboard. This left him enough rations ashore to last him into January, when he hoped to have the *San Pelayo* back. It was after midnight on September 10 when the *San Pelayo* sailed, and when dawn broke, the Spanish seamen and soldiers were unloading munitions near the St. Augustine bar when the French fleet suddenly appeared. Even though the tide was low, Menéndez was able to escape across the bar to safety. The French, after sailing around briefly, went off to the southward, seeking to find and destroy the *San Pelayo*.

On the second day after the French attack, a storm, which may well have been a hurricane, struck the area. It began with strong and heavy north winds, which (as Menéndez sensed at once) prevented the French from returning immediately to their base. His instincts also told him that the French had left no great garrison at Fort Caroline and had probably put their best troops into their marine assault. He was told by friendly Indians that one could reach the lower St. Johns and Fort Caroline by way of the Matanzas River, and could thus take the French works from the rear. Pedro Menéndez decided to attack, left fewer than 300 men at St. Augustine under the charge of Bartolomé Menéndez, and set out on September 18 to assault Fort Caroline. Menéndez' 500 arquebusiers, led by their captains, were guided by Pedro de Valdés and the adelantado himself in the general direction given by the Indians. Once they reached the vicinity of the fort, they would be guided by one of the French prisoners brought from Spain. During the storm, heavy rains had fallen; these continued for the next several days. The route of the Spaniards carried them along low areas west of the sandy coastal ridge and led them

---

34. Laudonnière's own account of the circumstances surrounding the departure of Ribault and his remaining garrison are found in his "L'Histoire Notable," from Suzanne Lussagnet, *Les Français en Amérique*, 2:176–78.

alongside broad, grassy sloughs. In normal weather, small streams wound through the marsh grass in these low areas, but the inundations of rain had converted these lowlands into lakes. The normal banks were overrun and the water rose into the tangled underbrush which lay beyond. In such conditions, the march was difficult and arduous. In the vanguard went Basque axmen who could prepare the way for the little army. By the evening of September 19, Menéndez estimated that they had come forty-five miles and were less than three miles from the site of the fort. The Spanish column left the low and marshy land, crossed open pine barrens, and finally reached rolling country. Here near the banks of the river was deep virgin forest, studded with many magnificent oak and maple trees and covered thickly by wild grapevines.

At nightfall the leaders and their captains labored to gather the straggling forces and camped for the night in great discomfort from the continuing rainfall. Sometime before daybreak, the men were aroused and the Frenchman began to direct the Spaniards toward Fort Caroline. At this point, Menéndez' purpose was only to try the defenses of the fort after an approach under cover of the woods on the south side.

The French garrison inside the works was markedly inferior in numbers to the Spanish force which approached, in a ratio of about one to two. The makeup of the garrison itself, moreover, rendered its inferiority even greater. Perhaps fewer than a hundred of those within the fort were capable of bearing arms. The worst weakness of Fort Caroline, however, was its lack of vigorous leadership, for authority for the garrison was divided between the Sieur de Lys and René de Laudonnière. As a result of this division of command and the illness of Laudonnière, little had been done to put the fort into a state of defense. Some work had been accomplished on the palisades, but a strong and vigilant guard was not being maintained.[35]

As the grey dawn of September 20, 1565, broke over Fort Caroline, some of the sentinels left their posts because of the pelting rain. The Spaniards drew near the fort, discovered a lone French sentry outside, and captured him. Pedro de Valdés then led the way with two battle standards carried by his side as his men quickly forced the poorly defended main gate. The Spaniards swarmed in after their flags and quickly took the fort. As the Frenchmen poured out of their lodgings in their nightclothing, they were cut down. One hundred and thirty-two were killed within the fort in what, by all accounts, must have

35. For the French commander's version of events prior to and during the taking of Fort Caroline, see ibid., 2:179–82.

been a confused, violent scene. A French eyewitness described the slaughter: "They made a pretty butchery of it, except for a small enough number, among which were the deponent, three drummers (one from Dieppe, the other two from Rouen), and four trumpeters (three from Normandy and the other, named Jacque DuLac, from Bordeaux)."[36] Forty-five men climbed the stockade and escaped into the woods or plunged into the river in an attempt to reach the French vessels anchored near the fort. Among these were René de Laudonnière himself, the carpenter Le Challeux, and the cartographer Jacques Le Moyne. Pedro Menéndez, who entered the fort after the first wave of attackers, called out to his men to spare the women and children huddled within the huts; about fifty were granted their lives.

When he had gained control of the fort, Menéndez held parley with Jacques Ribault, son of the French commander, aboard the *Pearl* anchored just off the fort stockade. When negotiations broke down, the Spaniards opened fire with a cannon and sank one of the small vessels. The men aboard the *Pearl* and the *Levrière* cut their cables and moved closer to the river mouth, to comparative safety.[37]

The adelantado surveyed the arms of the captured fort but found only a few bronze guns with some ammunition. The spoils of war also included 200 casks of flour and wine, some hogs, sheep, and donkeys, and a quantity of silver the French had obtained from the Indians. The victorious Spanish soldiery appropriated most of the booty, except for the food, artillery, and ammunition, which Menéndez put under guard. He also came into possession of two small French craft as well as the sunken ship in the river; another boat was found under construction near the fort.

By far the most interesting things found in Fort Caroline, however, were found in one of the huts inside the enclosure. In an apartment which the prisoners told him had belonged to Jean Ribault, Pedro Menéndez describes how ". . . there was found a small strong-box in which he had all his papers, provisions and titles, [including that as] captain-general and viceroy of that land, and the instruction as to what he must do. There were six decrees, signed by the admiral of France. In the instruction was a section which stated that, after having reinforced the forts which were in Florida and fortified others which might seem necessary to him, that which would serve God would be

36. From "Deposition of Jean Mennin," from Paul Gaffarel, *Histoire de la Floride Française*, p. 445.

37. For an outline of events concerning the Frenchmen captured by the Spaniards at various times, see Eugene Lyon, "Captives of Florida."

that he go to the coast of the Indies and give liberty to the slaves there. . . ."[38]

The adelantado began at once to negotiate with the nearby Indians for the release of those Frenchmen who had escaped from the fort and who had been captured by Saturiba's people. The nobles among the captives were valuable properties whose families in France would ransom them for large sums. Two of these men, the Sieur de Lys and Pierre d'Ully, were turned over to Menéndez when he promised to return them safely to France.

Pedro Menéndez asked the Sieur de Lys about the documents he had found in the fort and why they were signed by the admiral of France. The Frenchman replied that "The admiral of France had given a petition to the royal Council describing how Jean Ribault had discovered and had begun to settle and fortify New France, a very great and good land; [he said] that this would result in a service to the King and in growth of the kingdom. Ribault asked for aid in the form of men and money and a contract so that the [effort] might go forward. The Council had replied by decree that it was very pleased with how he had discovered New France, and that they would require him to continue the settlement and conquest, although for the present the Council was not disposed to provide any funds or men. In order, however, that the King of France could never take from him the land which he might gain there, the Council agreed that the admiral should give him provisions and instructions; in order that these might remain in force for all time, [it was agreed that] those of the Council would first decree it, and that the signature below would be that of the admiral."[39]

The rejoicing and feasting of the victors was somewhat tempered by the discovery in the fort of some of the books and symbols of the Huguenot religion. These gave the Spaniards deep disquiet, as did the presence of the heretic women and children. Menéndez prepared to send the French dependents away as soon as possible.[40]

38. From "La Florida," *Envío* 25-H, no. 162, *Archivo del Instituto de Valencia de Don Juan*. Philip II described the finding of the papers in the fort to Guzmán de Silva, his ambassador in London, for de Silva acknowledged receiving them and discussing the matter with Queen Elizabeth in a letter dated March 30, 1566, from A.G.S. *Estado* 819. The adelantado generally described his taking of the fort with its booty and the ships he captured in his letter to the Crown sent from St. Augustine on October 15, 1565 and found in A.G.I. *Santo Domingo* 231 (Stetson Coll.).

39. Ibid. The rescue and ransom of the French noblemen Pierre d'Ully is described by the adelantado in his letter to the King sent from St. Augustine on October 20, 1566, and found in A.G.I. *Santo Domingo* 115 (Stetson Coll.).

40. The unease felt by the Spaniards about the presence of the French women and children is described by Hernando de Baeza in "Los despachos que se hicieron en la Florida," from A.G.I. *Escribanía de Cámara* 1,024-A.

Those surviving Frenchmen who had escaped the searches of the Indians and Spaniards gathered aboard the little cluster of anchored vessels near the mouth of the St. Johns. After hurried consultation between Jacques Ribault and René de Laudonnière, the three smaller craft were scuttled and sunk in the river. On September 25, the Frenchmen set out for their homeland in the *Pearl* and the *Levrière* without any attempt to rejoin Jean Ribault. Concern about Ribault's whereabouts then moved Pedro Menéndez to return to his base at St. Augustine and protect it against possible assault. On September 23, the adelantado set out across the same country he had traversed the week before. He left behind a garrison commanded by Gonzalo de Villaroel in the captured fort, now renamed San Mateo for the saint on whose day it had been taken. At St. Augustine, the welcome for Menéndez and the celebration of his victory were tumultuous.

In deep contrast, there was no joy whatever among the men who had been aboard Jean Ribault's ships. The storm which had lashed the coast and interrupted the raid on Pedro Menéndez on September 11 had driven the ships southward. Desperately, the shipmasters attempted to claw their way out to sea, but as the strong winds shifted and they lost sails, masts, and rudders, the vessels were driven toward the shore. One by one, they stranded and broke up in the heavy surf. Three of the heavier ships were wrecked in the vicinity of the Mosquito (Ponce de León) inlet, and many of their men drowned in the churning seas. The flagship *Trinité*, with its commander and crew, grounded intact not far from Cape Canaveral and most of its men came safely ashore. One smaller craft managed to make its way free of the winds and seas. Its crew decided to leave Florida waters and go to the Caribbean.[41]

The shipwrecked men found themselves lost upon a hostile shore, with their supplies destroyed or damaged in the storm. As Indians appeared along the beaches to raid the scattered survivors, the castaways gathered into two large parties for mutual defense. One of these was formed of survivors from the *Trinité*, the other of men from the other ships. After some communication the separate groups began a long trek northward, headed for Fort Caroline.

41. The estimate of the location of the three major French shipwrecks was given to Pedro Menéndez by survivors of the first massacre at Matanzas. From the same source he learned that the *Trinité* was grounded some five to ten leagues from the other vessels. See his letter to Philip II from St. Augustine on October 15, 1565, from A.G.I. *Santo Domingo* 231 (Stetson Coll.). The story of the small French craft which survived the storm and sailed to the Caribbean is found in "Papers relating to various Frenchmen who came as prisoners in the fleets and were captives in the jail of the Contratación of Seville; 1571," from A.G.I. *Patronato* 267, no. 2, ramo 7.

In the meantime, Pedro Menéndez had begun to take stock of his resources, to be ready to strike again at his enemies. Having disposed of the French fort, he was mostly concerned with the marine striking force of Jean Ribault. He was now ready for the *San Pelayo* to return with his reinforcements from Santo Domingo and Havana, for he realized that the supplies aboard his galeass would soon be sorely needed in Florida. He sent Gonzalo Gayón in the *San Andrés* to search for the *Pelayo* in the islands and dispatched Juan Rodríguez on the same errand in the *San Mateo*, a renamed vessel which had once been French.[42] It was also necessary to resupply the soldiers sent by the Crown and outfitted at Cádiz, for many of them, Menéndez claimed, had left their arms and clothing aboard the *San Pelayo* in the haste of its departure. Pedro Menéndez furnished the men from his own stores, and the men signed a document agreeing that they had received 150 reales' worth of goods apiece.[43]

On September 28, friendly Indians brought the adelantado the news that many Frenchmen had gathered on the south shore of a small inlet of the sea eighteen miles from St. Augustine. With one company of men, Chaplain Mendoza Grajales, and a French prisoner for interpreter, Menéndez set out and arrived at the inlet at dawn on September 29. After some shouted exchanges across the water, Menéndez and his interpreter spoke at length with a French pilot and shipmaster. The Frenchman told Menéndez frankly the situation of his marooned countrymen. After Pedro Menéndez broke the news of the taking of Fort Caroline to the envoy, he sent him back to his fellows with the message that he was their enemy, bound to pursue them with a fire and blood war to extermination. Shortly, a French nobleman came to parley with Menéndez, asking for their lives in return for surrender. The adelantado claims that he said that they could place themselves at his mercy, but that he made them no guarantees of safety.[44]

42. See "Los despachos que se hicieron," A.G.I. *Escribanía de Cámara* 1,024-A.

43. See the hearing before the Casa de Contratación in Seville in February and March of 1572, found in A.G.I. *Justicia* 817. Menéndez claimed a total of 4,080 ducats for this aid to the Crown soldiery.

44. I will not attempt to render judgment upon the vexed question of the good faith of Pedro Menéndez de Avilés in the episodes at Matanzas. Rumor that he had in fact offered Ribault and the others their lives and then had them killed in contravention of his word was transmitted from Madrid by the Sieur de Fourquevaux in letters to the French rulers sent from Segovia on July 5, 1566; from "Lettres et Papiers d'état de Fourquevaux," in Paul Gaffarel's work, *Histoire de la Floride Française*, pp. 439-41. In his own letter to his sovereign, Pedro Menéndez states that he obtained the surrender of the French without any specific promise as to treatment, and then simply had them quickly and systematically killed. He evidently neither asked nor expected any further justification of his actions than that dictated by the exigencies of war and supply and

As a practical matter, the options open to the French at Matanzas were few and poor. If they turned away to the southward, they could only expect starvation, death, or captivity at the hands of the Indians. The friendly base to which they had been marching was now occupied by their enemy. They chose to surrender and were ferried across the inlet in small parties. Their hands were tied, and they were taken a short distance beyond, to a place out of sight behind the dunes. Pedro Menéndez removed the French pilot, four carpenters and caulkers, and twelve Breton sailors from the group of bound men. He spared their lives and had the rest put to the knife.[45]

Menéndez returned to St. Augustine with his prisoners. Since he had learned that Jean Ribault still lived, he feared that Ribault might refloat his flagship and threaten the Spanish settlement. The adelantado placed cannon at the St. Augustine bar and posted sentinels and lookouts. He began his first report to his King since the taking of the French fort. Writing with an obvious feeling of elation, the Asturian recounted the events of his victories over the enemy, listed the booty found in the fort, and described his general strategic situation. He emphasized anew the continuing threat posed by the French to the whole Atlantic coastline and to the galleon routes. To counter the danger, he proposed to build a fort further south, to anchor the Bahama Channel and complement the works at Havana and St. Augustine. He then shifted his subject to a major interest—his future settlements in the north.

Menéndez stated that he would go first to Santa Elena to found a colony. Then he would pass along to the Bay of Santa Maria, where, he again reminded Philip II, lay the key to the entire continent. It was there that the great waterway to the southwest, which offered a new and shorter route to return the New Spain silver to Spain, lay waiting. He planned to protect this route by fortifying a town in the Province of Coça, inland at the foot of the mountains. The great kingdom thus secured would be rich in cattle, vineyards, and sugar plantings. Its timber resources would provide naval stores, so that shipbuilding could flourish along its coasts. In Menéndez' view, his mission in the vast stretches of land called Florida was to "fix our frontier lines here,

felt himself to be fully empowered by royal authority to carry out his action. See the description of the executions at Matanzas in Menéndez' letter to Philip II written from St. Augustine on October 15, 1565, from A.G.I. *Santo Domingo* 231 (Stetson Coll.).

45. Observers at the scene of the first slaughter at Matanzas differed as to the number of those who died and who had been saved. Father Mendoza says that 111 were killed, and "ten or twelve" were given their lives because they were Catholics; see "narrative of Francisco López de Mendoza Grajales," in Bennett, *Laudonnière and Fort Caroline*, p. 163. Solís de Merás, in contrast, states that eight were saved and 200 were executed (*Pedro Menéndez de Avilés*, p. 115). The adelantado gave no total of the slain.

gain the waterway of the Bahamas, and work the mines of New Spain."[46]

The King's adelantado reminded his sovereign of the expenses he had incurred in his Florida effort. He advised that he had committed a thousand people so far to the enterprise, counting those en route to Florida but not yet arrived. Although the contract obligated him to bring only 500 persons for the conquest, he had asked Pedro del Castillo to send 300 soldiers in addition to the 1,000 already committed. Menéndez urged the King to increase the royal forces in Florida to the level of the promised 500. For his own costs, the adelantado stated that he would need 30,000 ducats. He pledged his willingness to devote all the funds he could earn or borrow from his friends or kinsmen but begged that the King hasten the payment of monies due him in Seville.

Pedro Menéndez' letter writing was interrupted at this point. First, news was brought to him of the burning of Fort San Mateo. He dispatched food and munitions to the place at once by sea and realized that supplies would now be more scarce than ever. Then there came another urgent message to the adelantado: more Frenchmen had come to the inlet where the first group had been killed, and among them was Jean Ribault. This time, Menéndez took 150 armed men and arrived at the place at dawn on October 11. The drama played out on the banks of the inlet now called Matanzas followed much the same course as before. After almost an entire day of negotiation, the French leader came himself under a flag of truce to see the adelantado of Florida. When the two antagonists faced each other personally for the first and last time, they met under vastly different circumstances from when the two fleets had clashed off the St. Johns River mouth a month before. Although he attempted to do so, Ribault could not move Pedro Menéndez from his terms of surrender: the Frenchmen must yield themselves entirely to the mercies of the Spaniards. The next morning, half of the French force chose to retain their liberty—they retreated southward away from the Spaniards. Jean Ribault, together with several of his captains and seventy of his men, came to surrender and be taken across the water. A few of the Frenchmen were taken as captives; the rest were killed, among them Jean Ribault. The major enemy figure had now been eliminated, together with the greater part of his forces.[47]

46. Pedro Menéndez de Avilés to Crown, St. Augustine, October 15, 1565, from A.G.I. *Santo Domingo* 231 (Stetson Coll.).

47. The adelantado estimated the number who surrendered at 70; Solís de Merás put the figure at 150. While Pedro Menéndez stated that he spared 5 men, Solís de

Menéndez commissioned Diego Flores de Valdés to sail at once in the *San Miguel* to carry the tidings of victory to Philip II. At the same time, he dispatched Francisco Genovés to Puerto Rico with fifty Huguenot women and children, all survivors from Fort Caroline. Genovés was also to seek and inquire further about the whereabouts of the *San Pelayo*, now gone from Florida more than a month. At this moment of triumph for Pedro Menéndez, he had no way of knowing that his great ship had been seized by heretic mutineers aboard and was even then on its way to Europe where it would soon be lost on the coast of Denmark.[48]

Within two weeks after the second slaughter of the French at the inlet of Matanzas, word came that many survivors from the lost Ribault ships had gathered and fortified themselves at Cape Canaveral. Pedro Menéndez determined to make a foray into the area of the great cape. The expedition would expunge the remaining French, explore a section where he hoped to plant a fort, and search further for Juan Menéndez. In the last of October, Pedro Menéndez left St. Augustine with 250 men divided into a land and a sea force. Three small craft commanded by Diego de Amaya sailed southward close to shore. Along the beaches marched the adelantado with 150 of his soldiers. The boats offshore carried the bulk of the supplies and munitions for the expedition.

One early dawn in the first days of November, Pedro Menéndez approached a point just a few miles above the headland of Cape Canaveral. There the Frenchmen had created a rough earthworks surmounted by six bronze cannon from the *Trinité*. Nearby, they had a small boat well along in construction. Huguenot sentries gave the alarm as they spied the morning sun flashing upon the helmets and armor of the Spaniards. From the sea they could see three boats closing in upon them. Alarmed, the Frenchmen fled over the sand ridges through the low palmetto into deeper woods to the west. The adelan-

---

Merás said that the lives of 16 were saved. See Solís de Merás, *Pedro Menéndez de Avilés*, p. 115.

48. The adelantado mentioned sending Flores; see his letter of October 15, 1565, from A.G.I. *Santo Domingo* 231 (Stetson Coll.). The dispatch of Genovés is described in "Los despachos que se hicieron," A.G.I. *Escribanía de Cámara* 1,024-A. The loss of the *San Pelayo*, through its seizure by "Lutherans" aboard and its subsequent shipwreck, is described in expository statement by Pedro Menéndez introducing his case against the Crown. It bears no date, but is probably from October 1567, and is contained in A.G.I. *Escribanía de Cámara* 1,024-A. The event is also described in "Ship Losses of the Adelantado," n.d. (November 1567), from the same legajo. News of the loss of the *San Pelayo* had come to the Spanish Court by April 9, 1566, on which date it was transmitted to the Queen Mother of France by her ambassador Fourquevaux; the letter is from "Lettres et Papiers d'état de Fourquevaux," found in Paul Gaffarel, *Histoire de la Floride Française*, p. 436.

tado sent a French prisoner, a trumpeter, to offer safety to the enemy if they would surrender. Except for a few of their leaders, the Frenchmen came in and yielded to the Spaniards. Perhaps seventy-five were thus captured. The crude fort was burned, the boat destroyed, the cannon buried in the sand, and the expedition continued southward.[49]

As his land forces, swollen by the number of the French prisoners, slogged along the long expanse of beach which stretches like a crescent moon south from Cape Canaveral, the adelantado of Florida entered a new and distinctive part of his kingdoms. As the marching men moved down the narrowing island they soon caught glimpses of the broad open waters of the Indian River. Menéndez could quickly see that the waterway would afford protected navigation by small craft which would enable more rapid and secure communication along the central east coast.

The Spaniards had also entered a very different cultural area of the Florida Indians. The people who lived in this area, who were called the Ais, had built a long and stable culture organized almost entirely around the sea. Their life was sustained by turtles, fish, and shellfish from the river, inlets, and ocean. Over twenty years of acquaintance with Spanish shipwrecks along the east coast had accustomed the Indians to the taking of white prisoners and the salvage of ships. By 1565, they had already built a reputation for ferocity and cruelty which compelled the advancing Spaniards to move with caution. When they came to the place where the land between river and ocean was a mere sandspit, they arrived at a thick cluster of Indian villages and the dwelling place of the chief of the Ais.[50]

49. Pedro Menéndez described the taking of the French force at Cape Canaveral in his letters to Philip II dated December 5, 1565, at Matanzas, Cuba, from A.G.I. *Santo Domingo* 115 (Stetson Coll.) and dated January 30, 1566, from Havana, from A.G.I. *Santo Domingo* 168 (Stetson Coll.). Irving Rouse, in his *Indian River Archaeology*, p. 192, lists a site numbered BR 84 not far above the extremity of Cape Canaveral. He believes this to have been a possible site for the French works.

50. Although the Indian background of the Indian River area has not been thoroughly developed by historians and anthropologists, some very useful studies have been made. The basic theory of the location of the Ais culture center was developed by Homer N. Cato of Micco, Florida, who has done much fruitful field work in a number of Ais sites in the vicinity of the Sebastian River and the ocean inlet opposite it. His work on the Spanish salvage site and on the Cato site led to later investigations by Dr. and Mrs. Ripley Bullen and Carl J. Clausen. See Homer N. Cato, "Found—Ancient Sebastian Man," and Ripley P. Bullen, Adelaide K. Bullen, and Carl J. Clausen, "The Cato Site near Sebastian Inlet, Florida." Charles D. Higgs studied some sites and wrote "Some Archaeological Findings and Investigations in the Land of Ais" and "Spanish Contacts with the Ais" (esp. pp. 25–30). Irving Rouse summed up the archaeological publications to 1950 in *Indian River Archaeology*. Work was also done by Hale G. Smith; see *Two Archaeological Sites in Brevard County, Florida*. I attempted to summarize the

The first meeting between the Spanish and the Indian chiefs went very well indeed. Although communication was difficult between the men, Pedro Menéndez and the *cacique* Ais concluded an agreement, in which the Indian swore fealty to Philip II and promised peace and obedience. Menéndez sealed the treaty with gifts of clothing and personal jewelry. He undertook no direct trade for bullion, but noted the gold and silver ornaments worn by the Indians. A number of the soldiers did engage in trading for the precious metals. Since the need of the Spaniards who had come by land for food was becoming acute, they welcomed the coming of the three supply boats with joy. When Amaya landed, there was momentary relaxation from the tension which short rations had brought, and the place was named "Puerto de Socorro." It was soon realized, however, that the foodstuffs on hand could not last the Spaniards and their French prisoners for long and the Indians had little food which the Spaniards would eat. To return to the forts in the north would be no solution, for they had no reserves after the burning of Fort San Mateo. The adelantado decided, after consultation with his captains, to proceed with his original design to fortify the area and determined to leave Captain Juan Vélez de Medrano there with 200 men and 50 of the French captives. His intention to populate the Indian River area was shown by the appointment of Vélez de Medrano as civil governor as well as military commander of the district.[51] He himself would take two of the small craft, fifty men, and twenty of his prisoners and proceed directly to Cuba to link up with the reinforcements coming from the north of Spain or with the New Spain capitana which was to await his orders in Havana. After relocating his men in a better site somewhat to the south of the Indian village complex immediately surrounding that of the chief, Menéndez put to sea in the two small ships, pushed toward Cuba by the strong north winds of winter. For the adelantado, the first phase of the conquest of Florida had ended.

ethnology of the Ais in "More Light on the Indians of the Ays Coast." As to the culture boundary between the Ais and Indian groupings to the north, it is fairly well established by the "Useful, profitable, and totally correct geographical course-description of the rivers, inlet-channels, lagoons, woods, villages, stream-crossings . . . from the city of St. Augustine to the bar of Ais," written in 1605 by Captain Álvaro Mexia and found in A.G.I. *Santo Domingo* 224 (from a recent translation by Homer N. Cato and Eugene Lyon). The cultural line is also emphasized by Fray Francisco Pareja in *Catecismo en lengua Timuquana y castellano*, in which he pointed out that speakers of the languages of the south coast could not be understood by the Timucuans.

51. The appointment of Juan Vélez de Medrano is found in "Testimonio de los documentos de Capt. Juan Vélez de Medrano," in A.H.P., *Protocolo* 646, fol. 256–59. More data are found in his request for salary payments for his Florida service, in A.G.I. *Justicia* 894, no. 8.

The Consequences of Victory

New Outreach Begins

When he arrived in the Cuban port of Bahiahonda, Pedro Menéndez had just finished a remarkable small-boat journey. It had been more than just a hasty voyage through rough autumn seas, impelled by the urgencies of supply. It was a trip of exploration and discovery. As the two *barcos* had threaded their way southward along a low shoreline and the features of Florida's southeast coast were gradually revealed to the eyes of a master seaman, Menéndez had made an important navigational discovery: one could sail southward inside the north-setting Gulf Stream with a vessel of any usual draft. He had also found and reconnoitered two ports suitable for Indies ships seeking refuge from storm or corsairs. The discovery of easy round-trip navigation from Florida to Cuba suddenly made Cuba very important to the adelantado, for it offered the best way to channel supplies and reinforcements from the Indies to the Florida garrisons.[1]

Pedro Menéndez did not remain long in Bahiahonda. By November 13, he was within the great harbor of Havana, where many vessels were anchored.[2] He shortly found that at least one part of his Asturias fleet had arrived—his nephew Pedro Menéndez Marquéz had come with the two Gijón ships and a Portuguese prize they had taken. Gonzalo Gayón and Francisco Genovés were also in harbor with the

1. See Menéndez' assessment of the navigational discoveries in his letter to Philip II from Matanzas dated December 5, 1565, from A.G.I. *Santo Domingo* 115 (Stetson Coll.). An excellent description of the journey of the adelantado from Florida is found in Solís de Merás, *Pedro Menéndez de Avilés*, pp. 129–31.

2. García Osorio states that the adelantado arrived in Havana on November 13, in his letter to the Crown from Havana, December 18, 1565, A.G.I. *Santo Domingo* 115 (Stetson Coll.).

San Andrés and the patache *Espíritu Santo*, after returning from their unsuccessful search for the *San Pelayo*. Menéndez could also see the *Santa Catalina*, the promised capitana of Pedro de las Roelas, anchored in somewhat deeper water.

From his nephew, Menéndez learned that the whole northern fleet had also had a stormy passage from Spain. After a halt at the Canary Islands, where they met Captain Luna, the ships had reached San Juan badly damaged and Juan Ponce de León gave them substantial help.[3] Off the north coast of Hispaniola, the convoy had sighted two Portuguese caravels and given chase. Esteban de las Alas took the larger vessel, while Marquéz captured the smaller. Since they were found to be present in the Indies without legal registry, the caravels were fair game. The fleet continued around the precipitous shore toward the port of La Yaguana and, on October 8, saw three vessels offshore. They were discovered to be an *urca*, a *fragata*, and a captured French patache with the Santo Domingo aid for Florida under the command of Captain Gonzalo de Peñalosa. It carried 250 men, 20 horses, and the necessary supplies and munitions. Peñalosa had also indulged in some corsair-chasing and had just captured a French *patax* when he met Esteban de las Alas. After the united convoys entered the harbor of La Yaguana for water, Pedro Menéndez Marquéz left with his prize and came directly to Havana. He brought 200 men and a quantity of arms and munitions, but little food.[4]

Gayón and Genovés had been utterly unable to find any trace of the great galeass *San Pelayo*. She had not come into any island port. The unavailability of the supplies that were aboard the missing ship only made Menéndez' need the more pressing. The supplies from Santo Domingo had not yet arrived. Menéndez also received another piece of bad news: the caravel *San Antonio*, outfitted at his expense, had been seized by French corsairs and then lost in a storm off Cuba. The French survivors had been hanged by the governor of Havana, García Osorio de Sandoval, but all the supplies were lost. Menéndez had little in the way of money at hand and began to explore all possible means of raising cash.

3. Ponce describes his aid to Alas' ships in his letter to the Crown, San Juan, April 20, 1566, A.G.I. *Santo Domingo* 71 (Stetson Coll.).

4. The send-off of Peñalosa and his subsequent adventures are described in "Copia de una relación que Capitan Gonzalo de Peñalosa dió de un viaje que hizo a la Florida con socorro de las armada del Adelantado Pedro Menéndez de Avilés," from A.G.I. *Patronato* 257, no. 3, ramo 22 (Stetson Coll.). The Audiencia of Santo Domingo discussed its role in the dispatching of the expedition in its letter to Philip II, sent from Santo Domingo on December 12, 1565, and found in A.G.I. *Santo Domingo* 71 (Stetson Coll.). The Royal Officials of that place also reported on the matter to the King in a dispatch dated November 26, 1565, A.G.I. *Santo Domingo* 74 (Stetson Coll.).

The adelantado began by selling the Portuguese prize and its cargo at public auction. With his share of the proceeds, he bought sea-biscuit, meat, cassava, corn, and some cattle and loaded these for Florida. The *San Andrés* was sent with supplies to St. Augustine and San Mateo under the command of Diego de Amaya, while the second captured French patax, renamed the *Santiago*, went to Puerto de Príncipe, Bayamo, and Santiago de Cuba to seek supplies.[5]

When he turned to examine the capitana of de las Roelas and learned the circumstances of her stay in Havana, Pedro Menéndez became embroiled in controversy. He learned that the ship had been detached at Cape San Antonio by Roelas, who had placed Captain Juan de la Parra in command of the ship, until he could turn it over to Menéndez in Havana. On his way to Havana, Parra also went hunting for prizes. Off Matanzas, he surprised and took another Portuguese caravel, which proved to be richly laden with hides, pearls, gold, and Negro slaves. The capture was escorted into Havana by Parra, who then made the necessary legal proceso against the Portuguese. As soon as it had anchored, the Cuban governor, García Osorio, sent his armed men to take charge of the caravel. The governor's men roughed up Parra's prize-master and Osorio had the captain jailed in irons.

When he learned of the arrest and confinement of Parra, Pedro Menéndez was furious. His anger was rooted in two things which always moved him powerfully: his authority and his money. Parra, the ship he had commanded, and the prize he had taken were now under Menéndez' authority, and the governor's action against Menéndez' subordinates was an affront to the adelantado. The Portuguese ship represented, moreover, a value of 13,000 to 14,000 ducats and his share would go far toward replenishing his depleted funds.

For three days, the two antagonists exchanged requerimientos. Since these had no visible effect, the men finally met and joined conflict personally. Other tensions lay between Pedro Menéndez and García Osorio. Menéndez had strong and long-standing affiliations with some of the members of the most powerful local faction, that of the linked Rojas, de Soto, Lobera, and Hinestrosa families, and Osorio knew it. Menéndez had further angered Osorio by moving into the house of Juan de Hinestrosa, the treasurer at Havana, and by hiring Gonzalo Gallego, Parra's maltreated prize-master, and sending

5. Menéndez described the sale in his letter to Philip II from Matanzas dated December 5, 1565. Hernando Baeza recounted the return of the *San Andrés* from Havana in "Los despachos que se hicieron en la Florida" from A.G.I. *Escribanía de Cámara* 1,024-A.

him to Florida as a ship captain. Pedro Menéndez represented still another threat to Osorio: he held direct evidence of royal favor in his asiento. Cédulas had come to Havana, bidding special attention to the needs of Florida, and Pedro Menéndez, with privileges from the King in hand, prepared to make demands and assert his authority against that of the royal governor. Both men were intensely proud personalities, jealous of their prerogatives and highly sensitive to any encroachment upon them, and their rivalry rapidly became a deadly one.

Pedro Menéndez and García Osorio were unlikely to achieve any meeting of minds. Menéndez asked for the release of Parra and the release of some of the goods from the prize caravel. If he could have these, Menéndez averred, he would use the money he realized to supply the royal troops in Florida. Osorio refused to release the ship or anything from it. Menéndez then asked for a loan, so that he could better supply his own men in Florida. This was also refused. Discussion of the royal order to furnish fifty supplied soldiers also resulted in deadlock. Menéndez needed no more troops in Florida, and Osorio would furnish no separate supplies. Finally, Pedro Menéndez tried to take possession of the four bronze artillery pieces which had just arrived for the fort at Havana. Osorio, anxious for the defense of the place and concerned about its weakness, refused this as well.

In any event, it is unlikely that García Osorio could have done much for the Florida supply. It does appear that the governor had an obligation to help to supply the royal men in Florida, if not Pedro Menéndez' private soldiers. Although Menéndez was already moving to meet his needs in other ways, the governor's obstructions did impede and embarrass him. While he outwardly concealed his deepest feelings about the governor, Menéndez began a campaign against him at the highest levels. He accumulated materials about the Parra case, made other procesos against Osorio, and prepared to send them to the King. He began to explore the possibility of obtaining the Cuban government for himself.

Having been rebuffed by Osorio, Menéndez attempted to obtain supplies from friendly Havana merchants. He established a warehouse, stored the munitions brought by Menéndez Marquéz to Havana, and began to sell or trade them for foodstuffs, but prices in Havana were high and food was scarce. Menéndez gave Hinestrosa his poder to handle business matters in Havana. From the captain of a fragata, Menéndez learned that the Santo Domingo support fleet had met with disaster, and that the urca had been sunk, but could find out nothing about the fate of Esteban de las Alas. He decided to outfit an expedition, search the old Bahama Channel for de las Alas, and attempt to negotiate a loan from the Audiencia of Santo Domingo. Most of all, however, he hoped to capture other valuable corsair ships. This was his best opportunity to realize enough money to relieve his financial necessities, and was, after all, in line with Menéndez' most deeply held inclinations and longest experience. Menéndez had to justify his taking the crown-leased New Spain *capitana* on such an adventure. In order to do this he established it as an anti-corsair expedition and later told Philip II that there was great danger that Jean Ribault's son, who had fled Florida with two "armada ships," would come to the Caribbean, join with other roaming pirates there, and assault the shipping and settlements of His Majesty's loyal subjects.[6]

In order to refit and to supply the vessels for the corsairing voyage, the adelantado spent or encumbered himself for 4,000 ducats. Menéndez hoped that this investment, probably realized from the sale of arquebuses and munitions and credit from Hinestrosa, would pay real dividends. To help cover his expenses, Menéndez dispatched Captain Luna to Vera Cruz with an urgent request that the Audiencia of Mexico lend him 3,000 to 4,000 ducats. At the same time, he asked the New Spain officials to send him Don Luis Velasco, the Indian from the Chesapeake Bay area, so that he might be available to Menéndez in his projected northern exploration and colonization in the spring.[7] Menéndez left Havana November 30, 1565, with his ships and men. At the very beginning, it appeared that fortune smiled upon the adelantado. A short distance to the east of Havana, his lookouts sighted a sail. Since it seemed to be a Portuguese caravel, Menéndez sent his nephew to chase it down. The vessel took refuge in the port of Matanzas, and Menéndez followed with his four ships. It turned out that the caravel was in reality a Spanish dispatch ship sent from Seville with messages to the authorities in Santo Domingo and Cuba. In one of those fortuitous accretions of information which occurred in an age of infrequent communications, the adelantado was suddenly brought up to date on events in Europe.

Nothing aboard the caravel was addressed to Pedro Menéndez, but he took the liberty of reading the cédulas the King had directed to

6. In reality, of course, young Ribault had returned to France. In any event, his feeble force would have posed little danger to Spanish fleets and could only have done scattered raiding. Menéndez outlines the supposed threat and the arming of the expedition in his letter to the Crown from Matanzas on December 5, 1565, A.G.I. *Santo Domingo* 115 (Stetson Coll.).

7. Menéndez mentions the Luna mission in the December 5 letter. Confirmation of the loan request is found in Royal Officials of Mexico to Crown, Mexico City, March 30, 1566, A.G.I. *Mexico* 323.

the Santo Domingo and Cuban officials. They contained a revelation. Obviously Menéndez' suggestions that a backup fleet be sent to reinforce and support his efforts against the French had borne fruit, for the King advised that he was sending many ships with 1,800 men to Florida by way of the islands and asked the Indies officials to provide supplies for the force for nine months.

This momentous news roused mixed feelings in the adelantado of Florida. While greatly relieved to hear that Crown-paid reinforcements were coming, Menéndez felt it imperative that the succor fleet save valuable time by sailing directly to Florida. He also felt a nagging concern that, if the royal forces were coming to Florida in the spring, he had best attend more decidedly to the supply and maintenance of the forts and garrisons he had left in Florida, or he might feel the weight of royal censure. Pedro Menéndez decided to protect himself and advance his cause by doing some corresponding of his own.

First, he wrote to the Audiencia of Santo Domingo and objected to the King's supply plan, proposing instead that he provide fresh meat from the islands and fresh fish in Florida at less cost to the Crown and with better results for the health of the garrisons. He also advised that he would not be financially able to return to Florida before March but was concerned that the men there be provided for properly. Next, Menéndez sent Philip II his first letter since October, reported on all that had taken place since the death of Jean Ribault.[8] He repeated the recommendations that he had made to the Santo Domingo Audiencia and noted that he was sending a pilot to Spain who could guide the ships directly to Florida. Menéndez also made complaint against García Osorio and sent along certain formal allegations in the Parra case.

Next, Menéndez looked beyond the immediate problems of logistics. He sketched out to the King his broad proposals to benefit the kingdom and himself by vigorous action on the sea. If Philip would grant him the title of "captain-general" of these parts of the Indies, Tierra Firme, and the Ocean Sea, Pedro Menéndez would provide and command a fleet of small, fast, and mobile fragatas. Two of these, to be equipped with oars and powerful guns, he had already ordered for delivery in the spring. With two more, Menéndez could secure the entire Atlantic coast from Newfoundland to the Caribbean islands. All he wanted in return, said Menéndez, was the title and a thousand slave licenses. He could sell some of these to finance his operations

8. See Pedro Menéndez de Avilés to Audiencia of Santo Domingo, Matanzas, December 2, 1565, from A.G.I. *Santo Domingo* 71 (Stetson Coll.). The letter to the King is the December 5 letter.

and would use the other licenses to obtain Negroes for the guard fleet.

While he was in Matanzas, the adelantado prepared to actuate his small vessel trade privilege. He told Philip that an error had been made in the asiento, when the tonnage of the shallops had been listed at 50 instead of 100 tons apiece, and he asked that the asiento be amended, thus increasing his tonnage permission substantially. While at Matanzas, Menéndez organized his trade fleet; he named Pedro Menéndez Marquéz as commander of the six shallops and four zabras, and prepared to send him to Spain with dispatches and to seek supplies to put into the Indies trade for the provision of Florida.[9] He was able to utilize the Portuguese captured by Menéndez Marquéz as galley slaves, as well as some of the French prisoners captured in Florida.[10]

Menéndez next turned to matters of personal privilege and appealed to the King for certain key appointments in Florida. For the principal royal posts in Florida, he exercised his adelantamiento powers and proposed four men. He described the Asturian hidalgos nominated: "They are people of confidence and high standing who have served your Majesty many years in my company, and are all married to noblewomen. Out of covetousness for the offices [for which they are proposed], and out of love for me, it could be that they might bring their wives and households. Because of these and of others who would come with their wives, it is a fine beginning for the population of the provinces of Florida with persons of noble blood."[11] Those proposed were Esteban de las Alas, Pedro Menéndez Marquéz, and Hernando de Miranda, as treasurer, accountant, and factor—the three royal financial posts in Florida. He also suggested Diego de Miranda, successor to the Miranda mayorazgo, as escribano mayor of Florida and secretary of the government there. Thus, before the struggling Florida garrisons had achieved more than a foothold, Menéndez looked ahead to the fulfillment of the dream he shared with his principal lieutenants and supporters. The letter was immediately sent to Spain in a patache, with a request that its crew be paid by the King or, failing that, by Pedro del Castillo.

In stark contrast to his exalted plans for gain and expansion ex-

9. The *nombramiento* is addressed to Pedro Menéndez Marquéz, dated December 4, 1565, at Matanzas, and is found in A.G.I. *Patronato* 257, no. 4, ramo 1.

10. The adelantado mentions the use of the Portuguese in his December 5 letter, A.G.I. *Santo Domingo* 115 (Stetson Coll.). The French are shown on ration lists for 1566 and 1567 as ship crew and found in A.G.I. *Contaduría* 941 (microfilm, P. K. Yonge Library).

11. Pedro Menéndez to Crown, Matanzas, December 5, 1565.

pressed to the King, Pedro Menéndez had to face unpleasant realities when he returned to Havana and abandoned his voyage. By December 12, he had received full news of the disaster which had befallen the Santo Domingo expedition. A storm north of Cuba had sunk the urca and the zabra of Candamo which had left Avilés the previous summer, with all the supplies they had carried, and a host of ship-wrecked sailors and soldiers were stranded 350 miles east of Havana. Pedro Menéndez Marquéz and Esteban de las Alas joined together to ferry the men across to the mainland. It was decided that the men should go to Bayamo or Puerto Príncipe to seek food at Menéndez' expense, and Menéndez sent them a letter of credit, drawn upon Juan de Hinestrosa. Pedro Menéndez commissioned Diego de Miranda to go to eastern Cuba with 2,000 ducats and establish supply sources in the Savanna of Vasco Porcallo, Puerto Príncipe, Bayamo, and Baracoa. He authorized his lieutenant to purchase more than 16,000 *arrobas* of meat a year, to build warehouses to store the provisions, and to draw upon Menéndez' credit freely in so doing. He also made arrangements in Puerto de Plata with Francisco de Zavallos to furnish supplies for Florida.[12] He also decided to dismiss the soldiers from Santo Domingo and reduce the expense of their maintenance. The prize caravel of Esteban de las Alas, still half laden with valuable hides, remained in Matanzas. Menéndez tried to sell the caravel and its cargo, but none would buy it sight unseen. Finally a deal was struck with Francisco de Reinoso, of Menéndez' entourage. Reinoso agreed to buy the caravel and the 2,000 hides remaining in it, for 4,000 ducats. He would cancel the 2,000-ducat debt already owed him, pay and supply the caravel crew, and give Menéndez 1,000 ducats in cash. The adelantado then sent one of the captured French barcos, renamed the *Buenaventura*, to the garrison which had been left

12. The events described here are outlined by Pedro Menéndez in his letter to the Crown from Havana dated December 12, 1565. Menéndez wrote that letter and mailed it separately. This separate letter is also included as a part of Menéndez' letter of December 25. It appears that, when he had recovered from his illness, he also mailed both letters together, thus repeating the contents of the earlier letter. In the Stetson Collection are found the combined letters of December 12/25, and also a separate copy of the December 12 letter, all from A.G.I. *Santo Domingo* 231. It is the separate December 12 letter which bears the marginal comment of Philip II. The letter of December 12, but not the one of December 25, is included in "Siete cartas escritas al Rey," 45 fol., from "Cartas de Indias," in the *Colección Navarrete*, vol. 14, fol. 281–326. The letter has been reprinted from the collection of Francis Parkman in *Proceedings of the Massachusetts Historical Society*, ser. 2, vol. 8 (1894):459. For the supply data, see "Instruction of Pedro Menéndez de Avilés to Diego de Miranda," Havana, November 8 [*sic*], 1565, from A.G.I. *Santo Domingo* 11. The arrangement with Zavallos is described in Menéndez' letter to Philip II written from St. Augustine on October 20, 1566, from A.G.I. *Santo Domingo* 115 (Stetson Coll.).

with Captain Vélez de Medrano at the Ais village with 10,000 pounds of sea biscuit, cassava, meat, and corn.[13]

Pedro Menéndez, worn by the strain of recent months, fell ill, seriously enough to require the attentions of a physician. After ten days' sickness, he recovered sufficiently to write a lengthy letter to the King. Menéndez complained again of the lack of cooperation he had received from Governor Osorio and noted that forty men had taken advantage of his illness to desert. He accused the governor of permitting some of these deserters to escape the city and flee inland. Another witness, more favorable to the governor, notes that Osorio had quite properly subdued many of the soldiers who had fled.[14]

Menéndez now redoubled his efforts to provide and send supplies to his Florida forts. Armed with the 3,000-ducat loan sent by the Audiencia of Mexico and the money he obtained from Reinoso, the adelantado shortly also received the remaining arms and munitions which had come from Asturias and Vizcaya. He established a warehouse in Havana, gathered foodstuffs and livestock from his Indies sources, and named Hernando de Baeza as tenedor de bastimentos for the Florida supply.[15]

The adelantado purchased Peñalosa's fragata and leased a Portuguese caravel named *La Asención* from its master, Álvaro Gómez. He sent the caravel to buy corn in Yucatán, where it was cheap and plentiful. By January 28, two small vessels had already been sent to Florida with hams, chickens, cassava, and corn when Diego de Amaya returned to Havana with more unpleasant tidings.[16] Amaya had gone first to St. Augustine, where he had found that an early and harsh

13. See "Despachos que se hicieron," A.G.I. *Escribanía de Cámara* 1,024-A.

14. Menéndez' letter is that of December 25, 1565. The royal accountant at Havana, Diego López Osorio, wrote to Philip II from Havana on January 26, 1566, found in A.G.I. *Santo Domingo* 115 (Stetson Coll., misdated December 26, 1565).

15. Baeza came with Menéndez on the Cádiz ships. His career is described by witnesses in "Cargo y data de la cuenta que dio Fernando de Baeça," Havana, February 10, 1569, from A.G.I. *Contaduría* 941 (microfilm, P. K. Yonge Library). His commission as a notary public in the Indies is found in A.G.I. *Indiferente General* 425, book XXV, fol. 233 and vto. Menéndez describes the establishment of the supply depot in his letter dated January 30, 1566 (see p. 129n49). Baeza's list of supply vessels from Havana is found in "Despachos que se hicieron," A.G.I. *Escribanía de Cámara* 1,024-A. In addition to Menéndez' letters and the ship dispatches of Hernando de Baeza, we are most fortunate in having the detailed list of supply vessels and cargoes sent by the adelantado from Havana from 1566 to 1574 contained in A.G.I. *Contaduría* 1,174. These data, collected by the Royal Officials of Havana at the request of the Crown, were gathered at Menéndez' request to support his position that he had supplied royal soldiers at his own expense. There is record of Baeza's dealing in Yucatan with one Juan Fernández of Campeche; see Declaration of February 17, 1569, from A.G.I. *Contaduría* 454.

16. Pedro Menéndez discusses Amaya's report in his letter of January 30, 1566, from A.G.I. *Santo Domingo* 168, which he directed to the King from Havana.

winter and the poor state of supply had led to more than a hundred deaths in the two forts. After leaving foodstuffs for the St. Augustine garrison, Amaya had sailed northward with the *San Andrés* with supplies for San Mateo, only to be caught in a strong gale off the St. Johns River bar. Amaya tried to cross the lines of breakers which marked the bar entrance, but the veteran *San Andrés* was driven ashore and broken up in the surf. The rest of the supplies were lost, and Amaya had to return to Havana in another vessel. On his return voyage, he could not locate the garrison at Ais and had sailed to a point just south of the St. Lucie Inlet when he sighted a small boat with Captain Juan Vélez de Medrano aboard. Vélez told a harrowing tale of hardship and mutiny. Soon after the departure of the adelantado the previous November, the garrison's rations had given out. The friendly Indians possessed no store of food sufficient for such a large body of men. As discipline disintegrated, bands of soldiers roamed the area seeking food. Friction between the Indians and the Spanish became outright war.

A soldier named Escobar persuaded one hundred of his fellows to desert and to march southward with him, seeking an escape from Florida and passage to New Spain. Captain Vélez followed in the small boat the adelantado had left him and found the mutineers encamped forty-five miles south. They had reached the north side of the wide St. Lucie River and could go no further. Keeping his distance from the rebels, Vélez told them he would go to Havana to seek supplies. Soon after he reached the open Atlantic, the two vessels met.

Diego de Amaya and the captain sailed together along the coast and found a promising harbor at the Jupiter Inlet, where the elevation commanded a good view of land and sea. There, on December 13, 1566, St. Lucie's Day, they built Fort Santa Lucía. Amaya left supplies and went on to Havana to report to Pedro Menéndez, while Vélez recovered his rebel soldiers and ferried them south eighteen miles to the new fort. Artillerist Diego López aided in the placing and siting of the cannon in the works, and the men began to trade with the Indians, called the Jeaga, for bits of gold and silver recovered from Spanish shipwrecks.[17] News that many men from Vélez' garrison had

17. Captain Vélez' recollections are from his "Testimonies," St. Augustine, May 15, 1566, from A.G.I. *Justicia* 999. A description of the sufferings of the men in Fort Santa Lucía is found in "Méritos y servicios de Diego López," St. Augustine, December 16, 1569, from the Woodbury Lowery Collection (microfilm, P. K. Yonge Library), I:2:414:265–290. In his narrative, López baldly stated that the Spanish in the Vélez garrison resorted to cannibalism. As to location of Santa Lucía, Woodbury Lowery, in *The Spanish Settlements*, Appendix S, 2:434, places it at the present St. Lucie River inlet near Stuart, Florida. On the other hand, Captain Juan de Soto placed the location of

died came to Havana with the supply ship. Discontent with Florida was expressed in many private letters which then spread from Cuba to other parts of the Indies.[18] Pedro Menéndez determined to relieve the garrison by March.[19]

When, at last, Esteban de las Alas had rejoined his chief in Havana, Menéndez could arm his ships and prepare his next move. He had established a supply pipeline from Cuba to Florida, even though it was poorly funded for any long-run operation. Help was coming from Spain: he knew of the large, heavily laden reinforcement fleet which should shortly leave Andalusia and come directly to Florida. In addition, the adelantado had sent by Menéndez Marquéz a request to Pedro del Castillo to furnish wine, shoes, and Indian trade goods, together with some settlers and their equipment. He could send no money but could repay Castillo with the slave licenses. He was still hopeful that the missing *San Pelayo* could be found.

Menéndez' plans now were clear: he would continue the mission of exploration and conquest interrupted by the expulsion of the French under Laudonnière and Ribault. His next expedition had multiple purposes. First, he would explore the lower keys for a passage east of Tortugas for the home-bound New Spain fleets on their way to Havana. Then, with pilot Gonzalo Gayón (who knew the area from the time of the De Luna expedition) he would skirt the western coast of the peninsula and seek a good port near the Bay of Juan Ponce.

Pedro Menéndez' settlement strategy was tied to his belief that the Florida peninsula was crossed by a navigable river system. He believed that the St. Johns emptied into the Gulf at some point on the southwest coast and wished to place his fort and found a settlement near that place. Thus easy water communication between his cities would facilitate the interchange of men and supplies and help in their mutual defense against any enemy. The southwestern port would be in the best position to receive supplies from Havana, from Yucatán,

Santa Lucía in "Xega" in his testimony in "Daños de los indios de la Florida," A.G.I. *Patronato* 257, no. 3, ramo 20. After working with Homer N. Cato of Micco, Florida, in the translation of the Mexia *derrotero*, I believe that the beginning point of the mutineers' southward journey was not far south of the Sebastian River in Indian River County. Their course, estimated at twelve to fifteen leagues in length, would have brought them to the north side of the wide St. Lucie River; from there it is about eighteen miles, or six leagues, to the Jupiter Inlet.

18. See Diego López Osorio to Crown, Havana, January 26, 1566, A.G.I. *Santo Domingo* 115. The news of trouble and disaster in Florida reached San Juan before the arrival of Sancho de Archiniega there in June of 1566. See Archiniega to Crown, San Juan, June 11, 1566, from A.G.I. *Santo Domingo* 71 (Stetson Coll.). Many deserters also carried the news to Santo Domingo and other places in the island Indies.

19. The adelantado's decision is mentioned in his letter to Philip II from Havana dated January 30, 1566, and from A.G.I. *Santo Domingo* 168.

and from his galleons in the New Spain trade. Settlers and missionaries could then solidify the establishments. Menéndez planned to leave Esteban de las Alas in charge of all the forts and direct his attention to eradicating the supposed French presence in Guale and to building his main base of operations at Santa Elena. Always in the background, as the matter of the highest priority, was Menéndez' search for the great interconnecting passage to the New Spain mines and the South Sea and the urgent need to deny the secret of it to the French. He would launch himself northward to explore and populate this area at the earliest possible moment. Another continuing motive was the hope that Christian prisoners, perhaps even his son Juan, might be recovered from Indian captivity.

On February 10, 1566, Menéndez made a proclamation in Havana, to justify his use of the New Spain ship *Santa Catalina* in his proposed expedition. He stressed the possibility of finding French corsairs and the need to eliminate the threat they represented to the Florida coasts, the other Indies, and the Spanish fleets. Next, he took formal control of the supplies and rations aboard the *Santa Catalina*. There were eighty-six soldiers and sailors still on board; some had deserted in Havana. Several months' supplies were turned over to Menéndez. He bought some additional materials of his own and prepared to sail.[20]

While Pedro Menéndez prepared to return to the scene of his triumphs in Florida, no solid news of the September clash between Frenchman and Spaniard had reached Europe by the first days of 1566. In the absence of any real intelligence, the military and diplomatic lines of action already decided upon by the King and his councils went forward. Concrete actions were begun to implement a heavy reinforcement of Pedro Menéndez with royal troops, and instructions were sent to the Casa de Contratación to embargo private ships for the new Florida fleet and to gather supplies of foodstuffs and ammunition. The difficult task of locating artillery, powder, helmets, and arquebuses for the journey was begun.[21]

---

20. There is much material about this ship arming in "Información de Pedro Menéndez de Avilés," Seville, 1567–68, which was assembled in an attempt to prove that Menéndez had spent much of his own money in feeding and supplying the crew of the *Santa Catalina*. This is found in A.G.I. *Contratación* 4,802 (Stetson Coll.). There are two lists of ships engaged in the expedition; one, in A.G.I. *Contaduría* 1,174, gives the sailing date as March 1, 1566; the other, from "Despachos que se hicieron," in A.G.I. *Escribanía de Cámara* 1,024-A, gives the date as February 20. Solís de Merás (*Pedro Menéndez de Avilés*, p. 138) sets the date at February 10.

21. On September 4, 1565, the Casa officials reported to Philip II that cannon and arquebus powder, matchcord, and lead were being gathered in the Seville warehouses for the expedition, A.G.I. *Contratación* 5,167, Book II. On August 15, they had been

The choice of a commander for the relief and reinforcement expedition had been made—on September 14, 1565, Philip II had selected Sancho de Archiniega, a Basque seafarer. On September 26, the King had written to his Florida adelantado explaining that he was sending him 1,500 soldiers. Philip was careful to spell out the touchy issue of jursidiction of the new force and rules that General Archiniega and Colonel Hernando de Orsuna would have full legal control over their troops once they left Spain. When they arrived in the adelantamiento of Florida, the King assured Menéndez that the commanders had instructions to obey and defer to him as "the person in whose charge was the enterprise of that land."[22] Philip II did urge Pedro Menéndez to cooperate with and seek military advice from these men who were so experienced in war. In addition to Colonel Orsuna, who would raise a company himself, Captains Juan Pardo, Pedro Redroban, Pedro de Andrada, Miguel Enriquez, and Juan de Zurita began to assemble their companies. They concentrated their recruiting in lower Andalusia.[23]

In the meantime, the Spanish King felt it was time to disclose to the French that Pedro Menéndez had been sent to Florida. He instructed Ambassador Alava to speak to Catherine de Medici and advise her that the Spanish had learned of "usurpers" in their land and had taken action to punish them. Before this formal notice was finally given them on November 23, 1565, the French already knew of the Menéndez expedition. When the announcement was made, a dispute then arose among Alava, the Queen, and councillors of the French King, in which the old arguments about territorial jurisdiction were repeated without any agreement.[24] In actual fact, the actions of Pedro

busy trying to locate ships; on that date, the shallop La Trinidad was embargoed in Port Santa Maria—see A.G.I. Contaduría 299, 12:3, 4. Evidently they had difficulty finding a proper capitana for the fleet and locating enough cannon; the King, in a letter to the Casa from the Bosque de Segovia, September 6, 1565, commented on their problems, and advised that he had sent to Vizcaya for a thousand arquebuses and helmets. The letter is from A.G.I. Contratación 5,012 (Stetson Coll.). The orders to the proveedores of artillery at Malaga and to the officials of Vizcaya and Guipúzcoa were dated the same day, and come from A.G.I. Indiferente General 738, ramo 7, nos. 74, 74-C, 74-E (Stetson Coll.).

22. Crown to Pedro Menéndez de Avilés, Bosque de Segovia, September 26, 1565, from A.G.I. Escribanía de Cámara 1,024-A. Archiniega's appointment is from A.G.I. Patronato 254, and his first day of duty was listed in A.G.I. Contaduría 299, 12:7.

23. Royal messages were taken to the captains recruiting men at Utrera, Port Santa María, Librijia, and Medina-Sidonia; see A.G.I. Contaduría 299, 21:2 vto. Difficulties and a lawsuit eventually arose out of the expenses incurred by Captain Pardo in the town of Tolox del Marqués, near Marbella on the Mediterranean coast, as the municipality sued for reimbursement. The case, dated January 27, 1566, somehow came to rest in A.G.I. Mexico 209, ramo 1.

24. Philip II gave his orders to Alava in a letter dated September 30, 1565, and

Menéndez in Florida had already made the question a moot one. The Spanish Queen had already warned the French Ambassador to Spain that Philip II would not tolerate any French colonies in his lands or near the fleet routes of Spain. Late in December, Ambassador Fourquevaux had an interview with the Duke of Alba on the question of Florida. The duke flatly told the Frenchman that, in spite of the lack of agreement on the question of territorial rights after the signing of the treaty of Cateau-Cambrésis, the Spanish position was that this treaty definitively denied any land rights in the Indies to the French. The Florida incursion would, therefore, be vigorously resisted and ejected.[25]

This position brought no relief for the Spanish from their concern over further French reinforcements to Florida. In August and September, reports had come to the court that a new armada for Florida was being outfitted in Le Havre.[26]

The eagerly awaited news of what had happened in Florida was contained in the adelantado's letter of October 15, 1565, entrusted to Captain Diego Flores de Valdés. It had been long delayed in reaching the Spanish court. The San Miguel, which carried the message, had been wrecked in the Azores, and Flores had had difficulty in finding another vessel to brave the winter gales and carry him to Spain.[27] Although Pedro Menéndez Marquéz was also en route to Spain, he had not arrived either.

It was after the first of the new year that any intelligence came from Florida to the Spanish King, and this news came by way of France.

found in A.D.E., vol. 8, no. 1, p. 150 (A.G.S., Estado, Legajo K, 1,504, no. 75). The ambassador's report on his meeting and argument with the Queen and her advisers was found in his letter to Philip II sent November 29, 1565, and from A.D.E., vol. 8, no. 1, p. 166 (A.G.S., Estado, Legajo K, 1,504, no. 89, pp. 144–45).

25. Isabel's comments to Fourquevaux are found in the ambassador's letter to the regent written November 3, 1565, from Celestin Douais, ed., Depêches de M. de Fourquevaux, ambassadeur du roi Charles IX en Espagne, 1565–1572, 1:63. The meeting of Fourquevaux with the Duke of Alba is described in a letter from the ambassador to the regent dated from Madrid on December 24, 1565, ibid., 1:17.

26. See testimony of Sebastián de Vacoli Pedrossa, taken by Juan Gutierrez Tello in Seville, from A.G.I. Indiferente General 738, ramo 7, no. 74-A, and the response from the Crown in a letter to the Casa sent from Bosque de Segovia on September 14, 1565, from A.G.I. Contratación 5,012.

27. The loss of the San Miguel and the subsequent delay in receipt of the news of Menéndez' victory is described in a letter from the Crown to the Casa de Contratación dated February 20, 1566, from A.G.I. Contratación 5,012 (Stetson Coll.). It is also contained in "Memorial de los navios cargados de bastimentos y municiones que se perdieron el Adelantado Pedro Menéndez yendo a echarlos luteranos que estavan poblando en aquella tierra de la Florida," in A.G.I. Escribanía de Cámara 1,024-A, n.d. (probably October 1567).

Philip received, by mid-January, a letter from his ambassador in France, advising of the arrival there of Jacques Ribault. Thus word of the taking of Fort Caroline, but not of the massacres of Matanzas, was communicated to the Spanish Court. Another, more direct messenger came shortly to Philip II. Pedro de Bustinçury, a Vizcayan prisoner aboard young Ribault's ship, escaped the French and made his way to Madrid. This man, the shipwreck survivor who had been an Indian captive among the Ais Indians on the Florida east coast, told the King of the Spanish victory at the French fort. He so impressed Philip II that he was commissioned to return to Florida to aid Pedro Menéndez in his relations with the Indians of that area.[28]

The vessel which had brought René de Laudonnière back from the tragedy in Florida had been much slower in arriving in France. His ship had arrived in England in mid-November. After experiencing illness and difficulty there, the Huguenot leader had finally reached the French court on March 18. Another captive Spaniard who had been kept on board Laudonnière's vessel also escaped and came to Spain.[29]

In the meantime, the long-awaited news from Pedro Menéndez finally came to Philip II in Madrid. Diego Flores Valdés arrived in Seville on February 13, and dispatches telling of his coming probably just preceded the arrival of the man himself at court.[30] When Philip II learned of the clear-cut and decisive victory of arms won by Pedro Menéndez in Florida, the monarch wasted little time in rejoicing. Because of the eradication of the French garrisons in Florida, he could change the extent and emphasis of his commitments in the Indies.

28. The letter from Alava to Philip II is dated January 6, 1566, and is found in *A.D.E.*, vol. 8, no. 1, pp. 184, 189 (A.G.S. *Estado*, Legajo K, 1,505, pp. 61–63). Fourquevaux wrote back from Madrid about the coming of the Basque to the Spanish Court in two letters, February 4, 18, 1566, from "Lettres et Papiers d'état de Fourquevaux," in Gaffarel, *Histoire de la Floride Française*, pp. 417, 421.

29. Laudonnière described his voyage in "L'Histoire Notable," from Lussagnet, *Les Français en Amérique*, 2:183, 184. Alava described the coming of Laudonnière to the French court and the incident of the second captive in a letter to Philip II dated March 16, 1566, from *A.D.E.*, vol. 8, no. 1,205, p. 271 (A.G.S. *Estado*, Legajo K, 1,505, p. 81) and one written on March 18, 1566, to Secretary Gonzalo Pérez, from *A.D.E.*, vol. 8, no. 1,206, p. 272 (A.G.S., *Estado*, Legajo K, 1,505, p. 84).

30. Philip II had not received the dispatches from Florida by February 10, when he issued a commission to Juan de Ubilla as almirante of the Archiniega fleet and urged him to go and expel the French from Florida. See cédula to Juan de Ubilla, Madrid, February 10, 1566, from A.G.I. *Contratación* 58. The arrival of the message and Diego Flores Valdés were acknowledged by Philip II in a letter to the Casa de Contratación on February 21, 1566, from A.G.I. *Contratación* 5,012 (Stetson Coll.). It is also described in Fourquevaux' letter to Charles IX dated February 18, 1566, from "Lettres et Papiers d'état de Fourquevaux," in Gaffarel, *Histoire de la Floride Française*, p. 421.

The King sent the news to Sancho de Archiniega and began to consider alteration of his military force. He also took immediate steps to reaffirm the contract obligation of his adelantado in Florida.[31]

Since the danger in Florida was clearly lessened, Philip II toyed with the idea of cutting the force the Crown was to send, from 1,500 to 1,000 men. He finally concluded that it could now be put to a wider use than duty in Florida and directed that the Archiniega force, under the direction of Pedro Menéndez de Avilés, should serve as the response to a widespread menace to the Spanish Indies. A part of the expedition would be used to reinforce the Florida troops, while the greater portion would become a mobile defense force for use elsewhere in the Indies. By the last days of March 1566, these decisions had been taken and notices of them sent to the Casa de Contratación and to Pedro Menéndez.[32]

The private side of the Florida conquest was not neglected by the Spanish King. In a letter to his officials in Seville, the monarch advised that he expected that Pedro Menéndez would supply and pay 300 of the men who were to go with Archiniega. Pedro del Castillo, who had already protested that he had not yet received the Casa de Contratación money due Pedro Menéndez, reacted strongly to this news. Castillo said that there was no way that he could underwrite any new draft of soldiers, or even supply the adelantado's own men currently in Florida, without the 20,000 ducats which were owed to Menéndez. Creditors were pressing him for outstanding obligations, and he pleaded also for payment of the additional charter fees earned by the *San Pelayo*. According to the accountants of the Casa, perhaps 16,000 ducats in all could be owed and Castillo had not yet presented all of the proper supporting papers. The King directed that Menéndez be paid 6,000 ducats, including reimbursement for the journey of Flores Valdés, even though the ship had not made the complete voyage to Spain. The Casa de Contratación did not make the payment.[33]

31. The Spanish King's letter to Archiniega was dated February 24, 1566, and is described in the auditor's summary of events affecting the Menéndez asiento in the first pages of A.G.I. *Contaduría* 941 (especially fol. 2) (microfilm, P. K. Yonge Library).

32. After consideration by the Council of the Indies on March 15, 1566, the King sent his decision to the Casa on March 21 from Madrid. The letter is found in A.G.I. *Contratación* 5,012 (Stetson Coll.). The cédula to Pedro Menéndez is outlined in A.G.I. *Contaduría* 941, fol. 2. In another letter sent from Madrid on March 21, 1566, the King also notified his officials in Havana that parts of the Archiniega force would be used to man the fort there. This is from A.G.I. *Contaduría* 454.

33. See Castillo to Crown, Cádiz, January 30, 1566, from A.G.I. *Indiferente General* 2,673. Castillo had also evidently written the King on February 15, for Philip II replied to him in a letter sent from the Escorial on March 15, 1566; this letter is from A.G.I.

As he made certain that the private obligations of his adelantado in Florida were not neglected, the King also moved to improve the supply of his own Florida troops from the Indies. On February 24, 1566, he directed the Royal Officials at Havana to furnish ample supplies for this purpose. Unfortunately for Pedro Menéndez, however, the order was not a very realistic one. In view of the poverty of the public treasury of the little community at Havana and the hostility of its governor, any such aid for Menéndez was as unlikely in 1566 as it had been in 1565.[34]

Seventeen ships, laden with supplies, sailed for Florida with the 1,500 men originally planned for on April 19, 1566.[35] The Archiniega expedition, originally intended to help in the expulsion of Jean Ribault and the capture of the fort built by René de Laudonnière, would now serve to reinforce the general defense of the Indies. The continuing menace to Spain represented by French marauders had served to encourage another substantial royal investment. The responsibility of utilizing this great force, whether in Florida or the Caribbean, had been put in the hands of Pedro Menéndez de Avilés.

In the meantime, the King's adelantado had left his winter base at Havana and sailed with his convoy toward the lower Florida Keys. The seven vessels, led by the *Santa Catalina* and the ship which had come with de las Alas from Santander, probed cautiously among the shallows and discovered an ample channel to the eastward of Tortugas. This was the passageway Menéndez had been seeking for the New Spain fleets. Sailing through the new channel, the ships continued in a northeasterly direction until they sighted the Florida coast in the vicinity of the Ten Thousand Islands. Then the vessels moved in closer to shore, seeking the Bay of Juan Ponce.[36] Leaving Esteban

---

Indiferente General 1,966, Book II. The trade officials discussed the matter with the King in a letter sent from Seville on March 6, 1566, from A.G.I. *Contratación* 5,167, Book III. On March 15, Philip had written the Casa functionaries, ordering them to make a payment of 6,000 ducats. This letter is described in a royal cédula sent to Casa representative Abalia in Cádiz, dated at Madrid August 28, 1566, from A.G.I. *Indiferente General* 1,966 (Stetson Coll.).

34. The cédula of February 24, 1566, to the Royal Officials at Havana was sent from Madrid; it is found in A.G.I. *Santo Domingo* 115 (Stetson Coll.). It is also referred to in A.G.I. *Contaduría* 1,174 and 454.

35. Led by the 480-ton galleon *Los Tres Reyes* as capitana, the Archiniega expedition carried four urcas, vessels of great capacity and relatively small draft, to transport supplies to Florida and enter its ports. The outbound ships are listed in A.G.I. *Contratación* 2,898 in *Yda*—1566. The successful departure is described in a letter of Francisco Duarte to the Casa on the same date, found in A.G.I. *Contratación* 5,185.

36. The departure of the expedition to Carlos is described in "Despachos que se hicieron," A.G.I. *Escribanía de Cámara* 1,024-A. Menéndez evidently sent dispatches to the King from Carlos, which were lost when the courier vessel, *Nuestra Señora del Rosario*, was taken off Spain; see "Memorial de los navios . . . que se perdieron," from

de las Alas offshore with the larger ships, Pedro Menéndez went to
shallower water and soon came to an inlet where he spied an Indian
canoe. In the canoe was Hernando Escalante Fontaneda, who had
been twenty years a captive. The adelantado described the young man
who came out to greet him: "very good looking, of noble parents, the
son of the late García Descalante, a conquistador of Cartagena . . .
[one] of two brothers, boys of 10 years of age: they were being sent to
Salamanca when their ship was lost. The people aboard escaped, but
over the years the father of this [chief] Carlos had killed 42 of the
captives, among whom was his elder brother."[37] Pedro Menéndez had
arrived in the land of Carlos, or the Calusa.

In his contact with the principal chief of Carlos, it was the
adelantado's purpose to assure the security of his communications
network and that of the settlers which he hoped to leave in the area.
He hoped to accomplish this by making friendly connections with the
Indian whose sway extended over much of extreme southwestern
Florida, the Keys, and the southeast of the peninsula as well.

The Solís de Merás narrative pictures the arrival of the adelantado
at the island kingdom of Carlos as one of considerable pomp. Accompanied by an entourage of arquebusiers with matchcords lit and
weapons ready, Menéndez landed at the village to the music of fife,
drum, and trumpet. The ruler of a large part of the southwest end of

---

A.G.I. *Escribanía de Cámara* 1,024-A. Because of this gap in Menéndez' correspondence,
one must rely upon the Solís de Merás, Barrientos, and "Barcía" narratives. The
adelantado does, however, give some details about Carlos and the Spanish prisoners
there in his letter to Philip II sent from St. Augustine on October 20, 1566, and found
in A.G.I. *Santo Domingo* 231 (Stetson Coll.).

37. From Menéndez' letter of October 20, 1566. De Escalante has usually been called
Fontaneda, and his striking memorial has appeared in a number of places. The best
and most recent edition is *Memoir of Hernando d'escalante Fontaneda*. De Escalante ap-
peared on a Spanish ration list of 1565–66, with another captive at Carlos, Alonso de
Rojas, as an interpreter. See "Lista de la gente . . . conquista de Florida," A.G.I.
Contaduría 941, fol. 9 and 10 (microfilm, P. K. Yonge Library). The culture of Carlos,
Calus, or Escampaba was a vigorous one, whose history is well described by Charlton W.
Tebeau in *Florida's Last Frontier*, pp. 25–32. John M. Goggin identified it as a Glades III
culture in "Cultural Traditions in Florida Prehistory," from *The Florida Indian and His
Neighbors*, edited by John W. Griffin. Lowery, in *The Spanish Settlements*, states his belief
that the capital city of Carlos was located at Charlotte Harbor (2:230–31n2). On the
other hand, Father Clifford M. Lewis posits the location of Mound Key in Estero Bay;
this view is expressed in a manuscript of his entitled "The Spanish Jesuit
Mission of 1567–69 in Southwest Florida: Search for Location." After reading the
description in Juan López de Velasco, *Geografía universal de las Indias*, esp. p. 164, I tend
to agree with Father Lewis. Father Lewis has expanded and revised his work on
Carlos into a chapter entitled "The Calusa," which will shortly be published as chap.
8 of *Tacachale: Indians of Florida and Southeast Georgia during the Historic Period*, ed.
Samuel Proctor and J. T. Milanich, Contributions of the Florida State Museum, Anthropology and History, no. 19.

the Florida peninsula was seated in state, to receive the homage of a large assemblage of his own people and to greet the Spanish leader as an equal.

Menéndez persuaded Chief Carlos to release the shipwreck survivors held captive there and to conclude an agreement of peace and friendship with the Spanish. The adelantado advised that he found five men, five *mestiza* women from Peru, and one black woman living as prisoners in the area of Carlos. The chief promised also to free three other Christians who were held captive at some distance inland.[38]

The adelantado and cacique Carlos exchanged gifts and entertained each other with food and drink. Carlos granted to Menéndez the highest honors that he could in light of his traditions by giving his sister, later christened and renamed Doña Antonia, to the adelantado as a wife. In order to seal this agreement, Menéndez felt it advisable to consummate the marriage while at Carlos. At this time, he did not leave religious missionaries or colonists at Carlos, but did reindoctrinate the shipwreck survivors who chose to remain there, and he left behind symbols of Christianity and of Spain. He had endeavored to some degree to instruct the Indians in the basic tenets of Catholicism and hoped to accustom them to worship of the cross.

Pedro Menéndez' approach to Carlos embodied many of the elements of his developing policies toward the Indians of Florida. He believed that the mouth of the strategic cross-peninsular waterway was nearby. When the friendship with Chief Carlos was sufficiently developed, he would anchor the Gulf entrance to this vital channel with a Spanish settlement. The threefold purpose of the conquest— colonization for economic exploitation, evangelization of the native peoples in the Catholic faith, and the establishment of a military base for Spain—would thus be accomplished.

Menéndez restrained himself considerably in the matter of the obtaining of trade through booty. While his men entered enthusiastically into the exchange of trinkets for gold and silver recovered by the Indians from shipwrecks, Menéndez did not do so. Whereas the men gathered perhaps 3,500 ducats worth of treasure, Menéndez simply received the gift of a single bar of gold from the chief. He then sailed away, doubled around the Keys, and proceeded north. The news of

38. From Menéndez' letter to the King, St. Augustine, October 20, 1566. Pedro Menéndez Marquéz advises that 18 captive Christians were rescued at Carlos; see "Daños de los Indios de la Florida," A.G.I. *Patronato* 257, no. 3, ramo 20. With Rojas and Escalante appear the name of "Luis, mulatto, interpreter of the land of Carlos"—from A.G.I. *Contaduría* 941, fol. 9 (microfilm, P. K. Yonge Library).

the expedition was sent back directly to Spain in the vessel which had been brought from Santander, so that the King might have word of the recovery of the shipwrecked Christians and of the alliance with Indians of Carlos.[39]

Pedro Menéndez turned his fleet northward on the east side of the Florida peninsula, sailing through rough seas. On March 19, 1566, as his convoy moved along the lower southeast coast, lookouts sighted the sails of a southbound caravel. As they drew closer, it was evident that the ship was the *Ascensión*, which had been loaded with corn in Yucatán and sent to supply the forts. When the adelantado boarded the caravel, he could immediately sense what had occurred: he had intercepted the escape of a shipload of mutineers! In addition to the crew of the vessel, the captain, ensign, and entire surviving garrison of the fort at Santa Lucía were aboard. In the last weeks before the relief ship came, rations in the little fort had been systematically reduced—for two weeks, the men received nothing but a bowlful of corn a day. The last four days before the caravel arrived, there was nothing: the supplies had run out. Only 75 of the 250 Spanish soldiers and French prisoners left at Ais had survived. When the ship came to anchor outside the Jupiter Inlet, the rebellious soldiers seized it and forced Captain Juan Vélez de Medrano and Ensign Ayala to come along in an escape from Florida. Grimly, Menéndez took command and turned the caravel around in the direction of St. Augustine.[40]

Worse troubles awaited the adelantado in the north. When he entered the port of St. Augustine on March 21, he quickly learned that there had been a general rising of the soldiery in that fort and at San Mateo. His coming interrupted a formal investigation being conducted by Maestre de Campo Valdés, who brought his superior up to date on the mutinies.[41]

39. See Menéndez' letter to the King, St. Augustine, October 20, 1566, from A.G.I. *Santo Domingo* 231 (Stetson Coll.).

40. Captain Vélez describes the incident in "Información que enbió el General Pedro Meléndez de Avilés sobre cierto motín que passó en la Florida," A.G.I. *Justicia* 999. The caravel can be identified from the list in "Despachos que se hicieron," A.G.I. *Escribanía de Cámara* 1,024-A, and is also mentioned in A.G.I. *Contaduría* 1,174. The description of the number of survivors of the garrison is found in the "Meritos y servicios de Diego López," St. Augustine, December 16, 1569, from the Woodbury Lowery Collection (microfilm, P. K. Yonge Library), I:2:414:265–90.

41. The author has utilized the detailed testimonies about the soldiers' revolts of March 1566 and later in that year which are found in several piezas in A.G.I. *Justicia* 999. It appears that some of this material had originally been located in A.G.I. *Contratación* 58, but is not now to be found in that legajo. The papers were evidently gathered in connection with appeals of the Redroban and Enriquez cases to the Council of the Indies.

Disaffection had begun in the two forts more than two months before. Although some supplies had come into the garrisons from Havana, rations were often meager. Also in short supply were opportunities for entertainment and loot, the basic expectations of the sixteenth-century private soldier. Foci of discontent arose in both forts, and correspondence between the two groups of malcontents was advanced by mid-January. Their purpose was to leave Florida as soon as possible. Pressure from the disaffected men forced Valdés to grant permission for work to begin on the uncompleted frigate left by the French on the ways near the former Fort Caroline. Sergeant Gutierre de Valverde came from St. Augustine to supervise the construction and persuaded twelve captive Frenchmen who were skilled at carpentry and shipbuilding to help get the ship ready for an escape to the Indies.

By mid-February, it was evident that Captains Recalde, Mexia, and San Vicente, some of their noncommissioned sergeants, and many of the men were affected by the rebellious mood—Licenciado Rueda, chaplain of the tercio at St. Augustine, was a leader in the plot. Several of the married settlers were also involved in the conspiracy. One night, while searching for food, a large group of soldiers assembled at the armory and forced Valdés to let them examine the building to see if any supplies had been buried there. They also searched the houses of Juan de Junco and Pedro de Coronas, who were known to be close associates of the adelantado and of Bartolomé Menéndez. None of the civil or military officials could do much in the face of such widespread disaffection. Significantly, those officials who remained loyal were all close associates or relatives of Pedro Menéndez—Pedro de Valdés, Bartolomé Menéndez, Juan de Junco, Captain Ochoa, Diego de Hevia, Pedro de Coronas, Antonio Gómez, Rodrigo Montes, and Martín de Argüelles. Valdés installed himself in the armory to guard the arms and munitions stored there. As things settled into an uneasy truce, it was apparent that only a spark was needed to set off a full-scale revolt.

That spark was provided by the coming of the fragata *La Concepción*, which arrived at the port of St. Augustine in the first week of March 1566. The vessel brought a quantity of corn, more than a ton of prepared meat, and wine, oil, and live hogs—more than two months' rations for both forts. As the news spread that a supply ship had come, the plans of the mutineers quickly took final shape. When the word reached San Mateo, Valverde and Captain San Vicente set out for St. Augustine. On the night of March 8, led by Sebastián de Lezcano, a large number of soldiers assaulted the armory where

Pedro de Valdés was lying ill. Shouting and beating on the doors with their halberds, the soldiers broke their way in and seized Valdés. Soon the other officials were in their power. The maestre de campo was confined in Captain San Vicente's house, and the others were placed in the stocks. The rebels next went to the shore, took small craft, and shortly controlled the fragata at anchor, which they began to prepare for their escape. It appeared that the authority of the King and his adelantado in St. Augustine had come to an end.

It would seem, however, that Pedro de Valdés was as resourceful as was Pedro Menéndez de Avilés. The maestre de campo escaped from imprisonment, freed Junco and the others, and gathered a small nucleus of loyal troops. With these, he hurried to the water's edge, where the mutineers were busily engaged in loading munitions aboard the captured frigate.

Valdés and his men assaulted and took the small boat into which the rebels were loading artillery from the fort. Lezcano was taken prisoner, and the loyalist forces again took charge of the city and the fort. The fragata withdrew to the bar and prepared to sail. Valdés mounted a bronze cannon in a small craft and went to parley with the mutineers, whom he urged not to leave the men, women, and children of St. Augustine without food and munitions. When negotiations broke down, Valdés fired several shots at the rebel vessel, and it sailed away.

Pedro de Valdés began formal legal hearings on the mutinies; he heard Lezcano confess his role in the uprising, and had him hanged on the public gallows. Many of the other guilty parties had departed with the frigate, while some fled inland and were killed by the Indians. About 120 from St. Augustine had left; a similar number had fled San Mateo in the other vessel. The mutineers took with them the books of the cabildo and other papers.[42]

Pedro Menéndez was infuriated when he arrived to find that such "great mutinies, disgraceful insubordinations and . . . treason" had occurred among his garrisons.[43] He moved immediately to restore the discipline of the troops and attempt to locate and punish those who had fled. In a *bando* proclaimed the day after his arrival, the adelantado labeled the actions of the rebel troops as mutiny and treason. He noted the sacrifices which had been made to undertake the *jornada* to Florida, and added that he fully expected another French attempt to

42. See "Order to hang Sebastían Lezcano," St. Augustine, March 13, 1566, from "El Fiscal de Su Majestad con el Capitan Pedro de Redroban," A.G.I. *Justicia* 999.

43. From statement about his arrival given on March 27, 1566, and found in "Información que enbió el General Pedro Meléndez," A.G.I. *Justicia* 999.

conquer the territory. Because he wanted no disaffected soldiers or settlers in his provinces, Menéndez offered to any who wished it the privilege to leave Florida, at their own expense.[44] A number availed themselves of the opportunity.

On March 24, word came to Pedro Menéndez at St. Augustine that the rebel fragata had sailed to the bar of the St. Johns, to await the other mutineers of the San Mateo garrison and sail together to the West Indies or to New Spain. He took three small craft, went directly to the spot, and loaded one of his vessels with corn, to demonstrate that supplies would be furnished to those who renounced the mutiny. Indeed, these seemed to be reluctant rebels. Some of the men returned to the fort at San Mateo, and the fragata delayed its departure while negotiations continued. The adelantado offered amnesty to the men aboard the ship, and some of the men ashore accepted the offer, but the ships finally left in a powerful storm which covered their departure. The mutinies of March had come to an end, but the trials continued so that action could be taken against those who had fled to other parts of the Indies.[45]

The desertions of 1565–66 and the deaths caused by illness, starvation, or Indian action had cut the original Spanish forces in Florida by almost one-half. The fresh soldiers which Pedro Menéndez had brought from Cuba were essential to maintaining a presence in the adelantamiento and to support the start of a new impetus of exploration and colonization. After the garrisons at St. Augustine and San Mateo had been reinforced with more than 200 men, the adelantado directed his fleet northward in early April 1566. He took his primary lieutenant, Esteban de las Alas, to begin the first exploration of the seacoasts of his northern dominions. From the time of the first Ayllón voyage to that of Ángel de Villafañe, much information about these coasts had entered the store of mariners' common knowledge, but this was a more systematic examination of the lands and waters which could yield substantial fruit in the prosecution of the Florida conquest. The official royal geographer, Juan López de Velasco, who used the accounts of Pedro Menéndez' explorations in his work, has described the shore which Menéndez saw: "From the river of San Mateo, the coast runs to the northeast to Santa Elena. The coast is made up entirely of great and small islands, which create many bars and inlets so that, although it seems to be a mainland, it is not."[46]

44. Statement of Pedro Menéndez de Avilés, St. Augustine, March 22, 1566, from "Información que enbió," A.G.I. *Justicia* 999.

45. Pedro Menéndez forwarded the procesos of the cases to the King with his letter written at Havana on July 1, 1566, from A.G.I. *Santo Domingo* 168 (Stetson Coll.).

46. López de Velasco, *Geografía universal de las Indias*, p. 168.

Across this maze of inlets, sounds, and sea islands, land communication was difficult, if not impossible. The Florida adelantado and his entourage, mariners all, chose to conquer, establish, and supply their provinces by sea. The sea route they pioneered was rapid and convenient—it would become the lifeline linking the Florida forts and settlements to the Havana supply base and other points in the Caribbean. A vessel of any size, Menéndez learned, could sail from the St. Augustine–San Mateo area all the way to Santa Elena in a safe depth of more than sixty feet of water. As the low coastline slowly unrolled before the appraising eyes of Pedro Menéndez, his evaluation of each inlet had to do directly with the amount of water over its bar. Thus the large and deep entry at the bar of Sena, where the St. Marys flows out to the sea at the south end of Cumberland Island, was marked down as a strategic place. Ships upward of 200 tons' burden could enter and find harbor there. Since the people who inhabited the area, the Tacatacuru, were allied with Saturiba and hostile to the Spanish, it might be necessary to fortify the river mouth. Other inlets to the north, Gualequeni, Osao, and Ospoque, were shallow and dangerous, and only fragatas or *chalupas* could traverse them.

As the *Santa Catalina* and the smaller escort ships that made up Menéndez' armada of discovery approached the next opening in the belt of shoreline, it became evident that it was a far more commodious and convenient port. The bar and its principal Indian settlements bore the name of Guale. It was evidently the pass at the south end of the island presently called St. Catherine's.[47] Soundings indicated a safe depth of nineteen feet over the bar at low water, enough for substantial vessels.

Leaving his armada at anchor in charge of Esteban de las Alas, Pedro Menéndez took two small craft with fifty men and entered the sound to the westward of the sea island. He moved with caution, as it was here that he expected the possibility of a colony of French, fled from the defeats or shipwrecks of the past year. At about a thousand yards from the bank of the sound, he discovered a village of Indians. The village, a few huts of wattle-and-daub thatched with sabal fronds, was no more impressive than its surroundings. The land west of the sound was marsh, interspersed with low oak hammocks and other

47. After comparing the Velasco derrotero with later maps, I would follow the identification of Guale inlets suggested by John Tate Lanning in *The Spanish Missions of Georgia*, p. 11, and seconded by Zubillaga in *La Florida*, p. 353, and by Verne Chatelain, *The Defenses of Spanish Florida, 1565–1763*, esp. pp. 35–40. The most complete record of the Guale visit in the spring of 1566 is in Solís de Merás, *Pedro Menéndez de Avilés*, pp. 199–210. The missionaries' letters cited by Zubillaga give by far the best view of Guale in the Menéndez years to 1572.

trees; what soil could be seen was sandy. The scant population of Indians eked out part of their living farming scattered cornfields, hunting deer and small game in the scrub or the deeper woods, and
fishing along the shores.

Menéndez did find his "Frenchman" here—a Spaniard who had
come to the area as a part of Ribault's 1562 expedition to Port Royal.
With this ready-made interpreter, named Guillermo, the adelantado
explained his presence and appealed to the Indians for obedience to
Philip II and acceptance of the Catholic faith. The chief at Guale had
heard of the triumphs of the Spanish at Fort Caroline and Matanzas
and was glad to acquiesce in Menéndez' demands. A cross was erected
in the village, and the Spanish and Indian leaders joined in evening
and morning ceremonies of litany and adoration of the Christian
symbol.

A central part of Menéndez' Indian policy was the bringing of
order to broad areas of his provinces—reaching across the parochial
culture boundaries of warring native groups to enforce peace in the
name of the Hapsburg monarch. Thus an overlordship of power
could pacify the land and pave the way for peaceable exploitation.
The adelantado had learned that Guale was at war with the Indians of
Orista, in the vicinity of Santa Elena in the north, where he hoped to
make a major settlement. Now he asked the chief at Guale to yield up
to him two captive Indians from Orista; in return Menéndez would
leave Alonso Menéndez Marquéz and seven other Spaniards as hostage. Menéndez assured the chief, however, that any injury to the
men would mean his return to cut off the heads of those guilty of the of-
fense.

In spite of its poverty, the Spanish retained favorable impressions
of Guale as a future site for colonization. The Indians seemed tractable, and there was a good port for marine supply and reinforcement.
If the soil was poor, then at least the spot could serve as entrepôt into
the interior, where richer lands and mines surely beckoned. As he
had done in Carlos, Menéndez evaluated Guale for its fitness in his
scheme of peripheral settlement at places of strategic importance easily reached by water. If friendly Indian relations could be established
at these key points, his rear would be protected and he would have a
safe path for retreat to the sea.[48]

The fleet left with its hostages and departed for the north. The
northeasterly course of the adelantado's ships carried them past sev-

48. Menéndez described his policy of peripheral settlement in his letter to Philip II,
written from St. Augustine on October 20, 1566, and found in A.G.I. *Santo Domingo*
115 (Stetson Coll.).

eral more inlets, none of which would admit vessels of any draft. They sailed by the shoals at the mouth of the Savannah River and soon approached the great point now called Hilton Head, but long known to the Spanish as the Punta Santa Elena. Beyond it lay the finest harbor in the provinces of Florida, which the French had named Port Royal.

As the Spanish rounded the point they saw a wide entrance, more than six miles across, containing several islands. The south bar lay deep enough to allow the *Santa Catalina* to pass within, but it was swept by strong currents. Pedro Menéndez brought the large ship to anchor and proceeded to explore the harbor in two bergantines with Alas and a hundred soldiers. He spied an island placed advantageously in the center of the harbor entrance. Its seaward point, he noted, held a white sand-hill eminence that would be ideal for fortification.[49]

The expedition passed further into the port and surprised a number of Indians near an old burned village. With the aid of the interpreter brought from Guale, they identified themselves, to the great pleasure of both parties. When the Indians discovered that Menéndez had brought back the captive Oristans, their delight increased, and a formal parley was arranged with cacique Orista. The adelantado of Florida utilized the ceremony of returning the prisoners who had been held in Guale to proffer Spanish peace and order and the Christianization of the tribe. Chief Orista retired to consult with his council and returned directly to accept the offer. Menéndez then agreed to leave men among them to learn their language and to teach them the rudiments of Christianity.

The Orista Indians lived in several groupings around and to the north of the main harbor of Port Royal. They were somewhat greater in numbers than the Guale people and they appear to have been more closely integrated in culture. Although dedicated to the cultivation of corn and other crops, they were still attuned to the rhythms of the acorn harvest and the seasonal runs of fish in the ocean and bays, and they moved their residence during these times.

The Spanish commander chose the site for his city with an eye to strategic considerations and in line with his desire to be near the centers of Indian population, yet not directly among them. The central

49. The descriptions of the port of Santa Elena or Port Royal are taken from the contemporary account of López de Velasco, in *Geografía universal de las Indias*, pp. 161, 169. The specific location of Menéndez' first fort there was also described in the "Derrotero que hizo Andrés González, piloto de la Florida, del viage que verificó al Xacán," from A.G.I. *Patronato* 19, no. 1, ramo 31.

island in the harbor, now named Parris Island, became the location of the second municipality founded in the adelantamiento of Florida. Here the dual entities—the city of Santa Elena and the fort of San Salvador—were built around the high sand bluffs, a little distance from the Ribault settlement of 1562–64. Although there was fertile soil to be found in some parts of the great bay, the island chosen for settlement and fortification did not have particularly good soil. Menéndez named Esteban de las Alas to govern both the civil and military elements of the district, making him alcaide of the fort and governor of the province of Santa Elena.[50] The municipal *regimiento* and cabildo was formed for what promised to be the center of the King's dominions in Florida. Again, the location of settlement was directly related to marine access and established in this case upon a fine deep-water port.

It was now time for Menéndez to begin the return voyage down the east coast of his territories, for it would shortly be necessary to return the large galleon and her crew to the New Spain fleet as escort for the homeward journey to Spain. On his way south, he would stop at Guale and then inspect the peninsular garrisons, still shaky in morale after the mutinies. At Havana, Menéndez would endeavor to pump more resources into his supply pipeline, which had continued to function during the late winter and early spring of 1566, bringing corn from Yucatán, and wine, biscuit, cassava, vegetables, pork, live chickens, goats, and sheep from Cuba.[51] Now that Santa Elena had been added to the route, the small ships would touch there also. The adelantado promised the men he had left in Fort San Salvador that he would send them supplies in very short order, but keeping that promise might be difficult, for Menéndez' resources were becoming slim indeed. If the promised fleet of reinforcement from Spain did not soon arrive, it would be difficult for him to continue the enterprise.

When Menéndez came to St. Augustine he found that raiding Indians had attacked and burned the fort built near Seloy's village. Many of the papers of the expedition, a quantity of food and munitions, and the French banners and trophies captured the previous fall were destroyed in the fire. The fire sharpened the problem of supply-

---

50. Alas' first appointment is affirmed in his later nombramiento as governor of Florida, found in A.G.I. *Contaduría* 941 (microfilm, P. K. Yonge Library), under the date of August 1566.

51. The shipments, carried from February through May, 1566, in the navios *La Ascensión, Santa Ysabel,* and *San Simón,* in the pataches *San Sebastián, Buenaventura,* and *San Mateo,* the fragata *Espíritu Santo,* and the bergantín *San Antón,* are detailed in A.G.I. *Contaduría* 1,174 and described in "Los despachos que se hicieron," from A.G.I. *Escribanía de Cámara* 1,024-A.

ing all of the forts, for there was little left in Florida, and another voyage to Havana had become urgently necessary.[52]

The adelantado arrived at the Cuban port in mid-May 1566. The supplies he had found aboard the *Santa Catalina* when it was taken for his service had been exhausted, and Menéndez had to supply the soldiers and crew aboard at his cost. Menéndez was not yet ready to release the big ship from his service, for he had another voyage to make. On May 25, 1566, he left Havana to make a rapid trip to Carlos. He wanted to further cement his relationship with the chief there, and had promised to bring Doña Antonia, his "wife," to Havana with other Indians for instruction in the Christian faith.[53]

The little fleet from Florida reentered the harbor at Havana on June 7, and Pedro Menéndez dismissed the large ship which had served him so well. The rough seas along the Florida coasts that winter had taken their toll, for the *Santa Catalina*'s owner complained that the vessel was returned in badly damaged condition. Four of the crew had died on the voyages (one at the hands of the Indians), and twenty-six remained in Florida.[54] The adelantado established the first household of instruction for the Indians of Florida in Havana; when the religious personnel arrived to take charge, they would have a body of potential Christians for their pupils.

Again the Florida leader attempted to obtain aid for the royal troops in Florida from the governor at Havana. For the second time, García Osorio refused to use funds of the Havana treasury for any such purpose; this time, a member of the Council of the Indies and the Royal Officials at Havana were also involved in his action. In February 1566, the King had written the Havana officials ordering them to give the Florida adelantado the supplies he needed, since they had not been forthcoming from Santo Domingo. When the royal cédula

52. Menéndez' promise to supply Santa Elena quickly was described by Licenciado Godoy in "Governor Osorio sobre los amotinados de Santa Elena," Havana, July 5, 1566, from A.G.I. *Justicia* 999. The burning of the fort and the destruction of its contents were mentioned in A.G.I. *Justicia* 817, no. 5, and in "Información ante el Alcalde desta Corte," Madrid, October 16, 1567, from A.G.I. *Escribanía de Cámara* 1,024-A.

53. The Solís de Merás narrative and the work of Felix Zubillaga appear to have confused and merged the two voyages to the Calusa area, that of February and that of May 1566. The register of ship sailings from "Los despachos que se hicieron," in A.G.I. *Escribanía de Cámara* 1,024-A clearly shows that the second voyage was for the purpose of bringing Doña Antonia to Havana.

54. Xímeno de Bretendoña, the owner of *Santa Catalina*, outlined the damages caused in the Florida expedition in his petition for larger charter fees in a petition found in A.G.I. *Indiferente General* 2,673. The return of the vessel is also mentioned in "Información de Pedro Menéndez de Avilés, Seville, 1567–68," A.G.I. *Contratación* 4,802 (Stetson Coll.).

was received in Cuba, the licenciado Gerónimo Valderrama, was present. The governor, Valderrama, and the King's officials met to discuss Menéndez' requests for supplies and aid. It was Valderrama's opinion that nothing should be given until a specific order should come from the Audiencia of Santo Domingo to that effect. García Osorio, for his part, said that Pedro Menéndez would have to pay for whatever he got.[55] Gerónimo Valderrama, who had been away from Spain for more than two years, was hardly in any position to have had much knowledge of the Florida venture. His involvement with Osorio, Menéndez, and the Royal Officials in Havana must have been nothing more than a matter of momentary judgment and was not a formal examination of the affairs of Florida. His record in New Spain indicates that the man was inclined to weigh all government matters in the light of strict observance of His Majesty's ordinances and stern protection of the royal fisc. His legalistic reaction was entirely predictable.

In the first week of July, and just before the departure of Menéndez for Florida again, both García Osorio and Pedro Menéndez wrote to the King. The adelantado's letter is disappointing to the historian, for it refers to a letter Menéndez had written Philip II from Santa Elena in early May and notes that Gonzalo Solís de Merás, who was coming to Spain, would furnish more particular information. Both men, in their letters, asked the King to seek further data about the Florida enterprise from Valderrama, who was returning to Spain with the same fleet after his visit to New Spain. In his dispatch, Governor Osorio refuted coolly the accusations Menéndez had made against him to the King, saying that he had done all he reasonably could for Menéndez, and that Valderrama would vindicate him.[56]

The adelantado obtained more cash or credit and was able to purchase additional supplies and munitions for his enterprise. On the same day he had written his letter to the King, Menéndez left Havana to carry supplies to his forts along the now well known route. As Pedro Menéndez returned to the Florida provinces, the expedition sent from Spain under the command of Sancho de Archiniega was completing its voyage. The ships had followed the usual route for ves-

55. The refusal to aid Menéndez is described in a letter from Juan de Hinestrosa and Juan de Carteaga to the Crown, Havana, December 24, 1568, from A.G.I. *Santo Domingo* 115 (Stetson Coll.). Solís de Merás mentions the episode in *Pedro Menéndez de Avilés*, p. 141. The visita of Licenciado Valderrama is detailed by Mariano Cuevas in *Historia de la Iglesia en Mexico*, 2:70, 95, 122, 180–90, 252–53, 324.

56. See Pedro Menéndez de Avilés to Crown, Havana, July 1, 1566, from A.G.I. *Santo Domingo* 168 (Stetson Coll.) and Garcia Osorio to Crown, Havana, July 3, 1566, from A.G.I. *Santo Domingo* 115 (Stetson Coll.).

sels outbound from Spain to the Indies; they had reached Grand Canary on May 4. On June 10, the worst of their journey over, the fleet entered the harbor of San Juan in Puerto Rico after watering at Dominica. Sancho de Archiniega wrote Philip II that he received a letter in Puerto Rico which described the sufferings and starvation of the Spaniards and French at Santa Lucía in Florida. It also told him of Menéndez' "marriage" to the sister of an Indian cacique—evidently a reference to the happenings in Carlos. Archiniega also advised his King that cannibal Carib Indians had killed most of the survivors from Pedro Menéndez' ship lost the year before in Guadeloupe.[57]

The further journey from Puerto Rico to Florida was routine, except that one of the vessels, the *San Salvador*, strayed from the rest and found harbor at Puerto de Plata on the northeast coast of Santo Domingo. There sixty men from the company of Captain Andrada became embroiled in controversy when their sergeant, Diego de Buytrago, attempted to lead them in the capture of a Portuguese ship which had anchored in that port. The arrival of the men in Florida was delayed while a case was tried; the Audiencia of Santo Domingo later sentenced Buytrago to three years at the oar in the galleys for murder.[58]

Great was the rejoicing in the fort and town of St. Augustine when, on June 29, 1566, a large fleet of Spanish vessels was seen off the bar. Their coming meant reinforcement, supplies, and the bolstering of the will to persist in Florida. Since the adelantado had not yet returned from his last voyage to Havana, Bartolomé Menéndez made the necessary formal welcomes in his name. Hernando de Miranda began his duties as royal factor by receiving the ships officially. Then he and Juan de Junco acknowledged receipt of the soldiers and cargoes that the vessels had brought. The King's reinforcements had arrived, and the belated royal support could not have come at a better time.[59]

57. The passage of Archiniega's ships and the accounts of his almiranta are discussed in a large pieza in A.G.I. *Contratación* 3,259 (Stetson Coll.). This legajo also contains a list of the Florida troops aboard; many of these same men can also be identified by later petitions for their back pay; these are found in A.G.I. *Contaduría* 310-B; I am indebted to Paul E. Hoffman for this citation. Archiniega's letter to the King is dated at San Juan on June 11, 1566, and is from A.G.I. *Santo Domingo* 71 (Stetson Coll.).

58. See "Peticion de Diego de Buytrago," seen in Madrid on March 31, 1568, from A.G.I. *Indiferente General* 1,220. The murder case is found in A.G.I. *Justicia* 1,000, no. 1, ramo 1.

59. A record of some of the formalities at St. Augustine when the fleet arrived there is found in A.G.I. *Contratación* 58.

The Struggle Continues

In contrast to his feelings of the previous summer, the Spanish King could feel a degree of satisfaction by mid-1566 about affairs in Florida. He had learned fully of the victory of his adelantado there and had dispatched to him a fleet of reinforcement. In a mood of approbation, Philip II wrote Menéndez late in the spring, praising his acts and acknowledging all of his dispatches sent from August through December of the previous year. The King advised that he was sending formal confirmation of the appointments of captains and officials that Pedro Menéndez had made; he noted his approval of Menéndez' seizure of the Portuguese caravel taken off Cuba, and he supported him in the Parra controversy with García Osorio. On the same date, a royal letter of commendation was sent to Bartolomé Menéndez.[1]

Another of Pedro Menéndez' protegés was soon to be honored, as the adelantado had wished. On July 5, 1566, Captain Diego Flores Valdés was named general of the Tierra Firme fleet which would next leave Spain for the Indies.[2] Thus the influence of the Menéndez coterie in the Carrera de Indias continued, even while many of its members were heavily engaged in the Florida enterprise.

1. The King's letter is dated at Madrid on May 12, 1566, and has been reprinted in Lawson, "Letters of Menéndez," 2:296–300. The letter to Bartolomé Menéndez is found in "Bartolomé Menéndez con el Fiscal sobre sueldo, 1570," from A.G.I. *Indiferente General* 1,219. The King also granted to Pedro Menéndez Marquéz a merced of 300 ducats for the news he brought in dispatches from Florida. This is cited by Martin Menéndez de Avilés in a letter dated at Madrid on June 9, 1633, and found in A.G.I. *Santo Domingo* 233.

2. The appointment of Diego Flores Valdés as Fleet General is from A.G.I. *Indiferente General* 738, ramo 8.

By spring of 1566, the news of the slaughters at Matanzas and Fort Caroline had provoked a formal reaction from the Valois court. On June 18, Ambassador Fourquevaux filed a second written protest on behalf of the French King against the acts of Pedro Menéndez in Florida. He presented his protest in an audience with Philip II, who took the matter under advisement. The French ambassador followed up his protest with a detailed letter about the situation of individual French prisoners being held in Florida, Cuba, Puerto Rico, and Spain. When the Spanish ruler gave Fourquevaux his reply, he decreed that all female prisoners and their children under fourteen years of age could return to Seville, where they would be freed. The men would also be brought to the Andalusian port, where their cases would be tried under Spanish law by the Casa de Contratación. Philip II refused, however, to categorize Pedro Menéndez or his acts as criminal.[3]

By midsummer 1566, events in the Netherlands dominions of Philip II clearly justified substantial concern. The King's efforts to enforce obedience to the Tridentine decrees he had proclaimed, together with some episcopal reforms of his own, had brought first passive and then active resistance. As Philip II pondered the conflicting advice of his counsellors in this matter, the directive he sent Margaret of Parma, the regent, was at first conciliatory. His decision finally to take a hard line was dictated by the outbreak of the iconoclastic fervor which swept Flanders in August 1566. After that time, rebellion and heresy in the Netherlands were fused in the mind of the King, and he determined to send an army shortly to enforce his will. A new battleground in the worldwide war against "the Lutheran sect" was about to open, but this did not make the needs of the Indies any less pressing. Having expended much upon Florida, Philip II was prepared to spend more. He had already authorized a shipload of supplies for the royal troops in Florida to serve as a backup for the original Menéndez and the Archiniega expeditions. The urca *Pantecras* was loaded with food and munitions and sent with its Flemish master at a cost to the Crown of more than 26,000 ducats.[4] It sailed June 28, 1566.

The urca contained a vital cargo of another kind: two priests, a brother of the Society of Jesus and an interpreter, sent to Florida to begin the great effort of evangelization of the Florida Indians. Thus the "shock-troops of the Counter-Reformation" would furnish the

3. For a discussion and documentation of Fourquevaux' plaint and the reply of the Spanish King, see Lyon, "Captives of Florida," pp. 18–20.

4. The cost of the *Pantecras* is described in items from A.G.I. *Contaduría* 294, no. 2b, 6:2–4; 304, no. 1, 102:4–103:1; 306, no. 2, 124:1. These citations were kindly furnished by Paul E. Hoffman.

necessary spiritual weapons in the struggle against heresy. Pedro de Bustinçury, the Basque who had for many years been a captive of the Ais on the east coast of the peninsula, would aid the missionaries in their communication with the Indians until they could themselves learn the languages of Florida.[5]

Pedro Menéndez had considered other religious orders for the work in Florida, but he had been in contact with the Jesuits for some time. His friendship with Diego de Avellaneda, the provincial of Andalusia, dated back to the time of his imprisonment in the Atarazanas in 1563–64. During his preparations for the 1565 journey in Seville, Menéndez had written Francisco de Borja, then vicar-general of the order, asking for missionaries for Florida. Within sixty days, Borja replied, giving his approval and advising that he would attempt to send three missionaries.

Although the necessary formalities with the Casa de Contratación were completed in time for Jesuits to sail with the Archiniega expedition, it appears that internal complications in the society prevented it. Examination of the correspondence of the missionaries with their superiors and of the qualifications of the men chosen for the task reveals the zeal and the quality of the Jesuit mission. The order which served as the cutting edge of conversion and religious restoration in Europe and overseas was characterized by organizational discipline and personal dedication. These qualities were now to be put to the test in the Jesuits' first commitment to American missions. The three men chosen were Fathers Pedro Martínez and Juan Rogel and Brother Francisco Villareal. They spent the time prior to the departure of the urca preaching to the men in the New Spain fleet and preparing themselves spiritually for the tasks ahead.

While the Spanish Crown was busily engaged in the supply and support of Florida, Pedro Menéndez' agents were no less busy. Pedro Menéndez Marquéz, who had come from Cuba with his uncle's

5. For the Florida Jesuit missions, I have relied upon a body of materials from Jesuit archives published in three fine works. The first, in point of time, is Ruben Vargas Ugarte, "The First Jesuit Mission in Florida." Next is Felix Zubillaga's *La Florida*, and the last is the work in which he published the documentation, *Monumenta Antiquae Floridae*. The mission had begun with a request from Pedro Menéndez de Avilés to Francisco de Borja sent from Madrid in March 1565, and reprinted in *Monumenta Antiquae Floridae*, pp. 1–4. Borja replied to the adelantado favorably from Rome on May 12, 1565 (*Monumenta Antiquae Floridae*, pp. 6–8). Royal approval of the mission was given by Philip II in a letter sent to Diego Carrillo, Provincial of the Order, from Ucles on April 9, 1565 (*Monumenta Antiquae Floridae*, pp. 42–44). The voyages of Pedro de Bustincury are described in a letter from the Casa to the Crown, Seville, February 17, 1568, from A.G.I. *Contratación* 5,168, and in a payment to him before his journey in 1566 authorized in A.G.I. *Contaduría* 294, no. 2, *data* 123:1–124:1.

dispatches, visited Pedro del Castillo in Cádiz. He then went to the court and thence to Asturias to restock the vessel *San Sebastián* for the journey to Florida. In the port of Cangas, Menéndez Marquéz' supervised the loading of the vessel. In addition to the items of food and drink permitted by the Florida asiento, he also loaded tar, rigging, ship fastenings, and cloth—illegal cargo under the King's contract.[6]

After Menéndez Marquéz' departure from Cádiz, bad news reached Pedro del Castillo there. One of Menéndez' pataches had been taken by Turkish galleys off the Andalusian coast on its way from Santo Domingo, the second ship from Florida to be seized in a few months. Castillo had other problems as well, for the Casa representative in Cádiz, Juan de Abalia, was delaying the sailing of other vessels of the adelantado. Pedro del Castillo protested about this to the King and also asked again for the payment of back charter fees due on the *San Miguel* and the *San Pelayo*. It was now known that the great galeass had been destroyed on the Danish coast.[7]

As the ships bearing supplies, reinforcements, and missionaries left Spain for Florida, the French were also preparing ships for an Indies venture. More than twenty vessels were being outfitted in Norman and Breton ports for a major raid upon Spanish and Portuguese commerce.

Meanwhile, in Florida, while the Archiniega expedition began to disembark its soldiery and unload supplies and munitions in St. Augustine, Pedro Menéndez had not yet returned from his most recent trip to Havana. His major lieutenants at St. Augustine, Pedro de Valdés, Bartolomé Menéndez, Hernando de Miranda, and Juan de Junco, agreed with the leaders of the expedition to send the two largest ships to Santa Elena with supplies. It was agreed that pilot Gonzalo Gayón, experienced from the Villafañe and Manrique de Rojas expeditions to that place, would guide the ships. Captain Juan Pardo's company of 250 men came aboard as reinforcement for the northern garrison. By July 18, the relief ships had arrived at Santa Elena.[8]

6. Menéndez Marquéz' voyage and the cargo of his ship are detailed in A.G.I. *Patronato* 257, no. 4, ramo 1.

7. The loss of Menéndez' patache is described in a letter from the Casa to the Crown, Seville, August 2, 1566, from A.G.I. *Contratación* 5,167. In a letter sent August 28, 1566, and found in A.G.I. *Indiferente General* 1,967, Philip II chided Abalia for delaying the sailing of Menéndez' ships. The loss of the *San Pelayo* is mentioned in "Memorial de los navios cargados de bastimentos y municiones que se perdieron el Adelantado," from A.G.I. *Escribanía de Cámara* 1,024-A.

8. See the declaration of Esteban de las Alas, from the city of San Salvador, punta of Santa Elena, July 18, 1566, from A.G.I. *Santo Domingo* 11 (Stetson Coll.).

When the adelantado landed again in Florida, he touched first at the St. Johns River and learned to his inexpressible relief and satisfaction that the Archiniega fleet had arrived. By July 10, Menéndez was in St. Augustine where he met with Sancho de Archiniega to arrange the disposition and division of the forces which he had brought.

The two men agreed that 750 soldiers, one-half of the new reinforcements, would remain in the Florida forts. Captain Pedro de Redroban, an experienced military engineer, remained in St. Augustine with his company to aid in reconstruction of the fort. Another officer who had arrived with Archiniega, Miguel de Enriquez, was also stationed at the first settlement. Colonel Orsuna had not come to Florida, and his company was assigned to Juan de Vascocaval. The company of Captain Martín de Ochoa remained at San Mateo; the fort there was still commanded by Sargento Mayor Gonzalo de Villaroel. Death and the desertion of some officers had left some companies decimated and others leaderless. Francisco de Reinoso was promoted to captain and assigned the men who would shortly leave for the new fort at Carlos. Captain Juan Vélez de Medrano of Ais and Captain Zurita would go with the adelantado on his voyage to reinforce the Caribbean islands. Until they left, the forces designated for the West Indies expedition could stiffen Menéndez' forces for special missions he had planned in Florida.

To replace the military organization he had used to defeat the French, Pedro Menéndez had prepared a system of regional lieutenants exercising civil and military powers under the overall command of another subordinate. As the adelantado planned a journey of some months in the islands and a lengthy voyage to Spain in the coming year, he decided to act as an absentee overlord and leave Florida to be administered by his norteño associates.

It was now time for Pedro Menéndez to go north for his final tour of inspection of the new settlements made there in the spring. After his vessels left St. Augustine, the adelantado paused at San Mateo on August 1 to commission an expedition to the north. It was Menéndez' plan that it probe for the "Bahia de Santa María" and the Western Passage while Don Luis de Velasco, the Jacán chieftain, made the first contact with the Indians there. The adelantado also instructed his men to reaffirm the Spanish dynastic claims by taking formal possession of the lands in the name of Philip II. An Asturian relative of Menéndez, Pedro de Coronas, was promoted to captain and directed to share authority for the expedition with Dominican friar Pablo de San Pedro. A skilled pilot, Domingo Fernández, and fifteen soldiers rounded out the contingent, which sailed in the patache *La Trinidad* on August 3, 1566.[9] Pedro Menéndez had already sailed for Santa Elena.

When the adelantado dropped anchor in the Santa Elena harbor, he discovered that the garrison had almost been wiped out in June by a mutiny which had followed much the same course as those in the south. The arrival of the promised supply vessel had precipitated a full-scale revolt. Trouble had flared earlier when a *junta* of dissatisfied soldiers forced Esteban de las Alas to permit them to wander inland seeking food from the Indians. Next the leaders of the mutineers seized the Spanish commander and Captain Pedro de Larrandia and put them in irons. The rebels divided the meager supplies and munitions in the fort and left some with the twenty-six men who chose to remain with their leaders at Santa Elena. The mutineers then deserted the enterprise of Florida by sailing away with the captured vessel and a French Huguenot pilot, Phillipe Buser. Their adventure ended at Tequesta in Biscayne Bay for some; for the rest, it ended in their capture by Governor Osorio in Cuba more than a month later.[10]

The infusion of men and supplies provided by the Archiniega expedition allowed Pedro Menéndez to turn around the situation at Santa Elena. When he arrived, Menéndez found that Pardo and de las Alas had the situation under control and had arrived at a modus vivendi, in which the captain scrupulously observed the jurisdiction of the senior official. The adelantado allotted enough soldiers to build and man a larger and better fort. With the rest, Juan Pardo was to undertake a lengthy exploration into the interior of Florida and was to seek the land and water route to New Spain, thus completing the unfinished work of Hernando de Soto. Menéndez' most significant action at Santa Elena was governmental, for he shifted the center of the adelantamiento of Florida. Esteban de las Alas was named chief lieutenant and was to exercise his control from Santa Elena, which became the capital of Florida. Alas' appointment as governor and as captain-general was dated August 1566.[11] In St. Augustine and at San Mateo, the regional governors Bartolomé Menéndez and Gonzalo

9. The abortive expedition to the land of Jacán has been depicted in an excellent monograph by Louis-André Vigneras, entitled "A Spanish Discovery of North Carolina in 1566." The main primary source is A.G.I. *Patronato* 257, no. 3, ramo 4 (Stetson Coll.), dated August 1, 1566. The names of the soldiers assigned to the expedition are found in the ration list in A.G.I. *Contaduría* 941 (microfilm, P. K. Yonge Library).

10. The best source of information about the Santa Elena mutiny is the testimony before Governor Osorio of Cuba taken in Havana on July 19, 1566, from A.G.I. *Justicia* 999.

11. "Nombramiento of Esteban de las Alas, Governador y Capitan-General," August 1566, Santa Elena, from A.G.I. *Contaduría* 941, fol. 2 vto. (microfilm, P. K. Yonge Library).

Villaroel would continue to exercise their offices. Juan de Junco remained in the office of tenedor de bastimentos at St. Augustine while Thomas Alonso de Alas carried out the same duties in Santa Elena.

On August 17, Menéndez paused at Guale, on his return journey south, to leave Captain Pedro de Larrandia, whom he had detached from the Santa Elena garrison. Six soldiers were left with him, and they began a small fort near the Indian settlements.[12] By the twenty-eighth of the month, the adelantado reached San Mateo and found that there had been a second rebellion in the peninsular garrisons. This time, the uprising had been quickly discovered and contained, and there was little for Menéndez to do but hear the legal appeals of the prisoners who were still alive. This time, the troubles had also begun in the garrison of Fort San Mateo.[13] Dissension centered in the company of Captain Pedro Redroban, although soldiers from other companies were also involved. Unhappy with the land and their assignment in Florida, the soldiers had become tense because of the continual Indian raids and had begun to whisper of desertion. In the forts, there was talk of treasure in the land of Carlos, there for any man to take. Redroban's sergeant, Pedro de Pando, and his cousin, Joaquín de Redroban, formed a party whose aim it was to go overland to Carlos. After making themselves rich, the rebels planned to make their way to New Spain and be forever freed of the misery of service in Florida. More than a hundred men banded together and set out, but had gone only a short distance when they were intercepted and halted by Pedro de Valdés. He promptly put the leaders of the party on trial. Gonzalo Villaroel arrested Joaquín de Redroban at San Mateo and his trial began August 13. On the twenty-fourth, Valdés issued a formal order that the man be hanged for his "enormous and atrocious guilt." As Villaroel prepared to carry out the order, Redroban approached the court through his *procurador* to make a formal appeal to the adelantado.

The time had come for Menéndez to grasp firmly the nettle of the Indian problem which his garrisons faced in the whole of the lower St. Johns. Throughout the year, the Spanish had continued to suffer casualties from Indian raids. Succinct marginal comments in the Florida ration lists indicate that many of the killed and wounded had

12. The names of the soldiers of Guale are found in the ration lists in A.G.I. *Contaduría* 941 (microfilm, P. K. Yonge Library), under the date of assignment of August 17, 1566.

13. Documentation of this mutiny is from "El Fiscal de su Majestad con el Capitan Pedro de Redroban," A.G.I. *Justicia* 999. Pedro de Valdés describes the events in his letter to the King sent from St. Augustine on September 12, 1566, from A.G.I. *Santo Domingo* 168 (Stetson Coll., incorrectly labeled from Juan de Valdés).

been caught in ambush. When the Indians suddenly attacked with bows and arrows, the Spanish were unable quickly to return fire with their arquebuses, and the little skirmishes often ended with several Spanish dead. Menéndez proposed to protect his men with padded cotton jackets (*escupiles*) which had been used in New Spain and Yucatán and further planned to augment his firepower with crossbows, which could come into action rapidly and cover the arquebusman while he prepared to fire his awkward weapon.

In contravention of his royal orders and contrary to his own expressed policy, Pedro Menéndez found himself forced to practice alliance politics with the Indians in order to lessen the attacks upon his men. The hostility of Saturiba and his allies, who occupied the lower St. Johns and the mouth of the St. Marys River, made some action essential. The adelantado chose to attempt to immobilize his opposition, and he prepared for a voyage up the St. Johns. Among the allies and enemies of Saturiba, still uneasy from the wars in the time of Laudonnière, he might be able to make some profitable treaties. At the same time, he could test his theory of a water route across the peninsula.

At the end of August 1566, with three small craft and a hundred men, Menéndez made his way upriver.[14] Not twenty miles from San Mateo, he came to the village of Utina, who had once been captured by Laudonnière. That chief was most wary of entanglements with the Spanish, as he had already suffered considerably from involvement with Europeans, and he refused to treat with Menéndez. The expedition passed on southward, camping at night under guard on river beaches on the cypress shoreline. The Spanish bypassed the towns of Chief Calabay, near the great double bend in the river near present-day Palatka, traversed Lake George, and found the river noticeably more narrow. Further on, they knew, lay the land of Mayaca.[15]

14. The adelantado analyzed the warfare methods of the Florida Indians and his suggested countermeasures in his letter to Philip II from St. Augustine on October 20, 1566, from A.G.I. *Santo Domingo* 115 (Stetson Coll.). A typical action, related by Pedro de Valdés in his September 12 letter (see note 13), ended in the death of three Spaniards in a cornfield ten miles from St. Augustine on September 7, 1566. Solís de Merás recounts the casualties in Indian raids in *Pedro Menéndez de Avilés*, p. 196. Deaths of men by Indian action are listed in the marginal comments on the ration lists in A.G.I. *Contaduría* 941 (microfilm, P. K. Yonge Library). I disagree with the chronology of the St. Johns expedition given by Solís de Merás in *Pedro Menéndez de Avilés*, pp. 237–52, and repeated by Zubillaga, *La Florida*, p. 262, no. 23, in which they fix the date at July 1566. The Valdés letter of September 12 fixes the limits of Menéndez' trip to Guale and Santa Elena as August 1 to August 28; this is confirmed by the appearance of the adelantado at the Redroban appeal on September 13. On this point, Solís de Merás was not an eyewitness—he had already left for Spain.

15. The outline of the lands under direct or indirect control of Chief Mayaca can be

Menéndez met with no success in dealing with the Mayaca Indians. After finding the main village empty and deserted, the Spaniards advanced in their boats until they reached a narrow point in the river. There they were threatened by hostiles with bow and arrow and they found the waterway blocked with stakes. There was no negotiation with Chief Mayaca; neither had the water passage to the Gulf been found. There was nothing to do but to return the way they had come.

On the voyage downriver, however, Menéndez realized some fruitful advantage from his expedition. After tentative but favorable contact with the Calabay chief, the Spaniards left some soldiers to begin the teaching of a simplified Gospel. This move stirred the jealousy of Saturiba and the interest of Utina and even of Mayaca. The adelantado was finally able to send catechists and gifts to Utina and Mayaca.

When he returned to San Mateo, Pedro Menéndez was in time to preside over the appeal of the mutiny case against Joaquín Redroban. The case was heard aboard a ship anchored off the fort and was very brief, for the adelantado simply noted that he was busily occupied with the dispatch of his West Indies expedition and remanded the convicted man back to Sargento Mayor Villaroel. Redroban was probably hanged; Valdés notes that three of the guilty were executed and three others sentenced to ten years' galley service. A continually widening circle of suspicion soon included Captain Pedro de Redroban. Although there seems no valid evidence that he was involved in the mutiny plot, Captain Redroban was arrested on September 12. The mutinies of 1566 had come to an end, but their unwholesome effects would continue to be felt.

After his return to St. Augustine, Pedro Menéndez commissioned his experienced chief pilot, Gonzalo Gayón, to make a journey to Mayaca. Gayón was ordered to take a small ship down the east coast and treat with the chief for the ransom of French and Spanish captives reputedly in his possession.[16] Menéndez also sent Francisco de

---

roughly estimated by consulting two Spanish derroteros. The first is "Provanza hecha a pedimiento de Gonzalo de Gayón," from A.G.I. *Santo Domingo* 11 (Stetson Coll.). Gayón was sent south in the fall of 1566 from St. Augustine to seek Mayaca from the seacoast, and stated that the villages near the coast owed allegiance to Mayaca. In the Mexía derrotero of 1605 (see pp. 129–30*n*50), the explorer wrote that "Mayaca and its surrounding towns are on the San Mateo River [the St. Johns], three days' travel from Nocoroco on a poor road." Nocoroco was an Indian town located north of the Mosquito (Ponce de León) Inlet. See John W. Griffin and Hale G. Smith, "Nocoroco—A Timucua Village of 1605 Now in Tomoka State Park." I feel that a line drawn south of Lake George eastward to the seacoast and one from the Orlando metropolitan area to the Cape would probably define the northern and southern boundaries of the Mayaca culture.

16. From "Provanza hecha . . . Gonzalo de Gayón" (see note 15).

Reinoso, promoted to captain, to establish a fort and colony at Carlos, near the other end of the supposed waterway. With him went twelve soldiers, six of them noblemen and six farmer-soldiers, the Indian heir to Chief Carlos, and two interpreters. The mission of Reinoso and the others was to win the confidence of the chief, build a fort, and begin the cultivation of the land.[17]

As he prepared the ships and men which were to embark with him on his anti-corsair expedition, Pedro Menéndez was saddened to learn of the unfortunate results of the voyage of the urca *Pantecras*. News was brought to St. Augustine that the relief ship had lost its way and put a small craft ashore to seek directions to St. Augustine. The boat, with Father Martínez, one of the Jesuit missionaries, aboard, was attacked by the Indians on September 29, 1566. The priest and three other men were killed, not far from San Mateo. Before their mission had fairly begun, the Jesuits had already obtained a martyr. The urca, unable to find the Florida ports, went on to Havana to unload its supplies.[18]

After establishing more firmly his system of government for the control of the Florida provinces, the adelantado next filled out his scheme with more detailed regulations. The lessons of the mutinies on the Indian River and at St. Augustine, San Mateo, and Santa Elena were not lost upon him. After due consideration by the cabildo in St. Augustine, Pedro Menéndez published seventeen ordinances for the governing of Florida. These regulations ran the gamut from military discipline, through religious instruction in the forts, to the powers and functions of the cabildos.[19]

By voice and trumpet, Menéndez had the ordinances proclaimed in the fort and city of St. Augustine and had them conveyed also to the other Spanish Florida settlements. The adelantado prefaced his laws with a discourse on why previous attempts to settle Florida had been a dismal failure; he felt that poor discipline and lack of firm authority had doomed the other efforts of conquest and evangelization. Now,

17. See Menéndez' letter to Philip II, St. Augustine, October 20, 1566, from A.G.I. *Santo Domingo* 115 (Stetson Coll.). The soldiers assigned to Carlos are listed in A.G.I. *Contaduría* 941 (microfilm, P. K. Yonge Library).

18. The adelantado described the loss of Father Martínez in a letter to Diego de Avellaneda written from St. Augustine on October 15, 1566, and reprinted in *Monumenta Antiquae Floridae*, pp. 89–99. Father Juan Rogel also related the killing of the priest in his letters to Pedro Hernandez sent from Monte Christi on November 11, 1566, and reproduced in *Monumenta Antiquae Floridae*, pp. 99–128.

19. "Ordinances which the very illustrious Senor Pedro Menéndez, Governor and Captain-General of the land and the coast of the Provinces of Florida for His Majesty and Adelantado of them provided and instituted in these said provinces of Florida," n.d. [September 1566], from A.G.I. *Justicia* 999.

he said, victory had been gained over the French heretics and His Majesty had sent 1,500 troops to support his untiring efforts in the land. So that this enterprise, too, should not fail, the regulations had been established.

The punishments set in the ordinances for deviations from military order and discipline were very harsh. Insubordination, blasphemy, or fighting with sword or dagger were punished by time in the stocks, whipping, deprivation of rations, months at hard labor on the fortifications, perpetual sentence to the galleys, or death. Attendance at mass and the learning of the catechism was obligatory upon the garrison, on pain of punishment.

In Florida, the ancient Spanish municipal institutions were utilized as the means for both civil and military government. In each fort, the cabildo was to meet twice weekly to consider current business. Its membership would consist of the governor, military captains, the royal treasury officials, the alcaldes, the procurador, a representative of the clergy, and the tenedor de bastimentos. The members would choose the alcalde, the procurador, an alguacil, and the alcaide of the public jail in annual elections. The whole body would deal with matters of community concern and legal matters, both civil and military. The clergy member was given a vote only in civil cases. Jurisdiction and authority were given to deal with legal cases and to execute sentence (barring appeal by the convicted party) in cases of mutiny and sentences of 10,000 maravedís or less. During military emergencies, the cabildo called to deal with such situations should consist only of the governor and captains. Appeals of the legal decisions of the alcalde and cabildo would be to the adelantado and then to the Council of the Indies.

On October 20, 1566, Pedro Menéndez de Avilés sailed from St. Augustine with a sizeable force of ships and men on his anti-corsair voyage. The adelantado had prepared his provinces for his absence by the appointment of regional lieutenants and of an overall governor at Santa Elena. He had fleshed out the structure of the Florida government with ordinances regulating its governance. He had staffed and financed a supply network to furnish the garrisons and settlements with food and munitions, even if this at times functioned haltingly. He had prepared the ground in Florida and in Europe for the coming of a band of dedicated missionaries who would undertake the conversion of the Indians of Florida. Important initiatives in the exploration of his far-flung territories had been undertaken or commissioned on both coasts and inland on the peninsula, north and west from the base at Santa Elena, and north to the Bahia de Santa María.

As soon as he left St. Augustine in the fall of 1566, the proprietor of Florida began a new relationship with the territories granted him by contract of the King. From this time forward until his death, Pedro Menéndez would lead a dual existence, vis-à-vis Florida. As adelantado, he would continue to act as the directing spirit of the enterprise. Between his visits there, lieutenants would govern the provinces in his name and in that of the King, while he sought preferment and profit elsewhere. The monies and benefits gained in this way would help support his efforts in Florida. The heightened menace of French attacks in the Indies, of which the Ribault and Laudonnière thrusts had been a part, furnished the rationale for his wider role. Menéndez' dual interests made heavy demands upon his time and energies, and often one area of his concerns would suffer from his momentary preoccupation with the other.

The first of these extra-Florida activities, the expedition to the Windward Islands, lasted from late October 1566 until the return of the adelantado to Spain in May of the next year. Except as they touch upon Florida, its details lie outside the scope of this work.[20] Suffice it to say that Pedro Menéndez and his chief lieutenant, Pedro de Valdés, passed systematically from point to point, fortifying the rim of the northern Caribbean against possible enemy attack and seeking French corsair ships. News of the French assault upon Madeira gave fresh impetus to his efforts. As he studied local forts and established garrisons in the major ports, Menéndez moved with his usual decisive rapidity. As they often had, these characteristics sometimes brought him into direct conflict with the jurisdiction of local officials.

When the adelantado reached Santo Domingo and began to treat with the Audiencia there, he found that body willing enough to cooperate in matters of defense. The Audiencia wanted the troops he had brought, but suggested that the adelantado return to Florida. When Menéndez attempted to bring action against Captain Juan de San Vicente and other deserters from Florida who were living at Santo Domingo, he found three of the oidores arrayed against him. Although San Vicente was indicted by the fiscal and was jailed, influence exerted by the three officials got him quickly freed.[21]

The problems of his Florida colonies were never completely out of Menéndez' mind. During his visit to Santo Domingo, he wrote the King, describing his Indies defense dispositions. He reminded his

20. An excellent account of the Windward Islands expedition of 1566–67 has been given at length by Paul E. Hoffman in "The Background and Development of Pedro Menéndez' Contribution to the Defense of the Spanish Indies."

21. This affair is related in "Probanza de Alonso de Grafeda," Santo Domingo, February 15, 1569, from A.G.I. *Santo Domingo* 12.

sovereign that supplies for Florida would continue to be an urgent necessity, and he hinted to Philip II of a secret which would serve greatly to increase the King's patrimony. This must have been the discovery of the great northern water passage, which he hoped his mission to Jacán would have found by that time. Menéndez told the King that he planned to revisit Florida early in the spring of 1567 and would thereafter come to Spain with news of the momentous discovery.[22]

By the first of the New Year, Pedro Menéndez had accomplished his main purpose in Puerto Rico, Santo Domingo, and eastern Cuba: the establishment of garrisons in key points. After leaving a small force in Santiago de Cuba in mid-January, the adelantado moved west along the south shore of the island, heading for Havana. Pedro de Valdés had already arrived there with the larger ships and the remaining soldiery. Until his chief should arrive, it was up to Valdés to represent Menéndez and to begin to prepare the defenses of Havana. On January 21, 1567, Valdés presented his credentials and displayed the King's order to Menéndez.[23] Governor Osorio and his cabildo coolly heard Valdés state that he had come with sizeable forces to strengthen Havana against enemy attack and proposed to build a watchtower and strong point at the Morro in Havana harbor.

The first to speak after Menéndez' lieutenant had made his presentation was García Osorio. The governor objected professionally to Valdés' fortification plans, but his strongest objections touched upon matters of jurisdiction. Osorio stressed the fact that he, as the King's governor and captain-general of Cuba, was the person responsible for defense in that island. The royal orders to Pedro Menéndez seemed to him a direct affront, and he proposed that the force of soldiers brought by Menéndez and Valdés should be given to him, and Menéndez should return to defend Florida, which was his own particular responsibility.

A vote was taken of the cabildo members on the question, and the majority backed the governor. Even Juan de Hinestrosa, long a friend of Menéndez, cast his ballot for García Osorio. In the new battle which was forming between the Florida adelantado and the governor of Cuba, Pedro Menéndez had lost the first round.

22. See Pedro Menéndez to Crown, Santo Domingo, November 29, 1566, from Lawson, "Letters of Menéndez," 2:309–20.

23. The documentation of Valdés' appearance in Havana, dated January 21, 1567, also contains a copy of the March 21, 1566, royal cédula to Menéndez about the Windward Islands expedition, and a copy of Menéndez' poder to Valdés, dated at Monte Christi on January 3, 1567. This material is from A.G.I. *Santo Domingo* 115 (Stetson Coll.). Another copy is in A.G.I. *Patronato* 257, no. 3, ramo 5.

Shortly afterwards, the adelantado himself arrived in Havana and took charge of his affairs there. He paid off the Crown ships and sent them back to Spain. The Cuban port was now heavily occupied with the comings and goings of the supply ships of the Florida proprietor. From Spain itself, and from the Indies, from San Juan to Yucatán, they converged upon Havana and were sent on to the forts in Florida by Hernando de Baeza. Menéndez found anchored at Havana the battered urca *Pantecras*, which had come the previous December with the surviving Jesuits. The valuable cargo which the ship had brought was intact and was transferred formally to Menéndez and his agent. Pedro Menéndez then bought the urca, rechristened it the *Espíritu Santo*, and put his own captain in charge. The large store of goods thus received was of vital importance to the Florida enterprise—it acted as a massive transfusion, renewing the flow of supplies. From the middle of February 1567 until the last of that month, foodstuffs, munitions, cloth, and apparel from the urca were parceled out and sent in several directions.[24] By written authorization of Pedro Menéndez, Baeza allegedly sent six shiploads of cloth and foodstuffs to St. Augustine and Santa Elena. An auditor, following up on the supposed deliveries, found that the Florida officials could not show receipt for all of the goods. In one case, that of the patax *San Christoval*, the shipmaster was supposed to have received oil and vinegar from the urca's cargo, but he later swore that he had received nothing.

It is evident that Pedro Menéndez diverted much of the royal property to uses not intended by the King, and that he converted some of it to private use. Although Menéndez continued to purchase and send large quantities of corn, cassava, and meat to Florida, a good bit of this was bought with the royal supplies, or with money obtained from their sale. Juan de Orduna, a servant of Pedro Menéndez, carried two hundred hats and a substantial amount of cloth from the urca to Yucatán to trade for corn, honey, and chickens which were then trans-shipped to Florida.[25]

Pedro Menéndez utilized the goods sent from Spain for the Florida

24. The controversial question of the distribution of goods from the urca *Pantecras* can be traced in several primary sources. Casa Factor Duarte's original list of goods aboard was received in Havana by Menéndez' representative, Juan de Hinestrosa, on December 12, 1566; this is from A.G.I. *Contaduría* 941 (microfilm, P. K. Yonge Library). In the same legajo is the body of material gathered by Andrés de Equino for his audit of Baeza's books in 1569. More material on the audit is found in A.G.I. *Patronato* 257, no. 3, ramo 8. The ship movements can be followed in A.G.I. *Contaduría* 1,174 and in "Despachos que se hicieron," from A.G.I. *Escribanía de Cámara* 1,024-A.

25. The Orduna voyage is confirmed by Bishop Toral in a letter written at Merida, Yucatán, on April 5, 1567, and found in Lawson, "Letters of Menéndez," 2:320–24.

garrisons to supply some of the soldiers he had posted in the Caribbean. The renamed urca was sent to Santo Domingo with a hundred pipes of flour for the garrison, and Menéndez turned over a quantity of clothing to Baltasar de Barreda, whom he had named as captain of the company he left in Havana. The adelantado issued thirty pipes of the royal wine and some of the oil and vinegar to his servant, Julian García, for his own use. An audit made two years later resulted in the charge, already current at the Spanish court, that Hernando de Baeza had openly sold a large quantity of goods from the *Pantecras* at public auction in Havana. To this charge Menéndez responded that if goods were sold in Havana and Campeche, the proceeds of the sales were used to send things necessary for the supply of the Florida soldiers of the King.[26] As a matter of fact, it appears that the intermingling of royal and personal funds and goods was such that the Crown had virtually no control over the use of its property. This situation resulted in part from the structure of an adelantamiento, in which the contractor had such personal influence that his control of operations within his little kingdom was almost total.

Bolstered by the infusion of supplies and money resulting from the arrival of the *Pantecras*, Pedro Menéndez greatly expanded his shipments to Florida. In addition to the biscuit, wine, oil, vinegar, cloth, and munitions directly unloaded from the *Pantecras*, Baeza sent meat in cask, large amounts of corn, live chickens and hogs, and (in April 1567) a shipload of horses and mares. For mounted defense, agricultural purposes, and breeding, these animals would help strengthen the colonies.[27]

The adelantado, looking beyond the exhaustion of the supplies which had arrived with the urca, wrote the King on February 10 asking for another shipment. Estimating the royal troops then in Florida at 900 in number, Menéndez requested eight shiploads of goods, including 2,000 pipes of wine and 500 tons each of flour and biscuit. This, he believed, would last for eight months.[28] Among other actions he took to raise money for the Florida enterprise, Pedro Menéndez had arranged to ransom some of his noble prisoners in their native France. One of these, Pierre d'Ully, had already been sent to Spain, and Menéndez awaited the ransom.[29] Although no records have sur-

26. See "Memorial of Pedro Menéndez de Avilés to the Casa de Contratación," Madrid, September 21, 1567, from A.G.I. *Contratación* 5,012 (Stetson Coll.).

27. The shipments are listed in A.G.I. *Contaduría* 1,174, under the date of 1567.

28. The adelantado's letter of February 10, 1567, dated at Havana, is found in A.G.I. *Contratación* 5,012 (Stetson Coll.).

29. Menéndez had told Philip II of his plans to ransom d'Ully in his letter of October 20, 1566, sent from St. Augustine, from A.G.I. *Santo Domingo* 115 (Stetson

vived to furnish proof of the allegations, Andrés de Equino, the Florida auditor, charged that Menéndez and his lieutenants used Crown property to barter for gold and silver with the South Florida Indians. According to García Osorio, quantities of this treasure had come into Havana from the north, and the royal percentage had been paid on none of it.[30]

The quarrel between García Osorio and Pedro Menéndez de Avilés had been diminished no whit by the coming of the adelantado to Havana, but was moving toward a major confrontation. When it came, the conflict centered on the matter of jurisdiction over the royal troops Menéndez had brought to Havana and featured Captains Baltasar de Barreda and Pedro de Redroban. Among the unfinished business before the adelantado in Havana was the completion of the trial of Redroban for mutiny, which had begun in St. Augustine the previous fall. The captain-engineer had been removed from command of his company, which had been given to Barreda, and had been stationed in Havana. As Menéndez prepared to leave for Florida, he formally put Barreda in charge of these troops, under his command, not that of Osorio. The governor immediately began secret negotiations with Pedro de Redroban, with an eye to a possible merger of their interests and the defeat of the Menéndez faction.

The adelantado next undertook another voyage to the west coast of Florida, where he proposed to continue the effort to find the water passage which would link up the east and west coasts of the peninsula. The failure of previous expeditions from Carlos and up the St. Johns only encouraged another attempt. Pedro de Valdés was sent to St. Augustine with instructions to try again from that coast, and Hernando de Miranda preceded the adelantado to the Gulf coast to begin the explorations there.[31]

As hostage for the good intentions of Chief Carlos, Captain Reinoso had sent Menéndez' "wife," Doña Antonia, to Havana, where she had passed the winter. Now Pedro Menéndez planned to return her to her brother in Florida and at the same time establish more securely the garrison there. Some Indians from Tequesta, on the lower southeast coast, had also come to Havana, and Menéndez could take them there

Coll.). The arrival and imprisonment of the French noble in Seville was recounted in a letter from the Casa to the King sent from Seville on January 11, 1567, from A.G.I. *Contratación* 5,167 (Stetson Coll.).

30. See charge number 24 in the audit, from A.G.I. *Patronato* 257, no. 3, ramo 8. Osorio's letter, dated simply "1567" at Havana, is from A.G.I. *Santo Domingo* 115 (Stetson Coll.).

31. See Menéndez to Casa, Havana, February 12, 1567, from A.G.I. *Contratación* 5,101.

and pursue Spanish objectives in that place. Father Juan Rogel and Brother Francisco Villareal would also go to Florida with the adelantado to make the first Jesuit mission establishment in the Spanish Empire. On March 1, a fleet of seven sails left Havana for Carlos, led by Menéndez in the new fast fragata *El Águila*. That vessel, which had been made to order in Havana, was commanded by Pedro Menéndez Marquéz.

When he arrived at the Indian settlement, Menéndez saw at once that the fierce and intractable nature of Chief Carlos and his people had been little affected by all of his initiatives toward them. The surface amity which had prevailed when Carlos had given his sister to Menéndez and had released the Christian captives had largely dissolved. The return of Doña Antonia was no palliative to the situation, for she told her brother that the "marriage" to Pedro Menéndez was artificial and unfulfilled. The proposal which Menéndez next made puzzled and infuriated the Indian chieftain: he urged reconciliation of the Calusa Indians with the Tocobaga nation, their hereditary enemies to the north. For the moment, however, Menéndez was able to persuade Carlos to come on an expedition to Tocobaga. It appears that Hernando Escalante also came, serving as interpreter.[32]

After coasting northward along the shoreline of the Gulf for several days, the Spanish ships reached the entrance of Tampa Bay and had passed into the land of the Tocobaga. Without being discovered by the Indians, the Spaniards entered Old Tampa Bay and approached the main village of the Tocobaga, located on the shores of Safety Harbor. Here Carlos showed that all of his instincts were intact, as he proposed to Menéndez that they attack the village, seeing that they had caught the enemy by surprise. Patiently the adelantado reiterated to Carlos that the mission on which they had come to Tocobaga was a peaceful one, but mollified him by promising that he would negotiate for the return of Calusa prisoners whom Tocobaga held.

After an initial meeting with the chieftain of Tocobaga, the Indian consulted with subchiefs and advisers from the surrounding country and finally agreed to a joint treaty with the Spanish and the Calusas. Tocobaga returned several prisoners to Carlos, and Menéndez left a garrison of thirty men, headed by Captain García Martínez de Cos. Since the adelantado had been unable to follow up the search for the supposed water route across the peninsula, Martínez' detachment

32. I base this supposition on the fact that Hernando de Escalante is described as being conversant with the language of Tocobaga as well as that of Carlos. This statement is found opposite the name of Escalante in the distribution of cloth and weapons for the years 1566–69 in A.G.I. *Contaduría* 941 (microfilm, P. K. Yonge Library).

could explore for the waterway and begin to accustom the Indians of Tocobaga to the Catholic faith.

Events on the voyage back to Carlos and after the party returned there made it clear that Menéndez' attempts at rapprochement between Indian groups had only exacerbated their hostility to the Spanish. Although Doña Antonia remained with the Christians, it was evident that Menéndez' "marriage" with her had failed to tie the Indians more closely to the Spanish. Tension between two noble factions among the Calusas brought Indians opposing Carlos into contact with the Christians through the little community of Spaniards who had been prisoner there, and any news could reach the Spanish in time to warn of danger. For example, when Pedro Menéndez decided to settle his colony on another island apart from that on which Carlos held his court, the chief offered canoes and men to help make the move. When the Spanish learned through their friendly grapevine that Carlos planned to overturn the canoes and drown the Spaniards en route, they used Menéndez' small boats instead. The fort-mission of San Antón de Padua had been born. In the prevailing atmosphere, Father Rogel was unable to preach directly to individual Indians, but had to confine himself to worship at the centrally located cross.[33] It was not a promising beginning for the Jesuit mission, but Pedro Menéndez had no choice. He could not remain; news from Havana forced his immediate return there to deal with a serious challenge to his authority. Menéndez received word that Pedro de Redroban had escaped from custody and that García Osorio had arrested Baltasar de Barreda and had assumed control over the garrison Menéndez had left there. After reinforcing the Carlos fort with fifty soldiers, the adelantado departed for Havana.

When Pedro Menéndez arrived in Havana in the last week of March, he found a conflict raging just short of armed combat. Baltasar de Barreda had escaped from confinement, and he and the adelantado quickly reassumed control over the royal soldiers Menéndez had left there. Menéndez found out the hiding place of Pedro de Redroban and seized the rebel captain. On April 12, 1567, Redroban was sentenced to be beheaded in the town square of Havana, but he formally requested an appeal to the Council of the Indies. Pedro Menéndez granted the request and agreed to take Redroban with him to Spain so that his case could be heard in Madrid. The battle between two rival power centers still continued in Havana,

33. Father Rogel depicts the situation at Carlos after the return of the Spanish from Tocobaga in April 1567 in a letter to Geronimo Ruiz del Portillo, sent from Havana on April 25, 1568, and reprinted in Zubillaga, *Monumenta Antiquae Floridae*, pp. 306–7.

but Menéndez had maintained and augmented his own position in that city, so important for his supply of Florida.[34]

At this time, as the adelantado prepared for one last visit to Florida before his voyage to Spain, Pedro Menéndez Marquéz' network of small supply craft was most active. In a report prepared at the end of March 1567, Hernando de Baeza noted that 150 men and more than 10 vessels were then involved in the effort. On March 25, he advised, the patches *Buenabentura* and *San Christoval* had left for Campeche to load corn for Florida, while the patax *San Mateo* departed the same day for the Savanna of Basco Porcallo to load meat and cassava. The bergantín *San Julian* had already gone to Tequesta to return the Indians to their village, and the fragata *Espíritu Santo* was loading horses, mares, and hogs for Florida.

The renamed urca, now also called *Espíritu Santo*, was still on its voyage to Santo Domingo, while yet another vessel by the same name had been lost off Havana while returning from Puerto de Plata with calves. Three ships, *El Águila*, a new shallop named *Buenabentura*, and the *Sevilla* were being prepared for Menéndez' planned voyage to Florida. Two more vessels, the patax *San Antón* and a large shallop, were being outfitted to go to Campeche for corn.[35]

The first stop made by the adelantado on his way north was the Indian settlement located where the Miami River flows into Biscayne Bay. Here lived the Tequesta, and it was at this place that rebel Spaniards had been shipwrecked in 1566. Pedro Menéndez halted at Tequesta to establish formally the Spanish mission. Evidently the earlier Spanish presence there had encouraged the Indians to break to a degree from their vassalage to Carlos, so that the adelantado was in a more favorable position in Tequesta than he had been on the west coast. Concord between the Spanish and the Indians progressed so well and so rapidly that Menéndez was able to leave Brother Villareal and a thirty-man company there to begin the erection of a fort and mission. When he departed Tequesta, Pedro Menéndez took with him three Indians, including the brother of the chief, to go with him to Spain.

34. The Redroban-Barreda case involving Pedro Menéndez and García Osorio is developed in "El Señor Fiscal con Capitan Pedro de Redroban, 1567," from A.G.I. *Justicia* 999. It is also featured in the body of Osorio's residencia; the charges are itemized in "Traslado de la sentencia que se dio contra García Osorio Gobernador y Capitan General desta Ysla de Cuba," from A.G.I. *Santo Domingo* 99. The best narrative of the dispute is by Solís de Merás in *Pedro Menéndez de Avilés*, pp. 230–32.

35. Data contained in Baeza's "Despachos que se hicieron," from A.G.I. *Escribania de Cámara* 1,024-A, can be confirmed by comparing the ships and cargoes listed in A.G.I. *Contaduría* 1,174.

As he had done the previous July, Pedro Menéndez made his land-fall first at San Mateo. At the fort there, his district governor, Villa-roel, quickly brought the adelantado up to date on occurrences in the vicinity of San Mateo since his departure. Another reconnaissance up the St. Johns, this time by Pedro de Valdés, had failed to yield the secrets of the water route from Mayaca to the Gulf. The soldiers at San Mateo experienced all of the unease of those within a besieged fortress; Indian raiders made any forays outside patently unsafe. On the previous November 30, Captain Pedro de Larrandia and several of his men had been attacked from ambush and killed on their way to San Mateo from the fort at Guale. In counterraids, Villaroel had been able to capture sixteen of Saturiba's warriors, including his son, Emola. Using the Indian hostages to draw the interest of Saturiba, Pedro Menéndez arranged a face-to-face confrontation with the Timucuan chief. The meeting took place near the St. Johns bar, where the adelantado anchored offshore while Saturiba remained back some distance from the beach. After some hours of fruitless par-ley, the Spanish suspected a plot to ambush their shore party and lure Menéndez to his death, while Saturiba refused to negotiate personally with the Spanish leader, and the meeting broke up in renewed mutual enmity. The uncertainty and hostility of the Timucuans in the vicinity of San Mateo would continue. Faced with continuing attacks upon his communications and forts, Pedro Menéndez gave orders for the con-struction of a protective line of blockhouses from Matanzas to Guale. One of these, named Alicamini, was located near the place of the par-ley with Saturiba, on the north bank of the St. Johns.[36]

Even though St. Augustine had been supplied reasonably well dur-ing the months since Menéndez' departure the previous October, the community and garrison had suffered the same uncertainties then current at San Mateo. Tensions between the faction of the adelantado, his brother, and other Asturians and that of the captains who had come in July 1566 with Sancho de Archiniega had flared up on sev-eral occasions.

This time, the trouble had begun the December before, after the cabildo had established a daily ration of one-quarter pound of bread per man. Captain Miguel de Enriquez, who had come to Florida with one of Archiniega's companies, objected to the decision of the cabildo and said that he would appeal it to the Audiencia of Santo Domingo. Witnesses testified that Enriquez had scoffed at the jurisdiction of the cabildo and had offered obscene comments about its authority.

36. The parley with Saturiba is narrated in Solís de Merás, *Pedro Menéndez de Avilés*, pp. 233–35.

Bartolomé Menéndez, whom his brother had left in charge as regional governor at St. Augustine, clashed with Enriquez on several occasions. The governor had intervened to punish one of the soldiers in Enriquez' company, whom he had apprehended giving cloth to a prostitute at the public fountain of St. Augustine. In another instance, Bartolomé Menéndez publicly rebuked the captain for the laxity of his men on the sentinel posts. His remarks upon that occasion are indicative of the tension in St. Augustine: "It is notorious that numerous French Lutherans have been expelled from these provinces, and the fort at San Mateo and other forts which they had occupied in the kingdom and jurisdiction of His Majesty . . . taken from them. It can now be expected that they may come and that they will come to revenge themselves for such great slaughter and destruction of their people. If this took place, it would be a great disservice to God Our Lord and to His Majesty, if we were found as careless and unprepared as we have been on the occasions when Captain Miguel Enriquez' sentinels were so careless."[37]

Miguel Enriquez was arrested and charged with insubordination. Beginning April 27, 1567, Pedro Menéndez heard testimony from Enriquez and from those appearing against him. The officer was adjudged guilty and was sentenced to lose his command and have his salary reduced. Enriquez also appealed his sentence to the Council of the Indies.

In the first week of May, Pedro Menéndez de Avilés bid farewell to his brother and to the other captains and officials at St. Augustine, and set sail in *El Águila* and another small ship for Santa Elena. With him went the Indians from Tequesta, the officer prisoners, Pedro de Valdés, and a small force of soldiers and seamen. He also carried three of the Timucuan Indians, including one who had been christened Juan de Valdés, to go with him to the Spanish court. Pedro de Bustinçury, the Vizcayan who had been captive of the Ais Indians and whom the French had taken to the Valois court, went with the Indians as interpreter.[38]

When he reached Santa Elena, Pedro Menéndez focused his attention upon the exploration and exploitation of the fertile continental areas of his domains and the discovery of a more rapid passage from Spain to New Spain and to the Pacific. Menéndez therefore called upon Juan Pardo to report on his four-month journey deep inland, in

37. Testimony of Bartolomé Menéndez from "La Florida, año de 1567, El Señor Fiscal con Miguel Enriquez," A.G.I. *Justicia* 999.

38. Bustinçury's return to Spain is mentioned in a letter from the Casa to the Crown, Seville, March 4, 1568, A.G.I. *Contratación* 5,168.

which the energetic captain had traveled more than five hundred miles and had reached the foot of the Appalachian Mountains. Pardo and his men had left Santa Elena on December 1, 1566, and had traversed a great variety of terrain, from the relatively warm seacoast to the snow-covered eminences of the Blue Ridge, all within the boundaries of the present state of South Carolina. At the sizeable Indian city called Joada near the mountains, Juan Pardo had founded a city called Cuenca, built Fort Joada, and left a sergeant and garrison to man the fort. The captain reported to Pedro Menéndez that he had found rich clay soils and heavy forest growth which promised great fertility. He also advised that the inland areas were watered and drained by several great rivers which could offer access for their development.

No trace had been found of the storied waterway which should lead to the viceroyalty of New Spain or to the South Sea, but the Pardo exploration was an important beginning. It established in Menéndez' mind the fertility of the vast inland areas and their suitability for his own future agricultural enterprise. The first contact was made with the Indians, and many new tribes had been marked out for evangelization and conversion.

The adelantado probably already knew that his Jacán expedition had failed. Instead of finding the homeland of Don Luis, it had landed near the Outer Banks of present North Carolina. After being discouraged by stormy fall weather, Pedro de Coronas and his men had returned directly to Spain, arriving in Seville by November 5, 1566. The "Bahia de Santa María" and the water passage would have to await future explorations.[39]

When he left Santa Elena for Spain on May 18, 1567, Pedro Menéndez de Avilés had behind him more than eighteen months' labor in and for his new provinces of Florida. His short-run military objective imposed by the presence of the Laudonnière garrison had been successful. The French fort had been taken and the reinforcing fleet of Jean Ribault destroyed.

The first actions had been costly, and not only to the French. Thanks largely to the work of Paul E. Hoffman, the cost of the Florida enterprise to the Spanish crown can be itemized rather precisely. To Hoffman's totals could be added the sums paid directly to

39. Record of the first journey of Captain Juan Pardo to the inland areas has survived in a report made at Santa Elena on July 11, 1567, by Francisco Martínez, a soldier on the expedition. This report has been reprinted by Ruidiaz in *La Florida*, pp. 474–80, and by Lawson in "Letters of Menéndez," 2:324–27. Payment to the friars and to Don Luis after their arrival at Seville from the ill-fated Jacán expedition are found in A.G.I. *Contaduría* 299; 3: 1, dated November 1, 1566.

the adelantado in conjunction with his contract. After making this adjustment, the royal cost at Cádiz, the expenses of the aborted expedition from Santo Domingo, and the shipments made in the urca *Pantecras* in 1566 total about 108,000 ducats. In addition, some charges attributable to Florida accrued when Menéndez used the fleet ship *Santa Catalina* and its crew and supplies during the winter of 1565–66. As to the Archiniega expedition, which Hoffman has demonstrated to have cost more than 130,000 ducats, it is felt that only about half of its expense should be allocated to Florida. Many of the Archiniega ships and men were sent in 1566 to the West Indian islands under Menéndez' command to provide for their defense. After making these adjustments, it appears that Philip II spent about 200,000 ducats directly on support of the Florida enterprise during its first phase—virtually all of the monies spent by the Crown for Indies defense during those years.[40]

The direct "private" costs of the Florida conquest in its first phase can also be approximated. Menéndez' initial outfitting cost has already been estimated at 47,000 ducats. Menéndez had spent 10,400 ducats in 1566 for the purchase of supplies in Havana for his Florida enterprise.[41] He had also spent at least 7,000 ducats in other Cuban ports, and had expended additional sums in Yucatán, Santo Domingo, Puerto de Plata, and San Juan, Puerto Rico. Menéndez also expended some 7,000 ducats in Spain. His costs probably totaled more than 75,000 ducats in the first phase of conquest.

The goods and supplies bought by Pedro Menéndez and his agents had to be delivered and there was substantial cost involved in the operation of his fleet of small boats. Another kind of cost, related to these shipping routes, was the loss of ships and men that had steadily eroded the Menéndez forces throughout the first year of the Florida conquest.

Within less than two years after Menéndez' first expedition sailed

40. Hoffman's most recent and explicit application of his research to expenditures in Florida by the Spanish Crown has been published as his "Study of Defense Costs, 1565–1585: A Quantification of Florida History." In this article, he has listed the total royal spending allocated to Florida defense costs for 1565–68 as 208,401 ducats.

41. See Appendix 5. In 1566, Pedro Menéndez had sent from Havana 505 loads of cassava, 854 *fanegas* of corn, 492 pumpkin-squashes, 26,700 lbs. of sea biscuit, 28 pipes of wine, 325 jugs of wine, 58 jugs of oil, 442 yards of cotton print cloth, 775 yards of coarse linen, 65,800 lbs. of jerked beef, 27 calves, 600 chickens, 80 goats or sheep, 550 sows, and 47 hams. These items, extended at the prices given by the Havana officials, total 10,396 ducats as shown in A.G.I. *Contaduría* 1,174. A witness in Mexico in 1591 testified that Menéndez bought, over an uncertain period, 2,700 fanegas of corn, 3,000 chickens, and beans, honey, wax, and hemp sandals from Yucatán; see Ruidiaz, *La Florida*, 2:622.

from Cádiz, eleven ships had been lost to the enterprise of Florida.[42] The sinking of these vessels, large and small, represented the loss of the greater part of the marine assets of Menéndez and his coterie. To offset these damages, there was little in the way of income. Ransoms and booty from the Florida conquest did exist but were not appreciable. Profits from the small cargoes carried by Menéndez Marquéz could not approach the potential that the *San Pelayo* would have represented in the rich New Spain or Tierra Firme trade. Faced with such losses, Pedro Menéndez had left Florida. His command of the Windward Islands expedition enabled him to sail at royal expense. During his voyage to Spain, he would endeavor to trade his deeds in Florida for royal recognition. The defeat and expulsion of the French colony of Laudonnière and Ribault would surely be rewarded by his sovereign, and soon.

Evaluation of the first phase in Florida also demonstrates that Pedro Menéndez' most vital contribution was that of acting as captain-general and entrepreneur on the spot. It was his own presence and leadership that had defeated the French. The Crown exerted a more passive, supporting role in the Florida conflict of 1565–66. During its active stages, the resources of the adelantado proved the more telling; much of the royal support was wasted or came too late to influence the outcome. Because of his slim financial reserves and because of the loss of many of his supplies and his largest ship, Pedro Menéndez and his men in Florida suffered many hardships and privations directly traceable to the single-minded way in which he had come to the task of erasing the French colony. Menéndez can scarcely be faulted for the zeal he displayed in striking out straightaway for Florida to meet the French, but the cost of this decision was a heavy one. Once his victory had been won, short supplies forced the adelantado to try to link up with his own missing forces and those promised by the King.

When he left Florida, Pedro Menéndez removed his unifying and commanding presence from the scene. The men he had left in charge of the separated garrisons had been unable to cope with the situations which arose. Indeed, it might have been impossible for any leader to deal with the independent-minded sixteenth-century Spanish soldiery in such circumstances. Men whose clothing and food supplies were low, fearful of death in a hostile land, might have rebelled in any event, but Menéndez' four-month absence seems to have been critical.

Once in Cuba, the adelantado sought with all means at his com-

42. The ship losses are detailed in "Memorial de los navios cargados de bastimentos y municiones que se perdieron el Adelantado," from A.G.I. *Escribanía de Cámara* 1,024-A.

mand to supply his Florida enterprise. The expedients he employed were generally successful. The charge that Pedro Menéndez deserted his Florida responsibilities to go hunting corsairs begs the question. He actually spent little time in this and the sale of the two Portuguese prizes yielded him some badly needed operating funds.

On the other hand, it does appear that the adelantado could have taken some rapid measures to relieve Santa Lucía once news of the difficulties there reached him in Havana. Menéndez' presence in St. Augustine and San Mateo could have forestalled the March mutinies. Instead, he sailed first to Carlos.

Pedro Menéndez' funding arrangements are subject to the same criticisms which one might level against those of the Crown: they had proven insufficient to provide ample and continuous support for the Florida enterprise. In spite of losses and setbacks, however, Menéndez persisted in his efforts. By early 1567, he had set up a viable pipeline for the supply of Florida through Cuba, and other Caribbean areas, was preparing further groups of soldiers and settlers in Spain, and had installed the first group of Jesuit missionaries. Menéndez left the Florida establishments in reasonably good condition. Fortified by the soldiery and supplies which had come in mid-summer 1566, the garrisons had been extended north and south of the initial settlement. The adelantado had founded cities at Santa Elena and St. Augustine and had set up regional government under major lieutenants. In view of widespread Indian hostility in this critical phase of colonization, internal defense continued to be essential. The task of exploring the new lands had proceeded remarkably well in a short time. Reliable navigation routes had been discovered, linking the Florida settlements and tying them to the supply base at Havana. The coastal features, harbors, and ports of a long shoreline had been studied and recorded. Pedro Menéndez had also discovered a short-cut for the New Spain fleets coming to Havana—the passage east of the Dry Tortugas, which would ever thereafter be in the official derroteros of the Carrera de Indias. He had taken formal legal possession of territories from the extreme south of the Florida peninsula to the North Carolina capes.

One may therefore evaluate the Florida conquest at the end of its first phase in early 1567. First, the immediate military objectives had been fulfilled by the expunging of the French forces. There remained, however, an uncertain quality to this victory. The Spanish had been unable to destroy French corsair power in the Indies, and new enemy incursions were expected momentarily at points along the long continental frontier which Pedro Menéndez had to defend. It seemed the destiny of Florida never to be free of peril, always to be an enterprise endangered. The vital elements in the conquest of a land—the construction of an economy and a society—were in a critical stage. The essentials of Spanish settlement—the military presence, the municipal institutions, and the evangelizing Church—were only tentatively established at a few outposts over a thousand miles of frontier. Profitable exploitation of the lands and native peoples of Florida through economically viable colonies was still to be realized. At great cost, the enterprise of Florida had been born, but its existence was indeed precarious.

Fort Caroline. (Photo courtesy National Park Service.)

The "bar of Ays," Indian River County, Florida. Pedro Menéndez passed here after destroying the French fort at Cape Canaveral in November 1565. Indian River in the background, Atlantic Ocean in the foreground. The star-shaped building is the McLarty State Museum. (Photo by Homer N. Cato.)

Matanzas Inlet, looking across to site of Ribault massacres. (Photo by Homer N. Cato.)

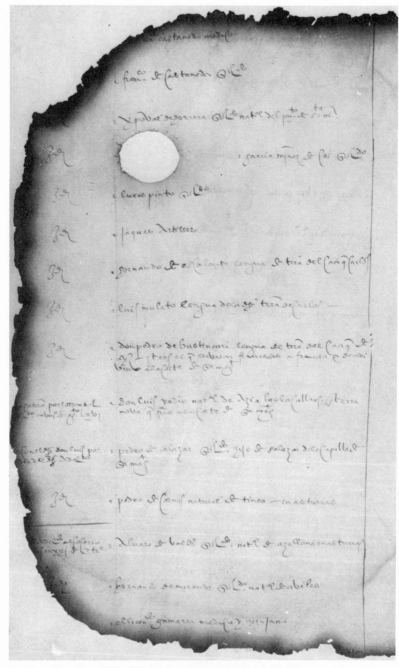

Florida ration list, 1566–67, showing Hernando Escalante Fontaneda and Pedro de Bustincury as Menéndez' interpreters. (From Florida accounts, A.G.I. *Contaduría* 941, microfilm, P. K. Yonge Library of Florida History, Gainesville, Florida.)

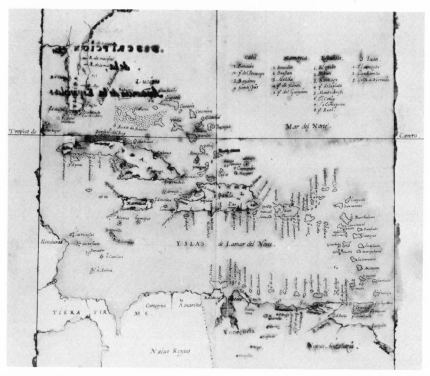

Juan López de Velasco map, dating from ca. 1574. (Photo courtesy John Carter Brown Library, Brown University, Providence, Rhode Island.)

Archive of the Indies. (Photo courtesy Archive of the Indies.)

The Enterprise Renewed

In the fast fragata *El Águila*, the Menéndez party made a very rapid Atlantic voyage indeed and reached the Azores in seventeen days. There Menéndez learned that Philip II might be going to the Netherlands to supervise military operations against the rebels. He therefore decided to sail directly for the north coast of Spain to intercept his King and report on the Florida enterprise.

On June 29, the Florida party arrived off La Coruña and was forced by the presence of corsair ships to put into Vivero in Galicia. There the two prisoners, Enriquez and Redroban, were made ready to be sent to Madrid under guard.[1] There Menéndez also learned that the King was still at court.

Pedro Menéndez was able to pass a few days in Avilés with his wife and other family before pressing on to the court, where he arrived July 20, 1567. The two captives had arrived three days earlier.[2] The Florida adelantado made a striking entrance into the presence of Philip II, accompanied by the six Florida Indians and preceded by his reputation of battle and victory, exploration and foundation. He found, however, a sovereign and court preoccupied with the events of an exciting spring and summer. The Spanish King had been pushed beyond his tolerance by the rebels in the Netherlands, and he had ordered the Duke of Alba to bring Spanish troops from Milan to enforce royal power in the Low Countries. While Calvinist Geneva held

1. See the certificate of custody, Graviel de Ayala, in Vivero, Galicia, July 2, 1567, from A.G.I. *Justicia* 999.
2. The notification of receipt of the prisoners, dated at Madrid on July 17, 1567, from A.G.I. *Indiferente General* 1,219.

its breath and all Europe watched in fearful anticipation, the world's finest army marched overland directly to Antwerp. By midsummer, the Spanish had begun a full-scale costly commitment in the Netherlands. The short but sharp actions against the Huguenot French in Florida, the wider-ranging expedition of Pedro Menéndez in the Caribbean, and the disciplining of the Netherlands were all seen by Philip as part of one war. Within Spain, tightening ideologies were also leading to disturbances. In November 1566, a pragmatic had been adopted which required the Moriscos of eastern Andalusia to change their Moorish customs as a part of their complete Christianization. Philip II was fearful that connections between the Moriscos and the Turkish enemy could lead to an invasion of Spain. After the new law was openly published on January 1, 1567, discontent began to grow among the Moriscos. Sooner or later, it was bound to result in open revolt.

The French representative at the Spanish court, Ambassador Fourquevaux, had continued to press for action on the prisoners Pedro Menéndez had taken in his Florida conquest. Philip's policy of the previous summer to release the captives had been carried out slowly after continual pleas by the French Ambassador. The Sieur de Lys was freed after a long term in the Madrid jail. In May, Philip had also released eight other Florida French prisoners who had been brought to Seville.[3] Still concerned with seeking some general recompense by the Spanish Crown for Menéndez' actions in Florida, Fourquevaux viewed the adelantado's arrival at court with interest and with malice. The Frenchman sought out Captain Miguel Enriquez and pressed him for details of Menéndez' circumstances. The Spaniard, awaiting trial before the Council of the Indies on the appeal of his case from Menéndez' service, told the French ambassador that the Spanish establishment in Florida was meager. He said, moreover, that Pedro Menéndez had come in part to defend himself against charges that he had permitted many men to die of hunger and that he had embezzled royal goods and sold them at auction in Havana. Fourquevaux passed word of his confidences with Enriquez to his own royal master.[4]

Prior to the arrival of Pedro Menéndez at Madrid, the King had already begun to act upon his request for a new royal supply expedition for Florida. The Crown had sent along to Seville in May Menéndez'

3. The King's order of release was directed to the Casa from Madrid on May 19, 1567, from A.G.I. *Indiferente General* 1,967. Royal policy toward the French prisoners is discussed by Lyon in "Captives of Florida," pp. 17–20.

4. See Fourquevaux to Charles IX, Madrid, n.d. [1567], from "Lettres et Papiers d'état de Fourquevaux," in Gaffarel, *La Floride Française*, p. 450.

order list for new supplies for the royal troops in the *adelantamiento*. In mid-June, Philip II sent another letter to the Casa, advising that he had cut the request for wine for Florida from 2,000 to 20 pipes, but had otherwise approved the supply list. On June 23, the trade officials replied that they had only 12,000 ducats available for such expenditure, and that it was already too late to send the goods in the New Spain convoy, for it was due to sail the next day. They suggested instead a shipment in a large shallow-draft *urca* direct to the Florida ports.[5]

When he had completed the formalities of his appearance before Philip II, Pedro Menéndez was ordered by the King to report by written memorandum to the Council of the Indies. The adelantado did so, narrating the history of his defeat of Jean Ribault and René de Laudonnière, the far-reaching explorations which had been made in Florida, and the forts and cities he had founded there. Menéndez went on to give his considered opinion on the state of defense of the Caribbean Indies against the forces threatening the empire there.[6] After he made his report, it appeared that Pedro Menéndez had faced down his detractors for the moment, and his return became a triumph.

After his initial duties had been completed, the adelantado inquired about the status of arrangements for the supply of the royal soldiers in Florida, and was taken aback to learn that nothing had yet been sent. The forts had only about three months' supply left when he had sailed, and the summer was now far advanced; thus it appeared that his own network might again have to bear the full burden of sustaining both royal and private soldiery. Menéndez pressed the King to speed up the provisioning and dispatch of the ships which were to go to Florida, but also objected strongly to the diminished amount of wine which was to be sent. Menéndez proposed, and the King passed along the suggestion to the Casa, that the supplies could be sent on one of Menéndez' own ships which Pedro del Castillo was then loading to go to Florida.[7]

After he had made his report of his services in Florida, Pedro

5. Philip's letters of May 24 and June 13, 1567, were both sent from Madrid, and are found in A.G.I. *Contratación* 5,012 (Stetson Coll.). The reply of the Casa came from Seville on June 23, 1567, and is from A.G.I. *Contratación* 5,167.

6. Apart from the letters of Fourquevaux, the best description of Pedro Menéndez' arrival at the court is from Solís de Merás, *Pedro Menéndez de Avilés*, pp. 241–45. The Solís de Merás narrative ends after that portrayal.

7. Menendez described his discomfiture at learning of the delay in the Florida supply in a memorial to the Casa dated at Madrid on September 21, 1567. The King sent to the Casa from El Pardo on August 13, 1567, his suggestion about using one of Menéndez' ships. Both documents come from A.G.I. *Contratación* 5,012 (Stetson Coll.).

Menéndez naturally expected some substantial royal reward for his deeds. His expectations, and the actions he took to bring these hopes to fruition, took two distinct channels.

First, Menéndez pressed for appointment to salaried office of high distinction and other mercedes from his sovereign. The second course of action he took was most illustrative of the nature of his position as a private conqueror. In September 1567, he filed suit against the Spanish Crown, seeking recompense for heavy expenditures and losses in the conquest of Florida. This action was not a suit between parties, but rather one between an individual subject of Castile and the royal patrimony, defended by the Crown fiscal. It was the duty of the fiscal to keep charge of the asientos and capitulaciones of the Indies adelantados, and bring charges against them where the interest of his King was at stake.[8] The legalism of Spanish life and the niceties of the relationship between Philip and his vassals are evidenced by the fact that the Crown prepared to reward Menéndez for his services in Florida at the same time that the lawsuit over the contract was being argued.

The body of testimony, allegations, and documents which make up this lawsuit remains the best single primary source extant about the contract with Pedro Menéndez de Avilés for the conquest of Florida.[9] The material included covers some seventy-five years. The corpus of the case begun by Menéndez in 1567 also includes a wide variety of biographical, geographical, and financial data about the Menéndez years in Florida.

The main line taken by Menéndez in his case was to attempt to prove that he had overperformed his contract for Florida, and to list and itemize his losses in the conquest, thus demonstrating overwhelming personal loss and damage in the effort. To this end, Pedro Menéndez and his attorney put on record plea after plea to prove

8. An excellent description of the powers and duties of the royal fiscal is found in "Powers of the Fiscal," from "Codice de Leyes," September 24, 1570, reprinted in *D.I.*, 16:431–35.

9. The case is in a single legajo—A.G.I. *Escribanía de Cámara* 1,024-A. Although the manuscript *inventario* for the *Escribanía de Cámara* section of the Archive of the Indies lists eighteen piezas in the legajo, only nine are now present in the bundle. Microfilm of the legajo is now in the P. K. Yonge Library. I believe the material so rich that I associate with it the Solís de Merás narrative, and think it may in fact have contained the "missing *relación*" from which both the Solís de Merás and Barrientos works were taken. See the cogent summary of parallels between the two narratives by Lyle N. McAlister in his Introduction, esp. pp. xxi–xxii (Solís de Merás, *Pedro Menéndez de Avilés*). It may be that the arrangement of papers for the Menéndez lawsuit against the Crown also paralleled the materials contained in the Revillagigedo archive. The asiento copy in *Escribanía de Cámara* 1,024-A is an original, signed by Philip II.

their case. On September 22, they filed a list of the ships with which Menéndez had sailed from Cádiz two years before.[10] On October 16, the adelantado and his associates testified that the Florida expedition had carried, in fact, many more men than Francisco Duarte had shown in his muster of June 1565.[11] There was added material describing the addition of the Luna contingent at Cádiz and the men and ships taken to Florida from Avilés, Gijón, and Santander.[12] Now Menéndez was ready to demonstrate his concrete losses in the enterprise of Florida. He filed a memorial describing the eleven vessels lost in the effort up to the time of his departure. He also detailed the performance of his network of small supply ships which had served Florida in 1566–67 from Havana and other points in the Caribbean.[13]

Pedro Menéndez had not as yet decided upon the amount of money or other considerations for which he might finally ask in recompense for his efforts and losses. His decision upon that point in the late fall of 1567 was also related to the benefits which the Crown was then in the process of granting to Menéndez. Also involved, as matters of his pride and prestige, were the Enriquez and Redroban cases, and the case of Captain Parra, which Menéndez had furthered. The latter two suits, of course, concerned García Osorio, against whom Pedro Menéndez was determined to gain satisfaction.

Although the adelantado's position in disciplining the two captains who had served in Florida was not upheld (both were given token fines and freed), the evidence presented against Osorio in the Redroban and Parra cases found its mark.[14] On October 24, 1567, Philip II issued a cédula naming Pedro Menéndez de Avilés governor and captain-general of Cuba, with no prejudice to his Florida titles. Menéndez would also have the right to serve in absentia through

10. "Información sumaria hecho en Cádiz por Pedro del Castillo," September 22, 1567, A.G.I. *Escribanía de Cámara* 1,024-A.

11. "Información ante Alcalde," Madrid, October 16, 1567, A.G.I. *Escribanía de Cámara* 1,024-A.

12. The Luna soldiery is enumerated in "Requeremiento de Luna a Castillo que le de para los fletes y costa de los soldados"; the northern effort is discussed in "La lista que hizo el [*sic*] de las Alas en Avilés de 257 personas," "Visita y registro de los navios y gente en Gijón, and Visita y registro del navio Espiritu Santo," all of which are from A.G.I. *Escribanía de Cámara* 1,024-A.

13. As previously cited, the ship losses are itemized in "Memorial de los navios cargados de bastimentos y municiones que se perdieron el Adelantado," while the supply sailings were listed in "Despachos que se hicieron," both from A.G.I. *Escribanía de Cámara* 1,024-A.

14. The end of the Enriquez case is documented under the date of August 24, 1567, in A.G.I. *Indiferente General* 1,219. The Parra case, which continued until 1570, is detailed in part in A.G.I. *Escribanía de Cámara* 952. Pedro de Redroban's appeal was finally successful; see the cédula to the Casa of August 2, 1568, from A.G.I. *Indiferente General* 1,967 (Stetson Coll.).

lieutenants as he had done in Florida. Osorio would have to undergo residencia at the hands of his hated rival and had still to answer the charges being developed in the Parra case.[15]

Of far more importance to Pedro Menéndez was the appointment which next came to him. On November 2, 1567, Philip II granted Menéndez the office, title, salary, and privileges of captain-general of a new royal armada which was to act as the main line of Caribbean and fleet defense. Menéndez' long past services and his most recent efforts in Florida and the Caribbean thus received substantial recognition. In addition to salary, the new captain-general would receive the King's fifth share of any prizes taken as well as his own share of the other four-fifths.[16] The twelve ships of his armada would be of his own design and were to be built in Vizcaya, under his supervision, by a close associate, Juan Martínez de Recalde. In prize money, paid appointments for a host of friends and followers, and the chance for profits through contraband, Pedro Menéndez stood to gain greatly from his appointment. In a sense, the captain-generalcy of the royal armada offered the conquerors of Florida an escape hatch and a safety valve for the pressures of financial insolvency which they faced. The royal appointment came none too soon; the next month Menéndez embargoed by his creditors for debt in Seville.[17]

The honors poured upon Pedro Menéndez de Avilés had not yet ceased. Philip II began the formalities connected with the granting to Menéndez of an encomienda in the military order of Santiago. Soon it was announced that Menéndez had been granted the title and revenues of the *comendador* of Santa Cruz de la Zarza, a property of the order located at Campos, near Palencia in Castile. It carried an annual revenue, which would help bolster his sagging finances.[18]

15. The Menéndez appointment as governor of Cuba of October 24, 1567, is from A.G.I. *Santo Domingo* 115. The adelantado named Diego de Miranda as secretary for the Osorio residencia on February 2, 1568, at Madrid; see A.H.P., *Protocolos, Escribanía* of Diego Rodriguez, no. 521. It appears that García Osorio had already been suspended from his office when the Menéndez appointment was made; on August 30, 1567, Philip II wrote from Madrid to Don Diego de Santillan as "our Governor of the Island of Cuba," ordering him to punish Osorio for his actions against Barreda. This is from a letter in A.G.I. *Santo Domingo* 1,122.

16. The cédula of appointment on November 2, 1567, is found, among other places, in A.G.I. *Contaduría* 454, no. 3. Menéndez' arrangement to receive the royal fifth of all prizes as well as his usual share is discussed in a cédula to the Casa sent from El Escorial on November 5, 1570; from A.G.I. *Santo Domingo* 24.

17. The embargo is described by the Casa officials in a letter to the King dated at Seville on December 24, 1567, and found in A.G.I. *Contratación* 5,167.

18. The income of the encomienda was at least 200 ducats per year, for Menéndez later pledged that sum from the revenues of Santa Cruz to Hernando de Miranda as part dowry for his daughter Catalina. See the dower agreement dated at Avilés on March 27, 1574, from A.G.I. *Escribanía de Cámara* 153-A.

Philip II also took steps to revise the Menéndez contract so as to make its trade privileges conform to the actual state of the ships which Menéndez now possessed. On October 6, the Crown ruled that the section of the asiento which granted Menéndez licenses for two 600-ton galleons be changed to allow for three 400-ton vessels. Another cédula sent the same day approved the change of the size of Menéndez' shallop licenses from 50 to 80 tons each. Menéndez now moved through Pedro del Castillo to send a galleon into the Indies trade.[19]

As the Florida adelantado moved from triumph to triumph, notably enlarging his sphere of influence and gathering the visible tokens of royal favor, his case over Florida losses and expenses continued. The documents he had presented in evidence and the entire status of his contract with the King were subjected to careful review by the chief auditors of the realm. The accountants issued a lengthy analysis of the case on October 22, 1567, setting forth all of the pertinent facts but making no conclusions. Lists were appended detailing the costs of the Crown and the adelantado at Cádiz. After placing Factor Duarte's original 1565 muster at Cádiz on record, the fiscal challenged Pedro Menéndez' contention that he had in truth carried five hundred more men than Duarte had shown. Since the muster Menéndez claimed to have made at the Canary Islands had been destroyed when the St. Augustine fort had been burned, it was difficult for the adelantado to prove his case.

Now Pedro Menéndez asked the Crown for 25,000 ducats for the value of the *San Pelayo*, a sum for the *aviso* he had sent Philip II in October 1565, and payment for what he had overspent in Florida. Altogether, he was asking for more than 50,000 ducats. On February 9, 1568, the Council of the Indies passed its definitive sentence in the case. Menéndez was to receive 500 ducats for the aviso *San Miguel*, sent with Captain Diego Flores Valdés and lost in the Azores, and a charter fee of six reales per ton for the *San Pelayo* during the four and one-half months she served in the Florida enterprise, altogether some 3,500 ducats. As for the rest, the Council left it up to Philip.[20] Shortly, the King granted a merced to Pedro Menéndez of 10,000 ducats for his services and losses in the enterprise of Florida. The

19. See Crown to Casa, Madrid, October 6, 1567, from A.G.I. *Indiferente General* 1,220. The shallop tonnage change is from a royal letter to Pedro Menéndez dated at Madrid on the same day, from A.G.I. *Indiferente General* 2,673. The dispatch of the galleon is described in a communication dated May 15, 1568, from A.G.I. *Indiferente General* 1,220.

20. The sentence is from A.G.I. *Escribanía de Cámara* 1,024-A, and is dated at Madrid on February 9, 1568.

adelantado made arrangements in Seville for a fellow Asturian, Diego de Valdés, who served as aide to the Archbishop of Seville, to collect the 2,000 ducats of the merced which was to be paid by the Casa.[21] The other claims Pedro Menéndez had made had not been finally settled by this payment, and the case of 1567–68 would be taken up again at a later date. Other minor requests for reimbursement—for the pay of Roelas' men Menéndez took from Havana and for supplies he furnished for the royal troops in Florida—would also be continued by the adelantado and his attorneys.[22]

It was apparent that Pedro Menéndez de Avilés had gained greatly as a result of his trip to Spain. In the face of much rumor and some fact about his misappropriations and carelessness in the Florida conquest, the adelantado had received evidence of royal favor. The concrete realization of cash sums from the benefits and offices he had received would be somewhat slower in coming. It is evident, however, that Castillo had by now received the back charter fees due Menéndez from 1563, and that he now had been voted those from the 1565 voyage. With more supplies coming to Florida and with the forthcoming collection of salaries and mercedes, the worst time seemed to be past. Best of all, the gaining of the fleet and Cuba offices would open many doors for Pedro Menéndez and his associates. Legal and illegal sources of funds would now become available, if properly exploited. His private trade could continue, and the grand design for the settlement of Florida could now proceed.

Most important, Menéndez could now begin to carry out the plan to populate Florida with settlers and their families—that key to conquest without which the adelantamiento could never prosper. It was common knowledge at court that the settlement of Florida was to be accomplished during 1568.[23] The previous year, Menéndez had contracted with one Hernán Pérez, a Portuguese, to bring from the Azores two hundred farmers and their families. The arrangement fell through, for Pérez and Pedro Menéndez disagreed and became bitter

21. The poder of Pedro Menéndez to Diego de Valdés is found in A.C.R., Legajo 2, no. 3, A7a (microfilm, P. K. Yonge Library). It bears the date "1568." The merced of 10,000 ducats was granted on April 11, 1568, by a cédula in A.G.I. *Indiferente General* 1,967 (Stetson Coll.).

22. Persuaded by Menéndez, the King wrote the Royal Officials of Havana from Madrid on February 2, 1568, and asked them to itemize the cost to Pedro Menéndez of the supplies he had shipped to Florida from Havana. This letter is from A.G.I. *Contaduría* 1,174.

23. The Baron Fourquevaux advised Charles IX that Menéndez was to leave in the winter of 1567–68 with 1,500 young married men and their families to make a massive effort to settle Florida. The letter was dated at Madrid on September 12, 1567, and was reprinted in "Lettres et Papiers d'état de Fourquevaux," in Gaffarel, *La Floride Française*, p. 452.

enemies.[24] Now, however, the adelantado could go ahead with his plan, using instead settlers from the province of Toledo, in Castile. Under individual contracts with each settler family, Menéndez agreed that their passage and freight would be paid for them. Upon arrival the adelantado would grant them lands for farms and pastures. Within two years, he contracted to furnish each farmer twelve cows and a bull, two oxen for plowing, two mares, a dozen sheep, goats, hogs, and chickens. He agreed to give the farmers shoots for their own vineyards. For each family, Menéndez would build a house, furnish a shepherd boy, and give one male and one female slave. Pedro Menéndez also hoped that merchants, learning of the richness of the Florida lands, would invest enough to create large stock-raising haciendas and sugar-mills, sizeable vineyards and grain fields. After ten years, he assured Philip II, the Crown would receive fine profits from such a land.[25] The gathering of the settlers in Toledo began, and Pedro del Castillo began to prepare to receive them in Cádiz to arrange for their passage overseas to Florida.[26]

Meanwhile, the royal agencies had finally begun to prepare the Florida supply shipment which had been under discussion since the previous summer. After repeated orders from Philip II, the Casa de Contratación selected and began to stock two urcas for the Florida voyage.[27] Once the winter had begun, the sailing was deferred until early spring.

Also to be sent in the urcas to Florida would be a number of persons returning to the provinces as well as a heavy reinforcement of the Jesuit Florida mission, led by Father Juan Bautista de Segura. The Indians who had come to Spain with Pedro Menéndez and their interpreter would also board one of the vessels, as would Menéndez'

24. Menéndez describes the agreement with Pérez in his letter to the King from St. Augustine dated October 20, 1566, from A.G.I. *Santo Domingo* 115 (Stetson Coll.). The rupture with Pérez is evident in the letter Pérez wrote on November 28, 1567, from Santo Domingo to the King, castigating Menéndez for selling royal property and accusing the adelantado of attempting to ruin him. The letter is from A.G.I. *Santo Domingo* 71 (Stetson Coll.).

25. See Pedro Menéndez to Crown, St. Augustine, October 20, 1566, A.G.I. *Santo Domingo* 115 (Stetson Coll.) for the adelantado's plan for the settlers and his arrangement for them.

26. The collection of the settlers from Toledo in early 1568 is described in material found with an order of July 26, 1568, before the Casa representative in Cádiz, from A.G.I. *Indiferente General* 1,220.

27. The royal orders were sent to the Casa on August 13, 28, 30, 1567; Philip II sent the Menéndez memorial of September 21 with another dispatch to Seville on October 1, 1567, and sent yet another letter there on October 15, 1567. These are from A.G.I. *Contratación* 5,012 (Stetson Coll.). Other letters from the King to the Casa were sent on November 3, 4, and 18; these are in A.G.I. *Indiferente General* 1,967 (Stetson Coll.).

new lieutenant governor of Cuba, Dr. Zayas. Diego de Miranda would return on the same ship to serve Pedro Menéndez in Cuba.[28]

It was, for Pedro Menéndez de Avilés, a matter of practical urgency and personal conscience that the Jesuit mission in Florida go ahead with all possible speed. Upon his return to Spain, he had pressed his monarch and the high officials of the Jesuit order for more missionaries. It was evident, by the fall of 1567, that Menéndez was exerting his influence so that a new contingent of Jesuits might be approved and sent to Florida with the relief ships.[29]

For their part, the Jesuits appreciated the sincere religious zeal of the adelantado and were cognizant of his power and influence at the Spanish court.[30] There were, however, obstacles to the Florida mission which Menéndez had to overcome. Widespread deprecation of Florida as a place of sterile soil and hostile Indians had come to Spain and was currently spoken of at court. The news of the death of Father Martínez had two effects: the dangers of Florida might dishearten the timid, but the possibility of martyrdom might encourage those of fervent faith. In an attempt to overcome any hesitations which the Jesuits might have, Pedro Menéndez appeared at their college in Seville on December 16, 1567. There he described the religious efforts in Florida to date and outlined his plan to establish a Jesuit college in Havana. In Cuba, the adelantado declared, the children of Indian leaders from Florida would be taught the Spanish language and the tenets of Christianity. They might also serve there as hostages for the safety of missionaries and soldiers at the Florida posts.[31]

Menéndez had delineated his design for the conversion of the Florida Indians in considerable detail; this he conveyed to the general

28. The Casa de Contratación acknowledged the King's order authorizing the Indians to sail on the relief ships in a letter sent from Seville on February 17, 1568, from A.G.I. *Contratación* 5,168. From the same legajo, on March 4, 1568, the approval for the passage of Miranda and "Pedro de Bacortoqui—the Vizcaíno who came with the Indians" was given. Payment of freight for the Indians and their interpreter is listed in A.G.I. *Contaduría* 299, 53:2 and 53:2 vto. Dr. Zayas later wrote a letter (from Seville, August 29, 1569) to the Crown telling of his voyage on one of the urcas of 1568. His letter is from A.G.I. *Indiferente General* 1,221.

29. Menéndez' influence in obtaining the royal letters of authorization for the missionaries was mentioned in a letter from Geronimo Ruiz del Portillo to Francisco de Borja, now General of the Jesuit order. The letter, dated September 25, 1567, has been reprinted in Zubillaga, *Monumenta Antiquae Floridae*, pp. 204–5.

30. Both points of view are expressed in a letter from Pedro de Saavedra to the general of the order, written from Madrid on October 10, 1567, and reprinted in Zubillaga, *Monumenta Antiquae Floridae*, pp. 206–7.

31. The Menéndez visit is detailed in a third-person narrative entitled "Anonymous Relation of a visit which Pedro Menéndez made to the Florida Missionaries in Spain," dated December 16, 1567, and reprinted in Zubillaga, *Monumenta Antiquae Floridae*, pp. 214–18.

of the Jesuit order at about the same time. From this plan it is evident that the post at Havana was to be only one of several regional colleges which were to deal with the vast areas of continental Florida, as missionaries arrived and were assigned to new areas. Menéndez included in his design the promising new fields opened up by the Pardo journey and a series of planned settlements on the Gulf coast route to New Spain.[32]

In a moving ceremony on January 1, 1568, in the great cathedral at Seville, the five Florida Indians were baptized in the Roman Catholic faith in the presence of the adelantado and the Royal Officials of the House of Trade. This baptism helped to dramatize the expectation that thousands of others would follow, and that the men going shortly to Florida would be the means for the gaining of many souls, to the glory of God.[33]

Loaded with supplies for Florida, the royal expedition left Sanlúcar de Barrameda on April 10, 1568. Its cost to the Crown had been more than 30,000 ducats.[34] This time the relief vessels would be going to a land in which there were established cities and means of supply were functioning well. It was hoped that the work of mission could proceed upon the foundations already well laid.

On June 19, 1568, the convoy of two urcas dropped anchor in the port of St. Augustine. The ships had been guided directly to Florida by Gonzalo de Gayón, who then formally turned over the cargoes aboard to the governor and alcalde at St. Augustine.[35] The foodstuffs, clothing, and munitions were sufficient to relieve the immediate needs of the garrisons.

Father Segura, newly arrived at the mission field placed in his charge, met with Governor Bartolomé Menéndez and Chaplain Mendoza Grajales to gain first-hand impressions and increase his knowledge of Florida. He was told that Father Rogel, who had recently come from the South Florida missions, was still on his voyage to Santa Elena and Guale and would shortly return to report to Segura. In the

32. Pedro Menéndez de Avilés to Francisco de Borja, Madrid, January 18, 1568, in Zubillaga, *Monumenta Antiquae Floridae*, pp. 228–34.

33. The baptism is described by Zubillaga in *La Florida*, p. 313.

34. The departure is mentioned in a letter from Gonzalo de Alamo to Francisco de Borja, sent from Havana on November 17, 1568, and reprinted in Zubillaga, *Monumenta Antiquae Floridae*, p. 349. Crown costs for the urcas are summarized in A.G.I. *Contaduria* 299, no. 2, 533; no. 5-B, 11–2. I am indebted to Paul E. Hoffman for this citation.

35. The date of arrival is given by Father Antonio Sedeño in a letter to Francisco Borja dated Havana, November 17, 1568; in Zubillaga, *Monumenta Antiquae Floridae*, p. 351. The order of Gonzalo Gayón to Martín de Argüelles, Alcalde, is dated at St. Augustine, June 22, 1568, from A.G.I. *Contratación* 58.

meantime, it was easy to determine that the St. Augustine garrison was almost demoralized. The Spanish were still in a state of shock: less than two months before, the French had landed, made a pact with the hostile Indians, and taken and burned Fort San Mateo! As the Jesuits learned about the disaster, it became clear to them that its roots lay deeper in the past. The two main causes of the loss of San Mateo seemed to lie in the nature of Menéndez' undisciplined soldiery and in the continued hostility of major components of the Timucuan Indians to the Spanish.

Soon after the departure of Pedro Menéndez, yet another mutiny plot had been uncovered at St. Augustine. Five ringleaders had confessed under torture and had been executed.[36] Even among the inner circle of Menéndez' faithful Asturians, moreover, dissent and argument had flourished during his absence. Martín de Argüelles and Bartolomé Menéndez had almost come to blows, and Esteban de las Alas had found it necessary to intervene and confine the two men until they could be reconciled. Under such circumstances, it was indeed difficult to maintain adequate discipline and to keep proper guard over the posts of Florida.

In the summer of 1567, the tensions between the Spanish garrisons and the Indians of Saturiba and his allies reached a climax. The Timucuan chief had joined with the Indians of the Nocoroco-Mayaca area and with those of Potano (located within present-day Alachua County) to wage war upon Utina. Although it was something which the adelantado of Florida had sought to avoid, the Spanish again found themselves playing out a role opposite that which René de Laudonnière had played. The enemies of the French had, perforce, become friends to the Spanish, and Indians who had allied with Laudonnière were now firmly united against the Spaniards. In August 1567, Captain Pedro de Andrada marched his company of eighty men deep into the interior of the peninsula to attack the stronghold of the Potanos. While passing a heavily wooded hammock, the Spanish company was attacked from ambush by a sizeable force of Indians. A cloud of arrows struck the soldiers, and Captain Andrada and many of his men died. Circumstances were now ripe for the very eventuality which Pedro Menéndez and Philip II had so strongly feared—the union of a French invader with hostile Florida Indians.[37]

36. Francisco López de Mendoza Grajales recounts the mutiny in his letter to Pedro Menéndez, written from St. Augustine on August 6, 1567, and reprinted in Lawson, "Letters of Menéndez," 2:328–32. The hanging of one of the mutineers, Alonso Lópes de Yepes on June 1, 1567, is mentioned in a marginal note opposite his name on the ration list for 1566–67 in A.G.I. *Contaduría* 941 (microfilm, P. K. Yonge Library).

37. The Andrada expedition is recounted briefly by Chaplain Mendoza Grajales in

It was left for a Gascon nobleman, Dominique de Gourgues, to mount in 1567–68 a French expedition of revenge for the death of Ribault and the other French killed in Florida. Although his voyage exhibited some of the characteristics of a normal corsair journey, its leisurely course to the Cape Verde Islands and westward to the Windward Islands led de Gourgues at last to Florida.[38]

Spanish and French sources agree that the three ships and two small craft of Dominique de Gourgues arrived off the St. Augustine bar on the afternoon of Good Friday in 1568.[39] The Spanish were already somewhat on edge because of the touchy Indian situation. On the last of March, at dawn, a force of 400 Timucuans had assaulted San Mateo, forced one side of the fortress, and withdrawn after wounding several Spaniards. Now, at St. Augustine, the Spanish fired two cannon shots to mark the port, if the sails were those of friendly ships. If they proved to be French ships, they would be warned that they would be met there with gunfire. The vessels sheered off and turned their course northward. Esteban de las Alas, who was ill of fever at St. Augustine, sent warning of the strange ships to his garrison at San Mateo, together with reinforcements.

When de Gourgues anchored his ships in the mouth of the St. Marys, he was greeted by Indians whose unfriendly aspect soon turned to joy when they learned that the strangers were Frenchmen. Shortly, Chief Saturiba himself arrived to parley with Dominique de Gourgues. Liberal gifts from de Gourgues and his enmity toward the Spanish sealed a bargain: the Spanish forts would be assaulted and destroyed. Intelligence provided by the Indians and confirmed by Pierre de Bré, a young Frenchman who had found refuge with Saturiba, gave de Gourgues a good understanding of the Spanish dispositions.

his August 7, 1567, letter; see note 36. The death of the captain and his men is mentioned in the ration list marginal comments in A.G.I. *Contaduría* 941. In 1569, Andrada's wife, Doña Constanza, received a 500-ducat merced from the King after pleading her case before the Council of the Indies. The matter was heard before the Council in Madrid on January 27, 1569, and the case is from A.G.I. *Indiferente General* 1,220.

38. The basic source for the De Gourgues expedition is "La Reprinse de la Floride par le captaine Gourgues," published in translation (Jeannette Thurber Connor) and reprinted in Bennett, *Settlement of Florida*, pp. 202–26. According to the narrative, the Frenchmen left Europe on August 22, 1567, and reached Florida by way of Dominica, Puerto Rico, and Santo Domingo.

39. The first Spanish description of the De Gourgues raid is a report from Esteban de las Alas, probably addressed to Juan de Hinestrosa in Havana, and dated May 9, 1568, at St. Augustine. It is from A.G.I. *Patronato* 254, no. 2, ramo 1 (Stetson Coll.), and is misdated 1569 on the cover sheet. The loss of San Mateo is narrated at length in the body of the legal case against the Spanish soldiers charged with its loss. This is from A.G.I. *Justicia* 1,000, no. 2, ramo 5 (Stetson Coll.).

Crossing with his Indian allies in two small boats, the French leader took a hundred arquesbusiers to the two small blockhouses which the Spanish had built on the opposite banks of the mouth of the St. Johns River. First one, then the other fort was taken and burned. There is a substantial discrepancy between the opposing accounts as to the strength of the Spanish garrisons and the actions which ensued at the little stockades. It is, however, evident that some of the Spanish got away to St. Augustine, and a few escaped to give the warning to San Mateo.

At that fort, the news inspired little but overwhelming fear. Instead of preparing to repel the enemy, and perhaps to withstand a long siege, the Spanish soldiers were panic-stricken. They grossly overestimated the number of the French forces, decided to flee, and began to cook up rations and get their possessions together. At dawn of April 25, the men began to slip out of the fort, leaving the guns unspiked and the artillery ammunition intact. None of their officers' orders had any effect—safety was their primary aim. They skulked through the thick woods, trying to find their way to St. Augustine. Some were killed or captured by the Indians. Later, a loyal captain returned to the fort with a few men and remained long enough to spike the guns.

When the French came against San Mateo, they took it without opposition. Two captives who had been caught by the Indians in their headlong flight were hanged outside the fort. Dominique de Gourgues retraced his steps to the ships anchored in the St. Marys; he was richer by the gaining of some nine bronze artillery pieces and other lesser prizes. Bidding farewell to the Indians of Saturiba and Tacatacuru, the Frenchmen left Florida to return to Europe.

An expedition from St. Augustine had the melancholy duty of visiting the burned forts and burying the dead. It found eight men hanging from trees near the two destroyed blockhouses and two more outside the shell of Fort San Mateo. A fire accidentally set by the joyous Indians of Saturiba had gutted the buildings inside the fort, and all the artillery was gone. The Spanish began the customary task of assessing the blame for the loss of the forts. Esteban de las Alas gave it as his opinion that, of 120 men in San Mateo, only a dozen or so would be free of the stigma of cowardice in the face of the enemy. A hearing was held, and the trial of the guilty began. The Spanish were determined to punish the Indians who had aided the French and also decided to build a strong outpost at the island of Tacatacuru to prevent further attacks by way of the hostile Indian communities near the St. Marys.

The French triumph at the scene of their earlier disaster was as cheaply won as had been Menéndez' own assault on Fort Caroline. Their chief gain was the satisfaction of a deep need for national revenge, for the capture of an empty fort and the hanging of a few men were little more than symbolic victories. The de Gourgues raid did not succeed in dislodging the Spanish from their foothold in Florida. In spite of this blow, the garrisons would remain. For their part, the Spanish had even less reason to boast of their performance in the action. The defense system erected and maintained at great cost and effort by the King and the adelantado of Florida had utterly failed its first test. If this was the manner in which the dominions of the King would be defended and in which the settlers now coming to Florida would be protected, it augured ill for the future of the enterprise.

After learning of the debacle of San Mateo, the new Jesuit vice-provincial and his missionaries were reminded afresh of the dangers and difficulties of their chosen field. Within a few days of their arrival, Juan Rogel came from Santa Elena to report to his superior and fellows. Father Rogel quickly brought the Jesuits up to date on the missions of South Florida and on possibilities for evangelization among the Indians of Guale and Orista and those in the uplands west and north of Santa Elena.

The tale Juan Rogel had to tell of events at the fort missions of San Antón in Carlos, at Tequesta, and at Tocobaga was one of struggle and disaster. At Carlos, the main station of the Jesuit, the tension between Spaniard and Indian had risen after the departure of Pedro Menéndez in the spring of 1567. The Spanish were like men besieged in their blockhouse—they dared not leave it without armed guard. Rogel, who had helped mediate between the opposing forces, left for Havana in early April 1567. Shortly after his departure, Carlos moved his women and treasure to another island, called in his subordinate chieftains, and prepared to massacre the Christians. When he learned of this, Captain Reinoso called Chief Carlos to him near the fort and killed him outright.[40]

The new chief, named Philip by the Spanish, was a man who had held a valid claim to the throne of the Indian kingdom. After the death of Carlos, Philip summoned the subchiefs of the surrounding Calusa towns to swear homage to him and to bring their usual gifts of women to the new King. Philip was now the accepted leader of the Calusa, and the Spanish could make a fresh beginning in that land.

40. Juan Rogel describes the death of Chief Carlos and events at Tocobaga and Tequesta in a letter to Geronimo Ruiz del Portillo dated at Havana, April 25, 1568, and reprinted in Zubillaga, *Monumenta Antiquae Floridae*, pp. 274–311.

Upon his return from Cuba with Pedro Menéndez Marquéz, Father Rogel went directly to the tiny settlement the adelantado had made in Tocobaga. There he found the garrison in good health and spirits. Chief Tocobaga and some of his principal nobles attended the Mass celebrated by the priest, but it was rumored that the chief was displeased at the possibility that the images in the Indian temple would be burned by the Spaniards. If that occurred, the interpreters told Rogel, the chief himself and his family had sworn to perish in the same fire.

When the Spanish returned to Carlos, Pedro Menéndez Marquéz confirmed Philip as chief, as a vassal of the King of Spain. Father Rogel then began in earnest to converse with the Calusa chief, recognizing that to win his conversion was a vital first step in the Christianization of his people. For six months, Rogel labored persuasively with Philip. As his mission moved from the shallow first stage of teaching the Indian children and a few adults the basic prayers and the adoration of the cross, the real difficulties began.

It now became clear that the Indians might be willing to accept the Christian God as a coequal or even superior deity in their pantheon, but that claims for exclusivity on behalf of God would meet dogged opposition. The Catholic doctrines of the afterlife, moreover, conflicted directly with the Indian view of a threefold soul of the dead which became, after transmigration, a nullity. The harsh condemnation by the Jesuit of strong cultural traditions, such as the sacrifice of children, the practice of sodomy, and polygamy for the chiefs, also raised a strong reaction on the part of Philip. Although the Calusa chief recognized the power of the written theology of the Christians, he persisted in his old ceremonies, while continuing to pray before the cross. For his part, Juan Rogel was determined to baptize Philip only when he truly reached the point of full understanding and acceptance of Christian doctrine. The Jesuit also vowed to deface and burn the Indians' idols and free Philip and all of his people forever from the heathen rites of their worship.[41]

From Brother Villareal in Tequesta, Rogel heard that the Indians on Biscayne Bay seemed more tractable and submissive than those of Carlos. Even so, the work of evangelization went very slowly in Tequesta. The chief permitted the Jesuit to catechize the children in the main house, where older Indians were often present, although they took no part in the prayers. After many months of work, only one old dying woman had accepted baptism. The Tequestas, who were sea-

41. The religious differences between Philip and Father Rogel are outlined in the priest's letter to Geronimo Ruiz del Portillo, cited in note 40.

sonal gatherers and moved their residence to the island keys in Biscayne Bay during the winter, had little to spare from their meager store of food. Indeed, the presence of the Spanish garrison began to be a troublesome burden, as the soldiers at times abused the Indians.[42]

At the beginning of December 1567, Juan Rogel had again made a trip to Havana to seek a more plentiful and reliable supply for the South Florida garrisons from Juan de Hinestrosa and Hernando de Baeza in Havana. Shortly after the first of January 1568, the Jesuit missionary returned to Florida with Pedro Menéndez Marquéz and three small craft. Again, the Spaniards directed their vessels first to the middle west coast of the peninsula and approached the village of Tocobaga. There they beheld an eerie spectacle. The Indian town was completely deserted, and nothing was found except the bodies of two dead Spanish soldiers. After further search, they learned that all twenty-four of the garrison had been killed by the Indians. Outraged, and unable to find anyone to punish, Menéndez Marquéz burned Tocobaga and returned to Carlos.[43]

On April 4, 1568, a small boat came into the harbor of Carlos with Brother Villareal and eighteen soldiers, the survivors of the garrison at Tequesta. Menéndez Marquéz had rescued them after the Indians had murdered four and surrounded the other men in their wooden fort. The immediate reason for the hostile acts of the Indians was the killing by the soldiers of a principal native leader. Shortly after the arrival of the survivors, Rogel and Villareal went to Havana. The priest from Carlos then sailed north with one of Menéndez' supply vessels to meet eventually with his fellow Jesuits.

Juan Rogel had much to tell the new company of missionaries from Spain about the northern settlements and forts established by Pedro Menéndez de Avilés. He had first stopped in Guale and had been impressed, as the other Spaniards had been the year before, by the mild nature of the Indians. Rogel noted that twenty-three affiliated chieftains in and around Guale spoke a common language, which was understood for a good distance inland. When he arrived in Santa Elena, Father Rogel was immediately struck by the similarities of the farmland close by to that of Spain. Wheat, grapes, and a

42. See Brother Villareal's letter to Juan Rogel, dated at Tequesta on January 23, 1568, from Zubillaga, *Monumenta Antiquae Floridae*, pp. 235–40.

43. The voyage to Tocobaga and the subsequent flight of the Spanish from Tequesta is discussed by Rogel in a letter to Geronimo Ruiz del Portillo dated at Havana on April 25, 1568, in Zubillaga, *Monumenta Antiquae Floridae*, pp. 274–311. Menéndez Marquéz and other witnesses testified to events at the two missions in "Daños de los Indios de la Florida," in A.G.I. *Patronato* 257, no. 3, ramo 20 (Stetson Coll.).

kind of wild olive grew well there, and the priest had seen a thriving vineyard at Santa Elena itself. During the time of his stay at Santa Elena, Captain Juan Pardo had just returned from his second lengthy journey inland. He discussed his discoveries with the Jesuit and shared his insights about the continental reaches of Spanish Florida with him.

Juan Pardo had left garrisons on his first journey inland, but instead of maintaining peaceful relationships with the Indians, the soldiers left in the forts had waged war upon the natives. In the fall of 1567, Pardo made a second inland journey of exploration. After renewing his garrisons at Guatari and Joada, the Spanish captain pressed on through the cool lands to the west. Skirting the south end of the mountain chain, he crossed extreme northern Georgia and entered present-day Alabama. Crossing the upper reaches of the Tennessee, Chattahoochee, and Coosa rivers, the captain noted the well-watered, fertile nature of the land. At the great Indian town of Cosa, or Coosa, Juan Pardo again crossed the trail of Hernando de Soto. Pardo continued on for seven more days until he came to Trascaluza, which to him marked the western boundary of Menéndez' land of Florida. From here, he maintained, it was only nine to eleven days' travel to New Spain—only about a hundred miles. Actually, more than a thousand miles stretched between northern Alabama and the closest point in Nueva Galicia or the nearest coastal settlement in Pánuco. Menéndez' chief geographic error—the foreshortening of continental distances—was thus continued.

After the end of his second continental trip, Juan Pardo sent reinforcements to his settlements at Guatari and Joada. By the time Father Rogel reached Santa Elena in June 1568, news had already reached the seacoast that many Spanish soldiers had been massacred by Indians at the inland forts.[44]

As the one man who was in an unusually good position to survey the entire colonization effort of Pedro Menéndez from the Florida west coast all the way to Santa Elena, Juan Rogel is a valuable witness for the historian. In July 1568, he gave the general of the Jesuit order

---

44. The second Pardo journey inland evidently lasted from September 1, 1567, to March 1568. The account which has survived is that taken by Juan de la Vandera at Santa Elena on January 23, 1569. I found a copy of this report in A.G.I. *Contratación* 58. It has been reprinted by Ruidiaz, *La Florida*, 2:465–73, and by Lawson in "Letters of Menéndez," 2:345–51. The deaths of several of the soldiers left in the inland forts are mentioned in the 1566–67 ration list in A.G.I. *Contaduría* 941, fol. 5–9 vto. (microfilm, P. K. Yonge Library).

his frank opinion of the state of the enterprise of evangelization in Florida.[45]

He thought he could discern one major obstacle which had impeded the religious mission in Florida—one thing which he believed had led to the many Indian uprisings in the two years immediately past. In his opinion, it was the behavior of the Spanish soldiers which had outraged the natives in every area of occupation. They had demanded food from the Indians, beaten and killed natives, and abused their women. The Spaniards had been, he asserted, overbearing, cruel, and harsh; this treatment had been the proximate cause of the loss of Santa Lucía, the troubles at Tocobaga, Carlos, and Tequesta, and the Indian attacks upon Fort Joada and other inland blockhouses. While the priest prayed for restraint of the licentious soldiery, he could also see one great hope for the Jesuit mission with the Florida Indians. If, he said, married settlers came in numbers, the land could be secured and the Gospel might then be preached in an atmosphere of community instead of one of lust and bloodshed.

What Juan Rogel could not see as clearly, or perhaps could not admit to his superior, was that the strict inculcation of Christian doctrine also posed a threat to the Indian cultures. Under the influence of the charisma of Pedro Menéndez' driving personality and exposed to the power and technology of European civilization, the Indians had taken the first steps to Christianization. The insistence on exclusive acceptance of Catholicism by the Indians would not be lightly imposed, however. Elimination of the old rites, ceremonies, and beliefs would imply a thoroughgoing change in Indian life. As they sensed, it would, in fact, mean the total alteration of their culture. The enforcement of such change would be accomplished only through heavy and consistent pressure by the Spanish over a period of time.

The framework in which Castilian religious and social values could best be instilled in the Indians was, as Rogel had stated, one of successful Spanish colonization. The only means by which the enterprise of Florida could succeed was that of greater population. As the first three years of the Florida asiento drew to an end, the greater part of the effort of settlement—the population of the provinces—had still to be accomplished. Adelantado, missionary, and soldier alike saw this to be the most important task.

To support the colonization of Florida, feverish activities were going forward in Spain in the face of some difficulty and opposition.

45. Juan Rogel to Francisco de Borja, Havana, July 25, 1568; in Zubillaga, *Monumenta Antiquae Floridae*, pp. 317–28.

While Pedro Menéndez de Avilés dedicated his remarkable energies to the construction and outfitting of his fleet of fast new ships in Vizcaya, his deputy Castillo continued to labor in Cádiz for the enterprise of Florida.[46] He had dispatched a caravel and galleon in the winter of 1567–68, and had encountered a degree of obstruction by the Casa officials in Seville.[47]

As the Crown moved slowly to pay the men who had served in the Archiniega expedition to Florida, the King made a ruling which favored Pedro Menéndez. Philip II agreed to pay the pilots who had gone on the original journey to Florida, even though the Casa de Contratación had disputed the payment.[48] The King wrote the Royal Officials of Cuba, asking that they pay the 200 soldiers Pedro Menéndez had left in Havana, so that their support would not become a charge upon the adelantado.[49] There continued, however, a strong reaction against the privileges and benefits the King had granted to Pedro Menéndez de Avilés. Unfavorable reports on Florida continued to arrive from the Indies.[50] The ruling by the Council of the Indies for Captains Redroban and Enriquez was a setback for the adelantado who had sentenced them. With characteristic conservatism and concern for the rights of the Crown, Philip II shortly took another step to offset some of the power which he had given to Pedro Menéndez. In view of the accusations, the King determined to reassert royal control over the Crown treasury in Florida, and on May 23, 1568, he named Francisco de Esquivel as treasurer of Florida. Evidently the monarch also thought of removing the accountant whom Menéndez had named.[51]

It was the controversy over the embarking of Pedro Menéndez' 200 colonists, however, which led to the major determination the Crown next made about the adelantamiento of Florida. Pedro del Castillo

46. The adelantado describes his preoccupation with the construction of the guard fleet *Galibrazas* in his letter to the King from Santander on May 12, 1568; from Lawson, "Letters of Menéndez," 2:336–45.

47. A January dispute over the dispatch of a galleon was heard before Antonio de Abalia in Cádiz on May 15, 1568; this is from A.G.I. *Indiferente General* 1,220.

48. Calculation of the pay due each man was made in A.G.I. *Contaduría* 310-B. The payment of Sancho de Archiniega is listed in A.G.I. *Contaduría* 299; 12:7. The payment of Gonzalo de Gayón and the other pilots was recorded in the same legajo at 38:4, 2.

49. The cédula is dated February 2, 1568, at Madrid, and is found in A.G.I. *Contaduría* 548.

50. See the letter from Hernán Pérez to the King sent from Santo Domingo on November 28, 1567, and from A.G.I. *Santo Domingo* 71 (Stetson Coll.).

51. Esquivel's appointment was dated at Madrid on May 23, 1568, and is from A.G.I. *Indiferente General* 1,220. The adelantado complained of the removal of his own people from their offices in his letter to Philip II dated at Santander on May 12, 1568, and reprinted in Lawson, "Letters of Menéndez," 2:336–45.

asked permission of the Casa representative in Cádiz, Antonio Abalia, to load the urca *Salvadora* with the large body of married settlers intended for Florida. Even though Menéndez' trade privileges had not expired, the three-year term of the asiento had ended at the end of June 1568. The Casa alleged, however, that since the term had then passed in which the adelantado was to have taken 500 settlers to Florida, the ships could not be sent.[52]

On August 23, 1568, the King granted specific permission for the ship with its colonists to sail to Florida. Three weeks later the order was followed up with a more detailed command to the royal trade representative in Cádiz. The 200 settlers should go immediately, and Menéndez would also have permission to embark other settlers direct from the Canary Islands to Florida.[53] Philip II had effectively renewed the Menéndez contract. The King had also made a key decision to aid his Florida adelantado to continue his population effort in Florida. As an intermediate stage between the haphazard means of supply previously used to support royal troops in Florida and a full-fledged subsidy, the King had agreed to provide regular support for a minimum royal garrison of 150 men. This would promote stability in royal support for Florida and would help regularize the financial requirements of both parties.[54] There would now be means to encourage the effort of population, upon which the future of the enterprise of Florida would depend. Both the parties to the adelantamiento of Florida were deeply committed to the continuation of their joint enterprise. Their expectations to date had led them into great expense but remained, as yet, unrealized.

52. Pedro del Castillo, in attempting to load the shallop *Nuestra Señora de la Consolación* and a caravel to carry the settlers and supplies to Florida, ran into opposition from Antonio de Abalia, representative of the Casa in Cádiz. Abalia swore that many Portuguese people were illegally aboard the ships. See "Información ante Abalia," Cádiz, July 26, 1568, from A.G.I. *Indiferente General* 2,673. Pedro Menéndez discussed the dispute and complained to the King about Abalia in a letter, n.d. [August 1568], from the same legajo. The Casa alleged that the actions of Abalia had been justified because the term of Menéndez' asiento had expired; the King referred to this charge and ordered that the Casa let the ships and settlers go, in his letter to Seville sent from El Escorial on August 22, 1568, from A.G.I. *Indiferente General* 1,967.

53. The King admitted that Menéndez had carried Portuguese on his vessels, but extended the adelantado's trade privileges and ordered that the violations be overlooked. This is contained in a letter from Philip II to Abalia, sent from El Pardo on August 17, 1568, and found in A.G.I. *Indiferente General* 1,967. A copy is also in A.G.I. *Indiferente General* 2,673.

54. The cédula of July 15, 1568, is cited and summarized in a later royal order of June 17, 1570, found in A.G.I. *Contaduría* 548. In a consulta of November 1569, the Council of the Indies noted that the Crown support for a minimum Florida garrison had been approved at a meeting in May 1568; this is from *Envío* 25-H, no. 164, *Archivo del Instituto de Valencia de Don Juan*.

Epilogue

Study of the background and events of the initial Florida conquest of 1565–68 discloses that it was accomplished by a conquest entrepreneur, or adelantado. The founding of Spanish Florida thus fitted into a long tradition in which much of Spanish expansion was done through royal surrogates, who underwrote the pacification and settlement of new lands in return for license to exploit them and the granting of titles, monopolies, land grants, and revenues. Philip II, caught between the urgencies of his dynastic policies and his limited resources, granted adelantamientos upon a number of occasions and promulgated royal ordinances in 1563 defining the place of private conquerors in Spanish expansion.

After the collapse of Spanish-French negotiations over New World spheres of influence following the treaty of Cateau-Cambrésis, the Spanish monarch learned of the French settlement at Port Royal. He ordered a punitive expedition to sail against the intruders and licensed Lucas Vázquez de Ayllón as adelantado for the settlement of the North American mainland. Neither of these efforts succeeded, but the French vacated Port Royal of their own volition, only to be succeeded by another Huguenot colony which established itself in Florida and built Fort Caroline. Deserters from that garrison went corsairing in the West Indies, and their capture and confessions eventually resulted in word of the French incursion reaching Spain late.

Meanwhile, the Asturian seaman Pedro Menéndez de Avilés had risen, through ability and influence, to be a minor power in the Indies trade and a major Crown official in the fleet system. He soon came into direct conflict with the merchants of Seville and the Casa de

Contratación over jurisdiction. After his conviction in 1563 and 1564 upon charges of smuggling and conflict of interest, Menéndez escaped his imprisonment in Seville and finally succeeded in having most of the charges against him annulled by the Council of the Indies. He then signed an asiento, or contract, with Philip II for the conquest and settlement of Florida.

Lamentably, historians have concentrated upon the striking events of Fort Caroline and Matanzas and thus upon the purely diplomatic and military aspects of the Florida conquest. This has resulted in general disregard of the fact that the Menéndez contract was signed before there was knowledge of René de Laudonnière's fort on the river May. It was only then that the dual nature of the enterprise of Florida began, as the Crown added troops, supplies, and munitions to Menéndez' own effort. Even though royal aid continued on a sporadic basis and resulted in 1568 in the King's guarantee of payment for a minimum number of soldiers, Menéndez' private government continued to control Florida and undergird its support during the entire period. The very nature of an adelantamiento, such as that in Florida, rendered Crown control over use of royal resources impossible.

Pedro Menéndez had to buy or lease ships, hire seamen, recruit soldiers, and purchase supplies for his expeditions to Florida; he was required to encourage and support settlers, and had to maintain his establishment for the term of his contract. Examination of the resources of the adelantado for the conquest discloses that he utilized all the cash, loans, and credit he could obtain in order to fulfill his obligations. Menéndez' origin, as a product of the north-of-Spain privateer culture and his relationship to its great noble families, insured that his Florida conquest was not to be a solitary effort, but a regional enterprise. Manpower, associates in leadership, and funds for Florida came from a network of fellow norteños, whose commercial and political reach extended to the south of Spain and to the Indies. The adelantado executed a contract with Pedro del Castillo of Cádiz, making him his surrogate and erecting a structure of powers-of-attorney which enabled him to tap commercial revenues and maintain his effort in Florida. The events of the conquest tested Menéndez' resources to the utmost. His decision to proceed directly to Florida from Puerto Rico in 1565 made his victory possible but cost heavily in ships, lives, and money. After royal aid promised to him in the Indies failed to materialize, the adelantado had great difficulty providing for the garrisons in Florida. The conquest also seriously reduced his private income potential through the destruction of many of his ships, and he underwent great tribulations with the unruly contract soldiers, whether those sent by the King or his own men. Their mutinies and rebellions cost Menéndez heavily, and their treatment of the natives undermined his Indian policies.

In spite of obstacles, Pedro Menéndez de Avilés and his norteño conquest group had achieved partial success in the realization of their Florida design. Their continental exploration had reached the Appalachians and the Carolina capes, and forts and missions had been built from the peninsular Gulf coast around the southeast cape north to Santa Elena. In spite of slow progress in converting the Indians, dedicated Jesuits persisted in their Florida mission in keeping with Menéndez' coherent plan for areal mission centers. Despite the soldiers' mutinies, Pedro Menéndez had imposed a detailed system for local and regional government upon his provinces. He made his establishments in complete accordance with ancient Castilian municipal institutions, which provided for the means of government, justice, and extension into the land under Spanish law. Menéndez had created cities whose cabildos would, he hoped, govern communities where settlers, soldiers, and missionaries could build a society that would include and instruct the native peoples. He made arrangements to bring hundreds of settlers to Florida, with whom he would share the costs and benefits of their establishment. Noble and commoner alike shared expectations of a land which would prosper in local self-sufficiency and in the production of hides and sugar for export. They also hoped that Florida would profit through discovery of a water passage to New Spain and the Pacific, and that naval stores production and shipbuilding would flourish there. The adelantado himself planned a large domain in the fertile lands north and west of Santa Elena, which might support the title of marquis, such as Cortés had enjoyed.

At the end of the first phase of the Florida conquest in summer 1568, Pedro Menéndez had been personally rewarded for his services in Florida by profitable offices, a bonus, and additional revenues. The King had also agreed to support a minimum Florida garrison of 150 men from fleet funds, while Menéndez' trade privileges were extended in return for his continuation of the efforts of colonization. In spite of the expulsion of the French at great cost to both contracting parties, only a foothold had been gained in Florida. The small number and wide dispersal of Spanish forces made real penetration and exploitation of the land impossible. Successful evangelization of the Indians and the creation of prosperous colonies were not yet realized. It had become ominously clear that only a sizeable Spanish population, supported by military force, could provide the matrix for a true pacification of the vast territory of Florida and its native peoples. The tasks of conquest had just fairly begun.

Appendixes

1. Agreement between Dr. Vázquez of the Council in the Name of the King, with Pedro Menéndez de Avilés, March 15, 1565

That which is agreed between Dr. Vázquez of the Council of His Majesty and in his name as party of the first part and Pedro Menéndez de Avilés, Caballero of the Order of Santiago of the other is as follows:

First, that the said Pedro Menéndez obliges himself that within the coming month of May, he will have ready and equipped to sail in Sanlúcar de Barrameda or Puerto de Santa María or Cádiz, to go with the first [good] weather, six shallops, each one of fifty tons, more or less, and four fast zabras, with their oars, artillery, arms and munitions, loaded with supplies and put in condition for war.

Item—He will carry five hundred men, one hundred farmers, one hundred sailors and the rest men and officers of sea and war, and among these there will be at least two clerics and other persons, skilled in stonecutting, carpentry, and farriers, blacksmiths and surgeons, all with their arms, arquebuses, crossbows, helmets and shields and with the other offensive and defensive arms that might seem fitting for the expedition.

Item—He will have ready within the same time-period his galleon named *San Pelayo*, which is of more than six hundred tons, new from its first voyage, which he will load and freight for any part of the Indies which he might wish. One-half or two-thirds of the cargo he may carry and the rest should be left vacant in order to carry in it up to three hundred men of the said five hundred, and some food and supplies which might be needed, as far as Dominica or Cape Tiburón or San Antonio, as he might deem best (which is seventy leagues from Havana, more or less, and about the same distance from Florida), because the said shallops cannot carry the said people, since they are small ships and not covered. They would sicken and die with too much sun and the heavy rain-squalls which there are in the said parts. Neither can they carry the supplies which are needed for these people for such a long journey. Having arrived as it has been said, at Dominica or some other place which seems best to him, he will transfer the people from the said galleon to the said shallops and the said galleon will go on its voyage. He [will go] with the said shallops and zabras, with the said five hundred men, supplied and prepared for war, as has been stated, to the Coast of Florida. There he is obliged to see and discover places which seem to him the best and most commodious, sailing along the coasts by sea and discovering and investigating by land, seeking the best site for a port and settlement and arranging to seek information. If there are on the said coast or land some corsair settlers or any other nations not subject to His Majesty, arrange to throw them out by the best means possible, which seem best to him. Take the land of the said Florida for His Majesty and in his royal name, attempting to bring its natives to the obedience of His Majesty. He will explore from the *Ancones* and bay of St. Joseph, which is in the western region of Florida to the *Cabeza de los Mártires*, which are in twenty-five degrees, and from there to Terranova, which is at fifty to sixty degrees of east-west, and all the coast north-south, to see and discover the ports and currents, rocks, shoals and inlets which might be in the said coast, marking and noting them as precisely as he can by their latitudes and bearings, in order that the secret of the coast and ports which are in it might be known and understood. This year he will do what he can and the rest within the three years for which he is obligated in this said asiento, and of all he shall bring testimony.

Item—He shall carry the necessary supplies for the said expedition for the five hundred men for one year, which year shall be counted from [the time] when the people are in the ships, ready to depart.

Item—That from the day when he sets sail, in the three years immediately following, he will put into the said coast and land of Florida up to five hundred men who might be settlers in it, of which two hundred shall be married and at least one hundred and the rest shall be farmers and officials, so that the land may be cultivated with more ease. They shall be religiously clean, and not of the prohibited [ones].

Item—With the said people, he shall build and populate in the said three years two or three towns in the places and ports which seem to him the best. In each one [there shall be] at least one hundred vecinos, and there should be in each one one great house of stone, adobe or wood, in accordance with the fitness and disposition of the land. [Each should have] its moat and draw-bridge, as strong as it could be made in accordance with the weather and lay of the land. Thus, if it be necessary, the vecinos could be gathered within it and sheltered from the dangers which might threaten from Indians, corsairs or other people.

Item—He will place, within the said time, among the number of the said people that he is obliged to bring at least ten or twelve religious of the order which seems best to him—persons who might be of good life and example. [He shall bring] four others of the Society of Jesus, in order that the preaching of the Gospel might take place in the said land, and in order that the Indians might be converted to our Holy Catholic faith and to the obedience of His Majesty.

Item—He shall place, within the said time, in the said land, one hundred horses and mares, two hundred calves, four hundred hogs, four hundred sheep, some goats and all the other livestock which seems fitting to him.

Item—He shall endeavor, in every way possible to carry out the said discovery and conquest in all peace, friendship and Christianity. The governing of the people in his charge shall be accomplished through Christian treatment, insofar as he can provide it, so that, in all things, Our Lord and His Majesty might be served, conforming to the instructions which might be given to him, which is that which is usually given to those who go to make similar settlements.

Item—He shall attempt to place, within the said three years, five hundred slaves for his service and for that of the people, in order that the towns might be built with more facility and the land might be cultivated. [They shall] plant sugarcane for the sugar works which shall be made, and to build the said sugar works.

Item—Since, upon the coasts of Vizcaya, Asturias, and Galicia there are shallops and zabras more serviceable than those of Andalusia and the same applies to skilled carpenters, blacksmiths, stonecutters, and farmers, it is understood that the part of this armada and people which depart from those places may go directly to the Canary Islands without coming to the city of Sanlúcar or to Cádiz, being first visited before the Justice or person whom His Majesty might name in the port.

Item—It is agreed that the said armada which he must take out [as has been said] must first be visited by one of the officials, in accordance with the customary regulation, in order to see if he goes with the order [prescribed by] and in compliance with the said asiento.

Item—He must give valid and sufficient bond that he will return to His Majesty 15,000 ducats of which he has made him merced, if he is not prepared to sail with the first favorable weather by the end of May, and if he does not have readied all which he is obliged to carry for the said period of time, in conformity with this asiento. He shall give the bond in this court or in the city of Seville, with submission to the royal Council of the Indies and to the other Justices of His Majesty.

In order to aid in the great expenses and labors which the said Pedro Menéndez must undergo in the discovery and settlement, that which is offered on behalf of His Majesty is as follows:

First, that there must at present be given and paid to him 15,000 ducats.

Item—That His Majesty must give authority to the said Pedro Menéndez so that he might be able to give repartimientos to the said settlers of lands and estates in the said land for their plantations, farms and livestock-breeding, in accordance with the qualifications of each and what seems best to him, without prejudice to the Indians.

Item—That His Majesty must give him five hundred slave licenses, free of all duties, with which they might be enabled to be taken to the said land, registered for it and for no other place.

Item—That he must be given the title of governor and captain-general of the said coast and land of Florida for all his life and for that of a son or son-in-law, with 2,000 ducats of salary, which he must have from the benefices and profits of His Majesty coming from the said land, and in no other manner.

Item—That he must be given the title of adelantado of the said land, for himself and for his heirs in perpetuity.

Item—If His Majesty establishes an Audiencia Real in the said territory, he must be given the title of alguacil mayor of the said Audiencia for himself and his heirs and successors in perpetuity.

Item—That His Majesty gives him in the said land, for himself and for his heirs in perpetuity, twenty-five square leagues in one or two locations [as he might wish it], which may be good land and in a place which might seem good to him—conveniently located, without prejudice to the Indians. With regard to the title of Marquis of the said land, which he asks be given to him, it is agreed that, the expedition being finished, and that which is contained in the asiento being complied with, His Majesty may make him the merced which would be fitting, in conformity with his services.

Item—Of fifteen parts, he must be given one of all the profits of mines, gold and silver, precious stones, pearls and benefices which His

Majesty might have in the said lands and provinces perpetually, for himself and for his heirs and successors, from which it is understood that the costs have been taken.

Item—He must be given two fisheries which he may select, one of pearls and the other of fish, for himself and for his heirs and successors in perpetuity.

Item—In the first ten years, the vecinos and settlers of the said land of Florida will not pay any almojarifazgo on the necessary supplies and provisions for their persons and houses.

Item—In the said first ten years, His Majesty need not be paid more than one-tenth of the gold and silver, pearls and [precious] stones which might be found and discovered in the said land, which said ten years shall begin to be counted from the day when the first smelting is done.

Item—That, when the said Pedro Menéndez absents himself from the said land, he may name and leave a deputy [who shall have in everything the same authority as himself] for as long as he wishes in order to come to these kingdoms and navigate in the Indies; this deputy whom he may name should be one who has the necessary qualities for the post.

Item—That in all the said three years that he must comply with this asiento, he need not pay any duties of almojarifazgo or of the galleys, or of any other things, whether of impositions upon ships or supplies, of arms or munitions, of barter with the Indians nor of any kind of food or drink. For all the above, he does not have to pay anything, as has been said; it is understood that this refers to items which are carried for Florida.

Item—That from the day he departs from these kingdoms, he may bring in the Indies navigation in any one year for a term of six years, two galleons of five to six hundred tons and two pataches of from one hundred fifty to two hundred tons, armed and equipped with artillery. They may sail as merchant or armada ships, within or outside of fleets, as might seem best to him. He may send them to any part or parts of the Indies which he might wish, together or singly, but they cannot go loaded with any merchandise except food and drink. Of the goods which he may carry and bring, and freight-revenues, and of the ships, he may not be required to pay avería for any armada or for galleys; this benefit is given him in aid of the costs and labors which he must experience in the said settlement and provision of it. Upon return from the Indies, he may bring [any] merchandise which he wishes free of averías, as it has been said, but he may not bring gold or silver, pearls or precious stones, except monies which belong to him and may be his own, and that which comes from freight-revenues from the galleons and pataches, of which he does not have to pay averia as it has been said.

Item—That for the period of six years, he may take from these kingdoms and from any part of them to the islands of Puerto Rico, Santo Domingo, Cuba, and to Florida, and from those parts to these, six shallops, and four zabras. [These may] sail together or singly, within or outside of fleets for the trade and commerce of the said Florida and to comply with the said asiento, and to carry there what seems best to him and may be needed for the people who may be in the said Florida. If he might wish to discharge some goods of eating and drinking which the said shallops and zabras carry in the said islands, he may do it, so that in place of those goods they may load livestock and things necessary for the said Florida. If some shallop or zabra should be left in those parts or might be lost, he may bring others in its place. The said six years must run from the month of June 1566. The masters and pilots who go in these ships must be natives, but may serve as masters and pilots even though they may not have been examined.

Item—That all [the ships] which he might take with the galleons, zabras, and pataches during the time of the said six years from the corsairs should be his or his heirs. Also, whatever prize might be taken from them—all the above to be without prejudice to the tercio [one-third Crown interest].

Item—It is agreed that, during the said six-year term, no one may in any way detain or embargo for His Majesty's service any of the said galleons, pataches, shallops, or zabras, in these kingdoms or in the Indies. If for some urgent and necessary reason any of the said ships may be embargoed, he may put others in their places, of the same tonnage. As long as the said six years might not have passed, he may bring them, in conformity with this said asiento all of the time for which they have been detained or embargoed. The officials of the Casa de Contratación of Seville or of Cádiz, or any other justices of these kingdoms or of the Indies where the said ships might arrive shall give him all favor for the rapid and good dispatch of them. They shall give the registries with all brevity, in order that they shall not be detained; they shall give all favor and aid to the captains and officials who sail in them.

Item—If God should carry off the said Pedro Menéndez before the end of the said three years in such a manner that he might not have been able to comply with his part of that which is contained in this said capitulación, that the person whom he shall name and designate may comply with it. In the event that no such person has been named, the person who inherits his estate may comply with it in order to enjoy all the mercedes contained in this said capitulación.

Item—That these said shallops and zabras which are to go during the said six years, as has been said, do not have to pay any averías on what they carry for the first time, when they leave on their voyage to Florida. When, however, during the said six-year term, they bring things from the said Florida or the islands, or if they take some things from this kingdom [whether supplies of food and drink or other necessary things for the said Florida], in such case they must pay the averías, which are divided up for the galleys which cruise this coast of the west of Spain, of which Don Álvaro de Bazán is captain-general. They must also pay the averías of the armada which goes to the Indies, if the said shallops and zabras go in convoy with them. If, however, the shallops and zabras navigate by themselves, and do not go in convoy with the said armada which goes to the Indies, they do not have to pay the avería of the said armada which goes to the Indies.

Item—With regard to the notaries public who must be carried [aboard ship]—insofar as the two galleons and the two pataches are concerned, the regulation shall be observed. Insofar as the six shallops and four zabras are concerned, however, for all of them together there shall not be named for His Majesty more than one notary, in consideration of the fact that they are the ships of the said Pedro Menéndez and that he must bear the cost personally of all the arms, artillery, munitions, supplies, and other things which they carry and must carry. They are, moreover, small ships and of small cargo, and for each one to carry its own notary public would cost him very much.

Item—His Majesty must give him the title of captain-general, in proper form, of this entire armada and the ships and people who go in it.

Item—Let all the above be given to the said Pedro Menéndez—the titles, cédulas, and provisions in the necessary form for that which has been given above with the favor which befits it, and of this asiento in order that one [copy] might remain in the possession of His Majesty and he shall carry the other one. Done in the town of Madrid, March 15, 1565.

(*rúbrica*)   (*rúbrica*)
Dr. Vázquez   P°Menéndez

SOURCE: A.G.I. *Patronato* 257, no. 3, ramo 3 (Stetson Coll.).

2. A Comparison of Provisions of Various Sixteenth-Century Asientos

Item	Lucas V. de Ayllón, Florida, June 1523	Pánfilo de Narváez, Florida, Dec. 1526	Hernando de Soto, Florida, April 1537	Lucas V. de Ayllón, Florida, June 1563	Pedro Menéndez de Avilés, Florida, March 1565	Captain Pedro de Silva, Omagua, Oct. 1568	Juan Ortiz de Zárate, Rio de la Plata, July 1569	Diego de Artiega, Costa Rica, Dec. 1573
Stated purpose of the effort	"Populate the land and build forts."	Populate and Christianize.	"Conquer, pacify and populate 200 leagues of coast."	"Population conversion and instruction of naturales."	Conversion of the Indians to the holy Faith; conquest, exploration, and population.		"Discovery, conquest and population; pacify the Indians."	"Discover and populate at your cost."
Required effort and duration	"Arm ships at your own cost."	Build 3 forts; put 200 men in two sites in a year; bring horses, other livestock from Hispaniola, Puerto Rico, Cuba.	Take 500 men with supplies for 18 months.	Take 3 caravels and 250 men (100 married). 6 months' supplies, 8 Dominicans, 100 calves, 100 horses/mares, 200 sheep; plant sugarcane, caña fistula, vines, and olives; 3,000-ducat performance bond.	Take, with a year's supplies, 500 men, of which 100 farmers, 100 sailors, rest skilled men-of-war; must, within 3 years, place a total of 500 settlers, including skilled tradesmen, 10–12 religious, and 4 add. Jesuits, 100 horses, mares, 200 calves, 400 hogs, 400 sheep; take galeass San Pelayo.	Take 500 men, of which 400 are men-of-war and 100 farmers; 4 ships, 6 clerics.	Take 4 ships at his cost; 500 men, of which 200 are farmers and skilled men; 4,000 cows, 4,000 sheep, 500 goats, 300 mares and horses.	Must spend 20,000 ducats; arm 3 ships, of about 400 tons, "well-provisioned," with 200 men, 100 of whom married, with supplies for a year; must go with fleet; survey and discover; 1,000 cows, 1,500 sheep, 500 hogs and goats, 100 horses and mares; 10,000-ducat performance bond.
Required founding of towns and forts	"Build forts."	Found 3 forts.	Build "3 stone forts at own expense."	Build 2 towns.	Establish 2 or 3 fortified towns.		Found 1 or 2 Spanish towns; build 3 stone forts.	Build forts in 3 sites.

	Governmental powers; duration	Titles and offices promised	Salaries	Tax exemptions and their duration
	General government; 1 life.	Adelantado; governor, 1 life; alguacil lieut., fort.	Governor, 365,000 maravedis; lieut., 100,000 maravedis.	No almojarifazgo, 1 life; no diezmo of precious metals or other duties.
	General government; military authority; 1 life.	Adelantado; governor, 1 life; capt.-gen., 1 life; alguacil mayor, perpetual; 3 fort cmdrs.	Governor, 150,000 maravedis; fort cmdr., 70,000 maravedis.	No almojarifazgo, 1 life on Florida materials; for vecinos, 5 yrs.; quinto reduced to 10 per cent, 3 yrs. No salt tax, 5 yrs.
	General government; military authority; 1 life.	Adelantado; governor, 1 life; capt.-gen., 1 life; governor Cuba; 1 fort lieut.	Governor, 1,500 ducats salary; 500 ducats *ayuda de costa*; lieut., 100,000 maravedis.	No royal payments on gold, 6 yrs.; no almojarifazgo for vecinos, 6 yrs.; pay 50 per cent on items from sepulchers; keep 5/6 Indian loot.
	General government; military authority; 1 life.	Adelantado; governor, 1 life; capt.-gen., 1 life; alguacil mayor.	Governor, 1,000 ducats.	No almojarifazgo, 10 yrs. Florida materials; quinto reduced to 10 per cent for 10 yrs.
	General government, 2 lives; military authority, 2 lives.	Adelantado, perpetual; governor/capt.-gen., 2 lives; alguacil mayor, perpetual marquis.	Governor, 2,000 ducats, from profits.	No almojarifazgo for all in Florida, 10 yrs.; quinto reduced to 10 per cent for 10 yrs. after 1st smelt; no avería—**larger** ships, or smaller if out of fleets; no almojarifazgo for Menéndez for 3 yrs.
	General government, 2 lives; military authority, apparently 1 life.	Adelantado, perpetual; governor, 2 lives; capt.-gen. and *justicia mayor*, app. 1 life; lieut., 3 forts; marquis.	Governor, 2,000 ducats; fort lieut., 100,000 **maravedis.**	No alcabala, 20 yrs.; no almojarifazgo, 10 yrs.
	General government, 2 lives; military authority, 2 lives.	Governor, 2 lives; capt.-gen., 2 lives; alguacil mayor, 2 lives; lieut., 3 forts.	Governor, 2,000 ducats, from profits.	For Artiega, no almojarifazgo on first voyage; for settlers, no almojarifazgo or alcabala for 20 yrs.

APPENDIX 2—*Continued*

Item	Lucas V. de Ayllón, Florida, June 1523	Pánfilo de Narváez, Florida, Dec. 1526	Hernando de Soto, Florida, April 1537	Lucas V. de Ayllón, Florida, June 1563	Pedro Menéndez de Avilés, Florida, March 1565	Captain Pedro de Silva, Omagua, Oct. 1568	Juan Ortiz de Zárate, Rio de la Plata, July 1569	Diego de Artiega, Costa Rica, Dec. 1573
Land grants and land privileges	15 leagues squared; may "divide lands and waters."	10 leagues, squared.	12 leagues, squared.	15 leagues, squared; may "divide lands and estates."	25 leagues squared; may "divide lands and estates."			
Trade privileges	6-year monopoly on Florida trade.				License for 2 galleons, 2 pataches, 6 yrs. in Indies trade; only slight limitation of cargo; no avería; out-of-fleet priv. License 6 shallops, 4 zabras, 6 yrs. after conquest year; tied loosely to Florida; no escribanos each vessel; out-of-fleet privilege.		2 ships a year licensed, free of almojarifazgo.	2 ship licenses to Costa Rica and to other parts for Costa Rica provisions.
Encomienda, repartimiento, and Indian tribute	"No encomienda."		"You may make encomiendas."	No encomiendas.	No mention in asiento; refers to *Ordenanzas*.		One reparti-miento.	May grant 2-life encomiendas in country, 3-life in new cities; 2-life repartimientos.
Slave licenses			50, free of duties; later 50 more.	8, pay duties.	500, free of all duties.		100.	20.

Other economic privileges		1/15 of profits; 500-ducat subsidy to raise silk; 2 fisheries.	4 per cent of royal profits, in perpetuity.	1/15 of profits; 500 ducats in juros; 2 fisheries; use Indian tribute for pension.	1/15 of profits, perpetual; 2 fisheries, 1 of fish and 1 of pearls.	2 fisheries.
Royal aid promised	500-ducat silk subsidy.				15,000-ducat merced, if sailed prior May 31, 1565.	
Citation of asiento	A.G.I. Indiferente General 415, Contratación 3,309; D.I., 8:224–45.	A.G.I. Indiferente General 415.	A.G.I. Contratación 3,309.	See p. 47n18.	A.G.I. Indiferente General 1,220.	A.G.I. Indiferente General 415.

3. Genealogy of the Enterprise of Florida

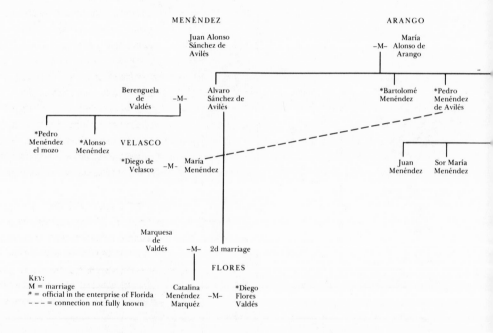

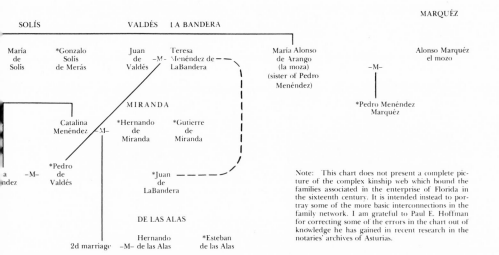

MARQUÉZ

SOLÍS   VALDÉS   LA BANDERA

| María de Solís | *Gonzalo Solís de Merás | Juan de Valdés | Teresa Menéndez de LaBandera | María Alonso de Arango (la moza) (sister of Pedro Menéndez) | Alonso Marquéz el mozo |

–M–

MIRANDA

Catalina Menéndez –M–   *Hernando de Miranda   *Gutierre de Miranda

*Pedro Menéndez Marquéz

a –M– *Pedro de Valdés   *Juan de LaBandera
ndez

DE LAS ALAS

2d marriage –M– Hernando de las Alas   *Esteban de las Alas

Note: This chart does not present a complete picture of the complex kinship web which bound the families associated in the enterprise of Florida in the sixteenth century. It is intended instead to portray some of the more basic interconnections in the family network. I am grateful to Paul E. Hoffman for correcting some of the errors in the chart out of knowledge he has gained in recent research in the notaries' archives of Asturias.

4. Crown Costs in the Cádiz Expedition, 1565
(in ducats)

Supplies and munitions	17,681
Merced paid to the adelantado	15,000
Payment to Pedro Menéndez in recompense for loss of Tierra Firme voyage	2,000
Advance pay on the *San Pelayo* charter	2,300
Total	36,981

NOTE: The Crown also paid at this time 11,000 ducats from avería funds for amounts due from the 1562–63 voyage.
SOURCES: A.G.I. *Contratación* 4,989-A, 4,680, 5,167, 4,344; A.G.I. *Contaduría* 310-B.

5. *Estimated Costs of Pedro Menéndez de Avilés
in the 1565 Florida Expeditions
(in ducats)*

Supplies and munitions purchased		
Cádiz	14,000	
Avilés	5,000	
Santander	2,800	
Gijón	2,200	
Cádiz (Luna ship)	50	
600 arquebuses	1,070	
		25,120
Pay advances		
Officers and mariners, the *San Pelayo*	1,460	
		1,460
Ship purchases, charter, outfitting		
Purchase 3 small craft, 2 ships	13,000	
San Pelayo work	4,000	
Charter *San Antonio*	3,000	
Charter 2 caravels	250	
Charter *Virtudes*	85	
		20,335
Expenses at Canary Islands		
Drafts drawn on Pedro del Castillo by		
Pedro Menéndez and Esteban de las Alas	450	450
Total		47,365

SOURCES: A.G.I. *Escribanía de Cámara* 1,024-A; A.G.I. *Contratación* 5,167; A.G.I. *Contaduría* 310-B; A.G.I. *Justicia* 879, no. 3, pieza 1.

Glossary

Adelantado. A Spanish and Spanish colonial official, appointed to represent the King's interest in frontier areas in return for grants of authority and certain revenues and exemptions, as stipulated in the contract or articles of appointment. Originating during the period of the Spanish Reconquest, the institution was transmitted to the overseas jurisdictions of Castile in the last years of the fifteenth century and was still active in the early seventeenth century.

Adelantado Mayor. A twelfth- and thirteenth-century adelantado whose functions were essentially legal.

Adelantado Menor. A full-fledged adelantado with substantial delegated powers, who had both military and civil functions; this office began in the thirteenth century.

Adelantamiento. The district controlled by an adelantado.

Alcabala. A Castilian tax paid to the Crown and levied upon goods as an excise; found in Spain and in the Indies.

Alcaide. The military governor of a fort or other fortified place.

Alcalde. The presiding officer of the governing council of a Spanish or Spanish-American community. He often possessed juridical authority.

Alférez. An ensign of a military company, or, as in *Alférez Real*, of a community.

Alguacil. The municipal peace officer; in the courts, a bailiff.

Alguacil Mayor. The high constable of a province, region, or *Audiencia*.

Almirante. In the Spanish fleet system of the sixteenth century, the second in command of an organized fleet, appointed by the Crown through the Council of the Indies for Indies fleets. The almirante sailed in the ship designated as *almiranta*, which guarded the rear of the convoy.

Almojarifazgo. The customs duties levied upon incoming and outgoing cargoes. These were collected and accounted for in Spanish or other European ports and in the Indies by the Royal Officials.

Armada. An organized fleet, squadron, or flotilla.

Armada Real. The royal guard fleet organized in 1567 and placed under the command of Pedro Menéndez de Avilés. Its mission was to provide escort for the treasure fleets at critical points and to control corsairs in the West Indies.

Armador. One who constructs and/or outfits ships, as for privateering or war.

Arroba. A Castilian unit of measure, by weight equal approximately to twenty-five pounds.

Artillero Mayor. The chief artillerist of a post or other jurisdiction.

Asiento. Any agreement or contract. In this work, the accord of an individual with a legally constituted authority.

Atarazanas. Generally, a marine warehouse, possibly affiliated with a dockyard. In Seville, the warehouses and workshops of the Casa de Contratación, located outside the old city walls in near conjunction with the Torre del Oro.

Audiencia. In Spanish and Spanish colonial administration, the highest regional appeals court, with some administrative functions.

Avería. An assessment levied as a percentage of the value of goods and bullion carried in the Indies trade (or other trade), out of which the costs of the defense and administration of that particular fleet were to be made.

Aviso. Intelligence or information, transmitted from one official to another. Also, the courier ship which carries such notices.

Ayuntamiento. The municipal government of a Spanish or Spanish-American community; also the structure in which its offices are housed.

Bando. An official proclamation.

Barbero. In sixteenth-century usage, one who exercises the skills of barber, healer, and surgeon.

Barco. Generally, any water craft. May apply to certain coastal vessels. Often used, however, for small craft used in harbor to transfer passengers or cargo.

Bergantín. A small, two-masted sailing craft provided with lateen sails.

Caballero. A Spanish nobleman (derived from horseman, knight).

Cabeza de los Mártires. A geographic term applied at different times to the entire chain of the Florida Keys east and north of the Dry Tortugas, and at times to one particular segment of them. The term is used on some maps to refer to the extreme northern keys and on others to refer to the extreme southern keys.

Cabildo. The municipal corporation of a Spanish or Spanish-American town or city; also the meeting of its governing body, attended by regular and ex officio authorities.

Cacique. A chieftain among the Indians. A term imported into Florida from the West Indies.

Caja. Literally, a chest. In sixteenth-century Spanish colonial financial administration, the royal strongbox, to which the three Royal Officials had access and in which Crown funds were kept. The term also applies to a regional royal treasury.

Capitana. The lead vessel of a Spanish fleet; the flagship of the fleet general, upon which all convoys formed and whose signals and commands were to be obeyed by all vessels in the fleet.

Capitulación. A formal accord of contractual relationship. In the context of this work, an agreement approved by the Crown.

Carrera de Indias. The Spanish maritime trade system in force in the Metropole and its Caribbean or continental American possessions during the sixteenth, seventeenth, and part of the eighteenth centuries.

Casa de Contratación. The Crown-appointed body which controlled the Indies trade from Seville after 1503, and which enforced royal regulations on navigation, ship licensing and lading, the fitness of persons to travel to the Indies, and the assessment of certain charges and fines.

Cédula. A written royal order, having the force of law. Cédulas were gathered, collated, and codified in works called *registros* or *cedularios*.

Chalupa. A small, decked craft, usually furnished with two masts, and rowed with six to eight oars per side, usually less than 100 tons in burden.

Comendador. The Crown-appointed official vested with the rights to the command of a military property and entitled to receive its revenues.

Concejo. The formal boundaries and jurisdictional area of a Spanish and Spanish-American community; the entity of local government.

Conquistador. One of the Spanish explorers and conquerors in the days of greatest Spanish colonial expansion in the sixteenth and seventeenth centuries.

Consulado de la universidad de mercaderes. The sixteenth-century guild of Spanish sea merchants involved in the Indies trade, whose headquarters was at Seville.

Consulta. The formal opinion of a royal council upon a particular matter, delivered to the King for his information.

Contadores Mayores. The chief accountants of the Castilian Crown, who served the Council of Hacienda and were the final reviewing authority of Indies audits.

Contra-corsario. Anti-corsair; refers to a type of expedition for which a shipowner could receive a letter-of-marque, and could at times operate under royal charter.

Converso. Literally, a convert. In medieval and early modern Spain, the term applies to those persons who had converted to Christianity from Judaism.

Corregidor. The Spanish or Spanish-American official in charge of a locality and its population, answerable to the King or to his viceroy for its administration, and responsible for the collection of tribute within his area.

Corsair. A commerce raider or other intruder in the Spanish Indies, not licensed by the Spanish Crown; in an age of privateering, applied at times to each side by the other.

Cruzada (also *Santa Cruzada*). A royal revenue granted by the Popes to the Castilian Crown in return for its support of the church mission in the *Patronato*; the revenue was received in return for the sale of bulls of indulgence.

Derrotero. A geographic and/or maritime route description, featuring major landmarks, navigational hazards, and other geographic features.

Diezmo. The tithe, to be collected from the faithful of a Spanish-American parish in colonial times, and to be accounted for as a royal revenue by the Royal Officials.

Doctrina. The Spanish colonial religious enterprise which involved the close relationship of a missionary or missionaries, a native settlement, and training in doctrine, often aided by Spanish and/or Indian youth.

Encomienda. The command of a military order. Also, the rights granted in the service and tributes of a Spanish colonial Indian community in return for the obligation of the holder to protect the Indians and provide for their Christian nurture.

Entrada. An expedition or entrance into a hitherto unknown land.

Escribano público. A notary public, commissioned by the Crown.

Factor. In Spanish colonial financial administration during the sixteenth century, one of the three Royal Officials who was commissioned to carry out royal policies and secure Crown property. The office was combined with that of *veedor*, and the position was abolished in the early seventeenth century.

Fanega. A Castilian measure for grain, equal to about a hundred pounds.

Fiscal. The prosecuting official whose duty it was to defend the royal patrimony before legal tribunals and to prefer and maintain civil and criminal charges in cases where the Crown might be affected.

Fragata. In the sixteenth century, a small sailing vessel, of lesser size than a bergantín, with or without decking. It was furnished with one or two masts and was also provided with six to twelve oars for propulsion.

Galeoncete. A small galleon.

Galeota. Galiot; a small galley, furnished with oars and sails.

Gobernador. Generally, any ruler or authorized leader. In Spanish colonial administration, the civil official in charge of a province, appointed directly by the Crown or by the viceroy.

Hidalgo. A nobleman; one certified to be of noble blood.

Jornada. A march, journey, or expedition.

Juro. An annuity granted by the Crown to be repaid from some royal revenue or revenues; often given in repayment for obligations to private persons or, at times, in recompense for the seizure of private bullion by the Crown.

Labrador. One who cultivates land for crops or pasture; one who raises livestock or engages in other husbandry.

Licenciado. One who has, through study in a Spanish university, become lettered through the achievement of a certain degree (*licenciatura*).

Lombardero. Artillerist who fires the smaller, open-breech pieces called lombards.

Maestre. An official aboard a Spanish ship whose duty it was to assume charge over all cargo and passengers aboard.

Maestre de campo. The military officer in charge of a sixteenth-century Spanish *tercio.*

Maravedí. The smallest unit of sixteenth-century Spanish currency, used as account currency. Thirty-four were required to make up a real, 272 to make up an ordinary peso, and 375 to make a ducat.

Mayorazgo. An entailed estate; the right to the succession in such an estate.

Memorial. A brief, report, or memorandum.

Merced. A gift or favor by the Crown given to a vassal or subject, often in response to a petition or given in return for services.

Mestizo. One of mixed European and Indian blood.

El Mozo. Used to designate a younger person from an older one with the same name; often equivalent to "junior."

Naturales. The original inhabitants of a land.

Norteños. Persons whose place of birth or family origin lies in the north of Spain.

Oidor. One of the members or judges of a Spanish or Spanish colonial Audiencia.

Parecer. A formal, written opinion given by a Spanish official or authorized body.

Patax, patache. A small sailing craft, often used as a reconnaissance or courier vessel by Spanish fleets, usually with two masts and at times a main lateen sail.

Patrón. Literally, "the boss." In Spanish or Spanish-American life, the person to whom another is socially, politically, or economically beholden.

Patronato, Patronato Real. The Castilian Crown's responsibility for support of the church, whether regular or secular; confirmed by several Popes.

Peso. A Spanish colonial monetary unit. There were several types of peso (*de oro, de minas*, etc.), but the most common was the Mexican silver peso of 8 reales' value, which was worth 272 maravedís.

Pleito. A legal suit or other proceeding at law.

Poder. A power of attorney, executed before a notary.

Proceso. The body of records and materials which constitute a lawsuit.

Procurador. An attorney, solicitor, or other duly qualified representative of a person or corporate body, empowered to be surrogate.

Quinto. The "royal fifth," an assessment collected by the Spanish Crown upon all mined or found bullion, booty, goods obtained in trade with the Indians, etc. Often reduced from 20 per cent to 10 per cent or even 5 per cent by Crown fiat.

Real. A Spanish colonial monetary unit, worth 34 maravedís.

Regidor. An alderman; a city councilman; a member of the cabildo.

Regimiento. The corporate, legal entity that makes up the Spanish colonial municipality.

Repartimiento. Literally, a division. In this work, the term applies to the division of lands or Indian service to Spaniards by an authorized official, such as an adelantado or viceroy.

República. In the sixteenth century, the term applied to the ancient liberties of municipal self-government in Castile.

Requerimiento. A formal request, demand, or summons served upon another person.

Rescate. A type of enforced trade between Spaniards and Indian peoples, evidently done at arm's length, at times involving the ransom of prisoners.

Residencia. The formal examination of the stewardship of a Spanish official (often performed by his successor) after the close of his term of office.

Reyes Católicos. Ferdinand and Isabella.

Royal Officials. In the sixteenth century, the three royal treasury officials (accountant or *contador*, treasurer or *tesorero*, and *factor-veedor*) to whom was confided the collection of and accounting for all royal funds and property of a particular jurisdiction.

Sargento Mayor. The executive officer of a Spanish *tercio*; a position of honor and responsibility, held by a hidalgo.

Señorío natural. The direct suzerainty of the Castilian Crown over certain lands and waters.

Sentencia. The culminating decision in a legal action, investigation or residencia, given by the authorized legal body.

Sobrecedula. A royal order or command sent simultaneously to a number of addressees or jurisdictions.

Solar. A building lot in or near the commercial and civic center of a Spanish or Spanish-American municipality.

Sueldo. Salary; also ship charter fee, paid on a per-ton basis.

Tenedor de bastimentos. An official in charge and accountable for the custody of royal property and supplies at a particular post.

Tercio. The essential sixteenth-century Spanish military formation, utilized in the Italian wars and thereafter, comprised of twelve to fifteen infantry companies.

Terra Nova. Newfoundland.

Tierra Firme. Literally, the mainland. In this work, applied to the South American mainland; the name became attached to the fleet which brought the goods of Peru (from Portobelo) and the New Granada hinterland (from Cartagena).

Urca. A ship type, Dutch in origin, which featured a large capacious vessel with fairly flat bottom contours, valuable for carrying freight across shallow bars.

Vecino. A citizen of a Spanish or Spanish-American municipality, formally admitted to citizenship by the cabildo.

Veedor. See Factor.

Visita. A special ad hoc investigation (performed by an individual or by a commission) into the governmental or ecclesiastical affairs of a Spanish or Spanish colonial jurisdiction, appointed by and reporting to a superior official.

Zabra. A small vessel, similar to a bergantín, used in Cantabrian waters.

Bibliography

I. Spanish Archival Materials

A. *Archivo de los Condes de Revillagigedo*—Madrid (A.C.R.) (material in microfilm, P. K. Yonge Library of Florida History, University of Florida, Gainesville)

Legajo 2, nos. 3, 3–B, A7a, 4, 5; *Legajo* 9, no. 21.

B. *Archivo General de Indias*—Seville (A.G.I.)
Contaduría: Legajo 294, 299, 304, 306, 310–B, 451, 452, 454, 455, 464, 466, 547, 548, 941, 942, 944, 1,174, 1,775.
Contratación: Legajo 9, 58, 135, 135–A, 2,898, 2,937, 2,946, 2,947, 2,948, 3,259, 3,309, 4,344, 4,680, 4,802, 4,981, 4,989–A, 5,010, 5,012, 5,101, 5,102, 5,104, 5,105, 5,167, 5,168, 5,185.
Escribanía de Cámara: Legajo 153–A, 154, 952, 956, 967, 970, 971, 1,009–B, 1,010, 1,011, 1,024–A, 1,184.
Gobierno:
Audiencia de México: Legajo 209, 323.
Audiencia de Santo Domingo: Legajo 11, 12, 24, 71, 74, 99, 115, 124, 168, 224, 231, 233, 1,122, 2,528.
Indiferente General: Legajo 415, 425, 427, 524, 614, 738, 739, 1,093, 1,218, 1,219, 1,220, 1,221, 1,222, 1,966, 1,967, 2,003, 2,058, 2,081, 2,673.
Justicia: Legajo 3, 212, 781, 792, 817, 821, 842, 855, 860, 861, 863, 865, 868, 869, 872, 873, 879, 881, 882, 888, 889, 893, 894, 896, 905, 908, 917, 918, 927, 956, 970, 999, 1,000, 1,013, 1,121, 1,155, 1,182, 1,183.
Patronato Real: Legajo 10, *ramos* 2, 4; 19, no. 1, *ramos* 8, 12, 14, 15, 31; 177, no. 1, *ramo* 25; 179, no. 5, *ramos* 1, 4, 5; 254, no. 2, *ramo* 1, 38, no. 3; 257, no. 3, *ramos* 2, 3, 4, 5, 8, 12, 16, 20, 21, 22, no. 4, *ramos* 1, 6, 8, 11; 267, no. 1, *ramos* 37, 41, no. 2, *ramo* 7.

C. *Archivo General de Simancas*—Simancas (A.G.S.)
Guerra Antigua: Legajo 18, 1,322, 1,327.
Junta de Hacienda: Legajo 44, 47, 67.
Estado: Legajo 816, 817, 818, 819, 820.

D. *Archivo Histórico de Protocolos*—Madrid (A.H.P.)
   1568: *Escribanía* of Diego Rodriquez, no. 521; *Escribanía* of Nicolas Muñoz, no.
   635; *Escribanía* of Francisco de Córdova, no. 646.
   1574: *Escribanía* of Juan del Campillo, no. 605.

E. *Archivo de Protocolos de Cádiz*—Cádiz (A.P.C.)
   1565: *Escribanía* of Alonso de los Cobos.
   1576–78: *Escribanía* of Diego and Marcos de Ribera; *Escribanía* of Juan de Medina.

F. *Archivo de Protocolos de Sevilla*—Seville (A.P.S.)
   1580: *Escribanía* No. 19, *Libro* IV.

G. *Archivo de la Real Academia de la Historia*—Madrid
   1565: 9–30–3; 6,271.

H. *Archivo del Instituto de Don Juan*—Madrid
   Envío 25–H (Florida) and 48–100 (Peru).

II. Microfilmed and Printed Document Collections

Archivo Documental Español (*A.D.E.*). 21 vols. Madrid: Real Academia de la Historia, 1950–.
Colección de documentos inéditos para la historia de España (*D.I.E.*). 112 vols. Madrid: Real
   Academia de la Historia, 1842–95.
*Colección de documentos inéditos relativos al descubrimiento, conquista y organización de las
   antiguas posesiones españolas de América y Oceania, sacadas de los Archivos del Reino y muy
   especialmente del de Indias* (*D.I.*). 42 vols. Madrid: Real Academia de la Historia,
   1864–84.
*Colección de documentos inéditos relativos al descubrimiento, conquista y organización de las
   antiguas posesiones españolas de Ultramar.* 2d ser. 25 vols. Madrid: Real Academia de la
   Historia, 1885–1932.
Connor, Jeannette Thurber. "Connor Papers." Typed transcripts. P. K. Yonge Library
   of Florida History, University of Florida, Gainesville.
Lowery, Woodbury. "Manuscripts of Florida." Transcripts on microfilm. P. K. Yonge
   Library of Florida History, University of Florida, Gainesville.
Navarrete, Martín Fernandez de. *Colección de viages y descubrimientos que hicieron los
   españoles desde fines del siglo XV. Con varios documentos inéditos concernientes a la historia
   de la Marina Castellana y de los establecimientos españoles en Indias.* 5 vols. Madrid,
   1825–37.
Smith, Buckingham. "Buckingham Smith Collection." Transcripts on microfilm. P. K.
   Yonge Library of Florida History, University of Florida, Gainesville.
Stetson, John B. "John B. Stetson Collection." Photostat cards and microfilm. P. K.
   Yonge Library of Florida History, University of Florida, Gainesville.

III. Secondary Materials

Alegre, F. J. *Historia de la Compañía de Jesus en Nueva España.* 3 vols. Mexico City: So-
   ciety of Jesus, 1842.
Altamira y Crevea, Rafael. *Historia de España y de la civilización española.* 4th ed. Bar-
   celona: J. Gili, 1928.
Arnade, Charles W. "Florida History in Spanish Archives. Reproductions at the Univer-
   sity of Florida." *Florida Historical Quarterly* 34 (1955):36–50.
———. "The Failure of Spanish Florida." *The Americas* 16, no. 3 (January 1960):271–81.
———. "A Guide to Spanish Florida Source Material." *Florida Historical Quarterly* 35
   (1956):320–25.
Asis, V. Fernández. *Epistolario de Felipe II sobre asuntos de mar.* Madrid: Editora nacional
   Fernández Asis, 1943.

Ballesteros Gaibrois, Manuel. *La Idea Colonial de Ponce de León: un ensayo de interpretación*. San Juan, Puerto Rico: Instituto de Cultura Puertorriqueña, 1960.

"Barcia" [Carballido y Zúñiga, Andrés González de]. *Ensayo cronológico para la historia general de la Florida*. Translated by Anthony Kerrigan. Gainesville: University of Florida Press, 1951. (First printed in 1723.)

Barrientos, Bartolomé. *Pedro Menéndez de Avilés; su vida y hechos*. [1567]. In *Dos Antiguas Relaciones*, edited by Genaro Garcia. Mexico City: Tip. y Lit. de J. Aguilar y Vera y Compañía, 1902. Facsimile edition, Gainesville: University of Florida Press, 1965.

Bennett, Charles E. *Laudonnière and Fort Caroline*. Gainesville: University of Florida Press, 1964.

————. *Settlement of Florida*. Gainesville: University of Florida Press, 1968.

Bishko, Charles Julian. "The Iberian Background of Latin-American History: Recent Progress and Continuing Problems." *Hispanic American Historical Review* 36, no. 1 (February 1956):50–80.

Bolton, Herbert Eugene. "The Mission as a Frontier Institution in the American Colonies." *American Historical Review* 23 (October 1917):42–61.

————. *The Spanish Borderlands; a Chronicle of Old Florida and the Southwest*. New Haven: Yale University Press, 1921.

Boyd-Bowman, Peter. *Índice geobiográfico de cuarenta mil pobladores españoles de América en el Siglo XVI*. 2 vols. Mexico City: Editorial Jus, 1958.

Bullen, Ripley P. "The Southern Limit of Timucua Territory." *Florida Historical Quarterly* 47, no. 4 (April 1969):414–19.

Bullen, Ripley P.; Bullen, Adelaide K.; and Clausen, Carl J. "The Cato Site near Sebastian Inlet, Florida." *The Florida Anthropologist* 21, no. 1 (March 1968):14–16.

Burrus, E. J. "An Introduction to Bibliographical Tools in Spanish Archives and Manuscript Collections Relating to Hispanic America." *Hispanic American Historical Review* 35 (1955):443–83.

Camín, Alfonso. *El Adelantado de Florida, Pedro Menéndez de Avilés*. Mexico City: Revista Norte, 1944.

Catholic Historical Survey. "Religious Index to the Stetson Collection." Typescript. St. Augustine: Catholic Historical Society, 1966.

Cato, Homer N. "Found—Ancient Sebastian Man." *Florida Sportcamping* 2, no. 3 (September 1966):32–34.

Céspedes del Castillo, Guillermo. *La Avería en el comercio de Indias*. Seville: Escuela de Estudios Hispano-Americanos, 1945.

Chamberlain, Robert S. "Castilian Backgrounds of the Repartimiento-Encomienda." Publications in Anthropology and History, no. 5, pp. 33–52. Washington: Carnegie Institution, 1939.

————. *The Conquest and Colonization of Yucatan*. New York: Octagon Books, 1966.

Chatelain, Verne E. *The Defenses of Spanish Florida, 1565–1763*. Washington: Carnegie Institution, 1941.

Chaunu, Pierre, and Chaunu, Huguette. *Séville et l'Atlantique: 1504–1650*. 10 vols. Paris: S.E.V.P.E.N., 1955–59.

Connor, Jeannette Thurber. *Colonial Records of Spanish Florida*. 2 vols. DeLand: Florida Historical Society, 1925–30.

Cox, Isaac. "Florida, Frontier Outpost of New Spain." *Catholic Historical Review* 17 (1931):151–74.

Cuevas, Mariano. *Historia de la Iglesia en Mexico*. 2 vols. Mexico City: Imprenta de el Asilo "Patricio Sanz," 1922. [Edition of 1946–47 is in 5 vols.]

Dánvila y Collado, Manuel. *Historia del poder civil en España*. 6 vols. Madrid: Fontenet, 1885–86.

————. "Significación que tuvieron en el Gobierno de América la Casa de la Contratación de Sevilla y el Consejo Supremo de Indias." In *España en América . . . Conferencias dadas en el Ateneo . . . de Madrid*, vol. 3, no. 12. Madrid: Real Academia de la Historia, 1894.

Davenport, Frances G., ed. *European Treaties Bearing on the History of the United States.* 4 vols. Washington: Carnegie Institution, 1917–37.

De Gourgues, Dominique. "La Reprinse de la Floride par le captaine Gourgues." Translated by Jeannette Thurber Connor. Reprinted in *Settlement of Florida*, by Charles E. Bennett. Gainesville: University of Florida Press, 1968.

De Roover, R. *L'évolution de la lettre de change—XIVᵉ–XVIIIᵉ siècle.* Paris: A. Colin, 1953.

Dirección General de Archivos y Bibliotecas. *Guía de Fuentes para la Historia de Ibero-América.* 2 vols. Madrid: Consejo Internacional de Archivos and UNESCO, 1966–69.

Domínguez y Compañy, Francisco. "Funciones económicas del cabildo colonial hispano-Americano." In *Contribuciones a la historia municipal de América*, edited by Rafael Altamira y Crevea et al. Mexico City: Pan American Institute of Geography and History, 1951.

Douais, Celestin, ed. *Depêches de M. de Fourquevaux, ambassadeur du roi Charles IX en Espagne, 1565–1572.* 2 vols. Paris: E. Leroux, 1896.

Duro, Cesaréo Fernández. *Armada Española.* 9 vols. Madrid: Est. tipográfico "Sucesores de Rivadeneyra," 1895–1903.

Ehrenberg, Richard. *Capital and Finance in the Age of the Renaissance.* Translated by H. M. Lucas. New York: Harcourt, Brace, and Co., 1928.

Elliott, J. H. *Imperial Spain, 1469–1716.* New York: St. Martin's Press, Inc., 1963.

Enciclopedia Heráldica y Genealógica Hispano-Americana. 86 vols. Madrid: Imprenta Comercial Salmantina, 1920–63.

Enciclopedia universal ilustrada europeo-americana. 70 vols. in 72. Barcelona and Madrid: Espasa Calpe, S.A., 1907–30; 10-vol. appendix, 1930–33.

Encinas, Diego de. *Cedulario Indiano.* [1596]. Facsimile ed. 5 vols. Madrid: Ediciones Cultura Hispánica, 1945–46.

Fairbanks, Charles H. *Ethnohistorical Report of the Florida Indians.* Tallahassee, Florida: Indian Claims Commission, Docket no. 151, 1957.

Fairbanks, Charles H., and Fleener, Charles J. "The Trial Ethnohistory Project at the University of Florida." *Florida Anthropologist* 17, no. 2 (June 1964):110–12.

Fisher, Lillian E. *Viceregal Administration in the Spanish Colonies.* Berkeley: University of California Press, 1926.

Flores, Bartolomé de. *Obra nuevamente compuesta.* Seville: Hernando Diaz, 1571.

Folmer, Henry. *Franco-Spanish Rivalry in North America, 1524–1763.* Glendale, California: A. H. Clark Company, 1953.

Fontaneda, Hernando d'Escalante. *Memoir of Hernando d'Escalante Fontaneda.* Translated by Buckingham Smith. Edited by David O. True. Coral Gables, Florida: University of Miami Press, 1944. (Dates from ca. 1575.)

Foster, George M. *Culture and Conquest: America's Spanish Heritage.* New York: Wenner-Gren Foundation for Anthropological Research, 1960.

French, Benjamin F. *Historical Collections of Louisiana and Florida.* New York: A. Mason, 1875.

Gaffarel, Paul. *Histoire de la Floride Française.* Paris: Firmin-Didot et Cie., 1875.

Gannon, Michael V. *The Cross in the Sand.* Gainesville: University of Florida Press, 1965.

García, Carlos Riba, ed. *Correspondencia privada de Felipe II con su secretario Mateo Vazquez: 1567–1571.* Madrid: Consejo Superior de Investigaciones Científicas, Instituto "Jerónimo Zurita," 1959.

Geiger, Maynard J. *The Franciscan Conquest of Florida.* Washington: The Catholic University of America, 1937.

Geyl, Pieter. *The Revolt of the Netherlands.* 2d ed. London: Ernest Benn, Ltd., 1958.

Goggin, John M. *Indian and Spanish Selected Writings.* Coral Gables, Florida: University of Miami Press, 1965.

Góngora, Mario. *El estado en el derecho indiano: epoca de fundación (1492–1570).* Santiago de Chile: Instituto de Investigaciones Historico-Culturales, Facultad de Filosofia y Educación, Universidad de Chile, 1951.

———. *Los Grupos de conquistadores en Tierra Firme, 1509–1530; Fisonomía Histórica-social de un tipo de conquista*. Santiago de Chile: Universidad de Chile, Centro de Historia Colonial, 1962.

Gonzalez Ruiz, F. *De la Florida a San Francisco; los exploradores españoles en los Estados Unidos*. Buenos Aires: Ibero-Americana, 1949.

Griffen, William B. "A Calendar of Spanish Records Pertaining to Florida— 1512–1764." Typescript. St. Augustine: St. Augustine Historical Society, 1959.

Griffin, Charles, and Hill, Roscoe R. "Descriptive Catalogue of the Documents Relating to the History of the United States in the Archivo Historico Nacional." Washington: Library of Congress, n.d.

Griffin, John W., ed. *The Florida Indian and His Neighbors*. Winter Park: Rollins College, 1949.

Griffin, John W., and Smith, Hale G. "Nocoroco—A Timucua Village of 1605 Now in Tomoka State Park." *Florida Historical Quarterly* 27, no. 4 (April 1949):340–61.

Haggard, J. Villasana. *Handbook for Translators of Spanish Historical Documents*. Austin: University of Texas Press, 1941.

Hammond, George P. "Oñate's Effort to Gain Political Autonomy for New Mexico." *Hispanic American Historical Review* 32, no. 3 (August 1952):321–30.

Hanke, Lewis. *The Spanish Struggle for Justice in the Conquest of America*. Philadelphia: University of Pennsylvania Press, 1949.

Haring, Clarence H. *The Spanish Empire in America*. 3d ed. New York: Harcourt, Brace, and World, 1963.

———. *Trade and Navigation between Spain and the Indies in the Time of the Hapsburgs*. 2d ed. Gloucester, Massachusetts: P. Smith, 1964.

Held, Ray E. "Spanish Florida in American Historiography, 1821–1921." Ph.D. dissertation, University of Florida, 1955.

Herrera de Heredia, Antonia. "Indice para las consultas del Consejo de Indias." Manuscript. Seville, 1969.

Herrera y Tordesilla, Antonio. *Historia general de los hechos de los castellanos en las islas y tierra firme del mar océano (1601–1615)*. 9 vols. Madrid: Imprenta Real de Nicolas Rodriguez Franco, 1726–27.

Higgs, Charles D. "Some Archeological Findings and Investigations in the Land of Ais." Manuscript, National Park Service, 1941.

———. "Spanish Contacts with the Ais." *Florida Historical Quarterly* 21 (July 1942):24–39.

Hill, Roscoe R. "The Office of Adelantado." *Political Science Quarterly* 28, no. 4 (December 1913):646–68.

Hoffman, Paul E. "The Background and Development of Pedro Menéndez' Contribution to the Defense of the Spanish Indies." Master's thesis, University of Florida, 1965.

———. "The Defense of the Indies, 1535–1574: A Study in the Modernization of the Spanish State." Ph.D. dissertation, University of Florida, 1969.

———. "Diplomacy and the Papal Donation." *The Americas* 30, no. 2 (October 1973):151–83.

———. "Florida and the Negotiations of Cateau-Cambrésis and Paris, 1559–1560: A Re-examination." Typescript. Laramie, Wyoming, 1972.

———. "A Study of Defense Costs, 1565–1585: A Quantification of Florida History." *Florida Historical Quarterly* 51, no. 4 (April 1973):401–22.

Hoffman, Paul E., and Lyon, Eugene. "Accounts of the *Real Hacienda*, Florida, 1565 to 1602." *Florida Historical Quarterly* 48, no. 1 (July 1969):57–69.

Hoffman, Paul E., and Mulholland, James. "A Tentative Calendar of Various Documents Relating to the History of Florida from the Buckingham Smith Collection." Typescript. P. K. Yonge Library of Florida History, University of Florida, Gainesville, 1966.

Horner, Dave. *The Treasure Galleons*. New York: Dodd, Mead and Company, 1971.

Hrdlička, Ales. *The Anthropology of Florida*. DeLand, Florida: Florida Historical Society, 1922.

Instituto Hispano-Cubano de Historia de América. *Catálogo de los fondos Americanos del*

Archivo de Protocolos de Sevilla. 4 vols. Seville: Compañía Iberoamericana de Publicaciones, 1929.

Iturribarria, Jorge Fernando. *Oaxaca en la historia*. Mexico City: Editorial Stylo, 1955.

Johnson, H. B., Jr., ed. *From Reconquest to Empire: The Iberian Background to Latin American History*. New York: Alfred A. Knopf, Inc., 1970.

Julien, Charles André. *Les voyages de découverte et les premiers établissements (xve —xvie siècles)*. Paris: Presses universitaires de France, 1948.

Keegan, Gregory, and Tormo Sanz, Leandro. *Experiencia misionera en la Florida*. Madrid: Consejo Superior de Investigaciones Científicas, 1957.

Kenny, Michael. *The Romance of Florida*. Milwaukee: The Bruce Publishing Company, 1934.

Lanning, John Tate. *The Spanish Missions in Georgia*. Chapel Hill: University of North Carolina Press, 1935.

LaRoncière, Charles de. *Histoire de la Marine Française*. 6 vols. Paris: Librairie Plon, 1910.

Lavin, James D. *A History of Spanish Firearms*. New York: Arco Publishing Company, 1965.

Lawson, Edward H. "Letters of Menéndez." 2 vols. Typescript. St. Augustine: Edward H. Lawson, 1955.

Lewis, Clifford M. "The Spanish Jesuit Mission of 1567–69 in Southwest Florida: Search for Location." Manuscript. Wheeling, West Virginia, 1967.

———. "The Calusa." In *Tacachale: Indians of Florida and Southeast Georgia during the Historic Period*, ed. Samuel Proctor and J. T. Milanich. Contributions of the Florida State Museum. Gainesville: University of Florida Press, forthcoming.

Lewis, Clifford M., and Loomie, Albert J. *The Spanish Jesuit Missions in Virginia: 1570–1572*. Chapel Hill: University of North Carolina Press, 1953.

Lockhart, James. "Encomienda and Hacienda: The Evolution of the Great Estate in the Spanish Indies." *Hispanic American Historical Review* 49 (1969):419–29.

López, Atanasio. *Cuatro cartas sobre las misiones de la Florida*. Madrid: Archivo Ibero-Americano, 1914.

López de Velasco, Juan. *Geografía universal de las Indias (1571–1574)*. Madrid: D. Justo Zaragoza, 1894.

Lorant, Stefan, ed. *The New World*. Reprint. New York: Duell, Sloan and Pearce, 1946.

Lowery, Woodbury. *The Spanish Settlements within the Present Limits of the United States*. 2 vols. Reprint. New York: Russell and Russell, 1959.

Luengo Muñoz, Manuel. "Sumaria noción del poder adquisitivo de la moneda en Indias durante el siglo XVI." *Anuario de Estudios Americanos* 10 (1951):35–57.

Lussagnet, Suzanne. *Les Français en Amérique pendant la deuxième moitié du XVIe siècle*. Vol. 2: *Les Français en Floride*. Paris: Presses universitaires de France, 1958.

Lynch, John. *Spain under the Hapsburgs*. 2 vols. Oxford: A. Blackwell, 1964–69.

Lyon, Eugene. "The Adelantamiento of Florida." Ph.D. dissertation, University of Florida, 1973.

———. "Captives of Florida." *Florida Historical Quarterly* 50, no. 1 (July 1971):1–24.

———. "A Descriptive and Annotated Index of Contaduría Records Relating to Spanish Florida, 1565–1602." Typescript. P. K. Yonge Library of Florida History, University of Florida, Gainesville, 1968.

———. "The Enterprise of Florida." *Florida Historical Quarterly* 52, no. 4 (April 1974):411–22.

———. "A Lost Son." Typescript. University of Florida, Gainesville, 1968.

———. "More Light on the Indians of the Ays Coast." Typescript. Gainesville, Florida, 1967.

Manucy, Albert. *Florida's Menéndez; Captain-General of the Ocean Sea*. St. Augustine: St. Augustine Historical Society, 1965.

Mariluz Urquijo, José María. *Ensayo sobre los juicios de residencia indianos*. Sevilla: Escuela de Estudios Hispano-Americanos, 1952.

Martínez Alcubilla, Marcelo. *Códigos Antiguos de España*. 2 vols. Madrid: J. López Camacho, 1885.

Massachusetts Historical Society. *Proceedings*, ser. 2, vol. 8 (1894).

Maynard, Theodore. *DeSoto and the Conquistadores*. London: Longmans, Green and Co., 1930.

Mecham, J. Lloyd. *Church and State in Latin America*. Chapel Hill: University of North Carolina Press, 1934.

Milanich, Jerald T., and Sturtevant, William C., eds. *Francisco Pareja's 1613 Confessionario*. Translated by Emilio F. Moran. Tallahassee: Division of History, Archives and Records Management, Florida Department of State, 1972.

Millares Carlo, Agustín, and Mantecón, Ignacio. *Album de Paleografía Hispano-Americana de los Siglos XVI y XVII*. 2 vols. Mexico City: Pan American Institute of Geography and History, 1955.

Ministerio de Fomento. *Cartas de Indias*. 4 vols. Madrid: Ministerio de Fomento, 1871.

Monicat, Jacques. "Les archives notariales." *Revue Historique* 214 (July–September 1955):1–8.

Moore, John Preston. *The Cabildo in Peru under the Hapsburgs*. Durham, North Carolina: Duke University Press, 1954.

Morales Padrón, Francisco. *Jamaica española*. Seville: Escuela de Estudios Hispano-Americanos, 1952.

Moreno, Frank Jay. "The Spanish Colonial System: A Functional Approach." *Western Political Quarterly* 20, no. 2, pt. 1 (June 1967):308–20.

Morse, Richard M. "Some Characteristics of Latin American Urban History." *American Historical Review* 67 (January 1962):317–88.

Muñoz Pérez, José. "El comercio de Indias bajo las Austrias y la crítica del proyectismo de siglo XVI." *Anuario de Estudios Americanos* 13 (1952):85–103.

Oré, Luis Geronimo de. *Relación histórica de la Florida*. Ca. 1604. First separate printing, 2 vols., Madrid: Imprenta de Romona Velasco, viuda de P. Perez, 1931–33.

Ots Capdequi, José María. *El estado español en las Indias*. 4th ed. Mexico City: Fondo de Cultura Económica, 1965.

Oviedo y Valdés, Gonzalo Fernández de. *Historia general y natural de las Indias*. (1535.) 5 vols. Madrid: Atlas, 1959.

Palau y Dulcet, Antonio. *Manual del Librero Hispano-Americano*. 7 vols. Barcelona: Librería Anticuaria, 1923–27.

Pareja, Francisco. *Catecismo en lengua Timuquana y castellano*. Mexico City: Imprenta de Juan Ruyz, 1627.

Paz, Julian. *Catálogo de manuscritos de America existentes en la Biblioteca Nacional*. Madrid: Tipográficas de Archivos Olozaga I., 1933.

Peña y Cámara, José María de la. *Archivo General de Indias de Sevilla: Guía del visitante*. Madrid: Junta Técnica de Archivos, Bibliotecas y Museos, 1958.

———. *A List of Spanish Residencias in the Archive of the Indies—1517–1775*. Washington: Library of Congress, 1955.

Perez, Luis Mariano. *Guide to the Materials for American History in Cuban Archives*. Washington: Carnegie Institution, 1907.

Phelan, John L. *The Kingdom of Quito in the Seventeenth Century; Bureaucratic Politics in the Spanish Empire*. Madison: University of Wisconsin Press, 1967.

Pike, Ruth. *Aristocrats and Traders: Sevillian Society in the Sixteenth Century*. Ithaca and London: Cornell University Press, 1972.

Powell, Philip W. *Soldiers, Indians and Silver*. Berkeley: University of California Press, 1952.

Priestley, Herbert I., ed. *The Luna Papers*. 2 vols. DeLand: Florida State Historical Society, 1928.

Pulgar, Fernández de. "Historia general de la Florida." MSS 29999, Biblioteca Nacional. In Woodbury Lowery Collection, MSS U–2, P. K. Yonge Library of Florida History, University of Florida, Gainesville.

Real Academia de Historia. *Catálogo de la colección de J. B. Muñoz*. 3 vols. Madrid: Real Academia de la Historia, 1954–56.

Recopilación de leyes de los reinos de las Indias. 4 vols. Madrid: J. de Paredes, 1681.

Ribault, Jean. *The Whole and True Discoverye of Terra Florida.* London: R. Hall, 1563. Facsimile ed., Gainesville: University of Florida Press, 1964.

Ricard, Robert. *The Spiritual Conquest of Mexico.* Translated by Lesley Byrd Simpson. (1933.) Berkeley: University of California Press, 1966.

Robertson, James Alexander. "The Archival Distribution of the Florida Manuscripts." *Florida Historical Quarterly* 10 (1931–32):35–50.

————. *List of Documents in Spanish Archives Relating to the History of the United States, Which have Been Printed or of Which Transcripts are Preserved in American Libraries.* Washington: Carnegie Institution, 1910.

Rodriquez Vincente, María Encarnación. "La Contabilidad virreinal como fuente histórica." *Anuario de Estudios Americanos* (Seville, 1967), pp. 1523–42.

Roncière, Charles de la. *Histoire de la Marine Française.* 6 vols. Paris: Librairie Plon, 1910.

Rouse, Irving. *A Survey of Indian River Archaeology.* New Haven: Yale University Press, 1951.

Ruidiaz y Caravía, Eugenio. *La Florida: su conquista y colonización por Pedro Menéndez de Avilés.* 2 vols. Madrid: Imprenta de los hijos de J. A. Garcia, 1893–94.

Sánchez Alonso, Benito. *Fuentes de la historia española y hispano-americana.* 3 vols. Madrid: Consejo Superior de Investigaciones Científicas, 1952.

Sánchez-Bella, Ismael. *La Organización financiera de las Indias, Siglo XVI.* Seville: Escuela de Estudios Hispano-Americanos, 1968.

Sapori, Armando. *The Italian Merchant in the Middle Ages.* Translated by Patricia Ann Kennen. New York: W. W. Norton, 1970.

Schaefer, Ernesto. *El Consejo real y supremo de las Indias.* 2 vols. Seville: Escuela de Estudios Hispano-Americanos, 1946–47.

————. *Índice de los documentos inéditos de Indios.* 2 vols. Madrid: Consejo Superior de Investigaciones Científicas, 1946.

Schoenrich, Otto. *The Legacy of Christopher Columbus.* 2 vols. Glendale, California: The Arthur H. Clark Company, 1949–50.

Scholes, France V. "The Spanish Conqueror as a Business Man; A Chapter in the History of Fernando Cortés." *New Mexico Quarterly* 28, no. 1 (Spring 1958):6–29.

Seaberg, Lillian. "Relations of Florida Indians with the French and Spanish, 1562–1568." Gainesville: Lillian Seaberg, 1953.

See, H. *Les origines du capitalisme moderne.* Paris: A. Colin, 1926.

Simpson, Lesley Byrd. *The Encomienda in New Spain.* Berkeley: University of California Press, 1934.

Smith, Buckingham. *Colección de varios documentos para la historia de la Florida y tierras adyacentes.* London: Trübner and Company, 1859.

Smith, Hale G. *The European and the Indian.* Gainesville: Florida Anthropological Society, 1956.

————. *Two Archaeological Sites in Brevard County, Florida.* Gainesville: University of Florida Press, 1949.

Solís de Merás, Gonzalo. *Pedro Menéndez de Avilés.* Translated by Jeannette Thurber Connor. DeLand: Florida State Historical Society, 1922. Facsimile ed., Gainesville: University of Florida Press, 1964.

Solorzano Pereira, Juan de. *Política Indiana.* 1st Spanish ed., Madrid, 1648. 5 vols. Madrid and Buenos Aires: Compañía IberoAmericana de Publicaciones, 1930.

Swanton, John R. *The Indian Tribes of North America.* Washington: U.S. Government Printing Office, 1952.

Tebeau, Charlton W. *Florida's Last Frontier.* Coral Gables: University of Miami Press, 1956.

————. *A History of Florida.* Coral Gables: University of Miami Press, 1971.

Ternaux-Compans, Henri. *Receuil des pièces sur la Floride.* Paris: A. Bertrand, 1842.

Tibesar, Antonio, ed. "A Spy's Report on the Expedition of Jean Ribault to Florida, 1565." *The Americas* 11, no. 4 (April 1955):590–92.

Torres Lanzas, Pedro. *Relación descriptiva de los mapas, planos, etc. de México y Florida existente en el Archivo General de Indias.* Seville: Imprenta de El Mercatil, 1900.

Vargas Ugarte, Ruben. "The First Jesuit Mission in Florida." U.S. Catholic Historical Society, *Historical Records and Studies* 15 (1935):59–148.

Vásquez de Espinosa, Antonio. *Compendium and Description of the West Indies.* (1626.) Translated by Charles A. Clark. Washington: Smithsonian Institution, 1942.

Vásquez, Manuel. "Index for the J. T. Connor Papers." Typescript. P. K. Yonge Library of Florida History, University of Florida, Gainesville.

Veitia Linaje, Joseph de. *Norte de la contratación de las indias occidentales.* (1672.) 2 vols. Buenos Aires: Comision Argentina de Fomento Interamericana, 1945.

Vela, V. Vincente. *Índice de la colección de los documentos de Fernández de Navarrete que posee el Museo Naval.* Madrid: Instituto Histórico de Marina, 1946.

Vicens Vives, Jaime, ed. *Historia económica y social de España y America.* 4 vols. Barcelona: Editorial Teide, 1957–58.

Vigil, Ciriaco Miguel. *Noticias biográficas-genealógicas de Pedro Menéndez de Avilés.* Avilés: Miguel Vigil, 1892.

Vigneras, Louis-André. "A Spanish Discovery of North Carolina in 1566." *North Carolina Historical Review* 46, no. 4 (October 1969):398–414.

Weber, Max. *The Theory of Social and Economic Organization.* Translated by A. M. Henderson and Talcott Parsons. New York: Free Press, 1947.

Wenhold, Lucy. "Manrique de Rojas' Report, 1564." *Florida Historical Quarterly* 38, no. 1 (July 1959):45–62.

Wright, Irene A. *Historia documentado de San Cristobal de la Habana en el siglo XVI.* 2 vols. Havana: Imprenta el Siglo XX, 1927.

———. "The Odyssey of the Spanish Archives of Florida." In *Hispanic American Essays: A Memorial to James Alexander Robertson,* edited by A. Curtis Wilgus. Chapel Hill: University of North Carolina Press, 1942.

Zavala, Silvio. *The Colonial Period of the History of the New World.* Translated and abridged by Max Savelle. Mexico City: Instituto Panamericano de Geografía e Historia, 1962.

———. *Los intereses particulares en la conquista de la Nueva Espana.* Mexico City: Universidad Nacional Autónoma de Mexico, 1965.

Zubillaga, Felix. *La Florida: La Misión Jesuítica (1566–1572) y la colonización española.* Rome: Institutum Historicum S.I., 1941.

———. *Monumenta Antiquae Floridae.* Rome: Monumenta Historica Societatis Iesu, 1946.

Index

Abalia, Antonio de, 55
Abalia, Juan de, 164
Absolutism, royal, in Indies conquests, 1
Adelantado, 2, 2n2, 4, 5
Adelantamiento, 2, 2nn3, 4, 5, 3, 4, 5n10, 208
Ais. *See* Indians, Ais
Ais, garrison at, 139–40, 150, 165
Alabama, 204
Alas, de las, family, 75, Appendix 3
Alas, Esteban de las, 16, 22, 23, 33, 36, 72, 72n3, 88, 89, 132, 137, 138, 141, 147–48, 153, 154, 157, 166, 198, 199
Alas, Thomas Alonso de las, 74, 167
Alava y Beaumont, Francis de, 59, 60, 67, 95–96, 143
Alba, Duke of, 59–60, 96, 108, 144, 187
Alexander VI, Pope, 3, 60
Alicamini, 180
Almojarifazgo, 52
Alvarado, Pedro de, 2
Amaya, Diego de, 74, 106, 128, 139, 140
Amboise: Insurrection of, 19; Pacification of, 33, 46
Ancones, the (St. Joseph's Bay), 49
Andrada, Pedro de, 143, 198
Antonia, Doña, 149, 158, 160, 176–78
Antwerp, 188
Appalachian Mountains, 182, 183
Arango family, 75
Archiniega, Sancho de, 143, 146, 160, 165
Archiniega expedition, 142, 145n30, 146, 147, 147n35, 159, 160, 164, 165, 180, 183

Arcos, 39
Argüelles, Martín de, 151, 198
Argüelles family, 75
Artiega, Diego de, Appendix 2
Ascension, 139, 150
Asientos 5, Appendixes 1, 2. *See also* Menéndez Asiento
Astudillo de Burgales, Gaspar de, 21, 35, 35n37, 81, 82n26
Asturias, family complex in, 75
Atarazanas (of Seville), 28
Audiencias, 4. *See also* Lima, Mexico, Santo Domingo, Audiencias of
Avellaneda, Diego de, 163
Avería, 9, 9n19, 13, 27, 27n17
Avilés, 8, 74, 75, 89, 191
Ayala, Gabriel de, 150
Ayuntamiento, 116
Azores Islands, 144, 187

Bacortoqui, Pedro de, 196n28. *See also* Bustinçury
Baeza, Hernando de, 139, 174, 175, 179, 203
Bahama Channel, 31, 43, 61, 105, 107
"Bahia de Santa Maria," 165, 182. *See also* Western Passage
Bahiahonda, 131
Bahia Phillipina, 61
Balboa, Vasco Nuñez de, 2
Baracoa, 39
Barreda, Baltasar de, 175, 176
Bastimentos, Tenedor de, 88
Bautista de Segura, Juan, 195

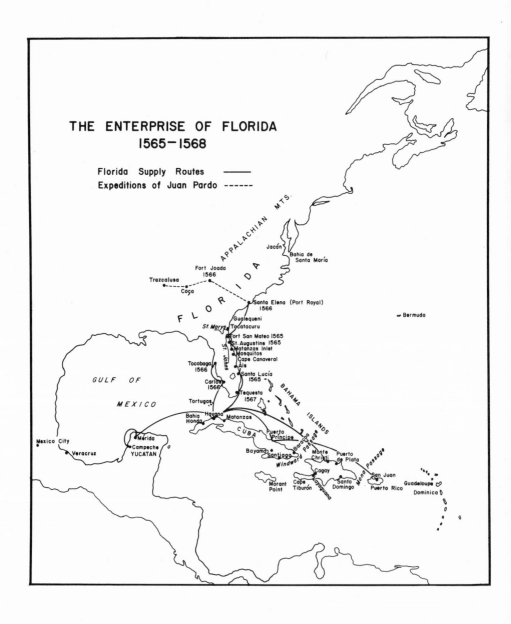

THE ENTERPRISE OF FLORIDA
1565–1568

Florida Supply Routes ———
Expeditions of Juan Pardo - - - - - -

APPALACHIAN MTS.

FLORIDA

Jacán

Bahia de
Santa María

Fort Joada
1566

Trazcalusa

Coça

Santa Elena (Port Royal)
1566

Bermuda

Gualequeni
St. Marys Tacatacuru
Fort San Mateo 1565
St. Augustine 1565
Matanzas Inlet
Mosquitos
Cape Canaveral
Ais
Santa Lucía
1565

St. Johns

Tocobaga
1566

GULF OF

MEXICO

Carlos
1566

Tortugas

Tequesta
1567

BAHAMA ISLANDS

Bahia
Honda

Havana
Matanzas

CUBA

Puerto
Príncipe

Mexico City

Mérida
Campeche
YUCATAN

Veracruz

Bayamo
Santiago

Bahama
Passage

Monte
Christi

Puerto
de Plata

Mona Passage

Windward

Cagay

Morant
Point

Cape
Tiburón

Guaguana

Santo
Domingo

San Juan

Puerto Rico

Guadeloupe

Dominica

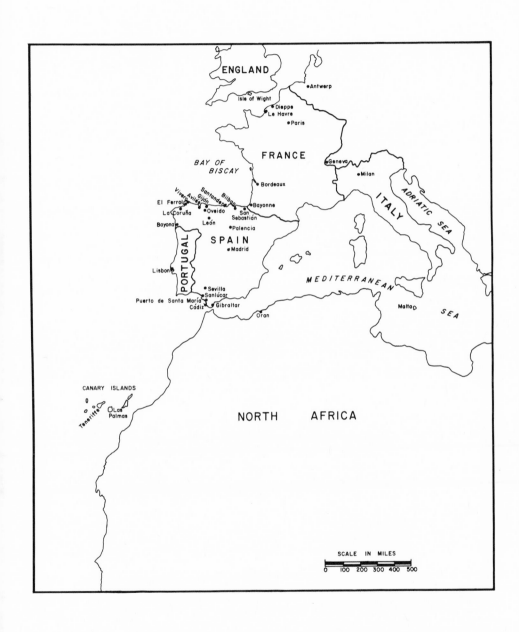

ENGLAND

●Antwerp
Isle of Wight
●Dieppe
●Le Havre
●Paris

FRANCE

BAY OF BISCAY
●Bordeaux
●Geneva
●Milan

ITALY

ADRIATIC SEA

Santander
Bilbao
Viveró Avilés Gijón
El Ferrol ●Bayonne
La Coruña ●Oviedo San Sebastián
León
Bayona ●Palencia
SPAIN
●Madrid

PORTUGAL

Lisbon●

MEDITERRANEAN

SEA

Malta●

●Sevilla
Sanlúcar
Puerto de Santa María
Cádiz ●Gibraltar
●Orán

CANARY ISLANDS
○
○ ○
Tenerife ○Las Palmas

NORTH   AFRICA

SCALE   IN   MILES
0   100 200 300 400 500

Adelantado: *A Spanish or Spanish colonial official, appointed to represent the King's interest in frontier areas in return for grants of authority and certain revenues and exemptions.*

from the Glossary, *The Enterprise of Florida*

Eugene Lyon adroitly explicates the role of private conquerors in Spanish expansion with what *Florida Historical Quarterly* has called a "magisterial" biography of Pedro Menéndez de Avilés. Using primary Spanish materials in Spanish and Florida archives, many studied for the first time, Lyon refutes the claim that the Spanish contract to settle Florida was signed with Menéndez in response to news of the French foothold at Fort Caroline. Not merely an expedition of military dominance or even of religious zeal, the Florida enterprise was primarily a joint commercial venture between Menéndez and the Crown, with the adelantado assuming most of the risks. Menéndez negotiated contracts for opening trade and agricultural centers, and he exploited family ties, particularly with his Asturian kinship group, who supported the adventure with men, ships, and money.

"Lyon has constructed a running account of the financial juggling act, promotional boosterism, political maneuvering, and seemingly eternal optimism of the Adelantado. Lyon is able to see the man whole as smuggler, entrepreneur, overbearing egoist, and religious devotee." — *The Historian*

"Menéndez emerges more deeply human than any previous biographer would have us believe." — *The Americas*
(Journal of the Academy of American Franciscan History)

"[*The Enterprise of Florida*] explains both the strength and the weakness of sixteenth-century Spanish imperialism [and] effectively displays the depth of understanding of early Spanish colonialism that may now be achieved." — *The Alabama Review*

"By far the clearest picture yet drawn of the founding of Florida." — *El Escribano*

About the author

Eugene Lyon, who is adjunct professor of history at the University of Florida, is also a consulting historian and writer. *The Search for the "Atocha,"* his book on a salvaged sixteenth-century Spanish treasury ship, was published in 1979.

A University of Florida Book
University Presses of Florida

ISBN 0-8130-0777-1